Date Due

MAY 12 1959 J O			
NOV 2 * 1961 L O			
DEC 11 1961 H V			
FEB 14 1964			
SEP 21 1965 M P			
JUN 9 1969 J R			
DEC 18 76 JL			

WITHDRAWN FROM
CORNELL UNIVERSITY LIBRARY

PRINTED IN U. S. A.

Cornell University Library
K M988 A3

Verdict! :

3 1924 031 058 476

olin

VERDICT!

Books by Michael A. Musmanno

VERDICT!
>   *The Adventures of the Young Lawyer in the Brown Suit*

JUSTICE MUSMANNO DISSENTS

ACROSS THE STREET FROM THE COURTHOUSE

TEN DAYS TO DIE

LISTEN TO THE RIVER
>   *A novel*

WORLD WAR II IN ITALY

THE SOLDIER AND THE MAN
>   *Story of a General*

AFTER TWELVE YEARS
>   *Sacco-Vanzetti Case*

BLACK FURY (JAN VOLKANIK)
>   *Warner Brothers Picture, starring Paul Muni*

CONSTITUTIONAL AMENDMENTS
>   *Attempts to alter law of the land*

VERDICT!

The Adventures

of the Young Lawyer

in the Brown Suit

BY MICHAEL A. MUSMANNO

Doubleday & Company, Inc.
Garden City, New York

1958

3/25/58
X

k

M988A3

169252B

7day

In the considerate interest of involved persons living,
or of families of persons who have passed away, an occasional
name or designation has been changed.

LIBRARY OF CONGRESS CATALOG CARD NUMBER 58–5951
COPYRIGHT © 1958 BY MICHAEL A. MUSMANNO
TYPOGRAPHY BY ANN BARBARA BENNET
ALL RIGHTS RESERVED
PRINTED IN THE UNITED STATES OF AMERICA
FIRST EDITION

TO
Madeline

Contents

Chapter 1

MY FIRST CASE

THE sky darkened, the planets paused in their headlong course, and mankind held its breath as I entered the courthouse to try my first case. Nothing in life can be so soul-stirring and momentous to any person as a young lawyer's first case is to him. His nerves are at razor's edge, his mind teems with plans and strategies for battle, his heart vibrates like a kettledrum. His feet scarcely touch the pavement, people and things acquire a fourth dimension, and a strange sound rolls through the heavens.

No wonder it seemed to me that the sky had lowered, that the planets had interrupted their plunging race around the sun, and that every man, woman, and child intently watched me as I resolutely advanced to the door carrying my brief case like a shield. Would I accredit myself well? Would I be a competent match for my adversary, who must, of course, have already had considerable experience in the arena of forensic combat?

The case I was about to try was not a murder case. Indeed, it was not even a criminal case unless one concluded it was a crime the way I tried it. The facts were simple. My client, Mrs. Margaret Patric, had been haled into court because of a fifty-dollar doctor's bill which, she protested, she had already paid.

Anyone who has not been a party to a lawsuit might be astonished at the spectacle of a doctor subjecting himself to the annoyance and expense of court proceedings, lawyer's fees, and great loss of time to collect fifty dollars. Even if he won the case, he would be out of pocket more than the amount he could recover. And then, considering his opponent in the controversy, why would she resist a fifty-dollar claim, when the resistance carried with it not only the anguish and harassment of a trial but the chance of losing the suit, coupled with payment of lawyer's fees and assessment of court costs in the bargain? But Mrs. Patric did not intend to lose. She hired for herself the best lawyer in Philadelphia. No, it was not I. She consulted John R. K. Scott, one of the most famous trial lawyers of the generation. Of course he at once informed her that she would be much better off if she paid the doctor's bill.

"But I have paid it!" she exclaimed, her face flushing with indignation.

"I mean the second time. It will cost you more than fifty dollars to defend the suit," Mr. Scott explained and, thinking to dissuade her from her intentions, he added: "I would charge you two hundred dollars to go into court."

Mrs. Patric at once wrote out a check for that amount and handed it to him.

Why was she paying two hundred dollars to defend a fifty-dollar lawsuit? Was it a matter of principle? Yes, but mostly personal pique. The same could undoubtedly also be said of the doctor. The doctor and Mrs. Patric had been friends. They quarreled. Their neighbors and acquaintances learned of the dispute, they fanned the controversy, and the grapevine telegraph did the rest. Personal pique precipitates more litigation than railroad wrecks.

On the Saturday preceding the Monday of the scheduled trial Mr. Scott said to Mrs. Patric, nervously waiting in his office for pre-trial advice: "Madam, I'll call in the lawyer who will try your case."

"Call in the lawyer!" she gasped. "Why, Mr. Scott, *you* are my lawyer!"

"Yes, Mrs. Patric, but I'm in the midst of a rather heavy calendar of trials just now. But have no worry——"

"Mr. Scott, think of my reputation! If I lose I'll be the laughing-stock of the town. I just can't afford to lose."

"Now, Mrs. Patric, don't worry. You'll be happy with the lawyer who'll represent you in court. He's a very capable young fellow."

Scott called for me and I appeared. "Here's your lawyer, Mrs. Patric."

If bewilderment had seized her before, stupefaction gagged her now. She had seen me in the office filing papers, putting away books, carrying messages, and occasionally she had witnessed me dusting desks and picture frames.

Without uttering a word her terrified eyes cried: "What, him?"

Mr. Scott correctly read her glance of dismay and replied: "Yes, he."

But our lady client was no more apprehensive about what was to happen than I. Like a student pilot who looks forward eagerly to his first solo flight, I had excitedly visualized my first trial, but I had always supposed that I would be forewarned weeks, even months, ahead of such a momentous and history-making event. However, like the unexpected rising of a river, the great event was suddenly only two days away.

Mrs. Patric made no effort to conceal her heart-fluttering alarm: "Mr. Scott, may I speak to you alone?"

"There's no necessity for that. I know what's in your mind. You want to tell me that you just have to win, and that's the reason you came to me in the first place, and you don't propose to have your case tried by an office boy. Now isn't that the complaint you want to register? Well, Mr. Musmanno is not an office boy. He is a lawyer—and he's smart, too."

Mrs. Patric looked me over. I tried to look smart but did not make much of a success at it. I felt myself blushing crimson to the roots of my chestnut hair. Mrs. Patric was embarrassed too. "Oh, Mr. Scott, I didn't mean to cast any reflection on Mr. M-M-Muskin—— I can't even pronounce his name. But since you've read my mind, I'm going to ask: How many cases has Mr.—ah—er—this young lawyer tried?"

"Musmanno, drop that dustcloth!" In my abashment I had picked up a hand towel and was polishing the life-size picture of John G. Johnson, nestor of the Philadelphia Bar, which rested in an enormous frame behind Mr. Scott's desk. "How many cases have you tried?" he asked.

Of course he knew the answer. I thrust the polishing cloth behind my back and shamefacedly confessed: "None."

"What?" she cried. "You're going to let him practice on me?"

It was out in the open now. She had looked me over and, so far as she was concerned, I could be returned to pasture. And I could not blame her much. I wore a rusty brown suit, the coat of which, cut square and boxlike, reached almost to my knees. A high collar scraped my chin. An obstreperous lock of my unruly pompadour kept falling into my eyes, no matter how often I brushed it back. I wore buttoned high-top shoes.

She did not want me. But even if I had been a model of sartorial and tonsorial elegance, as was my preceptor, Mr. Scott, I was still a beginner. And why should a beginner practice on her?

And who can say she was unfair in this attitude? I should not enjoy being a young surgeon's first operation. Nor would I care to have a newly made dentist grind my molars. When our own personal hide

is concerned, we all demand the best. But then, how do young professionals ever get started? It is an amazing but comforting reflection,
too, from the standpoint of the neophyte, that there is always someone
who turns up for that first ride on the newly built Ferris wheel.

Mr. Scott rapidly wrote out a check for the retainer she had paid
and handed it to her. She hesitated and then finally refused it. "Very
well," she said. "I'll take a chance with your—Mr. M-Mu—ah—
your young lawyer. But if he loses the case for me, I'll sue you, Mr.
Scott, I'll sue you!"

Those were the ominous circumstances under which I was pushed
into the ring of my first courtroom battle. I simply had to win. Saturday
afternoon and evening and all day Sunday I worked on my speech
to the jury. I read from the works of Demosthenes, Cicero, Patrick
Henry, Rufus Choate, Henry Clay, and Daniel Webster, and then,
gorged from this banquet of eloquence, I prepared what seemed to
me a masterpiece. I went over it several times, polishing it until it
glittered with classic allusions, and then tried it out before twelve
empty chairs in the empty waiting room of our office. The oration
began:

"Gentlemen of the jury, in the first book of Corpus Juris, com-
piled by the renowned Emperor Justinian, there appears the sen-
tentious pronouncement: *'De Iustitia et iure Iustits est constana et
perpetua voluntas ius suum cuique tribuena.'* This postulation has
come thundering down the ages, it has rumbled through the centuries,
it has roared in the councils of the mighty, it has detonated in parliamentary halls, it has vociferated in popular assemblies, it has been the
artillery of reason, the bombilation of righteousness. Justice, gentlemen
of the jury. But there have been times when its resounding cry has
dwindled to a whisper. Why? The hand of greed, infamy, and deception has clutched it by the throat and its voice faltered, its lips
stuttered—etc., etc., etc."

This beginning imparts an idea of the nature and flavor of the
entire speech.

And so, on a mild but memorable morning early in the month of
September, 1923, the momentous trial of Dr. Thomas Dantrus versus
Margaret Patric got under way before Judge Knowles and a jury of
twelve men* in the Municipal Court of the old Philadelphia City Hall.
The doctor's friends took over the right side of the courtroom while
Mrs. Patric's followers, like the cheering section of a girl's college,
streamed into the seats on the left. The plaintiff, Dr. Dantrus, beamed

---

* The law at the time did not yet permit women jurors.

with confidence as he conferred with his veteran counsel, Raymond
Phillips. Mrs. Patric, sitting at my side at counsel table, solicitously
asked me if I felt all right and if I knew just what I was to do. I smiled
at her and told her there was nothing to worry about.

Attorney Phillips, sixty years of age, rough and well seasoned,
looked me over with an expression which easily could be interpreted:
"This is too easy—a champion should at least have a *little* opposition."

The judge rapped for order and the trial was on. Mr. Phillips barked
out the names of his witnesses, who animatedly ascended the witness
stand and, under his deft questioning and leading jabs, quickly and
glibly told their stories. Phillips apparently intended to make short
work of the case as he briskly moved about the courtroom like a prize
fighter who, having taken the measure of his opponent, entertains the
audience with fancy footwork while he loads the lethal punch which
will set the birds to tweeting in the ears of his panting foe.

Dr. Dantrus was equally sure of himself in the witness chair as he
self-confidently related his matter-of-fact story. My cross-examination
did not even ruffle his aplomb, much less shake his positive testimony
that Mrs. Patric had refused to honor his bill after he had treated her
professionally for nearly a month. I could see lines of worry etching into
Mrs. Patric's face, but I patted her hand and reassured her that I had
everything under complete control. I was depending, of course, on the
heavy artillery of my closing speech.

Mr. Phillips now rested his case and I called Mrs. Patric to the
stand. In an excited manner she told how she had received medical
treatments from Dr. Dantrus and how, when his services had termi-
nated, she paid him fifty dollars, demonstrating to the jury with
nervous movements how she had counted out to him four ten-dollar
bills and two five-dollar bills. I asked her if there would be any reason
for her not to meet her obligations to Dr. Dantrus. In a shrill voice
and with eyes flashing she replied: "Of course not!"

Thinking to put her at ease, I said: "Mrs. Patric, I am sure the
Court and jury are very much interested in what you are saying, so
you may speak calmly."

"Calmly?" she shouted. "How can I be calm when that man"
—dramatically pointing to Dr. Dantrus—"is trying to ruin my reputation!"

Mr. Phillips leaped to his feet, expostulating: "This is outrageous
conduct, and I ask the Court to instruct this young lawyer to control
his client."

I rose and apologized to the Court for Mrs. Patric's outburst and made assurance it would not happen again. Mrs. Patric now took hold of herself and finished her direct examination with quiet emphasis, repeating that she had paid the plaintiff what she owed him and she could not understand why he should annoy her so. I was relieved that she had lowered her voice and now seemed entirely self-possessed, but when Mr. Phillips approached the witness stand for his cross-examination she received him like a tigress, which, of course, was a big mistake. In his skillful hands she became putty. By baiting her and taunting her with sarcastic questions, he got her to make several contradictory statements which did not sit well with the all-male jury.

The next witness, however, restored authenticity to our defense. Mrs. Mary Wilkin, a neighbor of Mrs. Patric's, testified that she was actually present when Mrs. Patric paid the doctor. My gratification over this substantive confirmation of Mrs. Patric's assertions was only short-lived. When Attorney Phillips aggressively advanced to cross-examine Mrs. Wilkin, she wilted. Phillips' huge bulk, booming voice, and machine-gun fire of questions so bewildered her that she could not remember the date on which she saw Mrs. Patric satisfy the bill, could not even say whether the transaction occurred in the summer or winter, and could not tell in what denominations of currency the bill had been liquidated. She left the witness stand very much shaken, her credibility even more so.

The next three to testify were women who associated with Mrs. Patric socially. They said that they knew Mrs. Patric well and that she was a woman who always paid her bills. Mr. Phillips objected to these witnesses, and one by one they were retired by the judge like baseball batters being called out on strikes under the deadly aim of a Christy Mathewson.

Manifestly things were not going too well for the vindication of Mrs. Patric's reputation, which she had entrusted to the masterful hands of Mr. Scott, who, in turn, had entrusted it to me, but I was not alarmed. I had by now shed all the apprehensions and timidity with which I had entered the courtroom, and I felt the assurance of the captain of a battleship steaming by shore batteries with guns of a shorter range than his own. I felt confident that we would win in the end. I glowed in visualizing that final scene when my argument to the jury would carry everything before it by the sheer power of oratory. At college, after participating in many debates, I had been elected to Delta Sigma Rho, renowned international collegiate debating fraternity, the gold key of which dangled proudly from the end of my watch chain falling through the buttonhole in the spreading lapel of my rusty brown coat.

Mr. William T. Connor, Mr. Scott's partner, came into the court-room to see how I was progressing. Sitting at the table beside me, he whispered: "You are too stiff. You walk and talk as if you were encased in armor plate."

I smiled. "Not armor plate, Mr. Connor, but sixteen-inch cannon that will pierce the stony indifference of that jury box and bring us such a victory as will cause Daniel Webster to look to his laurels," I replied in scrambled metaphor to myself.

The testimony now ended, Attorney Phillips advanced to the jury box and launched his attack—and what an attack. He stamped his feet, waved his arms, and pounded the rail while his powerful voice rose and fell through the vaulted chamber like the clamor of a storm at sea. To him the whole defense was ridiculous, and he thundered this to the jury; and the jurors, from all indications, were believing him. "There's too much of this evasion of honest debts," he vociferated. "Dr. Dantrus has done his work. Why shouldn't he be paid. Mrs. Patric says she paid. Preposterous! Where's her receipt? If she had a receipt, any scrap of paper to attest to the payment of the fifty dollars, you may be certain that her counsel would have had her present it. No lawyer, no matter how inept, would overlook anything so important as that."

Phillips swept a derogatory hand in my direction. My sixteen-inch cannon shrank at least to five-inch-gun size.

"I'm willing to stake my entire reputation as a lawyer on the out-come of this case," Phillips taunted. "If I could possibly lose so simple, so transparent, so self-proving a case as this one, then it could truly be said I am no longer a lawyer. We've proved my client did his work, we've proved he always gave a receipt for bills paid, and the defendant has failed to present any receipt, which she certainly would possess if she had paid the money. In my thirty-five years of practice, never did justice so clearly rest with the plaintiff. Gentlemen, you ought to decide this case in five minutes—and return a verdict for the amount legally and justly due my client."

My oratorical guns had shriveled to cap pistols, and I felt strangely tired and alone. As I struggled to my feet to reply, I could feel my throat as tight as a drumhead and my lips as parched as those of a desert traveler. Through some means of locomotion of which I was totally unaware, I found myself standing before the jury rail.

The twelve men looked me over with an indifference slightly tinged with curiosity as to what I would say, for, from all they had heard, there was not much for me to say. The courtroom spun dizzily as stage fright seized and swung me about its monstrous head. When I reached the floor again, the jury box had filled with twelve interrogating giants, each one questioning my very presence. My head alternated between hotness and coldness, while my hands became the most abnormal appendages, hanging grotesquely at my sides.

But my crowning incapacitation was that I had forgotten my speech! Not a word of that monumental oration which had overwhelmingly convinced the twelve chairs the evening before came to mind through the mist and fog which swirled about me. For a moment I grasped at the straw of relief flashing by in the rapids of panic that possibly this was all a nightmare, and I anticipated the moment when I should cast aside the blankets and laugh at this somnolent disaster.

A juror coughed. I coughed. I wiped my forehead. If only I could sneak out of that courtroom. From the corner of my eye I caught sight of Mrs. Patric, her face a picture of frozen horror. Her reputation, her reputation! I could hear her menacing words: "If he loses the case, I'll sue you, Mr. Scott, I'll sue you!" Despite this threat, Mr. Scott had insisted I try the case. He had reposed faith in me. A wave of determination rolled over me. I would collapse and die right there on the floor before I would fail that good man, the man who had given me a chance. I clenched my hands until my nails cut into the skin.

"Gentlemen of the jury," I rasped.

Where was that speech? If only I could seize a few words of it—for a start at least.

"Gentlemen of the jury," I repeated. The mist cleared slightly. "My worthy opponent has told you that he has been trying cases for thirty-five years." The fierce tension was moderating. I had actually formulated and spoken a sentence. "Thirty-five years," I repeated as I struggled to gain composure. "It is indeed a long time to be practicing law—and that explains Mr. Phillips' extraordinary ability. Thirty-five years. His client should be congratulated on having so experienced an attorney to represent him. And my client, poor woman, is entitled to sympathy in having so inexperienced a lawyer representing her, because, gentlemen of the jury, *this is my first case.*"

The expression on the faces of those twelve men before me changed like a dark landscape suddenly flooded by sunlight. Sympathy softened their countenances as dawn gilds the outlines of awakening nature. They looked up at me as if they were seeing me for the first time, and in that moment of surprise and commiseration for a young lawyer trying his first case they were eager to hear what he had to say.

I did not let them wait. I abandoned all effort to recall the Ciceronian opus I had concocted; I decided to speak to the subject which at that instant seemed to be absorbing their excited interest; namely, the trepidations and inadequacies of a young lawyer who feels for the first time the shot and shell of courtroom bombardment. I told them, more or less confidentially, that if, while deliberating in the jury room, they encountered phases of Mrs. Patric's case which appeared weak, they should keep in mind that the seeming feebleness was due not to any inherent defect in the proofs but to the immature manner in which her brand-new lawyer had presented it. And at the same time they should consider also that what might seem a very telling point in the plaintiff's favor was probably due to the skillful way in which Mr. Phillips, able and distinguished counsel that he was, had presented it.

I then moved up on the merits of the case. "My distinguished adversary has been practicing law for thirty-five years, but let me say that it does not require thirty-five years to see the injustice he is trying to perpetrate on my innocent client. Attorney Phillips claims that because of his thirty-five years' experience he can diagnose a case better than others, but let me say that penetration of vision is not limited to age; and my eyes, as young as they may be, can see and distinguish between black and white."

Here I proceeded to brand practically everything the plaintiff had presented as black and to portray everything my client had submitted as white. I recalled to them Mrs. Patric's testimony that she had paid the controverted bill and that a witness had corroborated the fact of payment, even though she did not remember the exact date of the payment. I asked them to drink from the fountain of logic: "Why would a woman of Mrs. Patric's standing in the community subject herself to embarrassment in court and the humiliation of a brutal cross-examination such as that administered by Attorney Phillips if she were not moved by a great principle—to defend her good name against the insinuations of Dr. Dantrus.

"Certainly, so far as time, effort, and expense are concerned, it costs her more to defend a fifty-dollar lawsuit than to pay fifty dollars. But the respect of one's neighbors, personal honor, and the retention of a good name mean more than the four ten-dollar bills and two five-dollar bills she paid into the hands of the *forgetful* Dr. Dantrus. Let us be charitable and say he *forgot*." Like a smoke signal rising from a distant hill, I believed I saw the suggestion of a sympathetic smile forming on the face of one of the jurors. I directed my immediate attention to him. "Is it any wonder that Mrs. Patric became excited on the stand as she was required to relate what no one had ever dared to question in her whole life, how she paid her just debts?"

I argued along this line for several minutes, but I intuitively felt that the vehicle on which Mrs. Patric might more likely ride to victory was the one that her lawyer was undergoing his baptism of fire. Thus, without being too brash about it, I never allowed that note to escape too far from the burden of my song. "Don't penalize Mrs. Patric because of the fault of her lawyer," I pleaded, "and don't reward Dr. Dantrus because of the great ability of his lawyer." And then, toward the end, so as not to seem to be plucking too strenuously at the minor chords, I said: "Members of the jury, forget about the lawyers. Decide the case on its merits—and its merits alone. On that basis I am confident that you will return a verdict for the defendant, Mrs. Patric."

But the jury could not forget about the lawyers. Phillips had thrust his personality into the case, and I had introduced myself as one of the figures to be considered. As the attorney for the plaintiff, Mr. Phillips was entitled to make the last speech to the jury, so that when I finished he strode to the jury box, again to excoriate people who welshed on their debts, as he put it. His voice again rose and fell like a storm at sea, again he eulogized his client, again he impaled Mrs. Patric on spears of scorn, and again he belittled her attorney, but he could not deny that her attorney was trying his first case, and that apparently was an item of monumental concern to the jury. After his speech, which was followed by the judge's charge, the jury retired for deliberation.

Five minutes later they returned with a verdict. My heart mounted to my throat as the foreman of the jury began to speak. The atmosphere rang with music, the courtroom burst into song, and bells sweetly chimed as there fell upon my ears the enchanting words: "VERDICT FOR THE DEFENDANT!"

Mrs. Patric had proved that she had paid her bill—and the young lawyer had won his first case.

Chapter II

"THIS CASE YOU'LL LOSE"

THE following morning Mr. Scott congratulated me and then, in a genial tone, added: "And now you are going to try a case which you will lose." For six months the case of Elsie Rondosky versus Henry and Mary Black had been ready for trial, but it was constantly being postponed because none of the other lawyers on Mr. Scott's staff cared to undertake the responsibility of trying it.

Our client, who was the plaintiff, Mrs. Elsie Rondosky, owned land which her neighbors, Henry and Mary Black, daily invaded. To keep them out, Mrs. Rondosky erected a fence. The Blacks tore down the fence, turned it into a bonfire, and fanned the smoke into the Rondosky home. The Blacks contended they had the right to cross Mrs. Rondosky's property because of uninterrupted use of a path over it for twenty-one years. Extraordinary as it may seem to a non-legal reader, it is a fact that if someone trespasses on your land and continues to trespass long enough, the law finally legalizes the imposition, and the resulting outrage is called an easement. Harry Black and his wife had other ways of reaching a public thoroughfare without passing over the Rondosky land, but because they were *that* kind of neighbor, they insisted on noisily tramping through our client's back yard. Mrs. Rondosky initiated a lawsuit to extinguish the alleged easement and obtain the full sovereignty of her land, to which she was entitled.

The case came on for trial in the Court of Common Pleas of Philadelphia County with the aristocratic Judge Mermiller presiding. After glancing at the documents on the bench before him, the judge quizzically eyed me and asked: "Are you representing the plaintiff?"

I rose and bowed. "Yes, Your Honor."

"Very well," he commented in a deprecatory tone which carried with it the surprising intonation: "Well, you don't have much of a case, but you can begin."

I made a short opening statement to the jury and called the plaintiff to the witness stand. I had only asked her two or three questions when the judge interposed and proceeded to catechize her as if on cross-examination. Did she build the fence? he asked her. Didn't the Blacks have the right to reach the street? he queried further. Mrs. Rondosky explained that the Blacks could reach the street without passing over her preserves; they could use Maple Lane. Maple Lane had nothing to do with the case, the judge tartly observed.

I could not believe my eyes and ears. I had always assumed a judge to be the very symbol of impartiality, but this judge, like the proverbial Sinn Feiner's neutrality *against* England, had taken up a blunderbuss of impartiality against my client. Without even a pretense at weighing the conflicting contentions, he had pushed aside the scales and was prejudging the issue before he could possibly know what the evidence would develop. I hoped, however, that after he had got over his first impressions he would allow the attorneys to try the case untrammeled by excessive intervention on his part. It was a vain hope. He was even more belligerent with the plaintiff's daughter, Bertha Rondosky, who followed her mother to the witness stand. In fact, he badgered all our witnesses to such an extent that the twenty-year-old Bertha, still smarting from the judge's sarcasm and ire, slid up to me at the counsel table and whispered, her pretty brown eyes flashing indignation: "Fight him, Mr. Musmanno, I think he is terrible."

But how was I to fight the judge? My only chance for a verdict lay in the possibility that I might get our story over to the jury in my summation. But the following morning, at the termination of the testimony, when I rose to address the jury, the judge asked in a voice which cut like a scimitar: "What? Are you going to talk to the jury? Isn't the question involved strictly a legal one for the Court to decide?"

"Your Honor," I replied, "since there are facts in dispute, I believe I should present our side of the case to the jury."

"All right, go ahead," he observed petulantly, "although I don't know what you can possibly tell them that will decide the real issue here."

I swallowed hard and advanced to the rail of the jury box. "Gentlemen of the jury," I began, my voice low.

"Young man!" Lightning flashed from the judicial Olympus. I swallowed again. What could be wrong now? I turned and faced the bench. The judge glared. "Don't stand so close to the jury box. Get back to the counsel table!"

I felt relieved that the judge's objection was not addressed to anything more serious, for, after all, it was an easy matter to speak from the counsel table. I had a good jury voice. Mr. Scott himself told me that. So I returned to the counsel table and bowed almost to an angle of ninety degrees. "I'm sorry, Your Honor, I incorrectly assumed that I should stand close to the jury box. I had seen other lawyers do so, but of course I shall gladly abide by Your Honor's wishes."

Then, turning on not quite the full power of my lungs but enough to let the jury know I meant business, I began anew: "Gentlemen of the jury, this is in effect a trespass case, because we seek to establish to your satisfaction that the defendants have no right to trespass on our property."

"You are not seeking anything of the kind!" was the next broadside from the bench. "What are you telling the jury that for? That isn't the issue at all."

I now resolved on a definite course of action. The judge's antagonism was so marked that it must have been obvious to everyone in the courtroom. Accordingly I decided that, instead of fighting him, as Bertha Rondosky had suggested, I would be humble, bowing like a reed in a storm before every wrathful demonstration from Mount Everest. In this manner I might possibly win the sympathy of the jury to the extent that they would take up cudgels for me against the tyrant towering at that moment over the whole legal universe. Thus I suppliantly turned to Nero and murmured: "I'm sorry, Your Honor, for that transgression."

"Well, don't let it happen again."

"I shall not, Your Honor."

I resumed. "Gentlemen of the jury, let us get to the roots of this controversy. Let us ask ourselves: What is the motive for the defendants' constant and wanton invasion of the tranquillity and peace of my client's property?"

"Mr. Musmanno! What has motive got to do with this case?"

The judge's face blazed red with fury and I bowed in contrition. In fact, I went so low in the arc of homage that I almost banged my head against the table. Then, turning to the jury, I begged forgiveness again: "Gentlemen, as His Honor has properly said in correcting me, motive has nothing to do with this case, and you will please ignore my referring to it."

And thus the sorry spectacle went on. In the course of a thirty-minute speech I was interrupted and verbally lampooned over a dozen times. The Blacks, of course, were laughing behind their hands at my discomfiture, and, so far as their attorney was concerned, he could never have done so well as his new-found Olympian ally was doing for him. When I completed my heckle-punctuated summation, he rose and, with unction dripping from every joint, he crooked his back even more than I had done and purred: "Your Honor, I will waive my closing speech, leaving it to Your Honor to present the respective positions of the plaintiff and the defendants."

It was heady wine and the judge accepted the flattery as an actor reaches for a bouquet handed up over the footlights. Gathering his silken robes regally about him, settling himself more comfortably in his chair, he turned to the jury and proceeded to deliver the *coup de grâce* to the plaintiff's case, which was already reeling from his previous blows. He said in effect that there was no merit in Mrs. Rondosky's position but that he was allowing the jury to pass upon the issue only because he wanted the matter ended once and for all. While, he explained, the jury had the right to decide either for the plaintiff or the defendants, he could not see how they could return any verdict except for the defendants. He then picked up a lawbook and from its pages extracted a few handfuls of jurisprudence which he flung at them without elucidation or interpretation, like a farmer feeding chickens. He wound up his charge, however, in language as clear as a cascading brook; namely, "I expect you to return in a very short time with a verdict for the defendants."

But the jury did not return in a short time with a verdict for the defendants. After five hours they returned with a verdict for the plaintiff, Mrs. Rondosky.

The judge exploded: "What do you mean by such an outlandish verdict?" almost falling out of his chair.

The foreman dared to throw salt into the open wounds of the jurist's vanity: "Your Honor, we mean that the plaintiff is entitled to everything that her attorney, Mr. Musmanno, has asked for, putting up the fence, keeping the Blacks on their own property and all that."

"You won't do anything of the kind!" he retorted fiercely, "and I'm ordering you to change your verdict right now so that it will read: 'For the defendants.' "

In ecstasy at the jury's verdict but in astonishment at what the judge was doing, I bounded to my feet with hand upraised and exclaimed: "Your Honor, I object, and protest legally, morally, and in every way possible to what Your Honor is doing."

He waved me down with a silk-draped arm and dictated a verdict for the Blacks, and it was so recorded. The jury looked on, dumfounded. I was stunned, and as the judge swept out of the courtroom with authoritative and triumphant stride, Bertha Rondosky burst into tears. "Mr. Musmanno, can he do that? I told you he was terrible." I tried to comfort her, while my own emotions tumbled before this phenomenon for which no study in my legal education had prepared me.

I stumbled back to the office, hurting in every atom of my being that I had been assigned a case which the other lawyers in the office had refused to try because it could not be won. Only several days before my heart had warbled a merry melody of victory; now it was tolling a melancholy bell of defeat. As I sat brooding and crestfallen at my desk, I felt a gentle hand on my shoulder, and a soft voice spoke: "Musmanno, I congratulate you."

"Congratulations?" I moaned. "I lost the case." I lifted my head to look up into the handsome face of John R. K. Scott. "Young man," he said, his countenance alight with amused contentment, "don't you realize what you did? You not only defeated the opposing lawyer but you beat the judge too. You used good psychology before the jurors and won them away from the judge. I was in the courtroom watching you. You did a good job and won a nice victory."

And so I won my second case, because the court *en banc* (three judges) reversed Judge Mermiller and reinstated our verdict.

Chapter III

METEORS OF DREAMS

How did I become a lawyer and what wheel of destiny took me to the office of the celebrated John R. K. Scott, who not only unfurled for me the horizon of a legal career but kept it clear when clouds of discouragement hovered? To tell that story I must lift the curtain on one of those nostalgic schoolboy days when I appeared with Arthur Young, a classmate of my age, in the office of the supervising principal to give an accounting of ourselves for fighting in the schoolyard. It all happened in Stowe Township, a semi-rural community six miles from Pittsburgh on the Ohio River, and we were twelve years old.

Professor Patton, the principal, sternly looked down at us as we stood before him with muddy faces, disheveled hair, and clothing torn in the furious fray. "I'm amazed at this exhibition of primitive battle," he observed. "I don't know what to do to you for this serious infraction of school rules." He paused for a moment, and then his face lit up with apparently a bright idea. "I'll leave it to both of you to decide what punishment I should impose."

Arthur, in a burst of bravado, spoke up: "Well, Professor Patton, since we broke the rules of the school, I think you should give us a whipping."

"Very well, Arthur. You have spoken like a brave boy." Then, turning to me, he asked: "Michael, what have you to say? Do you not agree with Arthur?"

"I certainly do not, Professor Patton," I replied, my Windsor tie rippling with indignation. "It is an easy thing for Arthur to speak of a whipping because he has been here a number of times for fighting, but you have never had me here, have you, Professor, except to confer on me the certificate of honor for making the highest marks of the year?"

"That's true, Michael," he admitted, a little taken aback.

"Well, even if I was wrong in fighting with Arthur, and maybe I was and maybe I was not, this is the first time I have been before you on a matter like this. And so I think I am entitled to a chance, don't you, Professor?"

"W-w-well, Michael, I don't know. Fighting is a very bad business, but——"

"I thank you very much, Professor, and since you have decided not to whip me, I ask that you also not whip Arthur."

"But I haven't really decided yet——"

"Professor Patton, you said that 'fighting is a very bad business, but.' 'But' would mean that you are going to forgive us, wouldn't it?"

"All right, Michael, I'll let you both off, but don't let it happen again." Then, as I was leaving the office, the forbearing pedagogue stopped me, patted me on the head, and said: "Michael, you certainly know how to argue. You ought to make a pretty good lawyer when you grow up."

A lawyer! Was it possible I could someday be a lawyer? That night the sky streamed meteors of dreams. The next day at my little oaken desk in the old country schoolhouse I kept looking out the window, building with my imagination, in the Ohio River Valley below, a marble courthouse with a golden dome. Would I ever see myself in that courthouse—a lawyer?

Several years later I was working as a clerk in a government department in Washington where, each Sunday morning after church, I reveled in a walk which began at the Capitol, carried me through the Agricultural and Smithsonian grounds, across the classic shadow of the Washington Monument, and ended at the beautiful Lincoln Memorial. I never failed, on reaching that magnificent marble temple, to enter it to admire and draw inspiration from one of the most dignifiedly dramatic statues of one of the very best of men in the whole panorama of history. While there I would see from time to time an aged man also studying Lincoln's statue with a reverence akin to worship. Of medium height, wearing the mustache and beard usually associated with the Civil War period, he bore a quaint charm and distinction which held me in a spell of irresistible fascination.

One day after the picturesque visitor had left I inquired of the guard at the Memorial if he knew who this person might be. For a moment the guard regarded me silently and then answered with a rising inflection in his voice: "Why, don't you know who that is?" I apprehended at once from his counterquestion that the man we were discussing must be some famous personage, and with tensed curiosity

I waited to hear the disclosure of his name. However, I never expected to hear what now fell awesomely from the old guard's lips. "My boy," he said, and he lowered his tone almost to a whispered hush, "that's Abraham Lincoln's son."

My heart stopped beating in the momentousness of the revelation. Then the story of Lincoln was real. It was not merely an engaging legend fashioned for school children and impressionable youths like myself. Lincoln actually lived, and he had a son as other fathers have sons, and I had seen that son. I had actually cast eyes upon the young man who had witnessed the surrender of General Lee at Appomattox and was the first person to carry the details of the dramatic meeting between Grant and Lee to his father in Washington. Perhaps I might even get to shake the hand of that boy who had walked over this very ground with the sixteenth President of the United States, and who, on that convulsive night of horror of April 14, 1865, had seen the tall oak of wisdom, goodness, and mercy totter and fall to the earth, leaving a void against the sky.

Every hour of every day of the following week a fever of desire burned in my veins to meet with and talk to Robert Todd Lincoln. By the time the Sabbath sun again gilded the path of my weekly constitutional, I had resolved that I would muster the necessary courage to approach him and at least touch his hand. As I waited in the rotunda of the Memorial, looking up into the eyes of his father seated perpetually in the marble chair of sculptor Daniel Chester French's masterpiece, I could feel the shadow of Robert Lincoln close by. There he stood as I had seen him so many Sundays in the past without realizing he was the living bridge between the present and the past. I turned and, through misty eyes which doubled every image, I made my way to his side and in a voice which seemed to belong to someone else and to come from a great distance, I managed to say: "I am—very sorry—to disturb you—Mr. Lincoln—but may—may I shake your hand?"

He lowered his gaze from the statue, where it had been fixed as if this were the first time he had seen it, and faced me. Time raced backward and I felt myself standing in the presence of Abraham Lincoln, the rail splitter, the lawyer, the statesman. I sensed all the sorrows and sadnesses of the lonely soul of the Sangamon. A strong, firm hand gripped mine and a pleasant and friendly voice said: "Of course you may. I have seen you here many times. Are you an admirer of my father?"

What could I say? It was like being asked if I admired St.

Paul. He noted my embarrassment and asked me if I was going to school, and when I nodded affirmatively he asked if I was preparing for any particular career. I was now able to stammer a reply: "I'd like to be a lawyer."

"It is one of the noblest professions of mankind because it is devoted to justice," he commented. And then, as if he were quietly addressing a group of young men in the rotunda, he went on: "My father often quoted Daniel Webster, who said: 'Justice is the great interest of man on earth. It is the ligament which holds civilized beings and civilized nations together. Wherever her temple stands, and so long as it is duly honored, there is a foundation for social security, general happiness, and the improvement and progress of our race.' " He paused and placed his hand on my shoulder. "To what greater ideal could one dedicate one's life than justice? And where could it be better fought for than in the arena of the law? Yes, my boy, you will make no mistake in studying law."

"Thank you so much, Mr. Lincoln, I shall always remember this blessed moment. I can't tell you how happy you have made me, how much you have inspired me. I just can't believe I am talking to the son of Abraham Lincoln. It is simply so wonderful—so wonderful—so wonderful——"

By this time I was in full tears, sobbing with excitement, pride, and happiness. As I mopped my wet eyes and cheeks, Mr. Robert Lincoln took me by the arm and we slowly emerged from the temple in which his father's statue is enshrined, as his memory is hallowed in the heart of the nation. As we walked toward Mr. Lincoln's automobile, which was parked a few hundred feet from the memorial, I saw a souvenir stand with miniature replicas of Daniel Chester French's artistic creation. "Mr. Lincoln," I said to my venerable companion, feeling now more at ease, "I'd like to buy one of those little statues, and it would make me very happy and proud if you would touch it—it would always be an inspiration to me."

"My boy," he said, "let me get it for you."

My heart soared. I was about to receive a gift directly from the hands of Abraham Lincoln's son. Suddenly, however, my cheeks were brush fires of embarrassment and self-humiliation. What was I doing? It seemed as if I were actually asking him to make me a gift. "Oh no!" I cried out in the utmost confusion. "I couldn't let you do that! I want to pay for it!"

But by this time a dollar bill from Mr. Lincoln's wallet had transferred to the pocket of the sidewalk merchant, who, all smiles and courtesies for his distinguished customer, whom he apparently knew well from previous visits, handed the statuette to the scion of the Rail Splitter, who now, in turn, passed it over to me.

Again my handkerchief was at my eyes as I sobbed joyously: "Oh, Mr. Lincoln, thank you, thank—you."

No matter where I have been and where I have traveled, that little dollar plaster-of-paris souvenir, from which I would not part for any money, has accompanied me, and it now occupies the most prominent spot in my home. And if ever tiredness overwhelms or weariness obtrudes, I have but to glance at this Abraham Lincoln of my impressionable and ever-sensitive youth; and courage with strength pours into my veins like an Edwin Markham poem.

I saw Mr. Robert Todd Lincoln several times after that first memorable Sunday, and on each occasion he took my hand warmly and wished me well in my ambition to become a lawyer.

There is perhaps no place in the world where a self-earning student can better study law than in Washington. The hours at the various universities are so arranged that, although employed during the day, one may still obtain a professional education by attending noon and evening classes. World War I interrupted my studies, but I immediately returned to them after I had put away my army uniform and donned civilian clothes again.

May 1923 found me in Philadelphia preparing to take the Pennsylvania bar examinations. Contrary to what may be the lay belief, American jurisprudence is not uniform throughout the nation. My studies in Washington had not equipped me for the searching questions on the statutes, decisions, and procedures peculiar to the Keystone State. Moreover, after I had obtained my Bachelor of Law degree at Georgetown University I went on, at the George Washington, American, and National universities, to acquire several other diplomas in the arts and sciences, so that in point of time and subject matter I was thus even still farther removed from the subjects which would be covered in the awesome test. A law professor in Philadelphia warned me it would be impossible to prepare myself in only fifty days (the time yet intervening) for the Pennsylvania bar examinations, rated in the academic world as among the most difficult in the nation. Other lawyers, whose opinion I sought, echoed the same alarm.

But with the inspiration of Lincoln firing my brain, I could brook no delay. If I did not take the current examinations I would need to wait eight months for the next examinations, and in the chronology of ambitious youth eight months is a decade, and to stand still for a decade is to die. Thus, impetuously, I dived headlong into the vast ocean of Pennsylvania jurisprudence and set out to swim to the other side—in fifty days.

By curtailing my sleeping time to five hours a night I was able to devote nineteen uninterrupted hours to my studies each day. Every morning at three o'clock, as the alarm clock jangled me into confused consciousness, I gulped a pint of black coffee, staggered to my feet, and attacked my books, standing up at the mantelpiece. If I allowed myself to sit down, sleep would lay me low like a blow on the head.

Determined not to allow a grain of sand in the fateful hourglass to be lost, I pasted pages of notes on the mirror and memorized their contents while I washed and brushed my teeth. Reducing dressing time to a minimum, I had only one cravat, an elastic affair which I could slip around my shirt collar in two seconds. I eschewed all entertainment, read no newspapers or magazines, took no physical exercise, visited with no friends. My meals consisted of sandwiches washed down with coffee, Coca-Cola, and ginger ale, all calculated to keep me awake as I unceasingly devoured treatises of law, volumes of statutes, and scores of textbooks.

Although fond of music, I could not abide it during this feverish hermitage. Somehow it reduced me to profound melancholy. I had a small room which a private family rented out, and here I lived, isolated from all social contact, a being apart from the world. When the landlord's family played phonographic records of sentimental numbers, which they did frequently, study became a precipitous mountainside impossible to climb. With my brain struggling to acquire and retain the abstruse formulae in the volumes before me, while at the same time fighting off the minions of sleep battering at the cerebral doors, I would find my consciousness slipping away on the wings of "Home, Sweet Home" or "Sweet Rosie O'Grady" as I detachedly saw myself turning blank pages of a never-ending book. On these occasions I would escape from this mystic captivity by fleeing to the Broad Street Station of the Pennsylvania Railroad several blocks away, not for the purpose of boarding a train, but to study in a place which could well be accepted as the last spot in the world in which to achieve studious concentration. I piled my books on a bench in the waiting room and studied there amid the steam blasts, bell ringing, and general noises of railroad locomotives puffing in and out of the vast train shed, oblivious to all the excitement of hurrying people shouting greetings and crying farewells. It seems that, psychologically, noises will disturb concentration up to the point that they engulf you and then cease to exist. Whatever may be the explanation for this extraordinary phenomenon, I know that for hours I would sit glued to a hard seat, wrestling with the dull pages of real estate law, partnership law, common law pleading, undisturbed by travelers who dropped their suitcases at my side and tripped over my wholly forgotten feet.

Alfred Smith, former governor of New York, once humorously remarked that his alma mater was the Fulton Fish Market. In the same spirit I could say I am a postgraduate student of the Philadelphia Pennsylvania Broad Street Railroad Station.

At last arrived the ordeal of the examinations, the anguished plying of pen and pencil which determines the law student's fate. Then followed the agony of waiting for the verdict.

One month passed with no word from the Board of Law Examiners. Another month dragged by, and in the soil of futile anticipation the dragon seed of worry began to sprout. To fail this test would shatter my self-confidence. Of course I could retake the examinations later, but a future vindication would not obliterate the misery of the initial frustration. I had never flunked an examination before. To falter now would suggest I could be proficient in every field of endeavor but my chosen life's work.

However, until I heard that some other candidate had passed, I could rest content that the semaphores of silence did not spell shipwreck for me. But came the catastrophic day when, striding along Chestnut Street, I met Charley Bent, his face an unmistakable beacon of bursting joy. "You did—did not—hear from the Board of Law Examiners?" I stammered, stopping dead in my tracks. A cloud of pity passed over the beacon.

"Don't tell me," he gasped in amazement, "that you haven't heard! I would have bet my money on you."

Chestnut Street rocked under my feet and I leaned against a building for support as I visualized the torment of another tedious preparation, another agonizing examination, and another possible shipwreck. I felt my spirit draining, my daring and self-assurance sinking.

"I'm sorry," Bent sympathized, "if I had known, I would have said nothing."

"You would not need to have said anything. As a matter of fact, you did not, but the news was written all over your happy face. Congratulations!"

I slowly walked away, climbed the steps to my room, threw myself on the bed, and sobbed. And to disaster was now added the torture of waiting for news of the misfortune. My ship had failed to come in, but no one yet had seen a floating spar which confirmed the disaster.

Two weeks of excruciating torture crawled by, and still the signal flags flashed no message. I could wait no longer. I determined to know the worst. I entered a telephone booth and forced a nickel into the slot like one plunging a lever to set off a dynamite explosion. "What record do you have on Musmanno?" I demanded of the female voice which answered in the office of the State Board of Law Examiners.

My only recollection through the years is that the voice mumbled a few words and I crumpled in the booth with the receiver at the end of the cord swinging in my face like the pendulum of a grandfather's clock. What had happened was that the letter carrying the news of my fate had been sent to a wrong address.

I had passed! I was admitted to the Bar.

But on the heels of this world-shaking event followed an astonishing revelation. No one manifested the slightest interest in the fact that I had become that most glorious of legal personages—a Philadelphia Lawyer. I applied at many large law offices in the city to offer my services, but no one wanted a young lawyer or even wished to consider if they might want one later on. It almost seemed that one had to be born into those offices or enter through an old men's home. I tried to obtain a position as legal research analyst in several law publishing firms, but here also youth was looked upon with disfavor. Two alternatives remained: one was to wait until some of the older lawyers died, the other was to open a law office of my own. But the latter was impossible since I had no funds and I was utterly unknown in the City of Brotherly Love, which at the time did not seem so brotherly to me. From the hope-kissed ways for the successful launching of a dazzling lawyer's career, I had slid into the shadow-filled troughs of a receding sea. I thought of entering the pedagogical profession. I wrote to sixty universities throughout the country for a position as teacher or instructor. I received sixty-two answers declining my services. Two universities turned me down twice.

In the meantime, with an eye on a possible literary career, I was writing articles and stories which were coming back with the same regularity and speed as the letters from the universities. However,

one effort found lodgment. The New York *Times* accepted an article
I had written on proposed amendments to the Constitution. They not
only accepted it, but much to my delighted surprise they paid me
thirty-five dollars for it. If it were not that I needed money for
such rather prosaic items as food and rent, I might have framed
the check. My name looked rather artistic on it.

Two weeks later I answered an ad in the Philadelphia *Legal In-
telligencer* for a legal assistant. The name of the advertiser did not
appear. I had already fruitlessly replied to several advertisements of
this character, and the day was now rapidly approaching when I had
to decide whether or not I should go back to my home town of Stowe
Township, admitting that the country boy had failed to make good in
the big city. The next morning, however, on a battered marble-
topped table in the hallway of my cheap boardinghouse I found an
acknowledgment of my answer to the anonymous ad. The letterhead
bore a name which opened my eyes wide—John R. K. Scott—the
most famous lawyer in Philadelphia and recognized as a legal lu-
minary along the whole eastern seaboard. He invited me for an interview.

When I arrived at his offices in the Lincoln Building directly
across from City Hall, which houses the courts in Philadelphia, I
found already some twenty-five or thirty young men waiting to be
interviewed. I felt I should depart at once for the railroad station to
buy a ticket back to Stowe Township. What chance could I have
against these native Philadelphians? But I was fascinated by the
spacious rooms, the crammed bookshelves reaching to the high ceil-
ings, the enormous framed pictures on the walls, the large waiting
room in which tarried, not only my potential rivals but troubled
clients seeking the advice, counsel, and guidance which might make
them happy again. And as I studied their anxious faces, trying to
catalogue them in the long list of people who call on lawyers—murderers, burglars, candidates for divorce, businessmen, salesmen—
I noted that the aspiring legal assistants were entering and leaving
Mr. Scott's office. Suddenly a young lady opened a door and said:
"Mr. Scott will see you now, Mr. Musmanno." I looked around. I
was the last of the applicants.

I could see my shirt front rising and falling over my pounding
heart as Mr. Scott, after a cordial greeting, proceeded to put questions
to me on my education and general background. Then, with a slight
smile, he reached into his desk, withdrew a copy of the voluminous

New York *Times,* handed it to me, and asked: "Did you see this article written by a man with a name exactly like yours?"

My shirt front fluttered like a bird's wing. "Yes—I——"

He broke in: "Did you write the article?"

With a suppressed tremor of excitement I replied: "Yes, Mr. Scott."

He now smiled broadly. "I knew that. That's the reason I held you to the end. It's rather hard to choose from so many applicants, but it seems to me you have something more than most young lawyers. You have the energy and desire for research. Nothing can be more important in the practice of the law than accurate knowledge of the law—and knowledge comes from studious application to the books, reading of law reviews, a familiarity with the statutes as they come from Congress and the legislature. A good lawyer must know how to burn the midnight oil. And I can see from this article that you have the spirit of research and a hunger for objectivity."

"Oh, thank you, Mr. Scott, thank you."

"More than that, I note that you have a good jury voice." He now paused and as I waited with my nerves tied in knots, for him to say: "I'll let you know if we ever have a place for you," he went on: "Come in tomorrow, and I'll assign you to an office."

The meteor of dreams which startled me in the Ohio River Valley on that memorable day Professor Patton had voiced his exciting prophecy had landed in my back yard. The great Attorney Scott had chosen me as a member of his staff and he said that I possessed a valuable adjunct of which I had theretofore been entirely unaware. Prior to that moment I never had been conscious of my speaking apparatus. Now I patted my chest gratifiedly and spoke unnecessarily loud to everybody. In a restaurant that evening I found myself ordering roast beef and mashed potatoes in a stentorian tone which caused diners at the adjoining tables to look around for the mass meeting I was addressing.

At last I was a lawyer! Large letters proclaimed to the world that fact on the door of an office of my own. I had tried my first case and won it, and I had not failed in the second. I rose from my desk to admire anew my name on the door, when it opened and Mr. Scott entered.

"Musmanno," he said, "I am sending you to court tomorrow to defend the Reverend Joseph F. Johnson, minister of the Manchester Baptist Church, in the case of Sanford versus Johnson. The plaintiff, Margaret Sanford, will be represented by Arnold Mercer."

"Not Mercer, the executive marshal of the Philadelphia Bar Association?"

"Yes, Mercer, leading spirit of the Philadelphia Bar Association, pillar of Philadelphia society, and veteran of the Philadelphia Bar. But don't let that scare you, my lad."

Chapter IV

A HAPPY RIDE ON HAPPY SHOULDERS

I COULD scarcely blame Arnold Mercer, veteran practitioner and high official of the Philadelphia Bar Association, for the cat-canary expression which overspread his features when he perceived that his adversary in the case of Mrs. Margaret Sanford versus Joseph F. Johnson turned out to be a young lawyer whose inexperience stood out like straw in a farm hand's tousled hair.

Mr. Mercer was attorney for Mrs. Sanford, who, on an assumed loan of four hundred dollars, had sued our client, the Reverend Joseph F. Johnson, Negro minister of the Manchester Baptist Church, which had become a house divided against itself. A fine-looking man —tall and broad-shouldered with a shock of thick gray hair— Reverend Johnson spoke in a melodious basso voice which carried a suggestion of melancholy—the melancholy of a steeple when a storm threatens to tear it from the crest of the church from which it has been looking for decades upon a sometimes sinning and sometimes contrite world. After twenty-five years Reverend Johnson faced an insurgent movement which sought to besmirch his name and leave him a pastor without a flock. The insurgents had prevailed on one of the parishioners, an elderly widow, Mrs. Sanford, to head the campaign of demolition through the medium of a lawsuit, innocent on its face, but deadly in its operation.

The lawsuit alleged that Reverend Johnson had induced one Ralph Harrison to borrow from Mrs. Sanford four hundred dollars, her lifetime savings, to put into his garage business, in which Reverend Johnson was an invisible but financially interested partner. It was claimed further that the four hundred dollars found its way to the coffers of Reverend Johnson, and since Harrison refused to pay the money back after a year's time, it was Reverend Johnson's legal obligation to do so.

If Mrs. Sanford prevailed in her action, Reverend Johnson would be compelled to resign his pastorship because he was being charged with a double-dealing which would strip him of all moral standing in the congregation, in the community, and in the Baptist Church generally. Reverend Johnson denied that he had any hand in the garage business and stated that his association with Harrison was purely religious, Harrison being a contributor to his church.

Unlike Mrs. Patric, Reverend Johnson had not protested my representing him, even though he had engaged the redoubtable John R. K. Scott and even though, if he lost the case, he stood to suffer the irreparable loss of his church and become flotsam and jetsam on the ecclesiastical seas. He was not, however, without friends in this battle for his ministerial life. Some one hundred fifty of his followers were present in court to show their fidelity and present a united front against the opposing faction, which had mustered an equal number in the thronged courtroom. During the trial the embattled partisans from time to time offered audible comment on this "Battle of the Century," and when one side scored or appeared to score an advantage over the other, the more demonstrative of the "winning" brethren lifted their voices in a resounding, enthusiastic "Amen, Brother!" After this had happened several times, the judge announced that any further participation by the audience in the solemn trial would result in his clearing the courtroom. This announcement produced the first and only unanimity during the trial: both sides protested. Nonetheless, despite the protest, both sides respected the order—more or less.

Mr. Mercer had assembled some fifteen witnesses to testify to the details of the transaction which allegedly transferred all of Mrs. Sanford's wealth from her cupboard cookie jar to the clerical pockets of the Reverend Joseph F. Johnson, minister of her church. All of these fifteen witnesses were ardently hostile to Reverend Johnson, who had at one time or another publicly castigated them for immoral and unchristian conduct. Thus, when I opened my case to the jury I said: "We will prove to your eminent satisfaction, members of the jury, that all of the plaintiff's witnesses are prejudiced against their pastor and that they are seeking to effect his ruin out of a desire for revenge because he has disciplined them for misbehavior——"

Mr. Mercer heatedly objected. "If the Court please, Mr. Musmanno's remarks are entirely out of order. This is a civil action, not a criminal case, and he may not introduce any evidence such as he adverts to, to show any supposed ulterior purpose behind Widow Sanford's meritorious claim."

"I will not need to introduce any such evidence," I replied. "I will wring it from the lips of the plaintiff's witnesses in my cross-examination."

No sooner had I spoken these words than I realized I had made a tactical error; I had disclosed to my adversary my trial strategy. Mr. Mercer was not slow in taking advantage of my blunder. He quickly redrew his battle plans. Instead of using the tainted fifteen witnesses, he decided to restrict his case to the plaintiff and one person not connected in any way with the church. In this manner he would prevent me from uncovering the bad faith behind the plaintiff's suit, the exposure of which I had firmly believed would win for Reverend Johnson the good will of the jury and, I hoped, an eventual favorable verdict.

Mr. Mercer called Margaret Sanford to the witness stand, and she testified that she loaned four hundred dollars to Ralph Harrison because she had been told that if Harrison did not pay back the money to her with interest Reverend Johnson would. In cross-examination I asked her who had made this statement and she replied: "Mr. Harrison."

I asked further: "Was Reverend Johnson present when Harrison made this statement?" and she answered: "No."

I turned to the judge. "If the Court please, I move that the statement referred to be struck from the record because it was made without any authorization from Reverend Johnson and not in his presence."

Mr. Mercer rose to protest my motion, but the judge ruled in my favor.

Mr. Mercer now called his second witness, a Harry Martin, who testified that he often heard the reverend talk about Harrison's garage business. The inference intended . to be conveyed here was that Reverend Johnson was using Harrison as a front behind which he carried on an enterprise for his own monetary profit. While it was possible to draw such a conclusion from this testimony, it did not seem to me that the inferential bridge rested on piers of sufficient evidence to support the charge that Reverend Johnson was the financial beneficiary of the Sanford loan. In the execution of his clever plan to prevent my cross-examining his soiled witnesses, Mr. Mercer had now fallen into a tactical folly worse than the one I had committed. In denying himself the benefit of the testimony of his fifteen witnesses, he had failed to present enough evidence to make out a prima-facie case. He did not realize, however, how short he had fallen of proving a claim against my client. Satisfied that he had completely squelched his brash young opponent who thought he was going to have a Roman holiday with his witnesses, Mr. Mercer casually stood up and with serene complacency remarked: "If the Court pleases, I rest my case."

Like an experimental chemist who knows he has the right formula but is still worried as he stirs the brew as to whether he will get what he wants and expects, I rose with outward calm but nervousness within and said: "If the Court please, I move for a compulsory non-suit. Mr. Mercer has completely failed to connect Reverend Johnson in any way with this financial transaction, and, under the Statute of Frauds, the defendant cannot be held to answer for the debt of another without a written promise to that effect."

I could not yet be certain whether the formula would effect the exoneration of my client, but there was no doubt as to the explosive reaction. Mr. Mercer shot to his feet and expostulated: "Mr. Musmanno's inexperience in a courtroom is now making itself too apparent. His motion is entirely out of order. I hold here in my hand a note signed by Mr. Harrison."

I stood up again. "If the Court please, Mr. Mercer is holding in his hand, not a note, but a statement. A note has a certain technical significance. I wish Mr. Mercer would use the proper term."

For a moment it seemed that Mr. Mercer would become apoplectic. It was simply ridiculous that this stripling lawyer, who only three months before had been cooling his heels outside the offices of the Philadelphia Bar Association for admission to the Bar, should be standing up in court and telling him, one of the accepted nestors of that organization, what term he should use. Leveling his forefinger at me, he said icily: "Young man! I don't need you to tell me what is correct phraseology. He then turned to the judge and said: "If the Court please, so as not to precipitate a controversy on an entirely irrelevant matter, I will refer to this document as a writing and not as a note."

"That's better," I commented, without even smiling. "And now," addressing the judge, "I respectfully renew my motion for a compulsory non-suit. Mr. Mercer has failed to connect Reverend Johnson with this transaction in any way. Reverend Johnson obtained no money or any benefit from Mrs. Sanford; he did not sign any writing; he never had any dealings with Mrs. Sanford or Mr. Harrison about the garage business."

The presiding judge was the same Judge Knowles before whom I had tried my first case, and he seemed to derive a great deal of amusement out of my baiting the veteran executive marshal of the

Bar Association. Comfortably leaning back in his chair, he said: "Mr. Musmanno, I'm inclined to agree with you."

Thoroughly angry now, but fighting to retain poise and decorum, Mr. Mercer was livid but his voice pale. "Your Honor, you cannot possibly consider a non-suit here."

Judge Knowles dryly remarked: "Why can't I? It does not seem to me you have established a prima-facie case."

Mercer seethed. "May it please Your Honor, I hope you are not taking seriously this immature, premature motion on the part of this young lawyer."

"Why is it immature, and why is it premature?" Judge Knowles replied, even rocking a little in his chair, thoroughly enjoying the discomfiture of plaintiff's distinguished counsel. "You have rested your case and Mr. Musmanno has moved for a non-suit. Why is that motion immature or premature? You may think that Mr. Musmanno is immature but——"

"Oh, if the Court please, I don't intend to reflect on Mr. Musmanno. I believe he will someday be a very able lawyer, but he certainly has a lot to learn about procedure. Let me present the law on this subject." He then argued for twenty minutes on what constituted a prima-facie case. It was quite apparent that what nettled him most was the possibility that a novice should be worsting him, a Corinthian column of the Philadelphia Bar, on a question of law. At least, if the case went to the jury and he lost, he could blame the defeat on the jury, but that a boy lawyer should tell him what the law was, was simply intolerable.

When Mercer finished his argument, Judge Knowles asked me if I had anything to say in reply. I rose and repeated: "If the Court please, I renew my motion for a non-suit on the ground that the plaintiff has not made out a prima-facie case."

Again the judge remarked: "I'm inclined to agree with you." Then, gathering up the papers on the bench, he conclusively decided: "The motion for non-suit is granted."

For a moment time seemed poised on the brink of eternal silence. Then, like a clap of thunder, applause shattered the courtroom calm. And in the wake of the triumphant turbulence, clouds of groans ascended from the defeated anti-Johnson faction. "God help us!" they cried. Chairs screeched and feet shuffled as the demonstrators cheered and moaned. Then, above the increasing pandemonium, a lusty voice shouted: "Hurrah for Reverend Johnson's lawyer!" "Hurrah! Hurrah!" others chorused. And as I reached for my brief case, I saw a hundred hands pushing through the overturned furniture to press congratulations.

"Order! Order in the court!" the tipstaves bellowed in the flood of disorder inundating the sanctum of the law. "Order!" the judge intoned as he banged his gavel and retreated to his chambers. Suddenly I felt myself being hoisted above the heads of the surging mass. Several of the reverend's more enthusiastic disciples had lifted me to their shoulders and clamorously proceeded to parade me triumphantly from the courtroom into and through the corridors of the startled courthouse. While the ride was a trifle on the rough side, I cannot say, in full verity, that I did not enjoy it.

Chapter V

MY FIRST CRIMINAL CASE

WITH the cheers of Reverend Johnson's enthusiastic supporters playing in my ears a delightful xylophonic concert, I glowed in the realization that I had now tried and won three civil cases. Although my brief case still vibrated with nervous apprehension each time I pushed open the courtroom door to face the storm and strife of a trial, I believed that perhaps I was acquiring an aptitude which might justify Mr. Scott's confidence in me and I now looked forward to trying my luck in a criminal case. The opportunity came quickly. The case carried the imposing title of The Commonwealth of Pennsylvania versus Sherman Tecumseh Grant.

It was not, in all reality, what might be called a *cause célèbre*. Newspaper reporters were not impatiently waiting with poised and smoking pencils to record the dramatic developments of the conflict, crowds were not fighting for admittance to the courtroom, photographers were not hanging in transoms to snap forbidden pictures of the celebrated defendant. The defendant, in fact, despite his illustrious name, was as obscure as a dotted figure in a photograph of twenty thousand fans in the bleachers of a double-header ball game. Nor was the nature of the criminal charge one to excite the absorbed attention of playwrights seeking material for courtroom drama. Sherman Tecumseh Grant was charged with nothing more world-shaking than stealing a bottle of milk. But to me the Loeb-Leopold, Dreyfus, and Thaw trials, all rolled into one, could not be as important as this one, because—this was my first criminal case.

There was another noteworthy factor involved: since John R. K. Scott was a nationally famous criminal lawyer, I felt I had the prestige of a great name to uphold. In and around the courtrooms the court attachés never referred to me as Mr. Musmanno; they spoke of me as "the young lawyer from Mr. Scott's office."

In addition to being charged with larceny, our client had been indicted also for aggravated assault and battery because, it was alleged, he had hurled a brick which hit a policeman who had followed him in hot pursuit. The transcript of testimony presented at the preliminary hearing before the committing magistrate revealed that the Commonwealth was prepared to prove that Grant had taken a bottle of milk under the eyes of Joseph Finch, who was standing on the porch of his home, where the bottles rested; that Finch tried to seize the culprit, who fled with Finch in his wake; that the chase traversed several streets and ended in an empty lot where Grant, concealing himself behind a stone wall, threw the telltale brick which caromed off the head of the startled police officer who thereupon arrested him.

With such avalanching evidence poised to engulf my client, I shuddered in the not unreasonable apprehension that my fourth courtroom battle could only end in a complete rout for Sherman Tecumseh Grant—and his lawyer. I blush to recall, after all these years, that in my professional and youthful zeal I was more concerned over the fact that I was about to lose my first criminal case than as to what was to happen to Sherman Tecumseh.

Grant had no witnesses to impart substance to his protestations of innocence except his wife, who related to me that when her husband left their home on the morning of the alleged crime he had consumed a breakfast which consisted of two pork chops, several pieces of bacon, a large quantity of fried potatoes, and many slices of bread, butter, and jam, all washed down with numerous cups of coffee. From this, of course, I could insist that one whose stomach was loaded down with a meal that would have slowed the flight of a pelican would scarcely be seeking a bottle of liquid nourishment, nor would he be able to propel his feet with the speed attributed to the actual milk purloiner. But I realized that this defense would scarcely be enough upon which to build a hope for acquittal. At best it was only argumentation. I had to find a weak spot in the prosecution's armor.

I visited the scene of the theft and mentally photographed the streets over which the prosecutor, Joseph Finch, according to his testimony at the magistrate's hearing, had pursued the culprit. I studied every inch of the rapidly changing routes and then, in studious reflection of this urban checkerboard, a bright idea loomed. If I could prove the prosecutor wrong in one phase of his testimony, I could assert he was mistaken in everything else. *Falsus in uno, falsus in omnibus.* "False in one, false in all." Thus I decided I would cross-examine the prosecutor relentlessly on the geography of the streets and the course of the flight and pursuit; that is to say, I would question him as to whether the milk snatcher had moved in a north, east, south, or west direction through the specific streets over which he fled. Somewhere in the whirlwind cross-examination which I intended to conduct and the fusillade of questions I proposed to fire, I was certain Mr. Finch would err as to what was north, east, south, or west, and I would charge him with error. He would probably assert with great emphasis that he was not mistaken, because witnesses who are adamant in one thing are apt to be adamant in everything else. I thought to myself with a smile: *Adamantinus in uno, adamantinus in omnibus.* Then when the prosecutor's cocksureness would have reached an ultimate and insufferable degree with his insistence that he knew what was east when I knew that the direction in which he might be pointing was west, I would swoop down with irrefutable proof that he was wrong. How would I do this? *With a compass.* That was the brilliant idea.

Thus, with the assurance of an experienced Arctic explorer, I purchased one of those magnetic, magical devices with its uncanny quivering needle. With it I visualized the dramatic moment I would score a *coup de main* which would rival Lincoln's melodramatic production of the almanac in the famous Montgomery murder case. I studied and practiced with this compass, familiarizing myself with its use as if I were preparing to sail an uncharted sea, which indeed, in many ways, I was. It had a luminous dial, and no matter what hour of the night I might awaken and glance at it, I knew, if I wanted to, how to head north.

But the trial took a different course from what I had anticipated and straightway sent my ship of confidence to the bottom of the Sea of Lost Hopes. When on cross-examination I asked the prosecutor Finch to state his occupation, he replied quite casually: "Civil engineer." Here was no one to be confused about north, east, south, and west! I dropped the direction angle like a hot rivet, which the compass itself had become. Furtively I endeavored to cover it with papers and slide it back into my brief case before anyone might see it and divine what I had been up to. Finch identified my client, testified he saw him take the milk, and insisted he was on his heels all the time until he took refuge behind the wall.

My whole fleet of plans had now disappeared from the face of the Ocean of Possible Victory. All I could hope was that I might salvage enough from the wreckage to demonstrate to Bill Gilderman, the office boy reporting to Mr. Scott on how I conducted myself, that I was still resourceful, even with the last lifeboat gone. I returned to the cross-examination:

"Did you recognize the man who took the milk?"

"No, I had never seen him before."

"What time was the milk taken?"

"At five-thirty in the morning."

"Wasn't it dark at that hour?"

"Certainly it was."

"At the time the culprit actually took the milk, you didn't know whether he was black or white?"

"No, but he was the same fellow I chased."

"But after he went behind the wall, it was possible, was it not, for him to escape and for some innocent person standing there to be arrested by mistake? Isn't that possible?"

"I don't know whether it is or not."

"Don't quibble. That is entirely possible, is it not?"

"Yes."

"That's all!"

I announced the "That's all!" with a rising inflection which told the world I had established a beachhead. From here I could launch an offensive of doubt. In order to win my case it was enough if I raised a cloud of uncertainty because a defendant may not be convicted unless the evidence convinces the jury of his guilt "beyond a reasonable doubt." With the witness's admission that it was possible that an innocent person could have taken the place of the guilty man behind the wall, I was ready to move forward.

However, the policeman who followed on the witness stand wiped away my beachhead as completely as a bulldozer passing over sand dunes. He testified that after the brick landed he dashed behind the wall from which the missile had emerged and found *only one person there—the defendant*. I strove for another beachhead:

"Did you see anyone steal milk that day?"

The prosecuting attorney objected to this line of questioning. "He never said that he saw anyone steal milk."

"Nor did he say that he did *not* see anyone steal the milk," I retorted. "However, in view of your concession, I assume we can assume that he knows nothing about the theft." To make doubly sure of this, I asked the witness: "Is that right?"

He replied: "Is what right?"

"That you did not see anyone take any milk?"

"When?"

"The day of the alleged crime."

Now Mr. Riser, the prosecuting attorney, broke in: "I object to Mr. Musmanno badgering the witness."

"Badgering? I'm the one who is being badgered. Why don't you have your witness answer questions instead of asking them? Also, I do not like your impeding my cross-examination. I want to know whether the policeman knows anything about the theft——"

"I must object to Mr. Musmanno's speeches." Riser turned to the judge. "I will admit this policeman knows nothing about the theft, but it must be kept in mind that our contention is that the man who stole the milk is the same man who threw the brick."

"But you must first prove who stole the milk," I added.

"We have proved that."

"You have certainly not proved that," I quickly put in, parrying his home thrust.

The judge brought the colloquy to an end by asking the assistant district attorney if he had any more evidence, and when he replied that he rested his case, the judge requested me to begin with the defense.

I bowed to the judge and made a short opening speech to the jury, ending with an outer display of confidence which would have had difficulty in finding a counterpart within: "And now, members of the jury, I am sure that after you have heard our defense, you will quickly return a verdict of not guilty.

"Sherman Tecumseh Grant, will you please take the stand?" I intoned the name as if I had been calling it on the fields of Shiloh. In a moment the defendant was in the witness chair, relating with an assurance that would have done credit to his multiple-illustrious namesakes how, on the morning of the alleged crime, as he was passing the Finch home on his way to work, someone yelled out in a threatening manner: "Now I got you!" Frightened out of his wits, he took to his heels, racing the dawn. He heard pounding steps behind him. He tried to outdistance his unknown pursuer. Then a policeman arrested him. That's all he knew. He was innocent of both the theft and the assault and battery. Oh yes, he had had a very big breakfast that morning. His wife followed him on the stand and confirmed the big breakfast. "I gave him pork chops, bacon, potatoes, bread, butter, coffee," she announced with the pride that any housewife would have the right to feel in cooking and serving so exemplary a repast at five o'clock in the morning.

That constituted our defense: a firm denial by the accused, plus a bountiful breakfast served by his faithful wife.

Three or four of Grant's neighbors offered to testify to his good character and I called them to the witness stand, where they declared that Grant bore a good reputation in his community for being a law-abiding citizen. One of the character witnesses stated that, with Grant, he was a lodge member in the well-known order of the Knights of Pythias.

I rested my case, and the assistant district attorney summed up devastatingly. With emphatic gesture, loud voice, and piercing argument he shouted to the jury that it was almost a waste of time to deliberate on this case, the guilt of the defendant being so obvious, clear, and incontrovertible. "If a thief cannot be convicted on out-and-out identification by the man who saw him commit the crime, how can anyone ever be convicted?" he asked the jury.

"If the Court please!" I sang out. "I must seriously object to Mr. Riser calling my client a thief. It is this honorable jury which will determine whether the defendant is guilty or innocent, and the district attorney is entirely out of bounds in calling the defendant names."

The judge, who apparently was thinking of other things as Riser spoke, started at my high-pitched interruption, but after a moment's orientation he said: "Objection sustained."

When the prosecuting attorney finished his summation I rose to speak, fully aware of the odds against me. The only stone in my slingshot of defense was the naked argument that a man with a pelican's breakfast under his belt would not be out looking for milk and trouble at five-thirty in the morning. But I told the jury also to be wary of starry-dawn identifications. I reminded them that only a month ago an innocent man had been released from Sing Sing Prison when it was established that he had been erroneously convicted on a mistaken identification—but in the meantime the poor wretch had served five years in prison.

The jury gave me rapt attention as I spoke, and as I got braver, I also became bolder. Suddenly I heard myself saying, and with heavy sarcasm too: "Now what does the Commonwealth present here? They present a witness who says that he saw Grant take the milk. *Now what kind of evidence is that?*"

Of course one might well assume that eyewitness testimony is about the most positive proof of guilt that can be presented, but I still felt, in spite of what had been said by the prosecution, that the police had got the wrong man. Lifting my voice in righteous indignation, I stormed: "In his irritation and vexation that morning, Finch was determined to catch *someone*. For a month he had been losing milk; he was wrathful; he had the right to be wrathful—but wrath must be properly channeled or it may work a grave injustice.

On the fateful morning which has become the subject of this criminal prosecution, Finch's vision was so bleared with mistrust and so myopic with suspicion that the first person who came within that range of vision would to him be the guilty one. And thus he pounced on an honest man who was on his way to work to earn his daily bread so that he might continue to have breakfasts like the one he had just enjoyed. If you here on the jury"—and I pointed to the third man in the rear row, who was wearing a Knights of Pythias button in his lapel—"had happened along Fifteenth Street that morning, you— who are a member of that superb and grand order of Knights of Pythias, as is the defendant—might have been accused by the prosecuting witness of this crime."

"I most vigorously object to this reference to the Knights of Pythias!" Riser snapped.

"May it please Your Honor"—I turned to the bench—"if I have done anything improper in referring to this superb and highly esteemed organization, celebrated for its charity, chivalry, and benevolence, I beg Your Honor's pardon."

The judge, who, like a lion half dozing in the cool of embowering trees, had been paying little attention to the speeches, came to full attention when Knights of Pythias was mentioned. After a quick glance around the courtroom he remarked with some heat: "I don't see why you should have to apologize for the Knights of Pythias. I belong to that organization myself."

"Thank you, Your Honor, I hope that someday I shall be fortunate enough to be admitted to this justly honored society, devoted as it is to the highest ideals of citizenship."

And now, concluding my summation, I spread-eagled somewhat: "Gentlemen of the jury, it is a tremendous power that you wield. Upon your verdict depends honor or disgrace, fame or infamy, happiness or misery. You have the power of kings. Each one of you occupies an invisible throne, each one of you wields the invisible scepter of a monarch. You wear the crown of reason and justice. Exercise that power of kings and free this innocent man."

As the jury filed out of the courtroom I asked Grant what he thought of my speech. He replied: "I liked that part about the kings, but I hope no one is holding a pair of aces!"

In ten minutes the jury returned with a verdict of not guilty.

Chapter VI

DAYLIGHT-SAVING TIME

THE lawyer is the only professional (with the exception of the prize fighter) who must battle an opponent—and beat him—before it may be assumed he has done his work well.

The doctor treats his patient, the engineer builds his bridge, the chemist perfects his formula, and though they all strive in a competitive world, none loses simply because his rival is successful. The winning attorney, however, must defeat someone else in order to be credited with an achievement. And the vanquished attorney, though he may have toiled and struggled valiantly in the contest, obtains only a zero for his efforts. In every lawsuit there must be a smashing victory and an irreparable loss. Every case in court must be ashes in the mouth to one attorney so that it may be a rose in the lapel to his opponent.

Thus, on an even division between cases won and lost, only one half of a lawyer's work will be chalked up as successful. And if one lawyer scores more victories than defeats, some other lawyer must suffer more defeats than victories, which means that more than half of his lawsuits will have been failures.

If there were an equitable and just way to compromise differences between disputing members of the human race, it would be a giant step forward toward the goal of universal contentment. However, there has been but little progress along this line because only a few people reflect on the cosmic symphony with its harmonization of the universe. The struggle for living, desire for advancement, thirst for promotion, and the conceit of self-aggrandizement create a separate little world for each individual. This world of his excludes the rest of the universe, which, however, is made up of all the other little individual worlds.

Thus, police and detectives with the most conspicuous record for arrests and convictions stand the best chances for bigger badges and salaries. Promotions in district attorney offices usually go to those who display unusual aptitude in sending defendants on their way to jail, penitentiary, or even the electric chair. A trial assistant district attorney is prouder of a first-degree murder conviction than a second-degree murder conviction. Although he may not consciously evaluate his actions in such proceedings, he will exert every effort toward persuading the jury in a given case to return a verdict of death or life imprisonment, whereas if he selflessly and impartially appraised the case strictly on its merits, entirely divorced from what its results could mean to him, he might be satisfied with a second-degree verdict or even an acquittal.

The ideal system of justice will not be attained until police, magistrates, lawyers, and all others associated with law enforcement are personally disinterested in the results of court trials. During the period of national prohibition, police agents employed various schemes and plans to catch their quarry, not because they necessarily believed these persons were defying the law, but because they built on the general assumption that a large number of jail convictions would entitle them (the police agents) to increased salaries, more privileges, and advancement in grade. My fifth case involved prohibition agents.

Two of them had charged Jimmy Brooks, an eighteen-year-old hotel bellboy, with violating the Pennsylvania Prohibition Enforcement Act. These agents, guests at the hotel where the boy was employed, had summoned him to their room and requested him to obtain a pint of whiskey for them. The boy refused. They recalled him a second and third time, and finally prevailed upon him to go to a bootlegging establishment (the address of which they supplied), paying him a dollar for the errand. The boy returned with the whiskey and the agents immediately arrested him.

I called at the office of Henry Morgan, the assistant district attorney handling the case, and asked him to nol-pros the charge because it was obvious no criminal intent was involved in my client's act. Lolling back in his office chair and lighting a big cigar, Morgan said: "Young lawyer, I'm glad you're using good sense in this matter. We have your client dead to rights, and if he'll pay a fine of one hundred dollars——"

"One hundred dollars!" I complained. "Where do you suppose a bellboy's going to get a hundred dollars?"

The self-satisfied official expelled a cloud of smoke and pushed his cigar through the center in a vain attempt to create a ring. "Now,

now, young man, don't try to play tricks with an old dog like me. Your poor bellboy probably got that much together to pay his lawyer."

"Mr. Assistant District Attorney, let me tell you something," I said as I cleared the blue vapor drifting toward me, "you get paid for every case you try because you're on a salary, but defense counsel is not always paid. It so happens that in this case the defendant has paid nothing, but I'm glad to defend him for nothing because I believe he's the victim of a frame-up."

"Frame-up? Look here, Mr.—— What's your name?"

"Musmanno."

"Look here, Mr. McManus——"

"I said 'Musmanno.' "

"All right, all right, you don't expect me to get a name like that on the first bounce," and he tried another smoke ring, this time by exaggeratedly pursing his lips. "I'll tell you what I'll do. I'll have the fine reduced to fifty dollars if you'll plead him guilty."

"I can't do that. Such a plea would stigmatize him with a criminal record—and he's innocent of any intentional wrongdoing."

"Don't get softhearted with me, Mr. Manomussen. He's guilty, isn't he?"

"No."

"He bought, sold, and transported liquor, didn't he?"

"Yes, but under coercion."

"Coercion nothing. He'll plead guilty and pay a fine of fifty dollars or I'll convict him and put him away for thirty days."

Fighting my way through the smoke, I left, angry and yet disturbed because the cigar smoker did have Jimmy Brooks "dead to rights" so far as the literal law was concerned.

A week later we went to trial. There was scarcely any doubt as to the facts, and after the prohibition agents and the youthful defendant had testified, Morgan turned to me and in a whisper that could be heard far beyond my ears, he said: "Well, Mr. Muslin, will you plead your client?"

"I will not."

"Well, you can't say I didn't give you a chance. I always believe in helping young lawyers, but if they don't want to be helped, let their blunders fall on the heads of their unfortunate clients."

I could feel my face going red while an icy shiver froze my spine. Suppose I was making a mistake and the judge, in the event of the boy's conviction, did send him to jail. It would be my fault. As I wrestled with indecision, Morgan was on his feet, facing the jury. And as he began to speak I saw in him a different person. Brusque, arrogant, and domineering in conversation, he was now all suavity, apology, and regret for what he was asking the jury to do: "Gentlemen of the jury, I have a rather disagreeable task to perform here and you will have an unpleasant duty to fulfill, but we are sworn to obey the law, and obey it we must. I feel sorry for this young defendant, and I feel sorry for his young lawyer——"

I half rose to object, not knowing just what I could or should say. Fortunately the judge motioned me down.

The A.D.A. went on: "Yes, I'm sorry for his young lawyer, Mr. Musket, but then, defense lawyers must take their cases as they come, good and bad——"

This time I stood up. "Your Honor, I object to his referring to this as a bad case. It is a good case—a good case for the defense——"

"Yes, Mr. District Attorney," the judge enjoined, "you had better leave Mr. Musmanno out of this."

"I'm very sorry," the A.D.A. said in a tone which was honey, treacle, and butterfly wings. "I'm sorry all the way around. Jimmy Brooks, the defendant, is a young man and perhaps did not realize the trouble he was getting into, but we must put aside all sentiment and sympathy. If we try these cases on sympathy, soon we will have no law at all. Let me tell you something about government. We have a state legislature which makes our laws. We elect that legislature.

"Last year that legislature met in Harrisburg; 208 representatives who were elected from 67 counties, and 50 state senators chosen from all parts of the Commonwealth convened in General Assembly just as the Constitution provides. There, in the magnificent capitol of our state, these spokesmen for the people met, and with all the majesty of government, with all the dignity of lawmaking, and with the spirit of William Penn, the original founder of our Commonwealth, guiding their deliberations, they wrote on the statute books the law which has been violated here.

"That law was signed by the chief executive, as the Constitution provides, and so far as we are concerned, that law is Holy Writ for us to follow. The defendant knew of that law and consciously violated it. It is not for us to make exceptions. If we except this young man from the operation of the law, why shouldn't we except the next defendant as well? Society is founded on the basic principle that everyone must be treated alike. Whatever mercy may be in order can be extended in the proper place. That power is not lodged in you. Your duty is simply to ascertain the facts and apply the law. The facts are admitted. The law is plain. It is for you to enforce it."

He now paused, looked at his watch, and added: "I will not make a long speech to you because it is three o'clock, and as we adjourn at four, I want to leave time for defense counsel to speak and have the Court charge you, so that you may still be out of here by four o'clock." And then, turning to me, he asked: "Is that all right, Mr.— Mr. Musmanner? I'm sorry that I previously mispronounced your name."

"Your error in that respect is not as great as your error in this case generally," I retorted, and with that opening shot I advanced toward the jury, wrathful that my opponent obviously assumed the jury would return a guilty verdict without even leaving the jury box.

On the rear wall of the courtroom hung a large clock with a sign beneath: "This Court operates on Eastern Standard Time." There had been much controversy in the state over the adoption or non-adoption of daylight-saving time. The larger cities favored the daylight-saving plan, but the rural population was opposed to it. The issue was finally resolved by the state legislature. Since the representatives from the rural areas surpassed in numbers the urban representatives, the daylight plan was rejected and a law was passed specifically making eastern standard time the official time of the Commonwealth. The larger cities in the state, however, ignored the law and advanced the clock one hour in accordance with the daylight-saving principle. This controversy over clock changing was still fresh in the minds of the people when the bellboy case came to trial.

Before beginning my speech, I took out my watch, glanced at it, and then said to the assistant district attorney: "Mr. Morgan, will you please tell me what time it is by your watch?" He appeared puzzled by the query and for a moment was obviously disposed to resent it, but, apparently remembering that he had made such a nice impression on the jury with his gentle and suave manner, he replied courteously: "Why, of course, Mr. Musa—— Yes, counselor, it is just about five minutes after three."

"Thank you," I said, and, facing the arbiters of my client's fate, I began: "Gentlemen of the jury, I quite agree with everything the learned assistant district attorney has said about the majesty of the law. I am in complete accord with him that the state Prohibition Enforcement Law, being on the statute books, is a law of the land— and must be enforced." Morgan smiled, probably wondering whether I did not intend to have my client plead guilty after all.

"He has painted for you an impressive picture," I continued, "of how that law was placed on the statute books, and I congratulate him on the word colors he used in producing his canvas. But let me, gentlemen of the jury, paint for you another picture, also true to reality. Last year, also, the same legislature which he has so well described to you met in Harrisburg. There, with all the majesty of goverment, and with all the dignity of lawmaking, the representatives of the people took their places in the magnificent capitol building, and there, with the spirit of William Penn guiding their deliberations, they placed on the statute books a law declaring that eastern standard time shall be the official time of the Commonwealth.

"And yet, gentlemen of the jury, in the pocket of the assistant district attorney, there ticks a watch in *defiance of that law!*

"The assistant district attorney, in answer to my request for the time, looked at his watch and said it was about three-five. Allowing for the five minutes I have been speaking, it would now be three-ten on his watch. But, members of the jury, look at that clock on the wall!" And I extended an emphatic index finger toward the large electric chronometer above the doorway. "It says that the time of the day is *two*-ten! And *that* is the official time of the Commonwealth, as declared through governmental lawmaking procedure. The assistant district attorney has ignored *that* time and the *law* which makes that time official. And he is an officer of the court. He functions in a tribunal of law, and yet he has violated a law which was passed with just as much solemnity, just as much dignity, and just as much majesty as attended the passage of the Pennsylvania Prohibition Enforcement Law.

"Gentlemen of the jury, many of you are carrying watches setting at naught the law of the Commonwealth. What does that mean? Does that mean you are lawbreakers? Not at all. It means that before the legislature ever met in Harrisburg to pass either the Prohibition or daylight-saving law there was a law passed by God Almighty—and that is the law of common sense. Common sense dictated to you to adjust your watches in accordance with daylight-saving time because it was convenient, logical, and sensible for you to do so.

"Common sense told the assistant district attorney to do the same. And common sense should tell you that this boy defendant is not guilty of violating the Pennsylvania prohibition law. What you and the assistant district attorney and the honorable judge on the bench did with your watches may have run counter to the letter of the Standard-time law, but it did not violate the spirit of the law. And the spirit, the intent of the law, is what counts. Eastern standard time is still the official time of the state, but you, for good practical reasons, have adjusted your watches to daylight-saving time.

"Before a crime can be committed, there must be an *intent* to violate a statute—there must be a *criminal* intent—there must be a conscious desire to set oneself at war with the law of the land. Can you say that Jimmy Brooks did that? He was coerced into buying whiskey by prohibition agents. They, the prohibition agents, are the real criminals. Instead of searching out the real violators of the law—the bootleggers, the manufacturers of the illicit liquor—they luxuriate and live high in high-priced rooms in a hotel—at your expense—and lure boys into lawbreaking.

"Gentlemen of the jury, this boy had no more intention of breaking the law than did the assistant district attorney when he set his watch in defiance of the statute passed on Capitol Hill. I ask you to return a verdict of not guilty and place the costs of prosecution on the two prohibition agents."

And that is what they did.

Chapter VII

THE ONE UNSELFISH FRIEND

IN OUR boyhood days my brother Sam, when in difficulty with our baseball-loving father, because of some infraction of home disciplinary rules, could always stave off a scolding and even a paddling by standing on a chair and declaiming at the top of his voice and with gestures, which I always thought highly exaggerated and inelegant, the baseball classic, "Casey at the Bat." I used a more subtle approach. When I saw Father's brow knit and a cloud pass over his countenance, I never stopped to examine my conscience as to what I had done that was wrong. Without any preliminaries I would say: "Papa, 'The one, absolute, unselfish friend that man can have in this selfish world, the one that never deserts him, the one that never proves ungrateful or treacherous, is his dog.' "

In that instant Papa would forget what I had done that merited punishment and I would climb upon a chair and continue, pulling out all stops of pathos: " 'A man's dog stands by him in prosperity and poverty, in health and sickness. He will sleep on the cold ground, where the winter winds blow and the snow drives fiercely, if only he can be by his master's side. He will kiss the hand that has no food to offer, he will lick the wounds and sores that come in encounter with the roughness of the world. He guards the sleep of his pauper master as if he were a prince. When all other friends desert, he remains.' "

By the time I finished, Papa would be sobbing and so would I, and as we mingled our tears I knew I was in safe territory for another week or two. Papa was very fond of dogs and could never resist the impulse to house and care for any itinerant mutt that stopped for a drink and a bone as he proceeded on his journey to heaven knows where.

From my many renditions of George Graham Vest's "Tribute to a Dog," I came to the conclusion that, next to Lincoln's Gettysburg Address, it was the one literary classic which was nearest to the American heart, and I never could imagine that anyone would ever challenge the integrity of its factual observations or the enchantment of its poetic imagery. But it was challenged by Attorney Ralph F. Fields in the case of Robert Fleming versus W. Q. Courtney.

Robert Fleming's dog, Rags, had met an untimely end beneath the wheels of an automobile, and Fleming told me all about it. Rags was not a pedigreed dog and he had never performed any outstanding feat in dogdom; he had never won a blue ribbon. In the eyes of the world Rags was probably a homely creature, but to Fleming he symbolized one of the most beautiful of relationships in life. When Fleming returned home of an evening it was Rags who met him, a being of quivering, barking ecstasy. Rags was a living token of perfect friendship, the ultimate in unspoken language of perfect understanding. Fleming explained all this to me with a slight suspicion of moisture in his eye.

"I sued Courtney," Fleming said, "not to get money from him, but just to show him that a dog has as much right to live as anybody else. When that skinflint came tearing down the street at sixty miles an hour, he still had time to stop, slow down, or swerve, but he kept on as if Rags was just a stone in the road. When the policeman finally stopped him and asked what he meant by traveling at that kind of speed, this blackguard replied that he was in a devil of a hurry because he had to attend a meeting of the board of directors of his company. Mr. Musmanno, I'd like to have you tell me, does the president of a board of directors have the right to disobey the law, even if it means killing a dog—my dog?"

"Of course not, no one is privileged to disobey the law."

At the alderman's hearing on the charge of cruelty to animals Courtney had been fined twenty dollars and Fleming fumed: "He should have gone to jail for a year, the rattlesnake! I bet if the situation was reversed and some poor duck had killed a dog belonging to him, then that sucker would go to jail." I did not try to straighten out Fleming's picturesque mixture of serpent, fowl, beast, and fish.

In preparing the case for trial, I asked Fleming what value he placed on Rags. "In order to obtain a monetary award you or someone else must declare his market value; that is, not what he meant to you, but what he would bring if he were sold publicly."

"Oh, Mr. Musmanno, I could never have sold Rags at all. Probably he would not have brought very much on the market, but to me that dog was priceless."

"Well, the law is rather cold-blooded about things of that kind. It places no value on sentiment, and I'm afraid that unless we can show an objective loss in dollars and cents we will encounter difficulties."

"Mr. Musmanno, I'm not concerned about money value. What I would like is to see that barbarian Courtney humiliated in court."

We went to trial in the civil branch of the Municipal Court, and I was gratified with Fleming's testimony. He made an excellent witness. He described with dramatic simplicity the accident which had snuffed out Rag's life and then added a touching biographical sketch of his deceased friend.

Attorney Ralph F. Fields, who always appeared in court wearing striped trousers and a flowered waistcoat, approached the witness stand to take up the cross-examination. A practitioner of extensive experience, Fields was usually to be found representing what was called the "silk-stocking trade." Elaborately pushing back the tide of white cuffs which overflowed his wrists, he asked Fleming in a liquid voice which suggested a pleasant, mellow beverage laced with a shot of strychnine: "Mr. Fleming, you have stated that this dog meant a great deal to you, that he brought you untold happiness, unceasing comfort, marvelous solace, and magnificent companionship, is that right?"

"Well, I don't know that I expressed it that way. All I know is that that dog meant a great deal to me."

"Yes, of course. Well, how will the payment of money bring back to you those priceless commodities which cannot be purchased on the market; namely, untold happiness, unceasing comfort, marvelous solace, and magnificent companionship?"

"If the Court please," I objected, "if Courtney has destroyed something valuable—and it *was* valuable despite Mr. Fields's uncalled-for sarcasm—it is not for him to complain that it is not replaceable. It may well be that Fleming is suing not to be enriched but to impress upon Courtney and men of his caliber that they may not brutally run down a man's companion or a child's pet just because he chooses to assume it has no monetary value."

"Your Honor!" Mr. Fields looked as much annoyed as if I had tramped on his highly polished patent-leather pumps. "I must object to my young friend's enthusiasm. He cannot interject a speech while I am cross-examining."

The judge smiled. "I have two objections here. I overrule Mr. Musmanno's objection and sustain Mr. Fields's objection."

Turning again to the witness, Fields asked: "What value in dollars and cents did you place on your dog, which you have already stated was not pedigreed, not blue-ribboned, but not unwanted?"

Fleming hesitated and then said: "I wouldn't take fifty thousand dollars for that dog."

"May it please Your Honor," Fields interposed. "I object to this answer and move that it be stricken, because obviously the standard of value is not what Mr. Fleming would take for the dog but what this dog—of which there are limitless hordes roaming, barking, and snarling through the streets of America—would bring on the glutted market for that type of animal."

"I object!" My voice shot to the roof of the building. "This is outrageous! Mr. Fields has no right to employ inflammatory language of this kind, and I ask the Court to so instruct him."

The judge smiled again. "Again I have two objections. Mr. Fleming's answer will be stricken from the record and Mr. Fields will refrain from testifying as he comments on the testimony of witnesses, which he should not do in any event. The characterization of witnesses and testimony, if at all, should be left to the summation speeches."

"Thank you, Your Honor," I said.

"Thank you, Your Honor," Mr. Fields said.

The defendant, W. Q. Courtney, took the stand and, with many aristocratic hems and haws, announced that of course he never intended to harm the plaintiff's dog which had darted into the street without allowing him a chance to stop to avoid hitting him.

The trial ended without our having placed a pecuniary value on Rags. When Mr. Fields moved for a compulsory non-suit on this basis, I explained that the dog's worth was a question for the jury to decide from all the evidence adduced, plus what was common knowledge to mankind. The judge overruled Fields's motion, and we went to the jury.

Drawing from his deep reservoir of dulcet tones, with all its gradations of emphasis, and bringing into play the not uningratiating manner of a justifiably annoyed Chesterfield, Fields began his summation: "Members of the jury, since no evidence has been produced to show that the deceased dog in this case had any market value, I submit to you, in simple logic and common sense, there can be no recovery in money at all." He paused, pulled down his fancy waistcoat, got closer to the jury box, and continued:

"My friends, let us summon your common sense in the disposition of this case. Let us get away from all the balderdash and silly sentimentality about dogs. Now, do not believe I dislike dogs. Quite the contrary. There is much to be said in their behalf. Some of them make excellent protectors of our homes at night, some of them are beautiful to behold, but to make a fetish and an object of adoration of every four-legged mutt is infantile and preposterous.

"Many of you, of course, have read Senator Vest's 'Tribute to a Dog,' which the plaintiff rather skillfully and probably at the suggestion of his youthful counsel referred to in his testimony, but I say to you, as I said to the Court, that canine loyalty, real or fictitious, has absolutely nothing to do with this case. Nonetheless, let me say that ever since the publication of Senator Vest's 'Tribute to a Dog,' much rhetorical tinsel has been hung on every mongrel that comes yelping down the pike. As a matter of fact, the dog is not all that Vest says it is, and you, members of the jury, know that as well as I do. To say that a dog is man's best friend is not only an insult to all mankind, but it is a palpable absurdity.

"Do I need to remind you of the countless children who have been bitten by dogs and have suffered agonies that my tongue could never describe? Is, indeed, a dog man's best friend? Why is it then that the most cutting reproof which can be administered to an ingrate is the one: 'Don't be like the dog that bites the hand that feeds you.'

"Does a dog, as Senator Vest proclaims, stand by his master in prosperity and in poverty, in health and sickness? And if that be true, why is it that there are so many homeless dogs? The answer, of course, is that their erstwhile owners failed to provide for them, and the dogs accordingly took to the road to more opulent or at least less unfortunate masters. A dog will stay with you when you feed and house him, and he will desert you when adversity evicts you and hard times disemploy you. He will protect you when you are within the strong protective walls of the citadel of your home, and he will stand guard when you have a shotgun on the rack and a mechanical burglar alarm system to call the police, but he will join the pack that snarls at your heels when you walk down the solitary path of misfortune or the world's reproof.

"Members of the jury, I call upon you to exercise your intelligence in this case. Do not make a mockery of justice, do not let oleaginous sentimentality induce you to betray your oath which requires you to return a verdict in accordance with the law and the evidence. This dog had no value that can be appraised in a court of law. Gentlemen of the jury, I thank you for your earnest attention and I shall confidently await your verdict in favor of the defendant."

With the stride of one who is conscious of his ability, pleased with his performance, and certain of his triumph, Fields returned to his seat at counsel table and looked almost with a pitying eye on me, for apparently he had devoured every argument in the pantry of human appeal, and I could speak only from empty shelves.

"Members of the jury," I began as I leaned against the clerk's desk. "I do not have the glibness of tongue nor the aptness of phrase possessed by counsel for the defendant, and perhaps he is right after all. If you believe that a dog is all that he says it is, then you should return a verdict in favor of his client, W. Q. Courtney, and turn us out of court."

Moving away from the clerk's desk and approaching a little closer to the jury box, I added almost apologetically: "If Rags had no value, then Fleming lost nothing, and therefore your verdict must be for the defendant. I never saw Rags, so I do not know whether he could have brought anything on the market or not. You have heard what he meant to Fleming. It is for you to determine whether that means anything in this court or not."

Here I stopped. Far above and beyond the jury box I beheld a picture, a picture which held me enthralled. For several moments I could say nothing, while the jury stared, wondering what had happened. Without seeing anyone in the courtroom I said: "I once had a dog. He came to me in a rather unusual way. As a little boy I often played on the banks of the Ohio River which flowed by our home. Nearly every year during the spring floods we beheld the wondrous spectacle of that swollen stream carrying on its broad and angry bosom shanties, chicken coops, doghouses, and other structures snatched from the river's edge by the mighty current and helplessly borne away to the distant and mysterious sea."

Here, for me, a miracle occurred. The mighty stream of my childhood broke down the walls of that courtroom and roared through its very center. On its eddying and turbulent surface danced the memories of the days that had passed away. As if in a dream, I went on:

"One day my eyes swelled in sympathetic alarm as they focused on a doghouse floating down the stream with a black shaggy dog straddling its precarious roof. Over the debris-strewn water could be heard his whimpering and supplicating bark. Up and down the bank I ran, wringing my hands and imploring some men close by to rescue the adorable creature on the little house sailing by.

"Just as I was entreating the owner of a skiff to please help, the little house capsized and my shaggy friend was thrown into the water. I clambered into the skiff—I was only eight years of age—and frantically untied the rope which held it to the shore. The owner, perhaps more moved by my emotional turmoil than the animal's distress, leaped into the skiff with the practiced step of the riverman and, with that one pushing bound, shot the boat from the river's bank into the tawny current. He at once fell to the oars, and the boat, under his masterful strokes, advanced with the speed of a mother seal speeding to the assistance of its endangered whelp.

"My little fuzzy friend was boldly paddling along, trying to recover his former home, every moment floating farther away. Logs and trees, with entangling branches, passed dangerously close, and I feared a disastrous collision before we could reach him. I whistled and called to him, using the universal canine name of Rover. He heard the call and turned his head as we approached him from the rear. Then I began a series of improvised long-distance endearments, and the little fellow attempted to reverse and swim upstream to meet us, but the current was too powerful. His eyes, however, smiled an acknowledgment of our efforts as I kept telling him to be brave until we arrived.

"At last we were at his side; eagerly I leaned over the gunwale and lifted him out of the rushing flood. He was just about spent, and he gratefully buried his head in my arms while I shouted hosannas and paeans of joy.

"I carried him home and he became our family pet and my companion. He was not a pretty dog, but he was intelligent, affectionate, lovable. For me the sun never rose in the morning, for me there was no dawn, no beginning of the day, until I saw our enthusiastic, grinning, flood-rescued Rover bound across the room, hurl himself into my arms, and send me delightfully crashing against furniture, or perhaps to the floor. This was always followed by a whirlwind romp about the house and yard until the place looked as if a tornado had struck it. And then, aglow with the sheer joy of living, I trotted off happily to school.

"For four years we had Rover, and then he went away. There was another flood. The Ohio once more overflowed its banks, and again habitations of man and beast were invaded by the ruthless stream, taking its toll of property and occasionally of life.

"I returned home from school one afternoon, but Rover was not there to bark joyfully his never-failing welcome. To my solicitous inquiries neighbors replied that they had seen him go to the riverbank. To the Ohio I raced. Anxiously I peered up and down the shore, and then turned my gaze upon the mighty flood moving by. I looked out upon that moving phantasmagoria as objects of every description, from empty soapboxes to full-sized dwellings, went unresistingly along. I lifted my voice loud and long for Rover, but only the shadow of echoes responded.

"After an hour's anguish of whistling and calling, there came three or four boys to tell me that Rover was in the river somewhere. They had seen him, with one paw uplifted, standing on the shore when he espied in the middle of the stream a detached door on whose flat surface crouched, afraid to move, four or five little puppies softly whining for help. Rover leaped into the water and made for the improvised raft bearing his unknown brothers. He was unable to overtake the raft, but he kept swimming on and on, until he disappeared from view.

"For weeks I patrolled the banks of the Ohio River for miles, looking and inquiring for my Rover, but he was seen no more.

"And now, each time I see a dog, a clutch comes to my throat as I think of the dearest companion of my childhood, and an involuntary prayer comes to my lips that whoever owns a dog shall be spared the agony of seeing his best friend go away—never to return."

I stopped talking. I had to. The knot which had been forming in my throat had reached the vocal cords, making further speech impossible. I turned to my seat and sat down.

The judge charged the jury, and it withdrew to deliberate. As they filed out, Fields leaned over to shake hands and say: "Musmanno, I want to congratulate you on your speech. At the beginning I was going to object because your argument was totally irrelevant to the issue, but I confess you had me spellbound. I like dogs myself, and I'm sorry I had to say what I did about them. They make life cheerful at times when we need some cheer."

The jury filed out slowly and the tipstaff closed the door behind them. He had scarcely walked away when the red light appeared above the door, proclaiming that a verdict had been reached. A quick light is generally interpreted by court habitués as a verdict for the defendant. Fields stood up smiling, confident of the result. Fleming looked away. Sure that I had lost the case, I tried not to hear precisely what the jury foreman had to say. Since his voice was low, I succeeded in this endeavor but I had no difficulty in making out what Fields said. Thrusting back his cuffs, he fumed: "I never saw such sickening, sniffling sentimentality over a dumb, dead dog."

The jury had found for the plaintiff in the sum of two hundred and fifty dollars.

Later the Court reversed the verdict on the ground that since no evidence had been presented to prove the market value of the dog the verdict could not be sustained. But Fleming was satisfied. He had achieved the victory he sought: he had vindicated Rags's memory, and he had proved that no one can ignore a dog and be loved by mankind.

Chapter VIII

THE BROWN SUIT

ALTHOUGH youth is assured that perseverance brings success, that everyone is master of his fate, and that fame and fortune are his to conquer if only he wills it, the fact remains that one's chances of reaching the glittering Port of Achievement can be considerably enhanced if the sails of his ship of destiny catch a few of the winds of good luck which, according to the law of averages (more strictly enforced by nature than many man-made laws), are bound to blow. Of course it must be acknowledged that those wind currents are also capable of disabling or even wrecking one's ship, but when that happens the resolute individual swims and battles his way to another ship—and again sails on!

Good luck had taken me into the office and within the tutelage of John R. K. Scott, one of the most colorful and successful lawyers of the generation. Hand in hand with his forensic talents went a most attractive courtroom personality. Tall and slender, with brown hair and friendly gray eyes, he was suave, eloquent, and dramatic; he was a figure that captivated, charmed, and conquered. In the Rosier trial, one of the most sensational murder cases of the 1920's (Catherine Rosier had killed her husband and his paramour), Mr. Scott played his most famous role. In his speech to the jury he drew a startling picture of a mind temporarily unbalanced under the hammer blows of continuing revelations of scandalous conduct between her husband and his stenographer. With rapier thrusts that flashed like lightning, and denunciation as sulphurous as accompanying thunder blasts, he annihilated the prosecution witnesses, and then, in the compassionate tones of prayer, he pleaded for protection of the sacred vows of matrimony and the acquittal of the pretty defendant. Reporters covering the trial said that even the great Shakespearean actors could not have excelled John R. K. Scott in his portrayal and mimicry of the various witnesses who had testified and whose testimony he dramatically re-enacted. The jury returned a verdict of acquittal in less than two hours' deliberation.

Mr. Scott's partner, William T. Connor, was as able and successful in the civil branch of the law as Scott was in the criminal. Mr. Connor could take the most complicated case in bankruptcy, engineering, or patent infringement and unfold it in court as if it were an Oppenheim tale of romance, mystery, and adventure. His jury speeches were masterpieces of unadorned eloquence. Of medium height, with a large barrel chest and massive head, he would stand before the jury box and with quivering finger pluck at the harp of emotions embracing all the scales of human feeling. If the case involved personal injuries, you saw the plaintiff not only as he appeared today but, through Connor's word pictures, which etched themselves into the very fiber of your being, you saw the plaintiff five, ten, twenty years from now—an object of pity, a shapeless figure of disablement and pain—all because of the recklessness, indifference, and wantonness of the defendant, which was usually a railroad company, a traction company, or some other large corporation.

If the victim of the accident was deceased, no Chopin could invest the trial with a more somber atmosphere than Connor. As he spoke, one could almost hear the funeral music and see the coffin descending into the cold grave while widow and orphans wept bitterly for the protector of the home, the beloved husband and father, the bread-winner for so many helpless ones, who was disappearing forever—all because of the heartless negligence of the defendant. Connor's speeches invariably won enormous verdicts.

I shall constantly be grateful to Lady Luck, who guided me to the offices of these two great lawyers, and in my breast a candle of gratitude shall always be lit to them for the opportunity they afforded me to develop whatever resources I may have possessed. They encouraged me and spurred me on by assigning me to increasingly important cases.

I was now handling a considerable amount of the divorce business in our office. This type of litigation usually perplexed me, and I harvested quite a crop of goose-pimples listening to the harrowing stories related by wife-plaintiffs. Most of them were young and attractive and must certainly have flattered the egos of their husbands when they were being courted and led to the altar or, as was true in so many cases, to the bar of the justice of the peace. What had happened? Why were they not attractive to their husbands now? Of course many of the stories of husbands' brutality were doubtlessly exaggerated, but even allowing for a measure of magnification, out of self-pity and a desire to escape the nuptial bonds, a nucleus of truth still remained in the wild and weird tales of cruelty inflicted by one person upon another who at one time must have seemed to the assailant the acme of all that was desirable and sweet.

Easily moved to sympathy, I always recoiled at the visualization of these wife-beatings, and I strode into each contested divorce trial aflame with indignation against the heartless brute who had brought pain and disillusionment to the weeping young woman holding onto my arm for protection and encouragement.

Occasionally I found myself forming a romantic attachment for these bruised but unwilted flowers. Injured innocence shining through tear-sparkling eyes, when framed in a pretty face, can be very appealing when combined with a wistful dependence on a zealous defender of that innocence. However, the attachment for one easily blended into the following one, the lily coalescing into the rose, the rose fading into the orchid, the orchid becoming the hyacinth. Winning for these charming people made the practice of the law a garden of blooms, but it was a garden not without brambles, briers, thorns, and nettles. And I suffered with my clients. Not unwillingly. In fact, I believe this vicarious hurting and exasperation only increased my determination and aggressiveness to vindicate what I quickly came to believe was a personal grievance against myself. Lawyers generally commiserate with the people they represent, but I did more. At the beginning of each case, whether it was a divorce, contract, tort, criminal, or equity case, I invariably would say to the client: "From now on, your troubles are my clients. Tell me the whole story, but let me do the worrying"—and the client usually did.

The law profession is engrossing and fascinating, but the emotional strain on overly sensitive lawyers surpasses the proverbial anxiety of any expectant father. Waiting for a jury verdict, especially in criminal cases, inflicted a Procrustean torture.

"Members of the jury, have you agreed upon a verdict?" the court clerk would intone as the perspiration drops on my forehead turned into icy beads and my heart raced like a pneumatic hammer. In another instant the world would be a heaven or a hell. It would be joy or misery, flowers or weeds, triumph or disaster. I would grasp the back of a chair for support, the choking breath in my lungs struggling against the barrier of my stifling tension.

Then as the foreman announced, "Not guilty," I would go limp with intolerable relief and, still shaking from the crisis, I would leave the courtroom like a disembodied spirit, haunting myself with the image of the catastrophe which fate had just averted.

I was lucky, extremely lucky. I won case after case until court habitués began to say among themselves that I carried a horseshoe in my brief case or that the Delta Sigma Rho key, which oscillated at the end of the watch chain suspended from the lapel of my rusty brown coat, was a supernatural charm. Of course I knew only too well that one day defeat would come—and the thought of that calamity, when it should arrive, conjured up an insupportable horror.

To a certain extent the court habitués were correct. I did have a talisman of good luck. It was the brown suit in which I had tried and won my first case. I still wore it. In all verity, I was afraid to wear another suit. I was winning suits with that suit; why should I gamble with another? Why provoke and tantalize the unknowable and the mysterious?

People occasionally were overheard to say: "That young fellow is a good lawyer, but I wonder who picks his clothes." Despite these remarks I could not get myself to put on a different suit. I probably fell into that classification of persons who assert they are not superstitious but why take a chance? I could spill salt, break a mirror, open an umbrella indoors, walk under a ladder, and still smile at Madame Superstition's threats of ominous reprisal. Amulets, wishbones, watch pendants, rabbits' feet meant nothing to me, but I had a "hunch" that my rusty, trusty brown outfit had something to do with the phenomenal record of successive legal victories I was scoring. At college and law school I always wore a green bow tie on examination days and never failed a test. Of course the results proved that I would have passed anyway, but after the first few examinations had brought me good grades I became somewhat apprehensive about not wearing that spinach-tinted cravat. Reason and logic argued strongly against belief in the influence of haberdashery on the marking of test papers, but if millions of people paid tribute to harmless sorcery by wearing all kinds of esoteric objects, why should I not offer one gesture of homage to Lady Luck and accept whatever benefit might come from the empyrean blue of sheer chance?

Some of the most celebrated figures in history made obeisance to the bizarre and the supernatural. Charles Dickens believed in dreams and lucky days. Napoleon selected certain stars in the sky as guardians to watch over him. Samuel Johnson always painstakingly persuaded his right foot to precede his left foot as he entered a dwelling. General Grant believed that if he dreamed of crockery, good fortune would visit him the next day. Admiral Nelson nailed a horseshoe to the mizzenmast of his flagship *Victory* before engaging an enemy ship. Sir Garnet Wolseley always tipped his hat to magpies. Sir Walter Scott believed in second sight. Alexandre Dumas assumed that the color of paper on which he wrote contributed to his literary success: for novels he adopted blue paper, for poetry yellow, and for magazine articles nothing but rose-colored sheets would satisfy. Macaulay always avoided stepping on the cracks in flagstones. Admiral Farragut, lashed to the mast of his ship as he steamed into Mobile Bay, listened for the words: "Keep on, keep on." Lou Gehrig, the baseball immortal, made a meal of pickled eel when threatened with a batting slump. Helen Hayes, the stage and screen star, treasures the rabbit foot with which she applied the rouge for her first play. The Phillies, it is reported, used to bury a rag rabbit to offset the pitching wizardry of Dizzy Dean. And so on, mumbo-jumbo, open-sesame.

All this, of course, cannot be sustained in the laboratory of the intellect and the classroom of reflection, still it is a species of self-deception which offers a comfort not to be despised. I could not ignore the record of that brown suit.

I lived alone in Philadelphia, occupying a small hall bedroom in a cheerless rooming house. Of a gregarious nature, I yet found myself as lonesome as Robinson Crusoe. I did not attend the theater or any public entertainment, I participated in no sports, I did not even own one of the primitive radio crystal sets which at that time had the world by the ear. I devoted all my spare time to study. When I retired at night I took to bed with me a large tome of the Pepper and Lewis *Digest of Laws*, so as to put to use even those few minutes between the time the ship of rest left the wharf of exhaustion and finally sailed into the open sea of oblivion.

In a word, with the exception of my professional engagements, I lived the life of a hermit, but the brown suit cheered me as a faithful comrade. In it I saw a career, perhaps a brilliant one which would lift me to the heights of legal stardom. So as to assure the suit as long a life as possible, I wore it only on court days. I knew I was making a fetish of it, and I determined from time to time I would cast the suit aside. But when in the morning I would open my eyes to the consciousness of the responsibility of a trial where I held in my hand the fate of a trusting client, I would advance upon the dark cupboard at the foot of my bed and take out that antiquated suit with the same solid confidence that knights of old climbed into their cast-iron trousers and clamped their Damascus-steel shirts around them.

Draped in this brown war panoply, I had now been victorious in forty-two legal battles and skirmishes. I was presently preparing for my forty-third combat. On the eve of the trial, Bill Gilderman said to me: "Mr. Musmanno, I think that if you wear that brown suit tomorrow they will slyly poke fun at it. I heard Attorney Robinson make some disparaging remark today about it, and he will probably fling it at you, keeping it up throughout the trial so as to irritate you. Why don't you fool him by wearing your oxford-gray suit?"

During my first several months in Mr. Scott's office I wore the brown suit for the unassailably cogent reason that it was the only suit I had. Now I had obtained a nice oxford-gray suit and Bill was urging me to wear it in court. "You will do that someday," he pleaded. "Why not start now? In this way you will throw Robinson off balance, for he will be thinking more about your suit than about his case."

"Very well, I will." So the next day I donned my oxford-gray suit. It fitted me well and conferred on me a trimmer appearance than the ancient sack in which I had been battling for justice.

The case I was about to try involved a motor-vehicle accident in which a nine-year-old child had been killed. As she made her way to school over a pedestrian walk skirting a country road, the rear end of a heavy truck slid from the cartway to the path and struck her, inflicting injuries from which she died in an hour's time. No one actually saw the truck at the precise moment of the impact, but there were witnesses who testified that they observed the child walking on the path, caught sight of the sidewise movement of the cumbersome vehicle, and afterward saw the child lying on the road bleeding and unconscious.

We produced medical evidence to show that the wound in the child's head corresponded precisely to the shape and configuration of the angle iron on the rear of the truck. Several people of the neighborhood testified that the defendant driver had traveled this road daily for many months prior to the accident, and this confirmed my contention that he knew of the tendency of his truck to skid at the very point the accident occurred. It was obvious that if he had employed the care and caution required under the circumstances, after seeing the child he would have stopped at once or swung away from the path to avoid the sliding motion which he knew was inevitable because of the defective condition of the road.

The jury gave every indication of appreciating the physical facts of the case, and many of them were nodding their heads in approval as I concluded my speech:

"And now, gentlemen of the jury, you have followed with a compassionate ear and a kindly understanding the story of this tragedy in the family of the plaintiffs. You have heard how on that cheerful and gladsome morning in May little Vivian, with a mother's kiss imprinted on her plump rosy cheek, started off to school. Bright, happy, healthy, and strong, she skipped out to the road with the throb of life within her body and a song of joy in her heart. When she returned, that heart had been stilled forever and the mother received back only the shell of what had been her joy, aid, and comfort. You are to determine what that loss means to the father and mother. In man-fashion we have presented the facts, and we know that you will render a verdict founded on evenhanded justice."

As I sat down, Bill whispered: "Musmanno, I'm glad you've won this case without your brown suit. You won't need to worry about it any more." I said nothing, but I felt a strange sensation in my chest. My shirt front vibrated beneath my oxford-gray jacket. The judge began his charge to the jury—and my shirt drooped like the sails of a ship when it enters the doldrums. This is what I heard the judge say:

"Gentlemen of the jury, I should have granted an involuntary non-suit at the termination of the plaintiff's case, but I am now satisfied that no evidence has been presented to establish that the defendant was responsible in any way for the unfortunate accident. You are hereby instructed to return a verdict for the defendant."

Chapter IX

REPAIR SHOPS

THE rosy world of promise and ever-happy anticipation had crashed. I had lost a case assigned to me by Mr. Scott; I had lost for deserving clients who believed in me and were supremely confident I would achieve for them the verdict which justice demanded. . . . I had lost my first case.

That night as I lay sleeplessly on my hard bed, I tried to loosen the fist of despair clutching my heart. Failing in this, I tried to break down the doors of somnolence before which I pleaded in vain. But the more I pounded at those portals of rest and unconsciousness, the more I kept unwittingly recruiting the opposing forces of unhappy wakefulness. Over and over I re-enacted the events of the day and of the case. What could I have done to avert the disaster? I had made a mistake somewhere. What was it? Of course I believed that the judge was mostly at fault, but still I could not shake off the failure which was my own. No one consoles a struck-out batter by blaming the pitcher. What gnawed most deeply at the vitals of hurtfulness was the fact that I had struck out in this particular case.

Vivian's tragedy had touched me deeply, and her parents had regarded me, in a cause so just, as their invincible champion. A successful termination of the trial would not have restored Vivian to them, but it would have accomplished a condolence in the pronouncement that the wanton negligence of a truck driver had not gone unnoticed and unredressed. A renewed faith in universal justice would have brought some balm to the grief-stricken parents. But now, with the loss of their child, went the seeming accusation of the law that Vivian was responsible for her own death. And in this bizarre situation I had become the hub of the shattered wheel of injustice.

I was aware that the day had to come when I would lose a case, but why did it have to be this one? Couldn't I have lost a simple assault and battery case, or a little contract action, or a lawsuit based on a meager debt? I winced in recalling, however, that my first case had been a lawsuit based on a meager debt. I would not have wanted to lose that case. In truth, I finally had to confess to myself—as I mentally portrayed the hypothetical cases I would have preferred to lose over this one—that I had not the stomach to lose any of them. And so, in that little hall bedroom, the walls of either side of which I could almost touch from the center of my bed, I agonized over this terrible thing which had happened in my life. In that dungeon of worry, frustration, and misery I wondered how I could go on.

What would be the reaction at the office? I was certain everyone would be nice to me, but how would that rebuild the fallen tower? And then, suppose I went on losing cases? What assurance did I have this might not happen again and again? I raised the blind and looked out the window at the dark back yard peopled with shadows of fences, garbage cans, and clothes poles, all of which, clothed in the raggedy garments of a mottled cloud-filled night, spoke of the futility of day and the helplessness of man caught in the web of circumstance which he cannot rend apart. In that doleful setting I made up my mind what I would do.

The next morning in my office I took a sheet of paper and wrote the following:

> My dear Mr. Scott:
> As I am not a member of your firm but only an employee I have no right to lose cases.
> Therefore, I hereby resign.
> *Michael A. Musmanno.*

I experienced such a sensation of relief, even a strange sort of pride, in what I was doing that before taking the letter to Mr. Scott's desk I showed it to Bill Gilderman and the other office boy, Joseph Sigman, as well as to Abe Koppelman, a young law student in our office. They all laughed. Koppelman said: "Of course you're joking about this?"

"Why do you say that? Of course I'm not joking."

Gilderman interjected: "I just can't believe you would voluntarily give up the excellent opportunities you have in this office."

"Yes, but a famous law firm like this one cannot afford to have an attorney who loses cases."

"Loses cases?" Sigman rhetorically queried as he slammed shut the lawbook he had been consulting. "You win forty-two cases in a row, and now because you're non-suited, through no fault of your own, you talk about losing cases. Why, there are lawyers in this city with big reputations who lose over one half of their cases. You'd better not let Mr. Scott or Mr. Connor see that letter. You can't say they haven't given you every encouragement and assistance."

"Yes, they have been mighty good to me."

"Well, don't let them down like that, no matter how you feel."

The idea which had seemed so logical, inevitable, and formidable in the hall bedroom the previous night began to fall apart under the combined attack of these energetic youths, and I tore up the letter. I also appealed the decision of the judge, although the appeal was turned down.

Several days later I tried another case. This time I wore my brown suit, and victory perched on its rusty shoulders once more. Again Lady Luck sprinkled her magic perfume over my brief case, and my train of success was on the tracks again.

But the faithful brown suit was showing signs of wear and tear, especially the trousers. It would not do, of course, to patch them. I took the coat to a pants store and got a pair of trousers to match it. This, I realized, was perilous business. What was I to do when the coat wore out? Would I then get a coat to match the trousers, and would it then be the same suit as before?

One may renew the blades and handle of a knife and still fancifully have the same knife, but one had to be careful about employing that same imaginative procedure when one was dealing with a suit with the responsibilities that suit had assumed.

I walked into court with some trepidation the first day I wore the new brown trousers. Madame Superstition did not notice the difference. We won that case also, but it was a strain on my nerves as well as on the suit.

But I would need to be a superman or a creature of fantasy to go on unceasingly winning. Such a feat would indeed fall within the realm of the supernatural. What is perfect can only appear to be perfect because as we weigh and analyze truth we inevitably conclude that perfection is only a figure of speech. The legal profession itself exists and functions only because of the mistakes, miscalculations, misapprehensions; in short, defects—mental, moral, and physical— in human beings. The medical profession equally has its honored place in the world of realities because of fault in the genus *Homo*. Men, women, and children ignore rules of health, and illness follows. They are careless, and accidents with controversies ensue.

One half of the businesses listed in the classified directories of tele-

phone books are repair shops. Shops that repair and mend everything
that man creates and therefore is imperfect; everything that man uses
and therefore becomes damaged. Shops that repair automobiles, type-
writers, sewing machines, fountain pens, shoes, suits, awnings, radios,
antiques, furnaces, artificial limbs, trunks, suitcases, bicycles, skates,
billiard tables, bowling alleys, bathtubs, showers, lights, furniture,
jewelry, pianos, plumbing, upholstery, etc., etc., etc.

And yet I expected to be perfect. Cicero, Daniel Webster,
Alexander Hamilton, Patrick Henry, John Marshall, Rufus Choate,
and all the immortals of the Bar, both ancient and modern, tasted
the unsavory salt of defeats, but I believed I had to enjoy the sugar of
victory in every case! In every field of endeavor, successful men
occasionally fail. The fabulous Babe Ruth, King of Swat, struck out
more times than he made home runs. The legendary Ty Cobb, who
stole more bases than any other player, also had the record of being
tagged out more times than any other base runner. Even Henry Ford
overlooked putting a reverse gear in his first automobile. Of course
today I realize how unreasonable was my attitude in 1924 when I
felt I just had to win every case, but I could see nothing illogical
about my position then. With full heart and soul I believed in my
cause and why should it not prevail? Each time I entered the courtroom I felt myself carrying the flag of Justice into the arena of vindication, and I could not bear to think that the flag should trail in
repudiation and defeat.

But I was doomed to disappointment and disillusionment nonetheless. Six weeks later I lost another case. This defeat came while
I was wearing the brown suit—but with the new trousers. From the
courthouse I proceeded directly to my lodgings and got out the old
trousers which I had tenderly put away as a fireman might store
away a helmet which had protected him from injury through years
of conflagrations. I took the trousers to a very skillful tailor and instructed him to employ that new system of repair which wove fresh
strands through threadbare areas with such finesse and precision that
when the job was completed one could not distinguish what was new
from what was old. The tailor did an excellent job and I rejoiced.

I donned the renovated trousers plus the old coat and, like a Spar-
tan going into battle behind a shield that had never failed him, I
marched into court with renewed confidence, courage, and zeal.

But it was to no avail, I lost again. Just a few new threads, but
Madame Superstition evidently recognised the trousers as not the same
old pants.

Then I lost another case. Three disasters in a heart-rending row! Happily the lost cases were not criminal cases. No one had to go to jail because of my failure, but to me every case was vital, regardless of the subject of controversy. I was now forced into the miserable realization that I could not depend on the brown suit any more. I did not, however, throw it away. Like a faithful horse that is put to pasture after its useful days are spent, I placed that suit in moth balls and I still have it as a reminder of the ebullient, confident, naïve days of my youth when I allowed superstition to pace determination and faith in one's cause.

I now started to wear my oxford-gray suit daily and with it began winning cases again, but I resolved that I would make no golden calf of it as I had of its predecessor. In point of fact, I liked the oxford suit better. It was really a fine-looking and excellent-wearing garment, and I did not need to worry about damaging it for fear of injuring its durability and thus my "infallibility."

I was now trying cases of major importance and magnitude and I was obtaining flattering results. Out of sixty-four cases, I had lost four. The sixty-fifth case was a contract action. I represented the plaintiff and had everything on my side: the documents, law, and facts; the witnesses were impeccable. I tried the case, I thought, exceedingly well.

Not to be immodest about the matter, I felt rather proud of the manner in which I exposed the other side. I shot holes through their defense, riddled the stories of their witnesses, ridiculed the pretensions of the opposing attorney, and made, as it appeared to me, one of the smoothest and most effective jury speeches in my career to date. The judge delivered a very fair and impartial charge. There could be no doubt that the jury would quickly return a verdict in favor of the plaintiff, my client. However, in an hour they returned and gravely intoned: "We, the jury empaneled in this case, find for the defendant."

That evening I wrote to Mr. Scott:

> My dear Mr. Scott:
>   I lost another case today and I am, with this letter, hereby tendering to you my irrevocable resignation as junior counsel in your office. When I lose a case I experience a threefold disappointment. I sense, firstly, the pang of loss that the client suffers; then, as the one responsible for the defeat, I personally experience the most intense personal chagrin and mortification; but

most of all I suffer in the realization that I have lost for you, you who have placed so much confidence in me. I shall never forget the chance you gave me, and I shall always be,

Most gratefully yours,
Michael A. Musmanno.

My rationalization, of course, left much to be desired, but my mortification was not because my life had been a cruise through the Tunnel of Love in an amusement park. I was by no means a child of fortune. I was only fourteen years of age when I began remunerative employment. My first job was that of a loader in a coal mine. I attended school at night. Later I was employed in various government departments in Washington, where, as already stated, I pursued a university education. Often I went without food in order to buy books and pay for tuition. But during all that battling on the gridiron of life, if I failed to score a touchdown or was thrown for a loss, I suffered alone. In the game of the law, however, the ground rules were quite different. Even in a prize fight, with which, for the purposes of this illustration, a contest in court may be compared, the psychological factors are quite dissimilar. A pugilist knocks his opponent to the floor for the count of ten or is flattened to the resin himself. Victory or defeat depends entirely upon his own skill, brawn, stamina. And the glory or gloom which crowns the encounter becomes exclusively his. He alone is pronounced the champion or he alone wears the badge of defeat in a broken nose, fractured ribs, or cauliflower ears.

But when a lawyer receives a solar plexus blow or ends up with his anatomy draped over the ropes of the legal arena, the ensuing pain and humiliation are not confined to himself. As much as he may ache from the pangs of defeat, it is his client who bends to the ensuing catastrophe, because it is he who loses his liberty or even his life, fortune, or reputation, or the trifling lawsuit against his neighbor which may loom as big in his mind as an involuntary bankruptcy.

On that melancholy day which shadowed my departure from Mr. Scott's office, my future in the legal profession was as uncertain as the state of the sea to a mariner in mid-ocean when his vision is blocked by a curtain of impenetrable clouds reaching from the sky to the water. Mr. Scott endeavored to persuade me in every way to alter my decision, but while I thanked him with all my heart and soul for his kindness and solicitude, nothing could change my resolution. As I had lost the case which precipitated my resignation, others could slip through my overeager hands with even more serious sequels. I brooded dark and dismal thoughts. Should I abandon a lawyer's career entirely? Was I too emotional? Did I feel too deeply to be practicing law? Was it impossible for me, in trying a case, to adopt an attitude of detachment? Did I always have to be like a surgeon operating on himself?

As I closed my desk for the last time, the other attorneys in the office, as well as the investigators, Sol Wittenberg and Ernest T. Wright, who had been very kind to me from my first day, came to me to follow up Mr. Scott's persuasions, but I had now crossed the Rubicon.

I needed a change of scenery for reflection. Perhaps after a journey to some place yet unknown to myself I might better decide what I should do. At any rate, I felt the great need of getting away from the courts as quickly as possible. Suddenly, on the wings of vague contemplation, came the solution to my enigma. Why not go to Europe? The winds of the sea would wash my mental and spiritual slate clean, and on another continent, while roaming among the pillars of the Old World civilization, I could decide what to do in the New. I had enough money to carry me along for two months, provided I exercised the strictest economy.

I had only one personal friend in Philadelphia, and that was Adrian Bonnelly, brilliant and eminently successful lawyer, formerly secretary to Congressman Felker. I called at his home to relate what had happened and outlined what I intended to do. He listened sympathetically and then, placing an arm around my shoulder, he said: "Michael, I know that you have been hurt badly and perhaps I could talk you out of your plans. But I wouldn't do that. Trust your instincts. I have faith in you." He helped me to obtain my passport quickly so that I could be on my way while I was still thrilled with the idea that my overseas odyssey would be the perfect poultice for my wounds. He recommended an itinerary which would take me into Italy, France, and England.

Within a week's time I was aboard a ship bound for Italy. To conserve funds I decided to travel steerage. Here I had turned to the wrong page on planning. Had Columbus lived as badly during those seventy days of his voyage to San Salvador as I did on my fourteen days to Naples, he might not have had the strength necessary to land and proclaim his great discovery.

During my days in the infantry I had complained with my brother soldiers about the food, but if on the fourteen days of my trip to

Europe we had had only one meal comparable to what we ate daily from our army mess kits, the voyage would have been a picnic. I always carried my meals from the kitchen, where they were served to us in little tin buckets, to the ship's rail to feed the fishes. The only reason I did not resign entirely from the bucket brigade was that I entertained the optimistic notion that someday the cook might forget himself and ladle out something fit for human consumption. The other steerage passengers, strangely enough, did not seem to mind what was handed to them. I subsisted on an occasional orange and piece of chocolate purchased at the ship's canteen. During the fourteen days' voyage I lost ten pounds in weight.

Chapter X

"WITH PASSION ONE DOES NOT REASON"

BETWEEN dining on oranges and chocolate bars I spent my entire time studying the Italian language, which was foreign to me except for a few words picked up in infancy from my mother. A fellow passenger by the name of Roberto Titone, who taught school in Naples, volunteered to tutor me, so that by the time our ship dropped anchor in the spectacularly beautiful harbor of Naples, I had acquired a fairly practical working knowledge of the language, and throughout my stay in Italy I continued intensively my study of Dante's idiom.

Titone had once been a law student and, although he never took a degree in jurisprudence, courts and trials always fascinated him. As our ship approached the shores of his native land he became pro-gressively excited over a murder trial on which the curtain was to rise in a Neapolitan court a day or two after our arrival. He had known the defendant as a boy and eagerly anticipated attending the trial. "Why don't you come along?" he urged me. "This will give you an opportunity to rest after the tedium of this long voyage. Mother is a wonderful cook, and she'll put back on your bones those ten pounds you've lost. And then I can continue to teach you, especially on your irregular verbs, which are a little weak."

"Weak!" I rejoined. "You flatter me, they're flat on their back."

His invitation was a generous one, enthusiastically and genuinely pressed, and as I had no immediate plans, I accepted. However, I was more interested in the prospect of continuing to receive his val-uable linguistic tutorship than I was in the trial which he looked for-ward to with such fervor. Before crossing the ocean, I had crossed the Rubicon: I wanted to hear nothing about trials, for a while, anyway.

However, still wearing the invisible knapsack of courtroom mem-ories which never fell from my back, I could not honestly feign disinterest in a murder trial. The defendant in the Neapolitan trial was named Albito Porta, a young man of patrician and aristocratic lineage, who had fallen in love with a beautiful and talented girl of plebeian stock whom he ardently wished to marry. His parents opposed the union and threatened to disinherit him in the event he defied their desires, but Albito nevertheless ran away with the girl. Up to this point it seemed to me that the plot was not, in the encyclopedia of love-making, a very unusual one. However, the drums of drama and the trumpets of tragedy now heralded a spine-chilling denouement. Count Porta, the boy's father, denounced Albito and warned him that if he married the girl he would not only disown him but would refuse ever to see him again. The girl, Pietrina, felt herself responsible for the abyss of filial banishment which her star-crossed lover faced and urged him to return to his father's roof. Albito declined her urgings. Her love meant more to him than all the titles, honors, and wealth his father could bestow on him. Pietrina now threatened suicide as a way out of her dilemma and self-adopted guilt. Albito immediately seized upon the monstrous idea and developed it to insane proportions. They would die together.

When, then, two days after we arrived in Naples, I saw Albito Porta in the courthouse of that city, my heart stumbled in its beat. A more piteous figure it would be difficult to imagine. Half of his face was shot away. With shotgun and revolver he had tried to prove the injustice of his father's denunciation. He had placed muzzle of the revolver in his mouth; and the shotgun, aimed also at his head, had been fired simultaneously with the revolver by an ingenious device set off by his foot.

And where was Pietrina? Alas, she was dead. Locking themselves in a room, Albito and Pietrina had proceeded to execute their appalling plan for self-destruction. First Albito transported Pietrina across the river of death, and then he set out to follow her.

Witnesses testified that they heard first one shot and then two other shots simultaneously. The doctor who had been summoned to the scene described the horrible spectacle which confronted him when he entered the room in which the lovers had spent their last moments together. "The girl was lying on the floor in a pool of blood," the doctor related. "Porta was on his knees, blood streaming from his head, his face unrecognizable. He could not talk, but he seized a piece of paper and wrote: 'Is she dead?' I replied that she was. Then he wrote: 'Doctor, let me die quickly.' "

Miraculously the doctor saved the life of the shattered lover, but when he left the hospital he was charged with the murder of Pietrina. As I sat in the drama-charged courtroom, more absorbed than one could be in any theater of Grecian tragedy, Albito Porta falteringly advanced to the witness stand. After my first glance I could not bear to look at him again. Once he had settled himself in the witness box, the judge asked him: "Signor Porta, what have you to say?"

Porta stared but did not reply. With lowered eyes I waited for his first words. A graveyard silence gripped the courtroom. One, two, three minutes passed by with the slowness of a glacier. Still not a word from the figure on whom all glances but mine were fastened.

Finally I heard a succession of noises which sounded like the rattling of stones falling on a casket. Porta was speaking, but the words were sepulchral. His mouth and throat had suffered excessive mutilation so that his voice, lacking tone, shade, and inflection, seemed to ascend from the bottom of a deep tomb. "What—do—you expect —me—to say?" were the first words, spaced by gasps and rattles.

A longer pause followed, and then I heard more sounds gaspingly forming into language: "Pietrina wanted—to die—and is dead. In fact—we are both dead, because I am only the miserable fragments of a wreck—without soul and without will—without hope and without fear."

"Could you not have left her, as your parents wished you to, and thus have averted the tragedy?" the judge put another question.

Again the reply from the living dead: "That would have been cowardly. On the altar of love we were ready to make sacrifice, and we did sacrifice our lives, so that no one could say that I attempted to find a pretext to abandon her."

The judge continued: "Would it not have been better, in spite of your parents' objections, to have married her? Why destroy two lives when a little thoughtfulness might have resolved your difficulties?"

Then came the answer which unlocks the mystery of much that is inexplicable in the storm-drenched mansion of tempestuous love. "Your Honor," the phantom voice spoke, *"con la passione, non si ragiona!* With passion, one does not reason!"

In the Italian criminal courts the victim or surviving relatives of a deceased victim of crime actively participate in the trial through private counsel. The private counsel here, representing the parents of Pietrina, strenuously pressed the Court and jury for conviction and imposition of the maximum penalty. He argued that the suicide plan was a simulated one and that Albito had premeditated the murder of Pietrina.

The prosecuting attorney, known as the Public Minister, opposed this contention. "The idea of suicide was born sincerely in the souls of two sensitive and lovesick youths. It is not human," he went on to say, "to ask of Porta why, instead of offering Pietrina the pallid hand of death, he did not proffer to her the rosy hand of matrimony. One might as well ask: Why was he foolish instead of wise, why was he mad instead of sane?"

It might seem strange that the Public Minister instead of defense counsel should be seeking to mitigate the demands for drastic punishment urged by private counsel. Defense counsel, of course, also speaks and defends to the utmost the rights of the accused. However, since private counsel is frequently motivated by a spirit of revenge instead of strict justice, it is the function of the Public Minister, whose office is considered quasi-judicial, to maintain an even balance between the zeal born of vindication, as exemplified by private counsel, and the enthusiasm of defense counsel which would excuse everything done by the accused.

In this case the prosecuting attorney was obviously convinced that Albito Porta had entertained no criminal intentions toward his sweetheart and that the object of the rendezvous was, without doubt, the one of accomplishing a double death. He was probably moved to compassion also, as everyone evidently in the courtroom was, by the intensity of devotion borne by each lover toward the other. Thus, in addressing the jury he spoke almost in the tones of a beneficent pastor seeking to bring harmony into a hate- and revenge-riven Capulet-Montague feud. With compassion and sympathy warming his words he pleaded: "Let my pacifying words of reason come like balsam to heal the aching hearts in this case, and whatever may be the response of justice, let hate cease and let revenge now be offered as a sacrifice upon the tomb of the little girl who loved and, to love, offered the perfume and the fragrance of her youth and the immaculate flower of her life. But let sentiment not touch us any more. I ask you to remove your eyes from the countenance of this unfortunate creature and I call upon you to adjudge him as we would adjudge a man."

Of course it would have been too much of an anomaly for the Public Minister to ask the jury outright to acquit the defendant—Porta had, after all, admitted killing Pietrina. Nonetheless, as he looked on the piteously mangled face of the accused he knew that the processes of law could never sentence him to the agony to which his own act had doomed him for the remainder of his wrecked life.

Only the grave could bring comfort and relief to that ruin of a man. Capital punishment had been abolished in Italy.

From the awesome threads of this tragic situation the Public Minister wove a plea which was one of the most moving, eloquent, illogical, and yet paradoxically logical, that I have ever heard in a courtroom. If the death penalty were still part of the law, he would ask that it be invoked, not out of revenge, but out of pity. "Jurors, if you had the power to pronounce that sentence which is no longer part of our code, I would be ferocious and ask that you be ferocious because such a ferocity would be an act of humaneness, but, according to our law, you can only condemn Albito Porta to live. You can only impose that sentence which he has been serving since the day the merciful hand of the doctor extracted him from the jaws of death, only to consign him to everlasting misery and unending unhappiness. Therefore, adjudge this man according to reason and according to justice."

Within an hour after the judge's instructions the jury returned a verdict of not guilty. Suddenly horror struck at every person in the courtroom as we beheld Porta sink to his knees and in his terrifying voice cry out: "Oh, Pietrina, why aren't you with me, or me with you?" His mighty sobs seemed to shake the very foundation of the courthouse. The guards released him, and he stumbled out into the world of his living purgatory.

Con la passione, non si ragiona.

With passion one does not reason.

Chapter XI

ROME

As I SAT in the Neapolitan courtroom excitedly following the movements and arguments of the battling lawyers, it seemed incredible that I should ever even have touched the hem of the thought of giving up the law. Just as sweethearts quarrel, only to be more attached to each other as the clouds of misunderstanding dissolve in the light of a renewed faith, I now realized that I had never really wavered in devotion to my chosen profession. I became impatient to return at once. Would my sweetheart forgive me? However, I reflected that since I was already in Italy I should not neglect the opportunity to visit Rome, the very cradle of the law of Western civilization.

Thus, after a two-week stay at the home of Signor Titone, I set out, equipped with a quiverful of Italian verbs, nouns, adjectives, and adverbs, for the Eternal City. Rome, whence comes Romance; Rome, the stamping ground of the Caesars; Rome, the Queen of History.

On the banks of the Tiber River, hard by the ancient Castle of San Angelo and within sight of the imposing Basilica of St. Peter, there rises in solemn majesty the Roman Palace of Justice. The enormity of the structure and its sheer massiveness fairly take one's breath upon first view. The approach from central Rome, leading over Ponte Umberto I, a bridge of imposing masonry, conducts directly to the principal entrance surmounted by the allegorical group of Justice.

On either side of the entrance, extending to the extreme corners of the palace, there stand, equidistant from each other, as if to guard for all eternity the sacred principles of justice they crystallized into law, the marble sentinels of the illustrious jurisconsults Vico, De Luca, Cicero, Papinianus, Bartolo, and Romagnosi.

Passing through the bronze gates of the building, one enters into a vast courtyard at one end of which rises a grand travertine double staircase leading to the Great Hall of the Court of Cassation.

At the approach to these formidable stairs stands THE LAW, personified in a large comely female figure bearing aloft in her hand a lighted torch. At her feet, in thoughtful posture and with wrinkled brow conning rolls of papyrus, sit the great quadrumvirate of the Roman Law: Hortensius, Paulus, Ulpianus, and Labeo.

In breathless awe I made my way through the titanic pile. All court buildings should wear a robe of majestic marble as does this one. Architectural massiveness in itself creates an atmosphere of commanding respect for the structure it proclaims. The United States Supreme Court building in Washington possesses this majestic projection. On its pediment appears the inscription: "Equal Justice Under Law." This same thought, expressed in slightly different wording, is gashed in stone on the Roman Palace of Justice: "*La legge è eguale per tutti.*" The law is equal for all.

As I moved almost on tiptoe through the corridors of the great building, a door momentarily opened offered a glimpse into one of the courtrooms. With wonderment and curiosity I stepped inside. It was the Court of Assize. Three robed judges sat on the bench and twelve jurors occupied the jury box. A large cage on the opposite side of the courtroom from the jury contained six prisoners. I thrilled at the prospect of witnessing a state trial. Were these defendants charged with treason? Why else would there be three judges in addition to the jury? My mind raced back to the old Roman days and the trial of the Catiline conspirators. But it was also possible that this could be a murder trial. At this moment the judge in the center addressed the defendants: "You have been charged with bastinadoing Francesco Scarpalunga . . ." I felt let down. Was this impressive personnel recruited and this formidable equipment assembled to try a simple charge of assault and battery? But this carping thought quickly vanished as I realized that I was a legatee of the rich testament of Roman Law. Immediately I sensed a pride, as well as inspiration, in the realization that in the Eternal City of Rome, with its mighty traditions of justice through the ages, the law speaks with ceremonious majesty, no matter what the accusation, no matter what the issue.

In this particular case the defendants were accused of beating one Francesco Scarpalunga for having, as they alleged, cheated in a game of *mora*. *Mora* is a game in which two opposing players swiftly and simultaneously display a certain number of fingers, each player announcing at the same time what he expects the sum total of the spread-out digits to be, the one guessing correctly winning the stakes. The process is a simple one, but with mental astuteness and experience a veteran player acquires a certain psychological skill which enables him to divine the number of fingers that his adversary, by force of habit, will cast. Then there is the talent of withdrawing a finger or two after observing one's opponent's hand, so as to make the sum total coincide with the number already announced. This practice is obviously not an approved one, and the person caught indulging in it is apt to end up almost anywhere. In this particular case the cheating player ended up in a hospital.

The presiding judge suggested a demonstration of the game for the benefit of the jurors, most of whom lived in the city and thus perhaps were unacquainted with the provincial sport. *"Quattro! Sette! Sei!"* rang through the courtroom, while fingers flew right and left. One witness revealed how the cheating was accomplished. He would throw four fingers and then withdraw one, but the fourth member disappeared with such lightning rapidity that my eye was unable to distinguish the vanishing act. Seeing only three fingers, I concluded that I had erred at first and that the player had cast but three digits at the outset.

It was over an argument about these ghostlike fingers which seemed to vanish in thin air that the fight began. All the defendants were convicted.

Following the trial I introduced myself to one of the attorneys, who immediately presented me to the judge as an *avvocato Americano*—American lawyer. The judge greeted me cordially and related proudly that he had one brother living in Cincinnati and another in San Francisco. He asked me questions on American trial procedure and expressed surprise that one of my youth should apparently have had so much experience. I replied: "Not only that, I had so much experience that for a time I believed I had enough!" When I related the shameful story of my withdrawal from the Philadelphia courts, he laughed and said he could understand my reaction. "But now that you are here," he added, "why not attend the University of Rome and study under the great masters like Enrico Ferri, today the world's greatest criminologist, and Pietro Bonfante, who holds the chair of Roman Law, and Orlando, our veteran war Prime Minister, who teaches constitutional law, and Salandra, also ex-Prime Minister, who holds the chair of administrative science, and Anzilotti, who holds the chair of international law, and Schialoia, our representative at the League of Nations and who sits as the Supreme Court of the Republic of San Marino?" I thrilled to the names of these altitudinous peaks in the Alps of jurisprudence. The judge went

on: "You have here the chance to study Roman Law where it orig-
inated, developed, and was codified twenty centuries ago—the Roman
Law which is the basis of all modern law." I felt a fire of eagerness
flaming within me. With it I burned my bridges. I would stay and
study in Rome.

Only one formidable obstacle obtruded: the one which has blocked
the fulfillment of many a meritorious desire—an empty treasury. I
sent off a letter at once to my brother Sam and acquainted him with
my plans, adding that if he wanted to see me again in Stowe Township he would need to send me money for the return ticket—I was
spending everything I had. He at once cabled me $250. At the
offices of the United States Lines in Rome I paid $90 for an eventual
return by tourist-cabin passage on the S.S. *Leviathan* which would
sail from Southampton. This left me $160 to the good. I matriculated
at the university.

It was a strange venture to which I was committing myself. Although already a lawyer and already launched on my professional
career, I was returning to school to study a field of law not essential
to American practice—simply out of love for jurisprudence and the
feeling that somehow this additional equipment would better qualify
me in the practice of my beloved profession.

However, in order to assure myself I was not making a mistake I
sought advice and counsel at the American Embassy in Rome. The
chargé d'affaires, with whom I spoke, advised me to abandon my
impractical idea. If I were a son of wealthy parents, he said, an extended stay in Rome would be pleasurable and gratifying, but since
I still had to battle my way in the world, an extended absence from
my profession would retard me to that extent in my climb to success.

But, like the impetuous youth I was, I ignored the very advice I
sought.

Eighteen years later my headlong decision found confirmation of
what almost seemed an uncanny foresightedness. Following Pearl
Harbor I entered the Navy as a lieutenant commander, and in 1943,
when plans were being formulated for the European invasion, I was
selected, because of my studies at Rome, for the Italian expedition.
Attached to the Fifth Army under General Clark, I participated in the
entire Italian campaign, later became General Clark's naval aide,
was wounded twice, served for a period as military governor of the
Sorrentine peninsula, and then went on, after the war, to become a
judge on the highest tribunal in the world, the International War
Crimes Tribunal in Nuremberg. But all this was still as far away

as the stars in the sky, which I studied at night, wondering what they held in store for me for the days to come.

And now I thrilled to student days again. Studying in an acquired language offered a challenge all its own and turned my lessons into rich explorations in new continents of learning. Attending classes, reciting, preparing papers—it was incredible and it was delightful. What can be more delightful than to have youth—and enjoy it as youth?

But with the excitement of school days went also the adventure of earning a living—in the land of the Caesars. Substantial as was the sum of $160, it still could not propel the ship of sustenance to the end of the course. I needed many lire. I hired out as tutor in English to Romans who had an eye on voyages to America and England. I did some translating from Italian into English for the Italian Ministry of Justice. I obtained a position as Rome correspondent for an English-language weekly newspaper printed in Florence.

This was the most profitable employment of all—not in financial returns but in general education. I received only one hundred lire (about five dollars) for each article accepted, but as a newspaper correspondent I had the authority to attend practically every public function in Rome. Thus, while mastering the immutable principles of the venerable Roman Law I was supplementing my education in the university of life itself. I covered all those events which interest and stir the world with glasses on its nose, the newspaper-reading public. I attended sessions of the Italian Parliament, got into theaters and operas on free passes, entered police lines at fires, riots, and parades.

It was during this period that Metro-Goldwyn-Mayer was filming in the outskirts of Rome the picture *Ben Hur.* I invaded the "location" to prepare a story on the production and ended up by playing a part in the movie, a fragmentary part to be sure—fragmentary as to the part of body exposed. My physique seemed to impress the director, Fred Niblo, as one which would do justice to a centurion uniform, and he hired me as an extra. Garbed in a short skirt, a brass breastplate, enormous silver (tin) bracelets, and spurred boots, I clanked about shouting orders to perspiring spear-carrying legionnaires. The crowning glory of my raiment was the helmet which enveloped my head as completely as an inverted macaroni colander, allowing me to peer through several perforations. The only visible part of my anatomy was my knees. Nonetheless, when the finished film was later projected in Pittsburgh, my nephews and nieces professed to recognize me by those knees. This was undoubtedly exaggeration on their part, and I believe that they really recognized me only because of the skillful manner in which I was able to make my way around, looking through the ventholes in the iron macaroni container decorating my skull.

I even performed in an opera. When in November 1924 the celebrated composer Giacomo Puccini died, his great success, *The Girl of the Golden West,* was revived at the Costanzi Theater. With the object of writing a story on opera as seen through the eyes of a supernumerary, I became a cowboy extra in this famous opera with its Wild West setting. At the first rehearsal the director manifested intense dissatisfaction with the non-singing actor who was to cry out: *"Al laccio!"* ("Lynch him!") in that climactic scene where the irate cowboys and gold miners surge around the hero, Dick Johnson, determined to hang him. Perhaps in derision the director exclaimed: "I'll bet that Signor Musmanno can do the job better than that. Try it." I took him at his word and threw into the rendition such feeling, gusto, and lung power that the director assigned the part to me. It was a tremendous responsibility which I undertook because the whole scene, without intending any pun, *hung* on those two words— "Lynch him!" Resolved to make my performance, which consisted entirely of those two words, a devastating one, I practiced them continuously. For the next two weeks, people walking through the extensive grounds of the Villa Borghese must undoubtedly have been considerably surprised at seeing and hearing a young man in an oxford-gray suit, with open book in his hand, yelling vociferously, *"Al laccio!"* at every tree and statue he passed. But on the night of the actual performance I outdid even myself. The whole theater rang, the beams probably trembled, and I'm sure the cast did, as I lifted my voice in a gale of a shriek: *"AL LACCIO!!!"*

Needless to say, when the final curtain came down on the opera, it came down also on the end of my operatic career.

I wrote stories on opera, drama, Tiber River regattas, parliamentary sessions, the royal family, Mussolini, wine-tavern vendettas— anything that would induce my editors in Florence to send along the much-needed hundred-lira notes. I wrote ten times more stories than were published, so that I hardly ever received more than five or ten dollars a week, but the events themselves always added one more page of instruction in the great book of experience, the wisest tutor of all. None of those events, however, was so rewarding, from all points of view, as will be noted quickly, as the session of the Supreme Council of the League of Nations in Rome.

It is asserted incessantly that the League of Nations never achieved much, but to this statement I must demur emphatically. It accomplished a great deal for me. The Supreme Council held its sessions in the Doria Palace, on the Corso Umberto, where in a large parlor an imposing buffet lunch scented the atmosphere to a heavenly degree. It is not known what Nero served his guests, but I doubt that his culinary major-domo could have improved on what was being served at the Doria Palace for the League of Nations delegates and the official visitors. White-aproned and white-hatted chefs presided behind steam tables laden with stuffed squab, roast spring chicken, broiled lobster, platters of spaghetti, ravioli, manicotti. Other tables sagged under antipasti, salads, fruits, and pastries. Ice cream, coffee, confectionery, liqueurs smiled and beckoned to you to partake of their hospitality.

Endowed by nature with an expansive temperament, I made it a point, when interviewing a delegate, always to invite him to the buffet table for the colloquy. "We can talk just as well, and far more satisfactorily, over some hot food and a glass of wine," I would say, "than we can here in this noisy assembly hall." And thus I would pilot my quarry to the tables glittering with silver bowls, percolators, and beautiful china, white with snowy napery and redolent of the delicious fragrances of dishes unsurpassed in any hostelry in the world. And here, with pencil on my pad and fork sunk into a broiled squab, I would discuss with my conferee the problems of the world as outlined on the agenda of the League of Nations.

If it happened that at the end of the day a salami or two and several loaves of bread, plus olives, peppers, and cakes were unconsumed, I would inform the head chef that I would do him the favor of taking the leftovers away in my brief case. He agreed with me that nothing could be more conducive to world peace than the articles I was writing on the efforts being made in that direction at these meetings of the League of Nations, and since I wrote better on a full stomach, it was important that I be kept well fed. Thus each evening I emerged from the Doria Palace with my head bursting with ideas, my stomach bulging with food, and my brief case distended with provisions for the lean days which would come when the League of Nations would have adjourned. Yes, I shall always have a kind feeling in my heart for the League of Nations.

Nor will there ever cool in the depository of my memory the warm sentiment which suffused me as I gazed upon that conference of world statesmen, that parliament of continents, that assembly of transoceanic peoples dedicated to the most attractive desideratum of the human race—World Harmony. On the agenda for discussion were such humanity-saving subjects as national security, international hygiene, control of traffic in opium and other dangerous drugs, strengthening of the International Red Cross, safeguarding of children, protection of women, execution of treaties of peace, international federation for mutual assistance in the relief of peoples overtaken by disaster, progressive codification of international law.

Aristide Briand, the French Premier, colorful and picturesque, dominated the Council. Listening to him, one could easily believe that the millennium stood at the very threshold of realization. Briand's voice has been variously likened to a bass fiddle, a violoncello, and a harp, and it did indeed possess the timbre usually associated with those instruments, but when I heard this masterful orator it was not difficult for me to believe a pipe organ was speaking. And the rich tones of his voice carried an even richer quality of sincerity. Peace! Peace! is what he pleaded for. Never again must marching armies trample over the breast of mankind. Austen Chamberlain of England agreed with him; so did Beneš of Czechoslovakia, and Hymans of Belgium, and Undén of Sweden, and de León of Spain. Over the ocean of years which separate me from that assembly of hope and yearning I can still hear the ringing words of Guani of Uruguay: "The acceptance of the principle of compulsory arbitration and the machinery contemplated to guard against and punish the international crime of aggressive war is welcomed by the American democracies as a substantial progress toward the ideal of an equality among the nations of the world and of justice and public law." This was one time that South America revealed a greater farsightedness than North America. If the United States had been an active, participating member of the League of Nations, the insanity of World War II could never have happened. Hitler would have been shut up in a museum with his *Mein Kampf,* Stalin would never have received lend-lease, and the raucous voices of the present world-disturbers in Moscow would have frozen into innocuous icicles in the arctic winters of the Red Square.

At the university I had for my preceptor the illustrious Enrico Ferri, leader of the Positive School of Criminology, member of the Italian Chamber of Deputies for forty years, author of some twenty books, lecturer, orator, and the greatest trial lawyer in Italy. When he pleaded a jury case he became a veritable tornado, sweeping everything before him by the sheer force of eloquence and personality. As the words cascaded from his lips I thought, as I watched him in action, that the very benches in the courtroom would melt under the impassioned torrent of his language. Without any reservation whatsoever, I would say he was the greatest orator of the period. Tall and slender, with white pompadour, mustache, and goatee, he looked like an intellectual Buffalo Bill. He always began his speeches in the lower register. Presently his voice would begin to climb and then, as he piled reason upon reason, fact upon fact, and circumstance upon circumstance, he engendered an excitement which brought his listeners almost to an exploding point. Then just before the emotional climax, just when the tension had reached a degree of absolute intolerableness, his voice would drop to a sweet whisper and delightful murmur. And now, having normalized the emotions of his audience, he would again soar to the mountain peaks of eloquence, carrying everybody with him.

In June 1925, Professor Ferri presided over the college of professors before which I defended the thesis I had written on the Italian jury system as compared to the American jury system. At the final faculty conference on my schoolwork I was awarded a somewhat unusual grade. One normally looks upon 100 percent as the highest mark one can possibly achieve, but Italian professors, with their love of superlatives, have established (at least it was so in 1925) a rating even higher than perfect! Thus my diploma of Doctor of Jurisprudence proclaims rather startlingly that in my studies at the University of Rome I attained not 100 percent, but 110 percent!

Chapter XII

PARIS

IN JULY, 1925, Professor Vittorio Emanuele Orlando conferred on me, in a colorful ceremony in the Aula Magna, the degree of *Dottore di Giurisprudenza*, and, hugging it to my bosom, I set off on the return home. Since I was to board the S.S. *Leviathan* at Southampton, I traveled northwardly through Italy, stopping at every large city not only to enjoy its own unique attractions but particularly to visit its *palazzo di giustizia*. Like a traveler gathering picturesque and vividly colored hotel labels for his luggage, I collected mental pictures of the courthouses in Florence, Pisa, Bologna, Turin, Milan, Venice, each one majestic and beautiful in its own right and in its own distinctive architectural style, but all dedicated to the great concept which would now always guide my life. Only one question knocked at the door of my consciousness as the train rolled over the continent and the locomotive announced to the world that I was homeward-bound; namely, would my sweetheart forgive me for having jilted her at the courthouse in Philadelphia? The car wheels kept answering as they passed over the rail joints underneath, but in the tumult of my emotions I could not decipher what they were saying.

And now, having crossed the Italian frontier, our train headed for the city whose name has become the symbol of uninhibited entertainment and sophisticated gaiety—Paris! In this great metropolis of theaters, hotels, cafés, restaurants, music, promenades, and magnificent boulevards, the thoroughfares led to but one place for me— the Palais de Justice. Aside from the fact that I did not have a single sou to spend for high life, I was too solemnly committed to a resumption of my career even to want to be a *bon vivant* in glorious Oui, Oui Paree.

And now, in this great French metropolis, I stood before the formidable citadel of the law, reliving its centuries of legal traditions. On that warm day in August 1925, I thought of the fiery period in

French history only a century and a quarter before, when judges were writing their decisions in blood. Here, amid this architectural forest of stone, during the Reign of Terror, Tribunals of Blood daily condemned to death personages whose names evoke history as gold produces glitter. Here Queen Marie Antoinette, King Louis XVI, Madame Roland, Danton, Robespierre, Charlotte Corday, and countless other hapless ones heard the judgments sentencing them to the tumbrels which jolted over cobblestone streets to the remorseless dripping guillotine while crowds alternately jeered and wept. Here blood ran in the streets until even the gutters must have revolted at carrying so much slaughtered human life in the names of Liberty and Justice.

I hoped I might witness a trial of today which would cause me to take away from the Palais de Justice a mental association less torrid and gory than the one which the present recalling of history imparted. In this wish I was singularly fortunate, for on that very day in one of the assizes there began a trial as spectacular and sensational as one which might have animated a chapter by Emile Zola, if only he had been present to record it.

A French Law student, Charles Carpentier, whom I had met that day and who spoke English fluently, offered to take me to the trial and to translate for me. With his assistance and my familiarity with the procedure, quite similar to the one I had studied in Italy, I had no difficulty in following the courtroom drama. The defendant, Aida Valette, a young woman of twenty-five, stood charged with having hurled corrosive acid into the face of her rival, who, her face and neck hidden beneath wide bandages, sat at the witness bench. Only the eyes of the victim were visible, but they told much. As from several fragments of a shattered statue one can mentally reassemble the original artistic creation, so one could divine from the orbs of Jacqueline Claremont and the golden strands of hair escaping from the fashionable turban encasing her shapely head that Nature had bestowed on her woman's most precious gift. The lambent quality of those eyes—deep, wide, and aquamarine—and the graceful slender lines of her figure corroborated the miracle of beauty which looked out from her photograph, made prior to the assault and which had been introduced in evidence.

The trial began with the judge, who wore long mustaches, calling upon the accused to explain why she had thrown the caustic chemicals at Jacqueline Claremont. Aida refused to answer, sullenly reproaching with her flashing eyes the judge, the lawyers, the audience, the witnesses, and perhaps all members of the human race. Undisturbed by her obstinacy, the judge, who is referred to as the president, stroked his mustaches and leisurely read into the record an account of what the pre-trial investigation had disclosed with regard to the conduct of the defendant. He then summoned the facially swathed Jacqueline Claremont to the witness stand and asked her to tell her story.

"I loved Charles Viviers," the witness began in a voice as lyrical as her face had once been enchanting. "Aida Valette also loved him." She paused. The jury leaned forward, as did every person in the crowded courtroom, and then, in a measured musical cadence, she resumed her narrative. "Aida was jealous and she demanded of me that I ignore Monsieur Viviers' attentions. I thought she was jesting. Naturally I could not abandon a love which was the very breath of my life. Then she threatened me with some dire punishment, never suggesting what it might be. Of course I had no idea she could be so fiendish——" Here the dikes of her reserve crumbled under a tidal wave of emotion, and the cast of bandages rose and fell with her heaving sobs. The public prosecutor leaped to her assistance, lifted a reassuring hand to her shoulders, offered her a glass of water, and urged her to continue.

"One day," the hidden lips spoke again, "it was just one year ago, while walking along the street, Aida suddenly appeared before me, carrying a large handkerchief covering an object of some kind. I feared she intended violence and screamed. She tore away the handkerchief and I caught a flash of a large openmouthed jar. In a second I felt a million needles in my face. Where the acid struck my clothes, the garment parted as if it were paper before a flame. I could feel the skin on my face and neck dissolving—— I can't stand it——" A piercing shriek finished her testimony and she crumpled on her chair, limp as a wilted flower, while every spectator's eye hurled a javelin of embittered resentment at the author of the atrocity sitting defiantly in the prisoner's dock. Unabashed, Aida glared back, but the audience retaliated with such audible volume that the judge felt obliged to lift a little bell from his bench and swing it once to the right and once to the left. The ensuing tinkle settled the tumult.

Mademoiselle Claremont, having revived, was taken to a seat by the side of the prosecutor, and the doctor, who first treated her following the attack, took the stand. As he finished describing in harrowing detail the mordant action of the chemical which had reduced the rapturous features of Jacqueline Claremont to a mask of spine-creeping grotesqueness, the defendant shouted: "Mr. President, I will tell the story—the whole story!"

"Very well," the president said, "conduct the prisoner to the stand," beckoning to two gendarmes at the dock. As she strode to the witness box, curiosity as to the nature of her defense stalked in the trail of her defiant stride. The courtroom had not long to wait.

Tossing her chin into the air and throwing back the cataract of black hair which surged about her belligerent face, Aida Valette exclaimed: "Charles never loved Jacqueline! She annoyed him with her pursuit. It is true I warned her to stay away from him. But it was only because I did not want her to be humiliated by his brutally telling her to keep her distance from him."

"You lie! He did love me!" Jacqueline's voice cried out with the desperate quality of one slipping over a precipice. The courtroom went into another uproar and the judge tolled his little school bell. But the commotion only momentarily stilled, ascended to peaks of sensation when Charles Viviers himself took the stand to deny Aida's charge and to declare in a choking voice: "I loved Jacqueline, and I love her now more than ever. And if she will have me, I will marry her today!"

"Monsieur President!" Aida's hand was waving frantically. "I would like to be allowed to approach Charles Viviers and ask him a question face to face."

"Mademoiselle, your request is a little irregular. Still, the law permits you to confront any hostile witness." The judge turned to the gendarmes. "Officers, conduct Mademoiselle Valette to Charles Viviers."

With one officer at either arm, Aida approached Viviers, who, palpably nervous, awaited her. The guards halted the bellicose defendant about two paces from the witness, whereupon in a surprisingly calm voice she said: "Charles, you have just said you will marry Jacqueline. But I know you do not love her. You only feel sorry for her. You would marry her out of sympathy, but once you saw her hideous face, you would hate yourself for your rash act. Witness now what you would have to look upon every day of your life!"

With this she broke loose from the guards and lunged at Jacqueline, trying to rip from her face the befriending cloth wrapper. The public prosecutor restrained her just in time, while the guards seized her and bore her, kicking and struggling, back to the dock. In a tone remarkable for its restraint the judge reprimanded the disturber and announced a recess.

When the Court reconvened twenty minutes later, counsel for the defense rose and, to the accompaniment of audible gasps from the audience, said to the judge: "Mr. President, my client is here charged with a grave offense, mayhem. A few minutes ago she asked that the alleged wounds of Jacqueline Claremont be exposed. I admit that the manner of her request and the reason assigned for it were improper. What Charles Viviers thinks of Jacqueline Claremont is utterly irrelevant, but I submit to the Court that this defendant has the right to demand that Mademoiselle Claremont's covering be removed so that the jury may see for themselves whether the crime of mayhem has actually been established. So far as we can know with certainty, Mademoiselle Claremont's claim may be merely a sham, and unless and until her supposed wounds are introduced as ocular evidence I move that the defendant be discharged on the ground that every element of the crime of mayhem has not been proved."

The public prosecutor roared to his feet: "Mr. President, in my twenty years' service in this court I have never heard so infamous and outrageous a demand! This act of counsel in joining with his client in her fiendish plan to wreak revenge on her suffering rival merits the condemnation of this court, the reprimand of every lawyer in Paris, and the rebuke of every decency-loving citizen in France. The only purpose that can be served in exposing this girl's pitiable condition is to alienate the affections of the man who has solemnly told the world that he loves her and wishes to marry her."

"It cannot be much of a love," counsel for the defense scoffed, "that would run away from the professed creature of his love only because she is not as beautiful as he would have her."

"If I were not in a court of law"—the public prosecutor's voice went into a falsetto—"I would demand an apology from you, the failure to render which would result in———"

The president's gavel shattered the remainder of the fiery challenge. "Counsel on both sides will at once cease their fulminations! Although personally regretting that Mademoiselle Claremont must be subjected to any embarrassment which may attend the exposure of her condition, trial procedure impels the granting of the defendant's request. Until the wounds are revealed, all the elements of the crime charged have not been proved legally."

"I will not permit it!" sobbed Jacqueline, spreading her protecting hands over the soft casing behind which she hid from the world.

"Mr. President"—the handsome figure of Charles Viviers was now speaking—"Mademoiselle Claremont need not fear that her poor wounds will rob me of my devotion to her." Then, turning to the distraught maiden, he added: "Jacqueline, I love you and will marry you today if you will have me." As he spoke he approached her. "Let me remove the bandages and let us both stand before the world unashamed and unafraid. I entreat you to let me do this."

"Charles, you might then not want me, but whatever you wish shall be done."

"You are still my Jacqueline, and nothing shall keep us apart," Charles assured her as tenderly he proceeded to the awesome task.

Gently weeping, Jacqueline Claremont yielded to her lover's compassionate fingers, while the courtroom stared in breathless expectancy. Not an eyelash flickered as Viviers unwound the first strips of white sheathing which, glistening in a shaft of sunlight falling through the window, became lace of mercy as it gathered in huge ovals at the feet of the quivering girl.

As the charitable ribbon descended, a sneer wreathed the defendant's lips. In a moment she would have her revenge. There were but two more turns of the bandage left when the judge spoke.

"Monsieur Viviers, stop for a moment! I warn everybody in the courtroom that there will be no demonstration when the unveiling process is completed."

Like a spiral of white smoke defying the law of physics and proceeding downward instead of rising to the ceiling, the last turn of the dressing floated to the floor. Only a large square of gauze now separated the harsh world from Jacqueline Claremont's cruelly scarred countenance. Tenderly lifting the upper corner of the protecting shield, Viviers easily detached it from the shapely head and it fluttered to the girl's feet.

The courtroom froze into immobility.

Everyone stared with incredulous eyes and said nothing. My own tongue cleaved to the roof of my mouth.

With a shriek of terror Jacqueline buried her head in her lap.

Viviers gently and lovingly lifted her to her feet and upraised her head. Still no one mumbled a word. Not a foot scratched the carpet of dead silence.

Finally a sob punctuated the stillness and Jacqueline moaned: "Get me a mirror and let me see this Medusa head which has paralyzed all of you."

A woman close by opened her purse and, as if in a trance, withdrew a small glass which she handed to the weeping girl.

Slowly Jacqueline lifted the glass, looked into it, and gasped: "No?"

In the frame of the mirror she saw perfection. Not a scar or blemish marred the exquisitely wrought face, not a wound or scratch disturbed the harmony of those matchless features.

What was this mystery? I turned to Carpentier: "W-what does this all mean?"

"Sh—sh," he cautioned, "let us listen to the girl, she'll explain———"

Jacqueline was now stammering: "I—I don't understand. At the hospital—I saw the pictures—taken right after I arrived there. I was so hideous—that I haven't looked—at my face since."

The Public Minister immediately subpoenaed the girl's doctor (a plastic surgeon) and court was adjourned until he should arrive. When in an hour he appeared, the mystery was resolved. He explained that he had performed several operations on the girl but had never told her of the extent of the skin graft employed, fearing to raise hopes which might not be realized. "But I am now happy to say," he went on, "that the operations were successful—and I can assure all her friends that her beauty has been permanently regained."

The statement came like a flash of lightning on a sulphur-charged day and, like the clap of thunder which is the audible manifestation of what precedes it, the audience burst into deafening applause. Everyone smiled, laughed, and elbowed his neighbor joyfully. In that instant the whole world had become beautiful. The defendant, however, gave no evidence of accepting any such metamorphosis. Her eyes widened in amazed incredulity, and then they seemed to catch fire as she bit her lips humiliatingly, like one who has been brutally deceived. Raising her hand as if to register protest against this dire plot which had been hatched against her, she broke into a violent general denunciation. The judge stopped her and pronounced his verdict: "Defendant, I find you guilty—and my sentence will be———"

"Mr. President, may I say a word?" Jacqueline interrupted. "I wish you would not be too severe with the prisoner. I believe she has already been punished enough by the trial itself."

When Viviers also joined in the request, it was the judge's turn to be incredulous. He paused, stroked his long mustaches, and then half smiled. "Very well," he said, "I will sentence the defendant to five years' imprisonment, but will suspend the sentence on condition that she never bothers either one of you."

"Who wants to bother them?" Aida sniffed, although she was obviously relieved at getting out of the scrape with a whole skin.

As we left the courtroom I asked Carpentier: "What moral, if any, do you draw from the whole affair?"

"I think it shows to what infamous depths hatred can descend. Don't you agree with me?"

"No, Carpentier, I would say that it reveals to what sublime heights *love* can *ascend*. Viviers loved Jacqueline. Nothing else mattered. She had been beautiful and to him she would always remain beautiful. He did not ask to look behind the bandages before he announced his willingness to marry her."

"But is not hatred as strong a force as love?" Carpentier countered. We were now outside the courthouse, promenading the banks of the Seine River, which had become a lake of empurpling quicksilver in the rays of the late afternoon sun. "The defendant was willing to face prosecution, undergo bitter condemnation, and, if necessary, go to prison to satisfy her hatred and revenge. Viviers, yes, was ready to marry the girl he believed to be disfigured, but he was not subjecting himself to a pain commensurate to what Aida would suffer in ignominy, shame, and incarceration."

"Carpentier, it is idle to speculate on which is the stronger. Did we not witness the conflict between hatred and love? Aida's bitterness was evidenced in the acid she threw at her rival. Acid cuts deep, yet we saw right there in the courtroom that love plumbs depths that poison can never reach. When Aida was convicted, Jacqueline did not seek revenge. Resentful as she could have been over Aida's act, which was intended to ruin her life forever, yet, in the sanctity and ecstasy of her love, now that she was sailing over a joyous sea with her skipper lover, she had no desire to sink the craft which had tried to torpedo her happiness. She allowed it to drift away over the horizon of forgiveness and forgetfulness."

"Musmanno, what is love?"

"Love is harmony, and harmony comes from justice. When the forces of justice succeed in righting all wrongs, the world will have come into the perfect state of happiness to which all mankind aspires."

Suddenly my attention was captured by a sunset so sublime that my heart stopped beating. "Look, Carpentier!" I pointed to the west, where the horizon blazed like a paint factory afire. Scarlet, yellow, and vermilion flames shot into the sky, throwing out embers of lilac, rose, and orange. The calmly rippling surface of the Seine mirrored the spectacular heavens miraculously transformed into a reservoir containing every shade and hue in the spectrum.

And then in the distance one perceived the advance guard of the twilight mists. A pink fog came steadily forward as if to lower the curtain on the drama of the day.

Soon it would be night, night in beautiful Paris. And then it would be day again.

And I was on my way home.

Chapter XIII

LONDON

LONDON!

The Tower of London, Parliament, Big Ben, Buckingham Palace, Westminster Abbey, Old Bailey, Waterloo Bridge, Magna Charta, Runnymede . . .

I had crossed the choppy English Channel from Calais to Dover and there boarded the London train, which was not an express—just a nice good, old, take-your-time afternoon train. The history of England, written in every purling stream, solitary farmhouse, serene village, and cheerful town, is too fascinating to dash through with the speed of a Twentieth Century Limited.

Settling back comfortably in a red plush seat which could have at one time accommodated Churchill or even Disraeli, my eyes drank in the green and gold panorama as I peopled it with figures from my imagination. Along the pleasant roads and by rivers' peaceful banks I recognized and waved to William Shakespeare, Samuel Johnson, Charles Dickens, Oliver Goldsmith, David Garrick, Sir William Blackstone, George Eliot, Sir Isaac Newton, Sir Walter Raleigh, and John Cabot, who apparently saw nothing strange in receiving greetings from someone beyond the frame of their own centuries.

Then the train stopped at a little ivy-covered station, the doors of my coach swung open, and through the aisles poured a flood of laughing, chattering, bright, blue-eyed lads wearing short jackets, Eton collars, and flowing Windsor ties. I smiled in my pleasant reveries. Weren't William Shakespeare, William Blackstone, and Charles Dickens at one time boys? English boys? Just like these boys?

With merry shouts and laughter sounding like a reveling carillon, the cherub-faced invaders clambered into their seats and burst forth into a jolly song which I then heard for the first time:

> "Oh, show me the way to go home,
> I'm tired and I want to go to bed,

> I had a little drink about an hour ago,
> And it went straight to my head.
> No matter where I roam,
> On land or sea or foam,
> You can always hear me singing this song,
> Oh, show me the way to go home!"

A bell of strange joy tinkled in my breast. What was it? Ah, yes, many moons had lighted the earth since I had heard English in massed voice. The impact of the language, the jubilation of frolicking youth, and the music of fresh throats threw me into immediate rapport with my surroundings. Was I not young too? And did not Shakespeare and Blackstone leave me a heritage also? And so, as the children reached the second chorus, I caught the tempo, and, with exulting soul, added a trebling tenor to the music of my little brothers:

> "No matter where I roam,
> On land or sea or foam,
> You can always hear me singing this song,
> Oh, show me the way to go home!"

Yes, I was on my way home—at last!

Arrived in London, I headed for Westminster Hall. Although I had left America to get away from courthouses, wherever I had tarried on the Continent the first building which engaged my interest was always the courthouse of the town. And now I entered England's oldest courthouse.

Prior to Magna Charta, justice traveled with the King. Thus, subjects seeking redress of grievances were more often than not denied a hearing because of the prohibitive expense and uncertainty involved in trying to locate the King, who was frequently on pleasure bent and not infrequently fleeing from some enterprising pretender to the throne, intent on separating him from his crown and even his head. It was the immortal Magna Charta, wrested from old King John on the plains of Runnymede in 1215, which declared that the Court of Common Pleas must be held "in some certain place." Westminster Hall became that *certain* place.

For six hundred years it was the seat of justice in England. Here the common law, which accompanied the colonists to America, took definitive form. Here developed the procedure which is the pattern of our own court routine. Here William Shakespeare visited to study not only judges, law, and lawyers, but all the human sensibilities, for it is in the law courts, more than in any other place, that the heart is revealed in its dramatic intensities and flinty cruelties as well as in all its manifold tendernesses.

The judicial seat of the British Empire has now passed from Westminster Hall to the Law Courts Building, also known as the Royal Courts of Justice, located on the Strand. In the Central Hall, some 238 feet long, 38 feet wide, and 80 feet high, one senses an ecclesiastical atmosphere, engendered undoubtedly by the lofty ceiling and the stained-glass windows. As I slowly moved through the throngs of barristers, solicitors, litigants, and witnesses entering and leaving the various courtrooms which open up into the cathedral-like vestibule, I suddenly confronted a colossal marble figure before which I stopped in hypnotic gaze. Here was the friend of my law-school days, my tutor for the bar examinations—William Blackstone! —the most formidable figure in every English and American law student's life. Although, like all other lawyers, I had studied Blackstone for years, because his *Commentaries* are the lawyer's bible (in a secular sense), I had never known what he looked like. Now I saw him three-dimensionally—a giant, a Hercules. In breathless enchantment I touched the stone hem of his Common Pleas robe. Blackstone!

Holding my breath, I stepped into one of the courtrooms. What I saw delayed a resumption of normal breathing still further. Never did I see so bright an array of juridical habiliments as those which graced the figure of the judge on the high bench. He wore a crimson robe with a black sash, and a wide blue bandoleer across his chest. His sleeves were of a mystic gray, and a white wig topped it all. The lawyers (called barristers) wore black robes and white wigs which were even more fetching than the one which surmounted the judge's head. Although the judicial wig was made of straight hair with no hanging braid, the lawyers' wigs were curly and sprouted two pert pigtails.

What impressed me even more than the colorful raiment and head-gear was the charming language which fell from the lips of all the legal gentry. It did not seem possible that these persons always spoke in so sweetly modulated a voice, so soft a cadence, and so musical and dulcet a key. One could easily believe that this was speech especially adopted for the occasion, just as the wigs and robes formed part of the costumery of a play.

The physical layout of a British court better responds to the speaking and listening requirements of a trial than that of American courtrooms. The judge occupies an elevated bench, as do the American judges; but, quite different from our setting, the rest of the British courtroom rises architecturally with the judge. The jury box, made up of double- or triple-decked tiers, also climbs, with the top tier attaining the level of the judge's perch. Solicitors and lay clients sit on the front bench in the well of the court. Leading counsel—i.e., Queen's Counsel —sit on the bench immediately behind. On the next higher bench, at the bar, but not inside it, sit junior counsel. The audience looks on from a lofty gallery.

The Central Criminal Court Building in Old Bailey, famous in legal chronicles and in Dickensian novels, occupies the site of the Old Bailey Court and the Newgate Prison. The symbol of Justice rising above this building departs from the traditional figures to which our eyes have been accustomed. Here Justice has not changed her sex and she still grasps in one hand a tilted pair of scales, but in the other she brandishes an admonishing sword. However—most startling innovation of all—her eyes are wide open! Yes, let the eyes of Justice be unbandaged. If Justice had not operated blindfoldedly in the early English courts, history would not have to recount shamefully the inhuman tortures inflicted in the name of the law prior to the eighteenth century; it would not stand condemned for the casual manner in which the law exacted death against the miserable wretch who stole a sheep, forged a signature, or lifted a farthing from the pockets of a fellow visitor at a county fair. In those dim-sighted days, some two hundred offenses were punishable by hanging.

It was on this site, then known as the Press Yard of Newgate Prison, that prisoners who refused to plead were crushed to death under heavy weights. If the accused admitted the charge against him, he forfeited his life, and his property was lost to the Crown; if he pleaded not guilty, his conviction was a certainty anyway and his property still reverted to the King. But if he remained mute, he could not be tried and his property thus could not be confiscated. Thus, as the pyramiding rusty plates ground his body into the dust, he comforted his last agonizing moments with the reflection that the government which was stealing away his last breath could not rob his loved ones of the roof, bed, and handful of shillings he left them.

The defendant's dock in an English criminal courtroom is an extraordinary piece of property. Built like a miniature wooden arena surmounted by an iron fence, it is planted in the very center of the room and is as large as a prize-fight ring. A policeman sits by the defendant. If the accused is a woman, a policewoman keeps her

company. If the defendants are both male and female, then policemen and policewomen join the population of this unhappy community.
The witness stand, which, with its projecting canopy, looks something
like a pulpit, is actually a stand, because the witness is not allowed
to sit down as he testifies.

But perhaps what strikes the American visitor with more impact
than anything else is the absolute quiet which prevails in an English
courtroom. There is no buzzing or whispering among the spectators,
a fault not uncommon in American courtrooms. The high sheriff sym-
bolizes order. And to preserve the pattern of contrast with the American
notion of things, the English sheriff appears in a dress wholly different
from what we usually associate with a sheriff. He wears velvet
breeches, silk stockings, slippers with silver buckles, a ruffled shirt,
and an open-front embroidered waistcoat. But I had no reason to
assume he lacked bouncing potentialities, considering the manner in
which he kept looking at me as I moved from seat to seat around the
courtroom, making notes of all that was filling my awe-inspired eyes
and ears.

As I entrancedly studied the costumery and architecture of the
English courtroom and continued to drink in the excellent diction fit
for a high-class theatrical performance, I could not help but feel that
I was looking upon a superbly acted play rather than a solemn trial
which was striving for the ascertainment of truth and the application
of the principles of justice.

And yet, stripping away the outer formalities, the colorful robes
and wigs, I perceived a facile similarity between English and American
trial procedure. If I could have accommodated myself to the theatrical
trappings of the barristers I would have liked to step down into the
colorful amphitheater to plead in earnest voice the cause of one of
the embattled litigants. The fire of the advocate burned in my veins.

Chapter XIV

BED AND BREAKFAST

A YEAR had passed since a ship had sailed from New York Harbor carrying a youthful passenger who, sick at heart and a little confused, hoped to find among the ancient ruins of the Old World the balm of Gilead for hurts and bruises received in the New World. His wounds now healed, the voyager yearned for home like a runaway boy who (contrary to his expectations) finds that his absence has not been mourned.

Although the S.S. *Leviathan* on which I was scheduled to leave was not due to sail from Southampton until seven o'clock on a Tuesday evening, I came dashing across the pier at seven o'clock that morning. The ship's officer at the gangplank held up his hand. "Just a moment. You've made a mistake. The ship sails at seven this evening."

I replied: "I made no mistake. I want to go aboard now."

He elucidated further: "You would find it very dull aboard, sir. The salons are closed, the musicians have not arrived, the shuffleboard courts are not ready——"

I broke in: "But are they serving meals?"

"Oh yes, you can have your meals."

"That's all I want to know." And I scurried up the gangplank faster than a war refugee. When I had arrived in London a week before, I had only enough money to pay for lodging. Fortunately, in many hostelries in London breakfast is included in the price of lodging, and the combination is known as "bed and breakfast." Thus, each morning before setting off for the courts I filled up on the traditional British breakfast of bacon, eggs, muffins, jams, toast, and coffee, which constituted my fare for the day. But no matter how much youth consumes for breakfast he wants lunch and dinner as well. So on the morning of the sailing I felt within me the ravenous cumulative appetite of seven unappeased lunches and dinners.

In all the history of good eating, not even King Henry VIII feasted more felicitously than I did during that five-day journey between Southampton and New York. At seven-thirty each morning fruit juice and black coffee appeared like magic in my stateroom. At eight-thirty, in the ship's dining room, I attacked a matinal repast of cereal, eggs, bacon, potatoes, and hot cakes. At noontime the table glowed, smiled, and chuckled with soup, steak, vegetables, salad, dessert, and coffee. At four o'clock tea, little sandwiches and cakes refreshed the oceanic afternoon, and at seven each evening a royal banquet unfolded in the large dining hall where one's eyes dilated as his belt yielded to appetizers, smoked oysters, celery, soup, roast fowl, vegetables, salad, nuts, fruit, pie, ice cream, and demitasse. At 10 P.M.—I skipped the chafing-dish supper available to those trenchermen who had capacity for it.

The voyage added nine pounds to my sparse frame. From the day I had left New York I had been living, not exactly on Oliver Twist rations, but far from what a healthy young man of twenty-six liked to have. My employment on the Continent hardly ever provided compensation commensurate with the human interest it afforded. There was the time that the *centesimi* and the half-lira coins in my pocket produced only enough of a jingle to call to my pantry box a large bag of black olives and two loaves of bread. With these provisions I held the fort for four days until a check arrived from the Florentine publisher. I have not been able to look at a black olive since. Not long ago I related this four-day olive story to a lady, expecting that the termination of my narrative would draw from her an expression of amused sympathy over my melancholy siege. I was considerably astonished, however, when she remarked: "You certainly were lucky! I just adore black olives!"

The voyage was an Odyssey of enchantment. I ate and slept better than any of the monarchs and princes of old whose castles I had visited in Europe, and I was returning to the greatest land in the world—to embrace again my sweetheart. How could one be happier? Not the slightest doubt entered my mind that Miss Law awaited me eagerly and that we would celebrate a felicitous reconciliation.

Aboard the *Leviathan* I achieved a rather unique fame, in no way associated with the law. Before leaving Rome I had sent my trunk ahead with directions that it be placed aboard the ship at Cherbourg, the eastern terminus of her run. Boarding the vessel at Southampton, I was informed my trunk could not be found. On the possibility that it might have been delivered to the wrong cabin, the purser allowed me to inspect the ship from stem to stern and to visit any cabin to look for the missing luggage. In this search I came into contact with practically every passenger and member of the crew, and I soon became known as "the young man who lost his trunk." Then it developed that Nazimova, the celebrated stage and screen star, also making the passage, had similarly lost her trunk, so we became the team of "Nazimova and Musmanno, the two who lost their trunks!"

Happily I looked forward to the moment when the great tragedienne would locate her missing property or become convinced it had been irretrievably lost. Inevitably she would hurl herself into a dramatic outburst worthy of her superb histrionic talents. For the time I forgot all about my own straying baggage and hugged myself in anticipatory glee as I visualized the dramatic treat of the century when Nazimova should emote over her wandering hatbox and mysteriously vanished trunk. But a desolate disillusionment ensued. When her luggage showed up on the Hoboken pier she merely shrugged a casual hip and remarked: "Well, it's about time."

My own trunk still played hide-and-seek. However, two months later it unobtrusively arrived at my home. I learned subsequently that it had been placed on the wrong ship, followed Columbus' route to the West Indies, returned to Cherbourg, and finally limped into Stowe Township, worn and battered but with its cargo safe.

But a more resplendent title awaited me than the one which identified me, as the traveler without a trunk. Aside from the time which I spent in the various dining rooms, which I admit was not inconsiderable, I devoted all my waking hours to working on a series of articles entitled "A Philadelphia Lawyer in the European Courts" for possible publication in legal journals at home. To the other passengers I must have seemed the proverbial bookworm. I never carried less than a half dozen books under my arms; I was constantly dropping papers and pencils which, as I walked, I stooped to pick up, only to lose a book or a pen or two. My fingers revealed telltale inkstains, my wearing apparel was indifferent, my hair was combed by the winds. I participated in none of the deck social life and engaged in no general conversation. I was a recluse and continued to be known as "the young man who lost his trunk."

One day while slouched studiously in my steamer chair surrounded by numerous tomes and notebooks, I overheard two fellow voyagers animatedly discussing the athletic contest scheduled for the ship's passengers when we should arrive in mid-Atlantic. Each of the two men was choosing a team of ten persons, the resulting teams to compete against each other on an individual as well as collective basis. It seemed they had already collected eighteen contestants, and each leader needed one more to complete his squad of athletes. One of the captains said: "Why don't you take the young fellow who lost his trunk?" and he pointed a casual finger in my direction. I did not lift my head but tensed a curious and windward ear. The other captain said: "What? Him? He wouldn't know a shuffleboard from a hundred-yard dash. All he knows is books, books, books."

The first captain rejoined: "Well, we've searched the ship over and he and that fellow from Cincinnati are the only ones left who could possibly qualify on weight. Suppose you take the 'trunk man' and I'll take the guy from Cincinnati."

"Oh no, you don't," the second captain flung back almost indignantly. "That's not fair. The Cincinnati fellow at least occasionally takes a hike around the deck. I'll tell you what we'll do. We'll toss a coin, and the man who wins takes Cincinnati, the one who loses takes the 'trunk guy'; that is, if we can get him away from his traveling library."

Thus was I shanghaied into the oceanic olympiad that memorable summer of 1925. The competitive sports included running, jumping, wrestling, swimming, and shuffleboard, which I had never played before. In view of the conversation I had overheard, I determined that I would show the team captains how wrong they were on the subject of my athletic capacity. I hurled myself into the games with the vigor and resolution of one fighting for his very life. Our team won the most collective points, and to the sheer amazement of everybody (but especially to myself) I won the first prize for the largest collection of individual points. That evening, however, I could not move a limb, and dinner was served to me in my cabin. Nor did any power of locomotion return to me the following day. Confined to my berth as I was, every muscle in my body protested and lamented, as must have protested and lamented the muscles of that turtle which beat the rabbit. On the eve of our arrival in New York, prizes were awarded at the final and farewell dinner. Several members of my team practically carried me hammock-fashion to the banquet hall, and there I was decorated with a medal which proclaimed me "The Mid-Atlantic Athletic Champion."

I highly treasure that disk of bronze which today has its place among its more austere brothers awarded during the war. The latter ones may have been gained at more risk of life and limb, but certainly not with any more win-or-die effort.

Ever since that wondrous voyage I have cherished a deep affection for the *Leviathan*. Prior to World War I, when she was the Hamburg-American liner *Vaterland*, she plied between French and English ports and New York, the largest passenger ship afloat. In 1914, at the outbreak of war, she was interned and then, in 1917, when the United States entered the conflict, she was taken as enemy property, converted into a troop-carrying vessel, and during the next two years ferried 240,000 troops across the Atlantic. Following World War I she was sold to the United States Lines and returned to the trans-Atlantic passenger service, and while in that service I became probably her happiest passenger.

Good old United States Ship *Leviathan*. When at last she became too old for active service and lay rusting at her pier in Hoboken, I never failed to visit her when I chanced to be in New York. In the end she was sold to a commercial firm in China, to haul sand, gravel, and scrap iron. I read this account in the newspapers, and as I did so I visualized with a melancholy heart that magnificent mistress of the yeasty deep now degraded to the menial tasks of a harbor scow. As I thought of her departing forever from the frothy American lanes over which she had long been queen, a knot formed in my throat and, taking out the medal I had won on her gleaming decks, a tear obscured but did not completely hide the fact that once, in my book-inundated life, I was the "Mid-Atlantic Athletic Champion."

Chapter XV

HOME!

I<small>T WAS</small> early evening and I rejoiced in a rocking chair on the porch of home, sweet home, a rambling frame cream-colored house trimmed in brown, the porch lazily nestling under the branches of a spreading mulberry tree which offered hospitable shade to those who stopped to say hello to the voyager anchored at last. It had been a gala homecoming. My brother Sam met me at the Hoboken pier, my brother Pasquale got on the train at Harrisburg, and the rest of the family—some twenty-five in number, including nephews, nieces, and in-laws—gathered me into their collective arms at the railroad station. "You look wonderful!" "You look good!" they all chorused as I kissed and embraced them one by one, my tears of joy playing havoc with the make-up of the younger girls. The fatted calf had been killed, there were speeches, toasts, and singing at the dinner table, and they all wanted to hear me talk Italian, which they half expected would have a Cockney accent.

And now I rested on the porch, the oscillations of the chair stirring vibrations in the floor of memory as my eyes lingered on the road which had borne the imprint of my bare toes as a child and whose dust today had been gaily churned by the returning feet of the wandering son. Beyond the road a quiet meadow rolled for a half mile to the Pittsburgh and Lake Erie Railroad tracks over which moved long lines of freight cars laden with products of mill, mine, factory, and farm. Next to the tracks glistened the wide silvery ribbon of the Ohio, stirred into foamy lace by frothy paddle wheels of steamboats pushing coal barges. The curtains of night were slowly moving into place as the river craft glided over the pavement of water now shining darkly in the gloaming.

Riding the northern embankment of the Ohio, some two miles away, the Pennsylvania Railroad tracks gleamed under the head lamps of whistling locomotives drawing endless lengths of cars carrying passengers and merchandise to and from the Gateway to the Middle West.

Pittsburgh! Coal mines, steel mills, railroads. To the east the skies flamed in the glare of open-hearth furnaces. Above the Monongahela, which flowed into the Ohio five miles away, the horizon resembled a gargantuan lemon with streaks of green and ocher as the flames from blast furnaces melted iron ores into liquid white metal.

Pittsburgh! The Workshop of the World. The center of a great territory comprising the teeming Ohio River Valley, the abundant Monongahela River Valley, the productive Turtle Creek Valley, rolling hills, extended plateaus, all dotted with hundreds of small towns still unfolding and expanding. Here lived the working people with their large families, people who toiled to build their homes, to send their children to school to enjoy the hope and promise of the beautiful American way of life.

At the confluence of the Monongahela and the Allegheny rivers which form the Ohio, there was erected in 1754 the log-and-mud redoubt known as Fort Duquesne over which the British and French clashed bitterly, but which finally, under Colonel Forbes, aided by George Washington, fell to the English and was renamed Fort Pitt in honor of the great English statesman, William Pitt. Hence Pittsburgh.

On the land formerly occupied by that little fort now rose skyscrapers, hotels, theaters, department stores, banks, all clustered within the fabulous "Golden Triangle." Pittsburgh was still growing and developing. Economically, industrially, commercially, politically, it was still youthful. It had the healthful dissatisfaction of growing pains. A vast fruitful region, agricultural and industrial, surrounded it. I felt that here was the place for the young lawyer. Moreover, I would be happier in western Pennsylvania, of whose soil I was indigenous, though as an adult I knew it scarcely at all. In Philadelphia I had been lonely. Here companionship would not be lacking.

Although I lacked capital with which to open a law office of my own, I was satisfied I would have no difficulty in finding a spot in an established law office. But I was destined for a disconcerting surprise. As had been true in Philadelphia, the large firms were apparently closed corporations on the subject of young lawyers. Hat in hand, I approached them all, but no matter how attractively I displayed my wares—tutelage under the famous John R. K. Scott and Enrico Ferri, graduation from several universities, and considerable trial experience—no one wanted to try a sample. Each morning I boarded a streetcar and jolted over five miles of rough track to the

Golden Triangle, only to be jolted successively by well-fed and well-dressed lawyers who informed me, one after the other, that they were not interested. What was I to do now? Although Mr. Scott had offered to take me back, I had irrevocably resolved to remain in Pittsburgh.

Then came what seemed a rift in the clouds. An important firm of corporation lawyers, whose offices I had already visited, asked me to prepare a brief in a very complicated tax case. In this way, the head of the firm said, they could test and evaluate my professional ability. For two indefatigable weeks I toiled at the task.

I made up my mind to dazzle that firm with the thoroughness of my research. I explored every textbook, treatise, and digest on the subject in dispute. I scoured through hundreds of decisions. I sweated and groaned over that brief; I wrote and rewrote it. It was a tedious job since the question involved was bare of the leavening of human interest, but I performed what I considered to be an excellent piece of work. Proudly I bore the finished product to the corporation lawyers. As I entered their luxurious, thickly carpeted offices I felt confident that soon I would be occupying one of the fine rooms into which I shot yearning glances.

I handed the sixty-five-page brief to the leading lawyer of the firm. While I did not expect him to slap me admiringly on the back, I was quite unprepared to see him take the sheaf of papers without comment and flip over the first page with an almost disparaging gesture. The second and third pages he turned with an even more deprecatory movement. In a few minutes he completed his perfunctory and apparently derogatory study and said: "This isn't exactly what we wanted, but we will hold this brief and then let you know."

With each belittling turn of the pages I shrank smaller and smaller in my own estimation. By the time he reached the end of my offering I was reduced to dwarfish proportions. I squeaked an apology and left. I was never called back to the office.

Several years later while looking over a shelf of printed briefs in the Allegheny County Law Library, I stumbled quite by chance on a legal argument which seemed quite familiar. It was the brief which had cost me a fortnight of intense labor and had earned me a heartache in payment. The lawyers had incorporated my argument bodily into their paper book which was presented to the Supreme Court. I then examined the Supreme Court reports and found that the position I had advanced and argued was sustained by that tribunal. They had won their case on my brief!

Six weeks had now fallen into the dustbin of time since I had disembarked from the *Leviathan* with the self-assurance that my sweetheart would join me in ecstatic reunion, if not at the pier, certainly in Pittsburgh. But in all this time she had not shown the slightest sign of forgiving me for deserting her in the City of Brotherly Love.

I began to think dark and brooding thoughts. What if she refused to allow me to make amends? Since I could not get into somebody else's office and I could not afford one of my own in Pittsburgh, how was I to acquire a practice? In Philadelphia a clientele awaited me the first day I entered Mr. Scott's office. If I had attempted to practice law in Philadelphia alone, I might have died of starvation. What assurance did I have that this might not happen in Pittsburgh? Although this was my home town, I had left it in my middle teens, so that I was completely unknown outside my immediate neighborhood in little Stowe Township with its less than ten thousand inhabitants, which, anyhow, already had two long-established lawyers. To return to Philadelphia was out of the question. I would never subject myself to the humiliation I felt I would have to undergo in picking up the thread which I had severed so decisively and so ingloriously.

While I did not have to fear any physical deprivation—living with my family, a bed, food, heat, and every necessity would always be provided—still, it has wisely been said that "man does not live by bread alone, even pre-sliced bread." Momentarily I would allow myself the comforting thought that as one swallow does not make a summer, neither does six weeks of frustration make a perennial winter of discontent.

But how was the winter to end? Suppose the uncanny good luck of the brown-suit era were to work in reverse? Therein lies the danger of believing that one's fate can be guided by a rabbit's foot or a cow's horn. Once the law of physics, chemistry, and mathematical cause and effect can be tampered with by the wearing of certain haberdashery, what assurance can there be that those who are opposed to us may not use the same forces of black magic against us?

One night I went to bed as disheartened as a galley slave. Over and over I berated myself for having allowed the brown suit to enter into my deliberations in Philadelphia: certainly I must have won my first case and many of the subsequent forty-one on the merit of the cause I represented and not because of the tint of the trousers I wore. But was this the end now? My career had begun so pyrotechnically in Philadelphia. It had gone up like a skyrocket, but was it now falling like a dead stick to the ground? Falling, falling, falling?

The mental image of that descent was frightening. I felt like hiding my head under the blankets as I was wont to do in boyhood, in this very bed, when inexplicable nocturnal noises used to create a terror which could not be combated. But while the picture of the plunging skyrocket was horrifying, it still held me in a grim and painful fascination. Almost sadistically I kept repeating, like the replaying of a motion picture, the vertiginous drop of the stick, which was I. It was torturing, but it was like the torture of a lovesick boy who cuts his finger to excite the sympathy of an indifferent sweetheart. Perhaps I felt that in the infinite spaces of the night the stars were witnessing that nose dive and shedding star dust of tears for the young man whose career had begun spectacularly but was now burned out—at twenty-seven.

I knew I was working myself into an odious state of self-pity, but I knew of no way to shut out the harrowing thoughts which had seized my consciousness and tied it to a stake of futility. Through the open windows I could hear the still, mysterious voices of a night in the country. The lament of the crickets, the doleful croak of frogs in a distant swamp, the dismal bark of a dog still farther away. And on the late-summer zephyrs which shook the curtains as they entered, there were borne the melancholy fragrances of flowers, grass, leaves, and weeds that would soon feel a decline under autumn's frosts and then finally death before winter's blasts.

Again I could see the dead stick falling. Then—crack! It finally struck the ground. I heard it splintering and breaking into pieces from the impact of its momentum against the earth. I waited for the echoes to die away, but they continued. Crack, crack, crack. Then followed a loud, resounding bang. I sat bolt upright, my heart in my mouth. Another bang shook me further. I leaped out of bed.

It was someone violently knocking at the door.

On unsteady legs I got to the window and made out the bulk of a man pounding at the entrance to the kitchen. "What do you want?" I called out. He ignored me and continued to hammer.

I lifted my voice: "Hello, there! What's the trouble?"

He kept on belaboring the door. I got into my trousers, raced down the stairs, and flung open the door. As soon as I did this, the unknown visitor seized me and flung me to the ground. Dazed, I scrambled back to my feet just as he charged head-on. I stepped back and swung in the dark. Although I thought my wrist had broken under the impact of my fist against his forehead, his violence did not abate. He threw an arm around my neck and began a vise-like pressure. By this time I had got over the shock of surprise and prepared myself for a strategic counterattack. Allowing him to believe that his choking process had succeeded, I went limp and sagged to my knees. As he relinquished his tight hold, I slipped away from his grasp and attempted a half-nelson grip. I accompanied this with speedy footwork, and as I applied force against the back of his head I simultaneously threw my right foot under his knee, tripped him, and brought him crashing to the ground with his head striking the concrete sidewalk beneath. I now succeeded in getting my fingers around his throat and asked: "What is it you want, my good man?"

In the meantime, however, I had been rending the skies with cries for help. My father, aroused by the commotion, came running down the stairs and, arriving on the scene, tumultously entered into action. Before I could tell him that I had the situation under control he leaped at me and got his strong fingers around my throat. He had assumed, in the dark back yard, lighted only by a vagrant ray of moonlight falling through the branches of our peach trees, that I was the combatant underneath. He had no idea what a wrestler and pugilist his lawyer-son could be in an emergency. My poor throat, which by this time had been entertaining various steely clutches, could not force a word of alarm to my lips. My head swam; I lost control of the invader on the pavement and he slid out from under me, stood up, and now seized my father about the neck. I can imagine my father's surprise when he found, as he thought, his own son choking him! As soon as I could form some words I stammered: "Papa, you were choking the wrong fellow. I was the one on top!"

In one grunt he expressed surprise and admiration that I had worsted my antagonist in the first round and also his regret that he had mistaken his boy's identity in the darkness. But there was no time for congratulations or sentimental observations. The assailant was choking my father. Once more I brought my half nelson into play. Around the attacker's neck went my arm, and under his knee my foot. He quickly released his hold on Dad and toppled to the earth. He now whipped a knife from his pocket and slashed out with the opened blade, cutting my father's hand and grazing his ear.

I seized his arm before he could strike again, and we closed in on him. And now, without saying a word, but with perfect unanimity of thought, my father and I carried him kicking to the rain barrel in a corner of the yard and thrust him in headfirst. He yelled and spluttered, and as he submerged I could hear the air bubbles forming and breaking. I said: "That's enough," and we pulled him out.

But we were premature. No sooner had he drippingly emerged

than he returned to the attack, but, now in unison, Dad and I overpowered him and started him for the barrel again. At this moment my stepbrother Dick arrived and we hurried him off for a policeman, who soon arrived and took the prowler into custody.

What has all this to do with the story of the young lawyer? After the police had jailed Fred Presser (that turned out to be his name) and he was charged with felonious assault and battery or attempt to kill, his wife came to ask me to defend him! She explained her husband had been drunk at the time of the nocturnal visit and did not know what he was doing. She added they had five small children and that if he went to prison they would be without support.

I made some inquiries and learned that Presser indeed was a heavy drinker—that is, a periodical drinker, one who could abstain for six months and then absorb whiskey until his brains floated in alcohol. While intoxicated he was capable of uninhibited violence, of which he certainly gave evidence the night he favored us with a call.

Released on bail, he came to our home to express his abject apologies. I asked my brothers and sisters if I should represent him. Sam said: "It would be too bad to turn down your first client." I offered to be his counsel on condition that I should not accept any fee. Sam remarked he couldn't see any profit in being a lawyer if I wasn't going to charge for my services. But I pointed out that since I was one of the victims of the assailant I could not be the assailant's lawyer! However, I promised to appear in court to urge leniency for him in view of his otherwise good record. At my urgent pleading the judge paroled Presser on condition that he totally abstain from intoxicating liquor, failing which he would be committed to the Allegheny County Workhouse for one year. Fred Presser became a sober man from that day.

Chapter XVI

COAL AND IRON POLICE

IT WAS inevitable that Presser should feel grateful. Thus when his neighbor needed legal advice on a property settlement he sent him to me. Later, when his cousin was arrested for simple assault and battery, he called to ask if I would defend him at the hearing before the justice of the peace. I replied that from that very moment his cousin was being defended.

The hearing took place in Snowden Township in the coal fields of Allegheny County, and I cleared my client easily. Apparently I did this job in a satisfactory, workmanlike manner because immediately after the hearing a coal miner in the audience approached me and asked me to defend his daughter, who had been arrested by Coal and Iron Police.

The Coal and Iron Police were private employees, paid and controlled by coal and steel companies but commissioned by the State of Pennsylvania. They constituted a hybrid in government because while enjoying the immunity of state officers they were not held to the governmental responsibility of state officers. Many of them were recruited from among thugs, gunmen, ex-convicts, and characters of the shadiest reputation, since their principal function was to terrorize the industrial and mining communities in which they operated —on the assumption that terror cowed the workers and thus made them more amenable to corporate control. Their concept of entertainment was to jump their horses over children playing in the street, shoot at dogs, and molest miners' wives and daughters. Assault and battery, mayhem, arson, and even murder were not beyond them. From a social-economic point of view, Pennsylvania at this time was at its lowest ebb under an industrial-political-dominated government which permitted this prostitution of the police powers of the state without shock or shame.

I shall not here relate the ignoble history of the Coal and Iron

Police of Pennsylvania. I wrote a book which portrayed the iniquities of that organization—a book which became the basis for the motion picture *Black Fury,* produced by Warner Brothers and starring Paul Muni. Later I led in the state legislature the fight which eventually eliminated this indefensible police system. But this all occurred years later.* My client in the present case was Miss Marian Ludlow, daughter of Johnson Ludlow, president of the United Mine Workers local in the Imperial area. She had been arrested by Coal and Iron Policeman Randall Thompeson when, in resisting his attempts at flirtation, she called him a "conceited prig" in the presence of many miners, who jeered him. He charged her with disorderly conduct, threw her into a cell in the Coal and Iron Police barracks, and held her there several hours until her father could obtain bail.

The coal company was becoming increasingly disturbed over the independent spirit manifested by miners in the Imperial district, and it was apparent that company officials were determined to use the arrest of Miss Ludlow, with her certain conviction and punishment, as a means of intimidating her father and his co-miners, who were "getting out of hand." It was an easy matter for the company to take the case before a justice of the peace known to be friendly to its interests. During this era certain industries in Pennsylvania, by liberal subsidies to the dominant political party, could name not only justices of the peace but legislators, mayors, and even governors and judges.

Over three hundred coal miners crowded into Justice of the Peace Rogam's office, which had once been a saloon, to observe and comment on developments. There was little conflict in the testimony as Miss Ludlow admitted she had spoken the words attributed to her by Thompeson. I contended that no words of themselves could constitute disorderly conduct unless they provoked disorder—and there had been no disorder except what Thompeson had himself created.

After the various witnesses had told their story, I stood up and addressed the justice of the peace with as much deference as I would have employed in presenting a case to the Supreme Court: "May it please Your Honor," and I bowed respectfully, "the defendant stands charged with disorderly conduct, and while this offense may seem trivial to some people, we know that every infraction of law and order is a serious matter. Particularly is it serious where the majesty of the law itself is involved; that is to say, where the alleged injured party happens to be none other than a police officer.

* See Chapters XXXVII and XXXVIII.

"The prosecuting witness in this case, Randall Thompeson, wears a uniform, and I have great respect for the uniform. The policeman's uniform is a symbol of security, it is a badge of protection, it is a token of honor, peace, and dignity. The American citizen, as he passes a policeman's uniform on his way home at night, is reassured that his home, which is his castle, will be inviolate and safe from attack and harm. In the blue of a policeman's uniform I see the color of loyalty, in the brass buttons I see intrepidity, in his trim fighting helmet I see courage in the face of every danger."

By this time Thompeson's chest had expanded until the buttons of his jacket were straining at their threads. He had expected to be ridiculed, roasted, and broiled by the seemingly aggressive young attorney for the defendant. Instead, defense counsel had become philosophical and even complimentary. This was indeed a surprise, a pleasant surprise.

The faces of the assembled coal miners, however, began to cloud and mantle with astonishment and rising indignation. They could not believe what their ears were telling them—that a lawyer representing the daughter of a coal miner should be praising Coal and Iron policemen, who symbolized to them the ultimate in Cossack brutality. I could see that a wave of resentment was forming and rolling toward the beach of audibility. I hoped to stop it in time. "And so," I said to the justice of the peace, pitching my voice so as to hold the ire of the miners suspended until I could fire the broadside I had been leading up to, "and so, I respect and admire the policeman's uniform; that is, when *it is occupied by someone who does honor to it.* A uniform can mean all the things I ascribe to it only when it covers a man. You cannot drape a uniform around a horse and say that that makes the horse a policeman. You cannot wrap it around a skunk and say that that will make the skunk a policeman. A skunk will smell through the drapings of a dozen uniforms. You cannot put a uniform on a criminal and expect that the uniform will make the criminal a respecting and respected upholder of the law. Thompeson, standing here, is a *disgrace to his uniform!* He sullies, dishonors, debases, and corrupts—he stains it with his criminality!"

The ex-saloon shook as if it had been hit by an exploding bomb. The miners shouted, applauded, laughed, and stamped their feet in thunderous glee. The justice of the peace, startled, rapped for order. Thompeson, his face livid with anger, leaped toward me with clenched fists. The coal company's attorney seized him. "Don't be a fool! Leave this to me. This is a legal proceeding."

"Squire!" the coal company's attorney sang out indignantly. "I must strenuously object to the language employed by Attorney Musmanno. He may not, because he is a lawyer, slander my client. By what right does he refer to my client as a criminal?"

"Because he is," I replied.

"What proof do you have?"

"Here is the proof." I plunged into my brief case and extracted certified copies of court records showing that Thompeson had twice been convicted of aggravated assault and battery. I handed them to my opponent, who glanced at them, gulped in embarrassment, and handed them back. He dropped his current objection and took up another one:

"But why did you call him a skunk?"

"Do you want to defend him on that ground?"

"Well—ah, er——" He appeared at a loss for words, fearing, I suppose, that I could produce some document which would prove that Thompeson was a full-fledged, full-pedigreed *Mephitis mephitis*.

"I did not say your client was a skunk," I continued, "but I would be pleased to have you tell me what he is after you read the details of what he has done. You will find that he spurred his horse into a crowd of women and children, inflicting injury on many. I would like to have you inform me what part of the animal kingdom would take him, if you learned that he struck a woman with a babe in her arms. I infer from your protest that he does not belong to the skunk family. I do not think he does so either. The skunk has *some* pride. . . ."

The former tavern again rocked with cheers and laughter as the miners back-slapped each other in joyous vindication. This is the type of castigation they had been waiting for, and it was particularly sweet to them because a man of the law was administering it.

Justice of the Peace Rogam decided against my client, as I had anticipated, but we appealed to the Allegheny County courts, where we obtained an easy reversal. This case carried my name into many of the mining communities in Allegheny County, and the miners' generous regard for me augmented with the years until at the Coal Miners' Convention of District No. 5, in November 1935, which embraced not only Allegheny County but parts of the adjoining counties as well, I was voted "The Coal Miner's Champion."

The Ludlow case led to other squire cases, which I always tried with earnestness and vigor, regardless of the supposed lightness of the offense or smallness of the amount involved. Many lawyers, and especially the younger ones, look upon the courts of the minor judiciary as unworthy of their best efforts, but here they err. An attorney, if not his client, is always on trial. As soon as he opens his mouth to speak, someone stands by to pass judgment on his ability. People often gather in offices of justices of the peace just to hear the attorneys argue. As the hearings invariably took place in the evening, they afforded to the workingman, in the days before television and all-blanketing radio, opportunities for an exciting show—free of charge. And then, aside from what his performance at the squire's hearing may mean to the lawyer himself, the client is entitled to the very best his lawyer can present—in any tribunal.

One evening I was arguing a case in Neville Township (an island in the Ohio River close to Stowe Township) before a justice of the peace who apparently prided himself on having read widely in the law. In addition to the usual dusty volumes of *Pennsylvania Assembly Pamphlet Laws* found in most squires' and aldermen's offices, he ostentatiously displayed several shelves of *Corpus Juris, Lawyers' Reports Annotated*, and a philosophical book or two on the development of the law through the centuries. In my remarks I praised the "learned justice of the peace who bases his decisions on the bedrock principles of justice gleaned from the books of the masters," and emphasized: "I must say that I am gratified indeed to find here a judge who gives no snap judgment, who renders no unconsidered decision, but who, with a scholar's thirst, drinks deep of the wisdom in these lawbooks which adorn his excellent chambers."

My opponent, following in my eulogizing footsteps, also threw in many flattering remarks about the literary taste of this member of the minor judiciary. When we had both finished, the justice of the peace remarked: "I agree with what you both say about books. They help me a great deal in settling—not deciding—cases." He then pulled down from the shelves one of the large tomes and exposed, standing behind it, a bottle of whiskey, which, considering its polished exterior, gave evidence of more loving attention than the books had ever received. He uncorked the bottle and with ceremony poured from it into glasses for both the litigants and the attorneys. And as the glasses clinked he said with an air of final authority: "And now over this cup of cheer I expect all of you to get together and settle this here case. People is made to get together and not to fall apart in foolish legal squabblings." We settled the case.

One evening while arguing a case before another justice of the peace I pounded at his bench with such force that the windows in his office rattled. A real estate man who happened to be there, shook my hand at the end of the argument and said: "I don't know whether you are right or wrong in this case, but you certainly impressed me with the way you fought for your client. If I ever need anyone to fight for my legal rights I certainly want you to represent me." And then he asked a question which always embarrassed me; namely, "Where is your office?" I had to tell him that I had not yet achieved the distinction of a law office. Surprised, he quickly said: "Listen, you can use the lobby of my office, free of charge." And thus, Anthony J. Barone (may his tribe increase) became the first man in Pittsburgh to offer me professional hospitality.

Chapter XVII

THEY CAN'T PUT YOU IN JAIL
FOR THAT!

THE perfect lawyer is the one who has worked at every trade, studied every science, practiced at every profession, visited every clime, lived with every people, fought in war, labored for peace, gathered flowers on the rugged mountain slope, penned poems to the sky, and loved in the light of the lambent moon. Universality is his name. He knows nature like a mother, science like a father—and the pages of the human heart turn under his sensitive fingers like the leaves of a treasured tome.

The perfect lawyer, of course, has never arrived, but when he does it shall be mankind's duty to elevate him to the supreme justiceship of nations—to the end that war, intolerance, and injustice may disappear from the face of the earth.

Although perfection is denied us mortals, we can always seek wisdom in further education and experience. One summer, at the age of twenty, I obtained employment as a temporary policeman on Neville Island, some three or four miles from my home. I particularly enjoyed the job because it supplied me with valuable experience in the very field from which much of the lawyer's work is drawn.

My father, who had worked most of his life as a coal miner and railroad section hand, was made a policeman in Stowe Township during his latter years. He was now retired and he turned over his uniform to me to wear at my new job. I did not have it altered because I thought that its over-size added some necessary years to my slight frame and thus might make me seem more formidable in the eyes of all potential lawbreakers.

I also had other original ideas on how a man of the law can outwit the outlaw. The chief of police having assigned me to a night beat which cut through a dark and lonely wood, it occurred to me as I moved over the black road, lighted only by the beam of my flashlight, that a desperate character wanting to cripple the watchful law could do it very easily—he would not even have to show himself. Ambushed in the all-enveloping darkness, he could accomplish his objective simply by shooting at the light.

Thus I conceived the idea of tying my flashlight to the end of a long pole which I carried horizontally and at right angles to my body, so that the flashlight, though it still pointed forward and lit up the road ahead of me, was off to my side about ten feet. As a result of this device the malefactor who shot at the light would never pierce the oversized uniform which contained me because—I was not behind the light!

It was an excellent stratagem, but I overlooked telling the chief about it. One moonless and starless night while patrolling my beat in the woods, the light holding its own at the end of the stick away to my right, I saw the chief advancing. Inquiringly he called out: "Is that you, Musmanno?" Cheerfully I replied: "Yes, Chief," but my voice did not emerge from behind the light where he naturally thought I would be. It shot at him out of the gloom far from the source of the illumination.

He started in alarm, his face paling. Thinking to have some fun with him (youth will have its joke), I swung the light from my right to the left side, lifting it above my head in a wide arc. Since he thought I was holding the light in my hand, he visualized me being lifted bodily and swept through the air by some supernatural force. He took to his heels, shouting: "Spirits! Ghosts! Help!"

I laughed loud and long, but when I arrived at the police station I found that I had laughed too long and too soon. I was suspended for scaring the chief.

During the period of my policemanship I became acquainted with many policemen. My father, who was quite proud of me in his uniform, which I wore constantly (it exempted me from payment for carfare and movie tickets), took me around to meet some of his former fellow officers. One of the men with whom he had served was one Charles Carelli.

Seven years later, my father, in bringing me up to date on what had happened during my absence from Stowe Township, related how a son of his former police companion, Albert, seventeen years of age, had been sentenced to the electric chair. The boy had been tried and convicted of holding up a saloon and shooting the bartender. Two others, implicated in the same crime, had been tried separately and were convicted, respectively, of second-degree murder and voluntary manslaughter, although the evidence had been the same in all three trials.

My father thought there was some doubt as to the boy's guilt.

Although Mr. Carelli was unable to pay any fee for my services, already having impoverished himself in the costly legal battle which had gone against Albert, my father urged me in behalf of his former police companion to look into the case and render any aid still possible. The execution date was only several weeks away.

It was a fearful responsibility to undertake. The Supreme Court of Pennsylvania had already affirmed the conviction, and if I failed in my attempt to save the doomed lad, I might, in the public mind, be charged with the loss of the case. Still, when I studied the record of the trial and talked to some of the witnesses who had testified, chills raced up my spine. I became convinced that justice had miscarried and that an innocent person was being dragged to ignominious extinction by electricity.

Albert Carelli was not a paragon of virtue. He might even be called a "bad boy." He had kept late hours, had associated with evil companions, and had previously been involved in minor scrapes with the law—but he was not a murderer. No one had identified him as a murderer. A confession had been extracted from him by brutal third-degree methods.

Albert had testified at his trial that on the night of the holdup which resulted in the killing, of which he was accused and now convicted, he was attending a county fair in Burton, Ohio, 132 miles from Pittsburgh. By train and bus I traveled to Burton, a little town not far from Cleveland, and discovered incontrovertible proof that Albert was in fact there at the time he said he was. He had been employed in Cleveland, where he lived with an uncle, and on the night of the crime in Pittsburgh had attended a dance at the Burton County fair. I talked with four or five girls who danced with him at the very time that the bandits were committing the robbery and making their escape in Pittsburgh. These girls exhibited to me their dance programs which carried Albert's name as a dancing partner. On that same night a fire had broken out in Burton and Albert helped the volunteer fire department extinguish the blaze. I spoke to several firemen who remembered Albert assisting with the bucket brigade. The barber in the town told me he had cut Albert's hair just before he went to the dance.

With the help of the boy's father and a young man called Frank Farini, I obtained affidavits, statements, and documents which exposed the state's conviction as shamefully unworthy of a niche in the temples of justice. Fortunately in Pennsylvania we have a tribunal to which one may appeal in a criminal case even after the Supreme Court has rendered its decision; namely, the Board of Pardons. I submitted my proofs to the Board of Pardons and petitioned for an outright pardon for Carelli. It was granted.

One of the happiest moments of my young lawyer's career quickly followed, when with the rolled-up pardon under my arm I passed through the grim and dirty gray stone walls of the Western Penitentiary to announce to Albert Carelli that electric chairs and penitentiaries were only a nightmare of the past—he was now free, free as the open air.

But the walls of the legal Jericho had no sooner fallen than the district attorney flung himself into the breach to re-erect them. No public official (or private individual, for that matter) likes to admit that he has been proved wrong. From time to time some noble soul will declare he is happy for the opportunity to rectify an injustice, but the district attorney here, confronted with the impossibility of upsetting the decision of the Board of Pardons, sprang into action to fight the Carelli case on another front. At the time of Albert's original arrest he was accused, in addition to murder, of a number of unsolved robberies and thefts, but when he was convicted of murder, the other charges were filed away. The district attorney, angry and chagrined by the complete release of a person the machinery of his office had convicted of murder, set in motion that same machinery to have Albert sentenced on the filed-away charges.

The pardoned youth, on the recommendation of his parents, had returned to Cleveland and his former employment under a Philip Genzal. In a short time the hue and cry raised by the district attorney of Allegheny County died down, and it appeared that Albert's ordeal was now buried in the graveyard of the past, tended only by the memory of the person who had been the victim of the cruel misadventure. Several weeks later, however, the ground under my feet shook from a bombshell explosion in faraway Cleveland. Philip Genzal telegraphed me that the police were seeking Carelli to arrest him on a charge of robbery committed in that city. Genzal wanted to know if Carelli, to whom he had offered refuge in his home, should be turned over to the police.

Every lawyer, as he goes about the discharge of his professional duties, is bound from time to time to encounter an unexpected snarling circumstance in his path, but nothing can trip him and send his self-confidence flying more thoroughly than a report which challenges his reliance in the innocence of a client in whom he has reposed unlimited faith. Was Carelli a bandit after all? Did he really commit the murder of which he had been convicted and which conviction, considerably due to my efforts, had been overturned and obliterated? I caught the next train to Cleveland, located Albert, and turned him over to the police authorities. I then plunged into an investigation of the new crime in which he was allegedly involved.

It appeared that on the night of the Cleveland robbery Carelli was riding in a car with a Harry Gibson who at a certain point got out of the car, professedly to purchase a package of cigarettes. When Gibson delayed returning, Carelli (according to his story) entered the store himself and found his erstwhile companion with drawn revolver rifling the cash register while the customers with upraised hands stood terror-stricken against the wall. When the grocer made what seemed to Gibson an aggressive move, Gibson shot, the bullet grazing his arm. The robber then fled, but was quickly apprehended. Carelli also fled and got safely to Genzal's home to tell him breathlessly what had happened, insisting vehemently that he had no previous knowledge of Gibson's criminal intentions.

Innocent or guilty, the law had lowered its boom on Carelli. It was difficult to believe that he could not have known that Gibson was a robber. Only one little ray of light illumined the whole ominous scenario. All of the customers declared that when Carelli entered the store he apparently recoiled in genuine astonishment and offered no assistance whatsoever to Gibson.

Albert explained to me that he had met Gibson at the Y.M.C.A. and that this new-found friend had never revealed to him he had a criminal record and at the time was a parole violator of the laws of Illinois, where he had been convicted of robbery.

Was Carelli a criminal type? If he did in fact take a part in the Cleveland robbery, he should be isolated from society, for if he could stray from the narrow path which had skirted the very brink of electric destruction, it could not be long until he fell into the abyss itself. On the other hand, if his earnest protestations of innocence were grounded in truth, he had once more become the target on a firing range of reckless and unconscionable sharpshooters.

As I felt my way through this dark labyrinth of conflicting hypotheses, a light suddenly blazed before me. In talking to the policeman who had caught Gibson I asked why it was that Gibson had not escaped in his car. The officer replied that Gibson did not have the automobile key. Carelli had it at the time.

"Say that again!" I broke in excitedly.

"Gibson could not get away in the automobile because he did not have the key. The other guy, Carelli, had the key in his pocket. And I don't see what you're so excited about."

"Why, Officer, don't you see? If Carelli was an accomplice of Gibson's, he would have remained in the car, wouldn't he, to help in the getaway? At any rate, he would have kept the motor going, wouldn't he? The fact that he locked the ignition and put the key in his pocket shows conclusively he could not have been aware of Gibson's plans. Isn't that right, Officer?"

The bluecoat removed his cap and rubbed his corrugating forehead. "Say, are you a detective or a lawyer?"

"But am I not right?"

"There may be something to what you say, but if Carelli wasn't in the holdup, why did he go into the store at all?"

"Well, when Gibson did not return, Carelli got out to see what had happened."

"All right, if he was innocent, why did he run away?"

"Well, he realized that, with charges pending against him in Pittsburgh, an arrest in a situation like this, no matter how innocent he might be, would make him look guilty, especially in view of the fact he had just been released from the penitentiary. He became confused, frantic, and ran away, which would be a normal reaction, considering all the circumstances. After all, he is only a boy. Don't you agree with me?"

The officer paused for a moment and then meditatively remarked: "I think you have something there, Sherlock Holmes," and walked away. Whether he was in earnest or being ironic, I was not certain, but I knew my logic was unassailable.

The automobile key which Carelli had retained in his pocket was the key which would unlock the prison door and restore him to freedom. The forthcoming trial would disclose *all* the circumstances in the case, many of which, seen only in the light of half-truth, had at first seemed so damaging to the Pittsburgh boy. I asked the Cleveland district attorney how soon we could expect the trial, but when he replied he had no intention of trying Carelli my heart leaped joyously. "Do you mean you will release him?"

"Oh no!" he retorted without offering any further explanation.

"Well, you can't hold him indefinitely without trial," I said.

The prosecuting attorney walked away, leaving his enigmatic observation shrouded in the darkness of official secrecy.

In the meantime the district attorney of Allegheny County had initiated extradition proceedings against Carelli, which I resisted in the

Court of Common Pleas of Cuyahoga County. After a spirited hearing in which I charged the district attorney with political motivation in seeking the extradition, the Court sustained the extradition. I appealed to the Court of Appeals of Cuyahoga County, then to the Supreme Court of Ohio, and finally to the Supreme Court of the United States.

In all these proceedings the Ohio and Pennsylvania prosecuting authorities constantly referred to Carelli as a bandit. Yet no court or jury had ever convicted him of robbery. What was even more unjust, however, was the fact that while unequivocally assuming him to be an accomplice of Gibson's in the Cleveland robbery, they refused to give him the opportunity to prove, as we claimed, that the scaffolding upon which that assumption was built rested on a slippery foundation and that it would come tumbling down once it received the slightest blow of impartial inquiry before a jury.

Then another bombshell burst. Gibson publicly declared that he had deliberately framed Carelli. He said that the Cleveland detectives, learning he was a parole jumper, threatened to return him to the Illinois penitentiary unless he involved Carelli. It was suggested to him that all he had to do was to lead Carelli into a situation from which he could not extricate himself without the implication of guilt spontaneously arising from the surrounding circumstances. Gibson followed directions and spun a crafty web. For this spider's masterpiece the Cleveland detectives, according to Gibson, were to save him from a forcible return to Illinois. However, those who made the promise either failed him or lacked the power to stop the juggernaut of the law now bearing down on Gibson; and Gibson, resentful at this "double-crossing," told all.

Was it possible that anyone associated with the administration of justice could be so devoid of conscience as to pervert the very law he was sworn to serve? We find such betrayals in novels, motion pictures, radio, and television programs. Unfortunately they are to be found also in the chronicles of truth. Of course the police denied Gibson's story, but what clothed Gibson's assertions with the garment of credibility was the persistent refusal of the Ohio prosecuting authorities to try Carelli for the Cleveland robbery, although he was being held in jail for the supposed commission of that very offense. This, in spite of the provisions of the Constitution and the principles of elementary justice which guarantee to every accused a speedy trial.

The old joke of the young lawyer who said to his first client that they could not put him in jail for *that*, when in fact he was talking to him through the bars, has had its serious counterpart in penal history more times than the average person realizes. I clamored, I insisted on a constitutionally guaranteed trial, but Carelli continued to remain in jail without trial and without bail. Each week I made my motion: "If the Court please, in the case of the State versus Albert Carelli, I move for an immediate trial of the accused." And each week the Court replied: "Motion denied."

They can't put you in jail for that!

Traveling back and forth between Pittsburgh and Cleveland played havoc with my attempts to build up a law practice. Still retaining desk space in the outer lobby of Mr. Barone's real estate office, I had made no progress toward obtaining an office of my own. The heavy burden which I carried in this case, the odds I faced, the increasing nervous strain to which I was being subjected, and the difficulties which beset me on all sides because of lack of funds invited a withdrawal from the battle, but I could not think of abandoning my client, from whom, nor in whose behalf, had I received a penny's compensation.

The many legal ramifications of the case imposed endless paper work. Each move had to be supported with briefs, all of which I typed myself. It often happened in Cleveland, when money for hotel accommodations was unavailable, that I would sleep in the library of an attorney who allowed me to use his lawbooks.

And so the case dragged wearily and exhaustingly along when one day an unexpected grenade detonated. Returning to Pittsburgh from one of my weekly fruitless journeyings to Cleveland, I learned that Pittsburgh detectives had just boarded a train for Cleveland to seize Carelli. Since the Supreme Court of the United States had not yet rendered a decision on my appeal in the extradition proceedings, this action of the Pittsburgh detectives amounted to potential kidnaping. How could I thwart the threatened illegality? I had to get to Cleveland before the detectives' train arrived. There were no commercial airlines at that time, but I induced an amateur aviator to make the trip in his open-cockpit biplane. He supplied me with goggles, leather helmet, and jacket, and we took off in a violent sidewise ascent from the Bridgeville landing field on a wild and erratic flight. At moments we were jaggedly cutting through clouds and at other moments we were hedgehopping over country fences. Strapped in with belts and ropes, I was able, in spite of our soaring, zooming, and fluttering, to prepare a petition for writ of habeas corpus which I intended to present to the federal court in Cleveland to prevent the detectives from carrying out what seemed to me an illegal act.

While we were yet some thirty miles from our destination the pilot shouted to me above the noisy propeller of our single engine: "Do you know we've run out of gasoline?" I don't know whether he expected me to reply to the question or whether, merely by posing the situation, he expected I could help in some way. However, without waiting for an answer he pointed the nose of the plane at right angles to the ground, which came rushing up with much more of an eager welcome than I could ever have desired. We crash-landed in a farmer's back yard. After the bewildered tiller of the soil had recovered from the shock of seeing a shrieking crate fall out of the sky into his vegetable garden and I acquainted him with the necessity of getting to Cleveland at once, he invited me into a Model-T Ford disconsolately parked in front of his house, and in it we finally got to the city. Still in my goggles, leather helmet, and flying jacket, I dashed up the steps of the Cleveland courthouse, but I was too late. Carelli was on his way back to Pittsburgh.

The Supreme Court of the United States had by now refused our appeal in the extradition proceedings, so there was nothing left to do but to submit Carelli to the mercy of the Allegheny County courts. The district attorney demanded severe penalties and the judge obliged with a twenty-six-year sentence. Later I appealed to the Pardon Board, and this sentence was reduced to ten years.

Albert Carelli was not a model youth. He was a wandering and mischievous lad, but I do not believe that intentional evil abided in his heart. I believe further that the long penitentiary sentence imposed on him was entirely out of keeping with the realities of modern criminological science. The fact alone that he had been erroneously convicted of murder and tortured with the specter of death in the electric chair should in itself have dictated a merciful disposition toward him when he came up for sentencing on crimes which *had not been proved by any court trial* and to which, at the time of the murder trial, he had pleaded *nolo contendere* (I do not contend) only because he was already confronted with the ultimate punishment of death.

It could well be that the demand made by the Allegheny County district attorney for heavy penalties was motivated to a great extent by the fact that a man whom his office had convicted of murder was later proved to be innocent.

They can't put you in jail for that!

Chapter XVIII

AUSTRIAN PETTICOATS

SHADES of a brown suit!

One evening three brothers came to my home to engage me to defend their married sister, Mrs. Josephine Rondish, imprisoned in the county jail on a charge of shooting her husband. One of the brothers, who hailed from Philadelphia, said he had seen me in court in that city, that he liked the way I tried cases, and that he particularly remembered the brown suit I wore. He said the garment resembled one worn by a cousin of his who lived in Poginsk, Austria. He had always admired it. When his sister in Pittsburgh had telegraphed him about her trouble, he called on Attorney Bonnelly, whom he knew as a very good friend of mine, and obtained from him my home address. He then contacted two brothers who lived in Buffalo, and the three came to Stowe Township to place in my hands the job of saving their sister from the fate which threatened her. Josephine, whom they spoke of as a tender violet, had critically wounded her husband and he was not expected to survive. When arrested she declared, according to the police, that for years her husband had maltreated her and that she could no longer endure his abuse. Therefore, she shot him as he lay sleeping on a couch. I made arrangements to call on the prisoner at the county jail the following morning.

What my visitors related electrified the atmosphere of our household. After they left, my sister Catherine enthusiastically clapped her hands and said: "Oh, Michael, they know all about your brown suit. And just think, you're going to try a murder case. That's so exciting!"

"No, no," I replied, my elation in getting an important case now considerably moderated as I realized it might become a murder case. "Their sister shot her husband, but he's not dead."

"But I heard them say he might die," Catherine continued.

"Catherine! You're not ghoulish enough to anticipate the man's death so that it will be a murder case?"

"Oh no, I don't want him dead. But from what those men said, he certainly deserved whatever he got."

"Catherine, I wish you wouldn't talk about serious matters like that. And let me tell you that this case needs more than the fortuitous and superstitious intervention of a brown suit."

"Oh, I'm sure you'll win it, with or without a brown suit."

But on the following day when I called on Mrs. Rondish at the county jail she refused to discuss the case. She said that if her husband died she also wanted to die. However, her husband did not die. In three weeks he was pronounced out of danger, and in three months more he left the hospital.

Josephine was now indicted on a charge of attempted murder and this seemed to change her attitude completely. She sent for me and declared she would fight the charges. She denied that she had shot her husband and refuted police reports that she had admitted shooting him. On the contrary, she asserted vehemently that *he* had tried to kill *her*. She characterized him as a brute and related a harrowing tale of how for seven years he had been breaking her on the wheel of marital despotism.

On the very first day following their wedding, she related, her husband, who was a much smaller person than she, bound her to a chair and administered stinging slaps to her face so that she might know he was the master, which she had never questioned. The slaps developed into punches, the punches turned into whippings, and the whippings graduated into chokings. Strangely, and yet perhaps not so strangely, it never occurred to her to leave him. To her, marriage was an indissoluble bond to be severed only by death. When she married Jabez Rondish in Austria she said she would remain with him unto the last day. That last day had not arrived.

She suffered seven years of unceasing physical abuse, and yet Nature—indifferent to storms, whether provoked by the elements or by man—presented the unhappy couple with three children, determined to preserve the race, regardless. Probably it was the children which kept Mrs. Rondish anchored in that unprotected conjugal harbor constantly lashed by domestic gales which might have sunk other nuptial craft.

Josephine was a beautiful woman. Tall and statuesque, with pale oval face, straight Grecian nose, large brown eyes, and raven-black hair, she carried herself as erectly as an Egyptian water carrier. It was as difficult to visualize anyone striking her as to imagine someone applying a whip to a marble statue. The community in which she lived was entirely non-Austrian and had been purposely chosen by Jabez so that his wife could not fraternize with others of her original nationality who might ally themselves with her against his tyrannizing sovereignty.

Preparing for the trial, I visited this community and learned from her neighbors that the unhappy defendant had been a woman of modest demeanor, simple dignity, and exceptional immaculateness. The American style of dress, which was running to scarcer and shorter garments in alarming diminution, had not influenced her attire in the least. She still dressed in the old European fashion, which called for corseted waists, ballooning sleeves, and ample, multifarious petticoats and skirts.

The first woman I asked about Mrs. Rondish volunteered: "Oh, she was a very good woman. She always minded her own business. The only time she went out was to look for her children, and when she went up steps or the wind blew you could see her beautiful white petticoats."

The second woman I spoke to remarked: "Mrs. Rondish—oh, glory be to God, I niver seen such a wonderful woman. She niver interfered with nobody in the town. If she didn't shoot her husband, begorry she should have, considerin' the way he always bate her, the baste. She was always wan to be takin' wonderful care of her children, and niver before have I iver seen such wonderful petticoats on a woman in me whole life."

The third neighbor commented: "She was soocha fina woman. And her hoosband, he was a bestia, an animala. She hadda soocha nice children and she always keepa them so cleena. And she always weara nicea white petticoats."

We went to trial, and as it got under way it appeared that our main defense was to be that the husband was a beast, that he deserved what he got, that the defendant was a good woman who minded her own business—and always wore beautiful white petticoats.

Mrs. Rondish performed well on the stand. She denied she told the police she had shot her husband. I later explained to the jury that it was quite possible the police had misunderstood her, in view of the excitement and confusion which surrounded her arrest, and particularly because of her imperfect English. What Mrs. Rondish had said or attempted to say to the police, and she so testified, was that *she* was lying on the sofa and that her husband came into the room with a leveled revolver, exclaiming: "Prepare to meet your Creator, for this is your last day!" She tried to deflect his aim. He grappled her; they struggled and fell. As they rolled on the floor the gun was discharged and he received a bullet in his stomach.

We called many witnesses who testified to the pit of torment in which Josephine had languished for seven years. Neighbor after neighbor testified to hearing her scream in apparent terror and pain. One woman declared that just a month before the shooting occurred she had been roused from her slumber by shrieks issuing from the Rondish house, that she flew to the window and by the light of an arc lamp saw Mrs. Rondish fleeing into the street, her dress smeared with blood. These neighbors said that scarcely a night passed but that they heard a moan or cry of distress from the Austrian woman.

Mr. Lownsdale, the prosecuting attorney, called in rebuttal a substantial-looking citizen who hurled a sputtering cannon cracker into our ranks by belittling the story of the defendant's nocturnal distress. He asserted that he knew Mr. and Mrs. Rondish very well and was quite familiar with their married life. Lownsdale continued the questioning:

"Where do they live?"

"Next door."

"How long have you lived there?"

"Two years."

"During that time did you ever hear Mrs. Rondish evidence any distress?"

"Yes."

"How many times?"

"Twice."

"So that in two years you only heard her complain twice."

"That's right."

With triumphant scorn the prosecuting attorney sang out: "That's all!" and then turned and practically sneered in my face. The jury, which up to that moment had been regarding the defendant with compassion and had even offered a glance of admiration for her defender, seemed confused at this turn of events. Two or three of them betrayed in their expressions the suspicion that the long tale of woe related by the defendant and her neighbors had been considerably exaggerated.

For a moment I wondered whether I should cross-examine this witness, even though I felt certain something was wrong. I was convinced that the narrative of abuse related by so many persons could not have been manufactured. It had been confirmed by too much circumstance for it to be fiction. Should a lawyer cross-examine in this kind of situation? There are able practitioners who insist that the better strategy is to avoid cross-examination and thus deny to the hostile witness an opportunity to emphasize further the damaging testimony already given. I am of the opinion that if the opposing witness's testimony is harmless or only mildly injurious, one may well let a sleeping dog lie. However, if the witness has struck a mortal blow, the cross-examiner should at least swish his saber in a few passes of incredulity, lest the jury assume he has accepted the evidence as beyond disputation. I was satisfied that a repetition of the present witness's testimony could scarcely cause any more damage than he had already wrought, and then there was the possibility that I might chance upon something to minimize the harm he had done. Accordingly I unsheathed the saber. In my fondest hopes, however, I could not have expected to hit such vulnerable spots which a few questions uncovered.

"Mr. Wensell," I began, "you say that in two years you only heard Mrs. Rondish complain twice."

"That's right," he replied with an intonation which clearly said: "You're not going to get anywhere with me."

"Is there anything wrong with your hearing, Mr. Wensell?"

"Why do you say that? I hear perfectly well, Mr. Musmanno."

"Well, didn't you hear these other witnesses testify to having heard Mrs. Rondish complain almost daily?"

"Yes, I heard them so testify, but that has nothing to do with me."

"Do you believe they are lying?"

"I object!" Mr. Lownsdale raised his arm. "It is not for the witness to pass upon their testimony. The jury can form its own conclusions."

"You are right," the judge affirmed, looking at the prosecuting attorney, and then, turning to me, "You may continue, Mr. Musmanno, but not along that line."

"Thank you, Your Honor. Mr. Wensell, do you have any personal interest in this case?"

"None whatsoever."

"Did the prosecuting attorney subpoena you to come here?"

"He did."

Again my opponent objected and again he was sustained. I resumed:

"Mr. Wensell, what work do you do?"

"Is that important?"

"Is there anything you have to conceal?"

"No, I have nothing to conceal."

"Well, then, why don't you tell us what work you do?"

"I don't think that has anything to do with the case."

I appealed to the judge, and the judge directed him to answer.

"I am a salesman."

"What kind of a salesman?"

"Why, a salesman, that's all."

"Where?"

"At Johnson's Pneumatic Tool Company."

"Are you there all the time?"

"No."

"Oh, you travel then?"

The witness hesitated, and then with some reluctance answered: "Yes."

"I noticed you hesitated with that answer," I commented as I got up from counsel table and approached the witness stand. "Is there anything wrong about traveling for your company?"

"No, why should there be?"

"I don't know. Your unusual hesitation caused me to inquire. Then I take it you are not home very much?"

"What's my being at home got to do with all this?"

"If the Court please, I request that he be required to answer."

The judge said: "You must answer."

The witness paused for another moment and then finally said: "No."

"The Johnson Pneumatic Tool Company sends its salesmen across the country at times, does it not?"

"Y-yes."

Feeling certain that I was on the verge of some important discovery, I now pointed my finger at him and asked: "Mr. Wensell, on your oath, now, honor bright, please tell this jury how many times you have been home during the last two years."

"Twice."

"And on both occasions that you came home you heard Mrs. Rondish cry out in distress?"

The witness lowered his head and mumbled: "Yes."

I walked over to Lownsdale's side of the table and, although addressing the witness, I sang out in the prosecutor's face: "That's all!"

The courtroom guffawed like a giant. Josephine had won the good will of everyone in the audience from the moment she had ascended the witness stand, when a flash of her pretty and voluminous petticoats gave objective confirmation to all that had been said about her fastidious and immaculate dress. Had the judge not rapped for order, the hands of her admirers, which, cymbal-like, had been raised to applaud, would have crashed out a salute to her with a brassy taunt for the prosecuting attorney.

This temporary setback to the Commonwealth's case, however, did not dampen the powder in Lownsdale's blunderbuss as he blasted against wifely sharpshooters. "Members of the jury," he shouted, "I don't care if occasionally Jabez Rondish did chastise his wife—she may have needed chastisement—but in any event this gave her no license to shoot him. There has been a calculated plan here to arouse your sympathies and becloud your judgment. They impressed you with her picturesque European dress. Well, she may wear European dresses, but she has already learned American methods about shooting husbands. And this has to stop! Where is it going to lead us if this husband-shooting isn't curbed?"

In my summation to the jury I agreed with the prosecuting attorney that there should never be an open season on husbands, but, aiming my own blunderbuss, I blasted that while husband-shooting had to stop, wife-beating must cease also! (There were three women on the jury.)

"Ladies and gentlemen of the jury," I stormed on, encouraged by the quick eager response of approval from the female contingent in the jury box, "there are men who believe that a wife should be a slave, a drudge, a lackey. They assume that not only should she bear a man's children, prepare his meals, wash and mend his clothes, and scrub her fingers to the bone, but that she should also bear his insults and gibes and from time to time feel the sting of his blows, the ugliness of his burly fists, and the ignominy and pain of his dastardly kicks.

"You have heard here a story that must have made your blood run cold. That such brutality and savagery should occur in enlightened America is almost incredible, but it did—and we are not restricted in our proof to the testimony of the defendant.

"You have heard related here, members of the jury, how this man struck his wife with a club and menaced her with a knife. Certainly you must have recoiled with horror as you heard how, while Mrs. Rondish was carrying his unborn child, Jabez Rondish scourged her until her injuries compelled immediate hospitalization. What kind of a man is that? I don't care what the prosecuting attorney or anyone else says, but I assert here that a husband who will strike his wife when she is in the sacred state of creating life, the husband who will whip his mate when she is suffering for him is not a man—he is a monster!

"He lashed his wife after childbirth too, and I say that the husband who will strike his wife as she struggles back to the mountaintop of life after having descended into the valley of death for him, the man who will do that is not a man—he is a fiend!"

The husband, of course, had denied having committed these aggressions, but he went too far in denying everything. He even denied ownership of the revolver which had done the shooting. He admitted owning a revolver but claimed that it was not the one with which he had been shot. On this point I believed we scored heavily with the jury.

"Rondish disowned his revolver. Why? He feared that by admitting the gun belonged to him he would in effect acknowledge he knew how the shooting occurred, because his story was that he was asleep on the sofa at the time the shot was fired. But why deny his revolver? She could have shot him with his own weapon, couldn't she? But Rondish denied everything! You heard him evade, side-step, quibble, and dodge. He said he couldn't tell from the exterior of the revolver whether it was his, but when I broke it open he couldn't tell anything from the inside either. You heard him say that he hadn't seen his gun for two years and didn't know where it was. You heard him declare that he had bought it for protection of his home, to defend his wife and children; and yet he didn't know where he kept it. And more. According to his story, the gun wasn't even loaded, and he didn't have any bullets!

"Here is a man who buys a revolver for defense, yet if a burglar had broken into his home he would have had to ask the burglar to help him look for the revolver and then, finding it, ask him for bullets!"

Another circumstance which I believed helped our case was that Rondish, immediately after the shooting, had hidden the revolver. "Why did Rondish hide the gun with which he was shot," I asked, "if he was innocent of wrongdoing?"

"Did he act like an innocent man?

"Did he act like the victim of an assault by his wife?

"Members of the jury, acquit this woman. Reflect on the kind of person she is. Even after her husband's brutal attempt to shoot her, she still wanted to help him. She sought permission to hurry to his hospital bed to attend the father of her children, but he refused to see her.

"Ladies and gentlemen of the jury, acquit this poor unoffending mother. What reverences, what sacrifices are conjured up in the sacred word 'Mother.' What a mother suffers for her children and for the father of those children, only a mother knows. Through her babes she feels all the ills and ailments that infancy is heir to. While the whole world sleeps, how often is she on her feet, holding her offspring in her arms, or sitting anxiously at his bedside, agonizing in double proportion with every ache, every twinge, every hurt that shakes the form of her darling child. This good woman has endured not only the pain of all mothers but, in addition, the agony and torture inflicted upon her by a man who vowed to defend, honor, and protect her. It should be the husband on trial here, not the wife. I ask you in all justice to acquit this much-abused woman."

After the judge's charge the jury filed out. Twenty minutes later they sent a note to the judge asking if they could find the husband guilty of anything. The judge instructed them that the husband was not the defendant. They then immediately returned with a verdict of not guilty.

The verdict, while quite satisfying, was not unexpected. The real surprise came a month later when I learned that Mrs. Rondish had rejoined her husband. When neighbors asked her why she did this, considering the brutal manner in which he had abused her for so long a period of time, she replied: "I love him."

Chapter XIX

A ROYAL CHAIR

THE castle in the clouds for which the imaginative child yearns is no more attractive to him than is an office to the young lawyer. An office is more than a place in which to meet clients; it is a symbol of stability and self-assurance that one is now a substantial integer in the pattern of organized society. The pride of the printer in his printery, the teacher in his classroom, the doctor in his surgery, and the sculptor in his studio derives from the fact that he has a place to which his fellow men may repair for the services he has to render. The scientist, doctor, and druggist are benefactors of humanity, but without their laboratory, surgery, and pharmacy they are moored to the wharf of futility. I needed a laboratory too, and at last I acquired one. I now had an office in the Commonwealth Building on Fourth Avenue. It was a room measuring about ten by twelve feet, containing a battered desk and a swivel chair which refused to swivel but constantly endeavored to throw the sitter forward on his face. Two straight-backed chairs for clients and a threadbare carpet completed the furnishings of this law office. But it was *my* law office!

Eagerly I came to it in the morning before the sky crews had thoroughly fastened back the curtains of the night, and reluctantly I left it at the end of the calendar day, never before the witching hour of midnight. Often I remained so late that I missed the last streetcar (which departed from Pittsburgh at 2 A.M.), and on those occasions I curled upon the floor and fell fast asleep. It is a marvel to me that my osseous structure (as yet!) shows no harmful effects from the countless times I made of the hard unyielding boards a couch for the night. Sleeping on the floor sounds like a hardship, and perhaps it is, but I did not so regard it at the time. I labored with such unflagging zeal and unbroken continuity that when at last I stretched out at the foot of my desk I had reached a degree of exhaustion that no bed could have been more comfortable or gentler to my body which cried for rest and surcease from the driving of my tyrannical will.

Work! If I had a case I toiled at it with the energy and concentration of a man building a wall against a falling avalanche: I investigated the scene of the accident or crime, I sought statements from all persons who might shed any light on the litigated circumstance, I consulted the authorities on the law involved. Since I had no stenographer, I did my own typing on a tenth-hand mowing machine perched on the top of my dilapidated desk.

If I did not have a case, I studied. I prepared articles for legal magazines, I indexed citations for ready reference on every subject of law I believed might come within the orbit of the practice I hoped to acquire. I wrote a column entitled "From Week to Week" for a community newspaper. And I made speeches.

Good heavens, how I made speeches! No society, group, or club was too small or too obscure for a speech from me, and I would regale them with no rambling fragmentary talk, either; I gave them an effort, a speech, an oration! I would talk fifteen minutes, a half hour, an hour, or an hour and a half, depending on the occasion and the subject matter. Since the ability to speak is no small part of a lawyer's stock in trade, I felt that every speech I made helped to equip me all the more effectively in upholding the standards of my profession in its service to mankind.

In those "good old days" there seemed to be more discussion among people on events of public interest than is currently true. The vast majority of the population today is satisfied to take its opinions already formulated for them, like pre-digested foods, from television and radio commentators, news analysts, and experts; but in the 1920's, spirited disputation was still the order of the day, and one topic which always inspired animated argument was the one of capital punishment. Thus, when Reverend John A. Orr, minister of the North Side Presbyterian Church, declared publicly that he favored the death penalty for the crime of murder, I challenged him to a debate. He accepted. Radio was just reaching the height of frenzied popularity at the time, so that the microphone became our podium and the whole radio population our auditorium. The newspapers as well as the radio station itself, WCAE, gave advance publicity to the forensic duel.

Speaking to the negative of the question, "Is capital punishment desirable in present-day society?" I larded my main speech, and rebuttal too, with many passages from the Bible. Since I was in effect defending what was generally regarded to be the more merciful side of the question and Reverend Orr was supporting the harsher point of view, a large part of the audience believed, especially in view of my Scripture-quoting, that Orr was the lawyer and I the minister!

Listeners to the debate were asked to vote on the issue presented. In the popular returns I received 56 per cent of the vote and the Reverend Orr 44 per cent. For some time many of my friends referred to me as "Reverend."

All my waking hours were devoted to my profession. I went nowhere unless the visit, call, or mission would in some way, directly or indirectly, contribute to preparing me to discharge better the responsibilities of my chosen work. I attended no social functions or activities. Being a lawyer was not only my occupation—it was my avocation, diversion, and entertainment. It was my wife, children, and grandchildren!

I never remained out of my office long. There was always a hopeful expectancy in hurrying back: a client might be waiting! One day I returned to find a customer I did not particularly welcome. His name was Vincenzo Bonini, and it appeared that he had once belonged to a group which had fought another group in a sort of backwoods feud or vendetta. He was charged with having fired a shotgun at his enemy, Pietro Gombetto, as he lay in wait for him behind a tree. Gombetto received flying buckshot in his legs. Bonini wanted me to defend him.

I had no stomach for this type of Criminal Court work because it had already happened in gory feuds of the prohibition era that rival gangsters had carried their total war to the point where they turned their guns on the opposing lawyers! I was a brave enough person, but how would bravery stand me in good stead here? And who cared about courage in this sort of controversy anyway? I needed the business badly, but not that badly.

Quickly I grasped for a reason which would convince Bonini I could not represent him. The only excuse I could think of at the moment was that I was very busy. Accordingly I pointed out that I had so many cases to handle that I could never devote to his defense the uninterrupted attention it certainly deserved. He replied that his case was just as important as anybody else's. I reminded him that there were many other lawyers in Pittsburgh, and quite a few not so occupied as I. While I said this I tried to look busy and prosperous and, at the same time, cover with the wastepaper basket one of the bigger holes in my carpet.

"No, me like you," he said. "I be in court one day and I hear you argue case—you wasa fine—you make lotta noise—and winna da case!"

I brushed aside the dubious compliment and then, sparring for time, said: "All right, I will need to think this matter over. You come in tomorrow and I'll see whether I can induce some of my other clients to release me for such time as may be needed to grapple with your situation. But I doubt that they will. I don't see why you don't go to another lawyer. There are many far more capable than I, and especially for this type of a case——"

"No, me lika you for mya lawyer," he stolidly insisted.

Why and how he developed this doglike faith in me, I do not know to this day. That night I thought the whole matter over and came to the irrevocable decision that, regardless of what he might say, I would refuse to defend him. How could it possibly profit me to have him as a client if the other side took down their shotguns and made a pepperbox out of me?

A voice within me urged: "Bravery!"

Another voice within me replied: "Coconuts! Bravery only embraces a principle. No principle is involved here. This is simply a mountaineering feud and there is no reason why I should step in between the blazing mountains."

The following morning Vincenzo Bonini arrived at my office early. Indeed he was waiting for me when I appeared. I determined to have the interview over with at once. "Mr. Bonini, it is useless for you to waste your time here. I will not take your case."

"Mr. Lawyer, I be innochenty. Why I should go to jail?" He seized my hand with the desperation of one about to be banished, and pleaded: "You gotta believe me. You make investigate. If you no find me innochenty, then you no needa defenda me."

As he spoke, tears rolled down his cheeks, and I paused to reflect: Could I justify the attitude I had assumed? For some inexplicable reason this man wanted me, and only me, as his attorney. If he was really innocent—and I had to admit that possibility—would the moral obligations of my profession permit me to turn him down only because I was conscious of some possible personal danger to myself? The ethics of the lawyer's code would not countenance a lawyer's refusing a case simply because the person in legal distress might lack funds with which to pay a fee. Would they excuse my ignoring the entreaties of an accused person because he did not have the associations I approved of? The only thing which should concern me was the truth of his protestations. After some mental debate I came to the conclusion that if I was convinced my persistent visitor was guiltless I could not conscientiously refuse to defend him.

"Very well, Bonini, I will investigate your case and if I am satisfied you are innocent I will defend you."

"Oh, thanka you, Mr. Lawyer," and before I could withdraw my hands he had seized both of them and kissed them.

I spent three days investigating the case and found that, approximately two years before, Gombetto had slashed Bonini's face with a razor. At the time, Bonini lifted a vengeful and prophetic hand, muttering that the day would come when Gombetto would pay dearly for what he had done. A week before Gombetto was shot, Bonini was seen purchasing a shotgun; and it was the Commonwealth's contention that the slugs which hit Gombetto came from a cartridge which could have been fired from a weapon such as Bonini had purchased. When Bonini was arrested, the police found in his pocket the old newspaper clipping which told of Gombetto's attack on him two years before.

It was an airtight case for the prosecution, with the facts leading to a conclusion of guilt with the certainty almost of an algebraic equation: (1) the parties had had a previous fight, (2) the victim had received a razor slashing and had threatened reprisal, (3) he carried around a clipping to remind him constantly of his avowed revenge, (4) he bought a weapon with which to accomplish that revenge, (5) there was a wounding of the previous assailant with missiles which fitted the purchased weapon.

With these disclosures I could feel my hands burning from the hot potato they had picked up, but before I could drop the scalding tuber I uncovered evidence which actually proved that Bonini was "innochenty." At the steel mill where he was employed I saw his time card with perforations which put him on the job at the very time he was supposed to be shooting Gombetto. Moreover, his foreman and fellow workers assured me they remembered Bonini being at work when the shooting occurred.

This was obviously a case where the accused was armed with considerable motive to commit the crime with which he was charged but had had no opportunity to carry the motive into effect. But you cannot punish a man because he calls on the evil spirits to send a storm which will destroy his neighbor's farm and, by coincidence, the farm is flooded. I asked Bonini if he really wanted to shoot Gombetto. He replied that there had been a time when doing so would have added a golden nugget of sweetness to the treasures of life, but that time had passed. His finger no longer itched for the trigger of violent vindication.

We went to trial and, with the alibi established for Bonini by his brother employees, we had no difficulty in winning an acquittal. Gleefully I returned to my office, chiding myself for having raised so large and formidable an umbrella of fears against a rain which had never descended. I laughed at myself. It was a good joke on me, I said, chuckling all the while.

But as I turned the knob of my office door and stepped over the threshold I perceived that I had been laughing out of the wrong side of my mouth. A shadow crossed my heart and silenced its happy song like a heavy hand on a harp's vibrations.

Who was waiting in my shabby little office but Gombetto, the victim of the shotgun shooting! And I saw a bulge at his hip where his hand significantly rested.

With the blood draining from my face—I could feel it hurriedly departing for distant regions—I continued like a tightrope walker toward my desk. I had to see the thing through now, but I remarked to myself: "That's what I thought in the first place. I should have listened to my own warning. Now, what a mess this office will be."

Gombetto stalked me to the desk and began:

"Mr. Musmanno, you be the lawyer who defenda that son of a gonya Bonini, who shoot me?"

"You are mistaken," I replied, "I defended the man *accused* of having shot you. Certainly there can be no doubt in your mind now that Bonini was innocent."

"Innochenty or guilty, you defend him."

"Yes, I did. Was he not entitled to be represented?"

"I no say that." On the dead pan of his face I could read no writing of his immediate intentions. But suddenly he whipped his hand from his hip. The lump in my throat became a goiter.

But to my electric surprise the hand was empty and he extended it forward in rough amiability. "I coma congratulate you because you be a mighty fina lawyer."

"Oh, thank you!" I exclaimed, grasping his hand with the eagerness of an acrobat seizing the hand of a fellow acrobat in mid-air. "It is certainly splendid sportsmanship on your part to congratulate me when you were the losing party," I went on, mopping the cold sweat on my forehead.

"That be righta, Mr. Musmanno. From now on I wanta you for my lawyer."

"Thank you very much indeed, Mr. Gombetto." Then the shadow of a suspicion flitted across my mind. "Say, you don't intend to shoot Bonini, do you?"

"Oh no, Bonini and me, we be friends now."

"Well, I'll gladly represent you in any civil case, but no criminal case. Understand! I believe I'll give up the practice of criminal law anyway. It's a little too exciting."

But of course I did not. Fortunately neither Bonini nor Gombetto ever came back to me, nor, so far as I know, did they ever oil up their shotguns except for animals in the woods, the shooting of which is permitted by the game laws of the Commonwealth.

Not long after this another potential client, Rodolfo Bino, treated me to a similar scare. Entering my shock-ridden office, he declared: "Mr. Musmanno, I wanta sue a son of a gonya who bombed me."

I lifted my hands in stark refusal. "Oh no!" I had conclusively decided by this time that no one could ever induce me again to take up a case which featured feuds or bombs. "I'm sorry, Mr. Bino, but I'm really too busy," I added with as much finality as if he had invited me to go over Niagara Falls in a canoe.

However, in the underbrush of my apprehensions chirped the cricket of curiosity. I looked Bino over and could not see where he had suffered much from the bomb. I thought people who were bombed had to be gathered up in a shovel or basket. I could not refrain from asking:

"You say you were bombed?"

"Shura, I was bombed and I wanna sue the bestia."

"I am sorry, but I really have too much business to attend to; you will have to go to another lawyer." The poverty-stricken appearance of my office made my explanation sound a little fantastic, but I was adamant—I would take no bombing cases. However, before the would-be client left the office I wanted to hear an answer to the query of the cricket as to just how he was bombed.

"You say you were bombed. Tell me how it happened."

"It was a very simpla tinga. I was bombed by an automobile."

"Oh! You mean you were *bumped* by an automobile?"

"Shura, thatsa watta I tella you. I was bombed by an automobile."

"Well, I think I can squeeze your case into my business schedule someway," I now said in a rapid mouthful. "I'm awful busy but I feel sorry for these poor pedestrian victims. I don't know what's going to happen to our country if we don't curb these automobilists who are running wild, crazy, mad on the highway with utter indifference to the rights of pedestrians. Now, just pull up a chair and give me the details and we'll have this suit filed in a jiffy." I eagerly reached for my pen, plunged it into the inkwell, and began taking notes.

Although I had determined I would not take any more cases which involved prohibition violence, I could not refuse to listen to Randolph Branche, who came into my office, placed a newspaper on my desk, and bade me read a front-page story to which he pointed with an indignant finger. "Mr. Musmanno, my reputation has been ruined by this newspaper," and he thumped the page. "Read, read," he urged, "and see if you don't agree I have been ruined."

When he finally removed his hand from the paper I read aloud: "'Among the persons who have felt the violence of the Stefano gang are John Steckeley, Randolph Branche——'"

"That's me!" he cried. "I'm ruined, don't you see? But read, read, and see what chance I will ever have to lead an honest life after this! I'm ruined," and he banged at his head with both fists. "I'm called a gangster—not only a gangster, but a wounded gangster. But read, Mr. Musmanno——"

I went on: "'Frank Truster and George Onconey. Randolph Branche was injured by a shotgun blast last February when on his way to——'"

"See, see, Mr. Musmanno, I'm ruined. I never saw a shotgun blast. I'm not a gangster, I'm not a bootlegger."

"Can you prove what you are saying?" I asked.

"Why, of course, Mr. Musmanno."

I devoted two days to investigating Randolph Branche's story, interviewing witnesses, studying police records, and came to the conclusion that the newspaper had actually erred in its reference to my client. Branche demanded that I sue the paper for fifty thousand dollars' damages. I agreed with him, but suggested that before we actually filed the suit we should speak to the newspaper owners and perhaps they might be willing to enter into an amicable settlement.

"Oh, if they will settle, that will be better," Branche concurred.

"How much would you take in settlement?"

He paused, entered into a mental computation, and finally said: "If they pay me right away, I'll be willing to settle for twenty-five thousand dollars."

We called at the offices of the Pittsburgh *Sun* and I got to see the managing editor, Ralph Mansinger. As soon as I mentioned Randolph Branche he said: "Mr. Musmanno, we discovered our error this morning. The man who really was involved was called 'Red' Branco. We regret the error and we are prepared to print a retraction."

"A retraction will be appreciated," I said, "but it can never undo the damage which has already been accomplished. Mr. Branche will never be able to live down the stigma of having been declared a gangster by your highly respected newspaper. My client is asking me to enter suit for fifty thousand dollars. Of course he would be willing to talk settlement."

"How much would he want?"

"He is waiting outside in your anteroom and I can call him in, but he has authorized me to accept settlement in the sum of twenty-five thousand dollars."

"I'm afraid, Mr. Musmanno, that that would be out of the question. If you would like to discuss the matter further with Mr. Branche, I shall be glad to wait."

I went out into the anteroom and related to my client what had transpired and asked him if he would take anything less than twenty-five thousand dollars. He said: "Mr. Musmanno, twenty-five thousand is already too little for the ruination of my reputation, but I will leave it to you if we should come down a little. You might offer to take twenty thousand, then fifteen thousand, but under no circumstances less than ten thousand. If he won't pay that, we will file suit at once."

Upon rejoining Mr. Mansinger I explained how wounded my client felt about the matter, but I went on to say that a lawsuit could only emphasize the wounds and scars and, in view of that fact, we would gladly take twenty thousand dollars, provided the papers were drawn up at once.

"I'm glad to see that your client is willing to talk compromise, but we could not think of paying twenty thousand dollars. He exaggerates in his mind the damage he has suffered. In a few days the people will forget that this story appeared——"

"I differ with you, Mr. Mansinger. Time will only magnify the damage. Each person who repeats the story will add something else until in the end they will have Branche a second Jesse James. If you will pay fifteen thousand dollars I'm sure I can get my client to withdraw his claim completely."

"Mr. Musmanno, I surely appreciate your reasonableness in this matter and I'm certain that with a little further discussion we can arrive at a reasonable figure."

We talked for a whole hour, and finally I went out to Mr. Branche and said to him: "We've agreed on a figure, but before we draw up a release, naturally you must approve. It's not quite as much as you had asked for nor as much as I had hoped, but I believe——"

"Well, tell me right away, Mr. Musmanno. How much will he pay?"

"One hundred and fifty dollars."

He gasped: "One hundred and fifty dollars?"

"Yes, that's right. One hundred and fifty dollars."

"Hell's fire! Don't you think that's pretty low?"

"It is, rather, but I leave it entirely up to you."

"But how about your fee? How much do you get?"

"Well, Mr. Mansinger has promised to buy me a straw hat."

"All right, get the paper ready and I'll sign."

In a half hour the release was signed, Mr. Branche had his one hundred and fifty dollars, and I had a new straw hat, sailor style.

I walked back to my office wearing the hat at a rather rakish angle. My young nephew, Neal, was waiting for me, and when he saw the hat he said: "Uncle Michael, you look like Maurice Chevalier."

It was indeed a good-looking hat. It cost one dollar and seventy-five cents.

And then finally there was the case of Philip August, who had been convicted of operating a still in the cellar of his home and was to appear in court on September 1 for sentencing. I was not his attorney at the trial, but Mr. August came to see me, stated he had dismissed his previous attorney, and pleaded with me to appeal his case. I said to him: "I doubt very much that an appeal would be successful."

This did not dissuade him. Looking at me with supplicating eyes, he said, most assuredly without intending any humor: "Mr. Musmanno, please take my case, because if you don't do something for me, the first of September will be the last of August!"

Little by little I was picking up clientele, and the birds in the mulberry bush in our front yard were singing more melodious tunes each morning as I left for the little office which seemed like a ship carrying me ever closer to the port of hope fulfillment. But with all my dreams I was still a little uncomfortable. When one sits for hours in a chair which is not only hard and unyielding but so much out of balance that it keeps throwing the sitter forward, the sitter by midnight feels that he has been fighting a catapult all day. I needed a good chair, but such an article cost sixty-five dollars, which was a king's ransom to me. A furniture salesman offered to let me have on credit the chair I craved, but I could never rest easily on a piece of furniture whose legs were planted in the quicksands of debt.

However, by missing lunch and occasionally doing without dinner, I set aside something each day from the little fees which were now trickling in with some regularity, and I at last got my chair. No royal throne could have afforded more comfort to its regal occupant than my roller-bearing, double-swiveled, triple-socketed, leather-seated, back-tilting chair now brought to me.

My desk was still old and battered. The carpet continued to look like the map of Asia, its various discolorations and holes making up the seas, lakes, and straits—but I was sitting pretty. I had a wonderful chair.

Chapter XX

THE BRIDGE OF SIGHS

IN ONE of the poorer sections of Pittsburgh on a drab and dingy passageway known as Mulberry Alley there lived for many years the Pollari family, consisting of father, mother, and five children. The father, Frank Pollari, sixty years of age and in failing health, eked out an existence for himself and family by peddling fruit from a little handcart which he wheeled through the surrounding community.

One night, while sleeping deeply from the exhaustion of his itinerant labors, he was awakened by a shattering of window glass and loud cries of "Get him! Get him!" Hurriedly dressing, he lifted a revolver from a dresser drawer, slipped it into his pocket, and started down to inquire. As he reached the foot of the stairs, the door suddenly swung open and, amid noises which explained no more than the enveloping darkness, he felt a blow which sent him staggering against the steps he had just descended. Stunned, he struggled to his feet and attempted to back up the stairs, when a voice shouted: "Kill him! Kill him!" Another blow fell on his face and he pulled the trigger of his revolver. A body fell.

When the police arrived, Frank Pollari was arrested and charged with murder. I was retained for the defense.

My investigation revealed that on the night of the slaying the young people of the Mulberry Alley vicinage had held a dance in an empty house next to the Pollari home. To the party came one Jerry Fishert, unhonored, uninvited, and undesired. Intoxicated and rowdy, he was ordered off the premises by one of the Pollari sons who had helped organize the neighborhood ball. Fishert left but returned a second and a third time. On the last visit he was thrown out, not overgently, by the Pollari boys. Smarting from his humiliating rebuff, Fishert gathered together a half dozen cronies at a nearby street corner and returned for "satisfaction." Among them was Clayton

Humphrey who, half drunk and ignorant of the preceding altercation, entered into the action picture "just for the fun of it."

When the roistering group arrived at the scene of the late dance, they found the building empty, but Fishert urged his followers on to the next house, which they proceeded to pelt with bricks and stones. Then they stormed the door and surged up the stairs. A revolver shot sounded, and Humphrey fell, a bullet in his heart.

The autopsy on Clayton Humphrey revealed a pint of moonshine whiskey in his stomach. He had put into his mouth an enemy to steal away his brains, and at twenty-one years of age he was in his grave. Had Humphrey survived, he probably, in his first sober moment, would have appraised his participation in the midnight adventure as madness.

But unhappily the dead do not speak and the living do not always think, and thus is much injustice perpetrated in this at times topsy-turvy world. The parents of the deceased Humphrey employed private counsel to assist the district attorney in his job of convicting Pollari and sending him "and all his kind to the electric chair where he belonged." Their grief was as disabling to clear thinking as whiskey had been to that of their son's, and accordingly, it was impossible for them to perceive any evil in Clayton's making war on a householder in his own home. However, not all of the Humphreys' vengeful and bitter determination to prosecute Pollari was due to faulty reasoning. They had been told that the shooting had not taken place in Pollari's house but out on the street; that Fishert and his companions had merely called to demand an explanation and apology from the Pollari sons for their rough treatment of Jerry; but, finding the dance disbanded and the Pollari boys gone, they gathered in the street to discuss what had happened and how to obtain the apology which would "set everything straight," when suddenly a window in the Pollari house flew open, a shot rang out, and Humphrey fell.

Since Frank Pollari did not know any of the boys and had no knowledge of the brawl which occurred at the dance that evening, why would he want to shoot Clayton Humphrey? The answer to that question was supplied by a theory of the private prosecution; namely, that Pollari's sons had informed their father of Fishert's rowdyism and that Mr. Pollari, resentful over what had been done to his sons, got his revolver and lay in wait at the window to shoot Fishert. The fact that he had mistaken Humphrey for Fishert would not mitigate the seriousness of the accusation because error in identification cannot lessen the offense of murder, once premeditation and willfulness are established. The theory had flaws, but in the hands of an able and vigorous prosecutor it could be, and was made to sound, very convincing.

So that the jury might more easily reconstruct in their minds the scene of the fatal night's encounter, I had photographs taken of the Pollari home to introduce at the trial. The abode was a crumbling, broken-down old brick structure in an alley of ramshackle habitations. It possessed no modern comforts and but few conveniences. A pump standing in the yard furnished the only water available for domestic needs.

I made extensive inquiries in the neighborhood about Frank Pollari and learned to my great encouragement that he enjoyed an excellent reputation for being a peaceful, sober, and law-abiding citizen.

Then came the trial. A murder trial. In all the dramatic phenomena of civilized society, none can surpass in human interest the spectacle of a murder trial. And for sufficient reason. A man's life is in jeopardy. And on defense counsel rests the harrowing responsibility of holding off the grim approach of the executioner.

Judge Long of Clearfield County is presiding in Courtroom No. 4 of the Allegheny County Courthouse. Frank Pollari stands in the gray light of the morning falling through the large windows while the clerk intones: "Are you guilty or not guilty of the charge of murder wherewith you stand charged?" Pollari does not understand the words. All he did was to defend his home, and now he is charged with *murder*. Bewilderment is in his eyes, fear is written deep into his ashen countenance. What must he do? What must he say? I stand up and answer for him: "Not guilty."

The clerk now asks: "How will you be tried?" The reply to this question must be spoken by the defendant personally. It is a formula coming down the centuries from the early Anglo-Saxon trials. Pollari stands in frozen muteness. The clerk whispers to him the response word for word—and word for word he stumblingly repeats: "By— God—and—my country."

Perhaps the law is not so brutal after all, because the clerk now says to the prisoner: "And may God send you a just deliverance."

The prisoner may now sit down. He is trembling like a leaf. I am nervous too, but fortunately I have a way of keeping all evidence of tremors on the inside.

Then comes the awesome procedure of selecting a jury. The clerk calls out: "Mary Rogers." A round-faced, blue-eyed woman advances to the witness chair. I hope we can retain her as a juror because round-faced people are supposed to be sympathetic and tenderhearted. The prosecuting attorney, James Raherty, questions her:

"Mrs. Rogers, do you have any conscientious scruples against capital punishment?"

"I do not understand your question."

"If the evidence convinces you that the defendant is guilty of murder in the first degree and merits the death penalty, would you on your oath return such a verdict?"

"I don't believe in capital punishment."

And the juror is excused.

The next person called is a round-faced man, Evan Miller.

"Mr. Miller," the prosecuting attorney asks, "do you have any conscientious scruples against capital punishment?"

"No."

"Have you formed any opinion on the guilt or innocence of this defendant?"

"No."

"The Commonwealth accepts the juror."

Now I examine the same juror. He favors capital punishment, and this runs counter to the supposed rule that round-faced people are opposed to the death penalty. Still he seems to have a kindly eye, and since only those who approve of capital punishment may sit on a murder case, there is no use in challenging him solely on that ground. I am only entitled to twenty peremptory challenges and I must not squander them, or I might find myself at the end compelled to accept a bad-looking juror (from the standpoint of acquittal) because I will have used up all my challenges. So I question him:

"Mr. Miller, are you married?"

"I am."

"Do you have a home of your own?"

"I do."

"Do you have any children?"

"Six."

I announce that I will accept the juror. Even though he would under certain circumstances vote to send a man to the electric chair, I doubt that as a home-owner and a father of six children he would, in this case, vote for a guilty verdict. Still the prosecuting attorney thinks Miller, under the circumstances, will vote for a guilty verdict. And that is how we try to outwit each other. Who is the better judge of a human countenance?

In a day and a half we have selected the jury of twelve. And now, collectively sworn, they are to remain together until the eventual verdict is rendered.

The trial is under way. My client and I sit at a large table facing the jury box with its twelve citizens: eight men and four women. I look for tenderness in their eyes, some expression which I can interpret to mean they will listen with compassion to the story of an abused poor old man on trial for his life. But this indeed is a strange observation. The prosecuting attorney has chosen these same twelve people because he believes he sees in their eyes a stern expression, an expression which he interprets to mean they will deal severely with that crotchety old misanthrope who shot down a defenseless boy. What a world of difference a point of view makes.

The people in the jury box do not seem unkind to me, yet neither do they offer a guarantee that my client will have an easy time of it. However, their countenances are open. I see no prejudice written there. The faces of these jurors, like their hearts, are untouched parchments on which it is up to me to write the words of deliverance: "Not guilty." Silently I utter a prayer for strength and wisdom which will guide me in writing these words.

On the Commonwealth side of the counsel table sit the trial assistant district attorney, private counsel for the prosecution, and three county detectives.

William Coleman, veteran criminal lawyer, volunteered to sit at the table with me to offer advice. Undoubtedly his assistance would have been invaluable, but I suggested that the spectacle of a little army of prosecutors on one side against the aged Pollari and his young counsel on the other side would perhaps produce a psychological sympathetic appeal to the jury in our favor. He agreed.

I had another reason for fighting the case unassisted. I worked better alone. When two or more counsel try a case together there is the constant inclination to confer and consult as to questions to be asked and strategy to be followed, and thus the principal lawyer loses initiative. Then co-counsel is frequently breaking into a line of questioning the principal lawyer is developing, or he is whispering suggestions which derail the speaking lawyer's train of thought. The biggest fault in multiple counsel, however, is that it divides responsibility. When I am confronted with an important task I do not fear accountability because I am thus compelled to do my best.

As Jerry Fishert had been the ringleader of the gang which had broken into Pollari's home, so also was he at the trial the spearhead of the Commonwealth's case. He testified that on the night of the shooting he entertained no thought of harming Pollari and that he was peacefully standing in Mulberry Alley with Clayton Humphrey and his companions when Pollari shot through his window.

Immediately after I had been retained for the defense I had called on Jerry Fishert in the Allegheny County Jail, where he was being held as a material witness by the Commonwealth. I cross-examined him about that visit:

"I visited you in jail, did I not?"

"Yes, you did."

"At that time you related a story quite different from the one you are telling now, didn't you?"

"No, I didn't."

"Well, look at this transcript of our conversation made by a stenographer. I call your attention to this statement: 'Clayton was there in the doorway when the shot was fired.' Did you not say that?"

I handed him the transcript. He studied the page closely, shifted about on the stand, and then said: "Well, maybe I did say that, but that isn't the way it happened."

"Didn't you want to tell the truth?"

"Yes, I did."

"I didn't frighten you in any way, did I?"

"No."

"You were entirely free to speak as you wished, weren't you?"

"Yes, but I was a little excited."

"Well, are you excited now?"

"No."

"Well, just how did the shooting take place?"

"Just the way I'm telling you now."

"So that when only you and I and the stenographer were present you were more excited than you are today in this courtroom with hundreds of people present?"

"Well, I didn't think it meant so much when I was in jail."

"Do you want to tell us that you were careless with the facts even though we were discussing a matter of vital importance and our discussion took place only two days after the occurrence—when your memory was fresh?"

"Yes, sort of."

"The fact of the matter is that when you were in jail you were telling the truth, but after you were released and you talked the whole affair over with your companions you felt that you wanted to adjust your story to fit in with theirs. Isn't that right?"

Fishert bridled. I pressed him:

"Am I not correctly sizing up the situation for you? Isn't that what happened?"

"I don't know what you are talking about, but I have the right to protect myself."

"And that is your idea of protecting yourself? By agreeing with your cronies to tell one identical story, even though it may destroy an innocent man who was protecting his home?"

Raherty strenuously objected. "If the Court please, Mr. Musmanno is going far beyond what is allowed in cross-examination. He is arguing with the witness, he is giving opinions of his own, he is——"

The judge intervened: "Yes, Mr. Musmanno, your question is argumentative. I sustain the objection."

By this time Fishert was sullen, evasive, and finally refused to answer all questions. I dismissed him with a curt "That's all!"

Raherty again took Fishert in hand and tried to rehabilitate his story, but the witness's credibility had by this time been considerably damaged. At least I hoped so.

The prosecution called four other members of the gang, and they emphatically insisted Humphrey was standing in the street when the fatal shot was fired. I could not budge them in cross-examination.

Still I had high hopes that when Pollari testified he would completely win over the jury with his simple and artless account of what had really happened. When he would relate how he had been attacked in his own home by a band of ruffians, I was certain the prosecuting attorney would not stride so cockily as he was now striding.

In his direct examination Pollari made an excellent impression on the jury. I noted that when he described how he had been manhandled in his home by people who were violent strangers several of the jurors whispered to their neighbors in a manner which suggested to me that they were sympathizing with the accused. However, when Raherty began his cross-examination, Pollari fell into a confusion which almost approached panic. The composure which he had maintained throughout the direct examination escaped him and he seemed as unstable as his little fruit cart might be amid a stampede of automobiles and trucks. The rumble of the prosecutor's powerful voice, the twelve pairs of eyes regarding him steadily from the jury box, and the hundreds of eyes in the courtroom studying him like some rare curiosity completely unsettled and unnerved him. In a storm of rapid-fire questions as to his exact position when the fatal shot was fired, Pollari hesitated, and Raherty made the most of his fright-laden hesitation.

When the skillful cross-examiner had finished with his bewildering fusillade of questions, he had Pollari asserting that he was lying on the floor at the time he pulled the trigger, which, if true, contradicted Pollari's main defense; namely, that he was retreating up the stairs when he fired in self-defense.

I knew that in his summation to the jury Raherty would make capital of this contradiction. He would argue that if Pollari lied on this most vital point in the whole case—where he was at the moment he pulled the trigger—the jury could assume that he had lied in all other matters, and particularly on the most important controverted point of all, the whereabouts of Humphrey at the time the shot was fired. I noticed that during the prosecutor's bombardment of the defendant on the latter's inconsistencies, several of the jurors averted their gaze when I looked at them. This was a bad sign.

As Pollari stepped down from the witness stand, my hopes stepped down with him. As he slowly made his way back to the counsel table I saw a phantom walking beside him. That phantom, made up of all my fears and apprehensions, seemed to be telling the jury the verdict they should return. "Guilty! Guilty!" said the phantom.

I did not sleep that night. In fact I had had very little rest throughout the trial. For eight days I lived in the courtroom and in my office. Each night I reviewed the testimony of the day, considered the strategic situation with regard to witnesses possibly to be called, and prepared trial briefs on points of law which might come before the Court for argument. It happened several times during the trial that I was still working at 2 A.M. and thus, with the last streetcar for Stowe Township having already departed, I reverted to the floor for a bed.

On the last day of the trial I resolved I would get home for a good night's rest so as to be completely fresh and alert for my address to the jury. I boarded the one o'clock trolley, but I was so exhausted that I fell asleep at once and was carried four miles beyond my stop. I then had to walk back to my home, arriving there about 3:30. At seven, unrefreshed and unrested, I was again on the streetcar on my way back to the courthouse.

However, once I entered the courtroom, all physical weariness disappeared. It is incredible the quantity of punishment the human body can stand without collapse. Let the cause be vital enough, and the battalion of nerves, like Victor Hugo's Old Guard, will never surrender.

But later in the day, as I rose to address the jury in that final effort to save Frank Pollari, I hoped that my voice would not betray the anxiety which was gnawing at my soul. This was a case which should not—must not—be lost. This case demanded an absolute acquittal, and yet if the jury believed the Commonwealth's contention, Pollari was doomed. And if doomed, the fault would be mine because it was my job to make it diamond clear, beyond the possibility of even the shadow of a doubt, that this was an out-and-out self-defense case—which of course it was.

"Ladies and gentlemen of the jury," I began, and then I stopped. I did not have myself wholly in hand. I paused to recruit my determination and then slowly resumed: "The verdict you are to render in this case can be a farewell to the defendant as he departs on one of three journeys." I paused again. "Your verdict can start the defendant, this old man, on that 'last long mile' from which there is no return; it can send him down the river to that grim pile where men lose the name of men; or it can order him home—free. I shall ask you, members of the jury and lovers of home, to give back to this poor old man the keys to his home. Send him back to the home he defended, return him to the home he protected for his children, direct him to the home from which he should never have been taken.

"Who is Frank Pollari? In all truth, he is not a person of any consequence as contemporary history calculates and appraises.

"In the broad scheme of life he plays a small and insignificant part. But yet, on that broad plateau of character, where there is no distinction between the rich and the poor, between the celebrated and the obscure; on that plateau of honesty, which is none too crowded, Frank Pollari occupies a place worthy of honor and respect.

"He came to this beloved country of ours thirty-five years ago. He toiled in the mills until the heat of the furnaces he tended and the glare of the white-hot steel he shepherded broke his health. He was a man of family and there were many mouths to feed. Without education or capital he turned to one calling which required neither. He became a small fruit peddler. He peddled his wares from house to house, supplying the housewife with that little order of fruit for the breakfast table, for the children, for the sick relative and the aged parent. Up with the dawn, he appeared each morning at the Fruit Produce Yards, picked up his supply of fruit for the day, and from there pushed his handcart rumblingly over the cobblestones to the residential sections of the city several miles away.

"But since May 1 the rumble of this pushcart has been stilled. The hello-ing cry of 'Fresh fruit! Fresh fruit!' has died away. The familiar figure of the fruit man is no longer seen in those sections where he was known so well. Since that fateful day Frank Pollari has been held tightly in the merciless clutches of the law—and today he looks to you for deliverance." I walked over to Pollari sitting meekly at the table and placed a hand on his shoulder. "You see Frank Pollari here as he has always been seen during these long years in America— humble, timid, unassuming.

"What has Pollari done that he should be here on trial for his life? Reflect, my friends, what *has* he done? And in that reflection, prepare to soothe the shock which must inevitably come to your sense of justice. Frank Pollari is here because he sought to defend his home!

"Defend his home!" I repeated, lifting my voice as well as my arms as I returned to the jury rail.

"Members of the jury, is defending one's home in America a crime? And if so, when did that startling change come about in our jurisprudence?

"My friends, the defense of one's home is perhaps the most sacred, as indeed it is the most fundamental, right in organized society.

" 'Every man's home is his castle.' Sir William Pitt, after whom our revered city of Pittsburgh is named, declared in a speech in the English House of Commons: 'The poorest man may in his cottage bid defiance to all the force of the Crown. It may be frail: its roof may shake; the wind may blow through it; the storms may enter, the rain may enter—but the King of England cannot enter; all his forces dare not cross the threshold of the ruined tenement.' What right, then, did a gang of hoodlums have to enter this defendant's home at one-thirty in the morning—a mob of drunken ruffians—to enter to do violence—to enter it, according to their own stories, 'to demand satisfaction'? What satisfaction? And from whom? What authority had they to demand satisfaction from anybody? If they were aggrieved, they had the law to turn to for redress of their grievance."

It was late afternoon, and the fading light of day falling on the jury box enveloped it in a lambent aura which softened its outlines and somehow brought it closer to me. All nervousness left me. Without any lessening of the realization of the grave responsibility which was mine—the responsibility of a man's life—I nonetheless felt a freedom of expression and an exaltation of spirit which had not been with me from the beginning of the trial.

"Members of the jury, the Commonwealth contends that Pollari fired from a second-story window at Humphrey standing in the middle of the street. If you can seriously believe this, then you must throw to the winds all reason; you must abandon all logic; you must cast away all common sense and human observation.

"There must be a cause for every human behavior, and before the Commonwealth can convince you that Pollari shot from the second-story window, it must show *why* he would do this. Pollari did not know Humphrey. Why would he aim at him? Why would he shoot him?

"The Commonwealth asks you to *assume* that Carl Pollari, the defendant's son, told his father about the altercation he had had with Jerry, but you cannot adjudge a man's life or a man's liberty on *inferences* or *imagination*. The dance ended at 1 A.M. The invasion and shooting occurred at one-thirty. Carl was not at home between one and one-thirty. His presence elsewhere has been accounted for. Will the Commonwealth argue that Frank Pollari is presumed to be clairvoyant and that in some occult manner he learned what happened at the dance?

"Because the autopsy revealed that the course of the bullet in Humphrey's body was downward, the prosecuting attorney argues that this corroborates Fishert's testimony that Pollari fired from the second-story window at Humphrey standing in the street. Mr. Raherty deliberately set out to confuse Pollari on the witness stand. And after an hour's bombardment he succeeded, and I trust he shall never feel proud of what he did. He so confused and perplexed the defendant that Pollari said he was on the floor when he fired the revolver; all this so that Raherty could argue to you that Pollari was not telling the truth, because if he really was on the floor when the shot was fired, the bullet could not have taken a downward course. But keep in mind, members of the jury, that in a contest of wits between the veteran of the Bar, the trial district attorney, and the frightened, bewildered fruit peddler—the first time in court, the first time called upon to defend himself in a verbal duel with a highly intelligent, shrewd, experienced duelist—keep in mind that in such a contest the district attorney was bound to win. He thrust his rapier of cross-examination at Pollari with such a bewildering succession of strokes that Pollari was lost in the maze. But the truth of the matter is that although Pollari was knocked down he had regained his feet before he fired. He was retreating and endeavoring to climb the stairs when he shot downwardly. This is how it happened."

I seized the gun and acted out the entire scene, even to the extent of falling to the floor, struggling to my feet, retreating up the stairs (climbing the witness stand for this simulation), and firing; that is, pulling the trigger of the empty gun.

"That, my friends, is why the course of the bullet was down," I resumed after regaining my breath from the exertions of the demonstration. "Did Pollari shoot Humphrey from the window? He would have had to be an expert pistol shot to hit a target at that distance, pulling the trigger only once, and there is no evidence that he had had any training with a pistol.

"Who is the real culprit in this case, members of the jury? It is Jerry Fishert, the man who refused to see he was not wanted. Jerry Fishert it was who lured poor Clayton Humphrey to his death. Jerry Fishert it was who assembled the gang to make war on the defendant's home. Jerry Fishert it was who punched the defendant in the face and kicked him in the stomach.

"I assert here that Jerry Fishert is as accountable for the death of Clayton Humphrey as if he had pulled the trigger of the gun. On his head will rest for all time the moral responsibility for that boy's untimely death.

"For the pathetic taking away of Clayton Humphrey I have only the deepest sympathy. No one regrets that tragedy more than the defendant or myself. But the man who made Humphrey's premature death possible was not Pollari but Jerry Fishert. He is the one who should answer to Mr. and Mrs. Humphrey for the empty chair at their fireside. . . .

"Members of the jury, before I finish, I am impelled to say a word about Lena Pollari, the defendant's wife, who has been stumblingly carrying the heavy cross of a family's burdens for seven months. In freeing the defendant you will also lift the crushing weight from her almost broken back. Ever since the catastrophe of May 1 she has been the breadwinner, the beast of burden of that family, taking care of her children by day and scrubbing floors by night.

"By your verdict, ladies and gentlemen, take the scrubbing brush from her water-soaked hands, lift her from her knees, reveal to her that the fountain of the milk of human kindness has not dried and withered, bring a smile to those lips which have forgotten how to smile.

"I will be frank to say that if it is possible for a jury to convict in a case of this character, then we will not know what to do when the monster of the night breaks into our homes. If we hesitate to defend ourselves, we may be murdered, and if we fight the beast who is seeking to destroy us and those we hold dear, we will be accused of crime. I do not believe you will impose upon American lovers of home and family any such dilemma. . . .

"The home of which we speak in this case is not a palace. It is not a country estate with broad lawns and neatly trimmed hedges. It is not an imposing mansion set back from a well-paved boulevard, with a grandiose drive and impressive entrance. I have seen some jails which were far more comfortable as human abodes than this house. We have here something that is but a little better than a hovel, a dwelling without modern conveniences, a dwelling with its water supply, like the well of old, out in the yard. But as poor as it may be, ladies and gentlemen, it is Home. . . .

"We are close to the Christmas season. Soon each one of you with your family will gather round the Christmas tree to exchange presents of love and devotion. Soon you will sit down to the festive board to enjoy the good things the holy Christmas season brings.

"In the humble Pollari home with its three rooms there will be no tinsel-decorated Christmas tree, there will be no shining toys for the children, there will be no sumptuous repast. But it is within your power to make it Merry Christmas for them just the same. You can offer them peace and contentment. It is within your power to give to that family the most wonderful Christmas tree in all the world; the liberty of their father and the liberation of their mother from the cross of agony they are bearing.

"Members of the jury, the case is now in your hands, and we eagerly, anxiously await your verdict of not guilty. As those two words fall from the lips of your foreman, they will sound like the golden tinkle of a Christmas bell to the heart of a lonely child. Make life more precious, our homes more secure, and bring happiness to this good man's heart with those two musical and magical words—'not guilty'!"

Raherty followed my summation with a blistering speech for conviction. He seized upon my reference to Christmas and shouted:

"Defense counsel talks about Christmas at Pollari's home. How about Christmas at the Humphrey home? What kind of a Christmas do you suppose they are going to have? Their boy is gone; he will not be there at the fireside; he will not be there to receive or confer presents. And it will not be only this Christmas but for every Christmas that follows. These good people, Mr. and Mrs. Humphrey, sitting here in the courtroom, will remember every Christmas what you have done to them. Give them something to be cheerful about at Christmas. It is because of what Pollari did that they will have that empty chair. Treat Pollari as he treated Humphrey——" and so on, with a flinty appeal for vengeance.

No opportunity was afforded me to say in reply that the jury could not restore to the Humphrey parents their boy; and if the Humphrey family had an empty chair, whose fault was it? If Humphrey's attack on Pollari, spurred on as it was by Fishert, had not been thwarted, there might have been an empty chair at Pollari's.

The jury got the case at five-thirty. They were taken to supper and returned to their deliberations at seven. I did not leave the courthouse. Judge Long, seeing me waiting around like a lost soul, called me into his chambers to ask why I seemed so distressed. I said that I thought Raherty's speech was a very effective one.

He said: "But it wasn't as effective as yours. Do you know that every woman on that jury is with you?"

"Do you think so? How do you know?"

"By the way they looked at you and your client. I could see that many times as you were speaking they were in tears."

What an extraordinary phenomenon is this business of tears. You listen to words or read them. They are only words. They do not collide with you, and yet they can be as effective as blows. The human race will always endure in dignity and honor so long as there can be tears. Tears are shed only for the good, never for the bad; tears flow because of ideals which are either being glorified or shattered, exalted or threatened with destruction. That gentle rain of the soul falls when one beholds overwhelming beauty, outstanding purity of character, a demonstration of love, pitiful injustice, or a sacrifice being made for the eternal principles of righteousness and justice. And so into my heart trickled a few cool drops of reassurance because the four good women on the jury had shed a tear for poor Frank Pollari, who needed sympathy, and for poor Mrs. Lena Pollari, who thirsted for compassion.

At eight-thirty my heart started like a bell ringing in the middle of the night. A tipstaff announced that the jury was ready to report its verdict. Deputy sheriffs hurried to the county jail to fetch the defendant; principals and spectators hastened to seats and standing places of vantage. I sank at the counsel table, a riveting machine of anxiety pounding in my chest, my forehead exuding alternately cold and hot sweat. Poor Pollari, sitting beside me, asked what I thought. I placed my hand on his shoulder and told him not to worry. I did not explain the reason why he shouldn't worry: at that moment I was worrying enough for the whole human race.

The jury filed in like twelve spirits from another world. I studied their countenances for a sign—a sign! What was it? Guilty or not guilty? Happiness or despair? One of the ladies caught my agonizing inquiry. An expression of surprise formed on her face, as if it said: "Why are you worrying?" Then she smiled. God bless you, lady. I shall never forget that smile. It was a rose cast upon a sea of torment. I know she would not have smiled unless there was good news for me. But could it have been a smile of condolence? No. The corners of her mouth were curved upward, her eyes were lighted.

The clerk is now questioning the jury: "Members of the jury, have you agreed upon a verdict?"

"We have," the foreman replied.

"Prisoner, stand up."

Pollari stands up unsteadily, his face plowed with years of hardship and trouble. His eyes plead.

"And how do you find the defendant—guilty or not guilty?"

"Not guilty," the foreman answers.

Mrs. Pollari embraces her husband in a scream of joy. This is followed by another scream—a wail of despair.

Mrs. Humphrey's cry of anguish struck away some of the sweetness of my jubilation, but nothing could still the hymn of gladness in my breast as I realized that liberation at last had come to poor Frank Pollari.

I returned to my office, as I did after every event, but my excited spirit would not sit down at the desk with me. I attempted to read mail which had been neglected during the trial, I tried to study the *Advance Reports*, but I could not adjust myself to routine. And that evening I learned something new. When you are happy, rejoice; when your heart is bursting with gladness, sing; when your soul spreads its wings for flight into the upper strata of ecstasy, soar. Let routine go, let drudgery escape, let happiness with flaming banners parade through your soul.

I dropped all papers, locked my desk, and started for home, to which I should have galloped on the steed of joy immediately after the verdict. As I dashed out of the Commonwealth Building, however, my thoughts and my steps instinctively headed for the courthouse, and in a moment of whimsey I followed them.

It was a cold and clear night, but the wintry air set my blood to tingling with cozy warmth. Arrived at the courthouse square, I drank in the rugged beauty of our Temple of Justice. To the extent that architecture is capable of imparting a mood, the Allegheny County Courthouse is a Magna Charta in stone. Silhouetted against a moon-filled December sky, with its dominating tower casting an awesome shadow across Grant Street, its castellated walls and massive arches symbolized the sturdiness and the majesty of Law through the ages. Next to it and connected with it by a stone span called the Bridge of Sighs rose another gray pile, the Allegheny County Jail. There was a time when hangings were conducted in the yard just beyond the high granitic wall. How many had crossed over that Bridge of Sighs never to return? Had I lost my case today, my client would have traversed that melancholic span into the darkness and the gloom of that ever-grim and ill-slumbering prison.

What were its occupants thinking if they looked through their barred windows at that resplendent moon riding high in the skies? And soon the bright star of Christmas would be suspended in the heavens. How many would be home to see that star gleaming at the crest of a glowing-green Christmas tree? As if in crystallization of my thoughts, the air now filled with swirling snowflakes, enveloping the courthouse in delicate white drapery. Through the dancing lacy curtains I perceived two figures, strangely familiar, walking arm in arm about the sheeted castle. They seemed in a daze. I walked up to them. They were Frank and Lena Pollari! The poor old dears. They could not believe that their trial had ended and that they were free to go home unpursued and unhaunted by the mysterious forces of the law.

Crime takes its undoubted toll from organized society, but society also at times descends with a heavy hand on the poor and unoffending. Frank and Lena Pollari were overwhelmed with the great good fortune which had come to them—liberty. And yet they had been awarded only what they were entitled to under the laws of God, the nation, and the state. I hailed a cab and took them to their little crumbling domicile, now home again. Mrs. Pollari said she wanted to buy a Christmas present for me. I implored her not to do this, emphasizing they needed their pennies for things far more vital than a gift for me. Mrs. Pollari observed: "I would sell my eyes to buy a present for the one who helped us in our hour of great need." My throat knotted like an oak tree.

I boarded a streetcar and headed toward my own home and the paradise of a warm bed and felicitous, dreamless dreams. Sleep I needed and wanted more than all the wealth in the world. Anxiety had robbed me of rest for two weeks. Now I could luxuriate in the garden of sweet nothing. I had done a job well and I had been rewarded with victory. What could be sweeter? I climbed into bed as physically exhausted and happy as a baseball pitcher who has pitched a triumphant twenty-inning no-hit game. I closed my eyes in ecstatic anticipation of the shooting moons which precede the delicious falling off into unconsciousness, but the moons did not arrive. I opened my eyes and discovered that I was really wide awake. I was too happy to sleep, and I thought how strange is this earth of ours when one cannot sleep because of worry and then one cannot sleep because of joy. Nonetheless, it is a grand old earth and I would not exchange it for any other planet or combination of planets in the whole solar system.

Chapter XXI

REVOLVER SHOTS IN THE FOG

On SATURDAY morning, April 12, 1924, Joseph Valotta, in the custody of a deputy sheriff, descended the steps of the Allegheny County Jail to enter an automobile which was to take him to the Rockview Penitentiary. Outside the stone walls stood Mrs. Valotta and five children, the oldest thirteen, the youngest two. They had come to say good-by to husband and father as he started on the journey from which he would never return.

Valotta threw one arm around his wife's waist. He kissed her in farewell and she swooned.

The children could not understand what was happening. They watched the jail attachés carry their limp mother into the building while their father, streaming tears, was being rushed to the waiting automobile. As the car roared away, they saw a hand lifted in sad adieu. In the bright morning light a bracelet gleamed at the wrist. The car turned into another street and the hand and steel jewelry disappeared. At that moment the jail door clanged. The children stretched out their arms and cried: "Papa! Mama!"

The following night Joseph Valotta, his head shaved, his trouser legs slit for the application of the death-dealing electrodes, waited in his cell for dawn, which would mean for him the rising of the sun on eternity. In five more hours, when the light from above would gild the grimy skylight in Condemned Men's Row, a priest would call on Joe Valotta and, intoning Latin prayers, accompany him to the chair which always becomes a vacant chair.

In the still watches of the night a bell tinkled. Was this the premonitory sound of the afterworld call?

A deputy warden answered the telephone and on his sensitive ear fell these words: "This is Mrs. Pinchot calling. The governor has granted a reprieve in the case of Joseph Valotta. Cease all preparations for the execution. A telegram in confirmation follows."

Through Senator John W. Vickerman of Bellevue and Miss Emma Baker, a music teacher in Pittsburgh, Mrs. Pinchot had learned that new evidence had been uncovered in the Valotta case. She awakened her husband, who had retired, informed him of what had occurred, and the reprieve was made official.

This was the beginning of the fight for a man's life which continued unabated for two years, and then Mrs. Pinchot again stepped into the picture, as will be unfolded later. During that time Valotta received ten more reprieves, the case was heard by the Pennsylvania Pardon Board, it was taken into the United States District Court, it was passed upon by the Supreme Court of the United States—and Valotta once more entered the death house. Again the death warrant was read to him, again came the preparation for the head shaving, again followed the experimenting with the electrodes.

Who was this man and what had he done?

Up until October 29, 1922, this obscure person, unknown outside the immediate circle of his family and co-employees, was a worker in the Pennsylvania Railroad shops on the North Side, Pittsburgh, where he had worked for seven years. In July of that year, labor trouble had disturbed the tranquillity of that section of the city and violence flared, becoming progressively worse. Riots, beatings, and street fights so ruptured the peace of the community that even people who had no part in the controversy feared for their safety, especially at night, as they passed through the strike-torn region. In one dreadful fracas a passer-by had been critically injured by a flying brick. Joe Valotta, inquiring of a policeman for protection for himself and his family, was advised to go armed, and the policeman himself sold Valotta a revolver.

In spite of this protection, Valotta exercised the better part of valor by remaining home of nights. However, on the evening of October 29, the customs and obligations of religion and kinship required him to attend a christening in a relative's home on the periphery of the turbulent area. The ceremonies and festivities lasted until after midnight, and at about 1 A.M. Valotta, with a friend, Joseph Palermo, started home. It was a very dark night and a pea-soup fog swirled up from the banks of the neighboring Allegheny River. As the men walked along Armandale Avenue, discussing the possibility of employing for their Christmas celebration the same excellent musicians who had performed at the christening, they saw under an electric light at the intersecting Irwin Avenue four men, later to be described by a police magistrate as "street loafers and no-account men." The judge, who was to preside over the subsequent trial, said of these same men that they "were practically, the whole day preceding the tragedy and up into the night, freely indulging in moonshine whiskey and were in a quarrelsome, disorderly, and belligerent condition."

Noting the provocative and belligerent attitude of the four non-descripts, Valotta stepped off the sidewalk into the street in order to avoid them. They, in their turn, rushed toward him, and Valotta took to his heels. Overtaking him, they gestured menacingly as Valotta backed up against the wall of a house. As Valotta was later, at the trial, to describe the scene, one of the men "said that he want to see the end of me and said, 'I will kill you, and I will show you how to treat the guineas.' " With this the man lunged at him and Valotta whipped out his revolver and fired. The figure fell, and Valotta fled through the dark, fog-blanketed street.

Behind him he heard the clatter of pursuing feet. There was lightning in their steps and they were gaining. Without turning, Valotta pointed his revolver behind him and emptied the weapon. The four shots took lodgment in one body.

Tragedy.

That body was the body of a policeman, Officer Edward C. Couch. He had joined the pursuers without announcing he was an officer of the law. The bullet wounds were fatal.

The first man at whom Valotta shot, Thomas Hopkins, also died. Valotta was indicted on two charges of murder. In the ensuing trial he was convicted of murder in the second degree for the Hopkins death and of murder in the first degree for the Couch death. The first-degree murder verdict carried with it the death penalty.

I was not in Pittsburgh at the time of the Valotta trial, but when I returned from my self-imposed exile in Europe I learned of the intense public interest the case had aroused. William L. Curry, distinguished Pittsburgher and philanthropist, who was convinced Valotta was not a murderer, volunteered to aid the accused railroad worker, who was without funds.

Weather reports and the direct testimony of witnesses emphasized that, on the night of the shooting, visibility, because of smoke, darkness, and fog, was almost negligible. The defense argued that in every likelihood Valotta did not know that his most immediate pursuer wore a policeman's uniform.

The Commonwealth controverted this conclusion so that the issue in the various appeals, as it was at the original trial, rested on the question: "Did Valotta know that the man who was about to seize him was an officer of the law?" If he did, then he fired to avoid arrest and, in doing so, acted with willfulness, deliberation, and premeditation, which elements would support a first-degree murder conviction. If, on the other hand, he believed Couch to be one of his previous assailants, the resulting homicide could not rise to the gravity of first-degree murder. In fact, he would be entitled to an outright acquittal because in that case he would have been justified in firing in self-defense.

William L. Curry died in March 1925. Before passing on, however, he wrote a letter to his brother, Grant Curry, expressing the hope that in the event of his death before Valotta obtained his freedom the fight in his behalf should continue. Let cynics assert that true altruism has disappeared from the face of the earth, that there is no more self-abnegation, and no more genuine philanthropy in the heart of man. In my own career I can produce countless noble instances to the contrary. And in those illustrations of magnanimous selflessness I see the noble benefaction of the Curry brothers standing out with the luminosity of a lighthouse at sea. With no kinship or social relationship linking them to a man they had never seen, these two brothers gave of their efforts, money, and energies to save this obscure human being from the unjust doom about to descend upon him. They did this not for reward, not for glory, but for simple justice.

In the spring of 1926, at Grant Curry's invitation, I argued the Valotta case before the Pennsylvania Pardon Board, made up of the lieutenant governor, attorney general, secretary of the Commonwealth, and secretary of internal affairs. Three votes were needed for a favorable decision. I related the often-told story of the original aggression, of Valotta's flight, and of his unawareness, owing to fright and the fog-filled night, that a policeman was in pursuit. The Board was very attentive, but the secretary of the Commonwealth commented: "Nothing has been presented to alter the essential fact that Valotta shot a man in uniform so close to him that he left powder marks, after he had already unjustifiably killed one man. I have voted to send many a man to the electric chair for offenses much less than this one." The Board voted two to two, and the death sentence thus remained unchanged. The date of execution was set for June 28, six days hence. Only one hope remained—an appeal to the governor himself. He was at the time vacationing at his home in Milford, near the New York border, and in response to my urgent request for an opportunity to present my plea, he invited me to Milford.

And so, on a bright summer's day, I arrived at Grey Towers, the governor's magnificent estate, reflecting on the extraordinary and momentous experience which awaited me. I was to plead a cause, argue a case, present a lawyer's defense in behalf of a man's life in a courthouse which had the sky for its ceiling, the horizon for its walls.

Breathing deeply the fragrance of the luxuriant vegetation overflowing the estate in a green flood, I advanced over a tree-arched path to the Pinchot mansion, pressed a doorbell, and a young lady appeared. Handing her my card, she called "Governor!" and Pinchot, the picturesque Bull Mooser, political veteran and Forester in President Theodore Roosevelt's administration, appeared, as vital and enthusiastic as one twenty years his junior. Greeting me with a firm and cordial handshake, he escorted me through a large reception hall crowded with trophies of forest and stream. Chatting amiably about the weather and commenting on a job he was currently engaged in, the building of a fish dam on his estate, the tall and slender chief executive, with "handle-bar" mustaches, led me out to a vast lawn where he presented me to Mrs. Cornelia Pinchot. The fame of Mrs. Pinchot in Pennsylvania was next only to that of her husband's. Literary and oratorical, liberal in her political views, she was a personality that inspired admiration and contention in political circles. With her crown of flaming red hair which gave her a very striking appearance, she always drew enormous crowds at political rallies.

Reaching out with a warm handclasp, she said in a cultured and throaty voice: "Mr. Musmanno, you are here to work this afternoon, Gifford tells me, so you'd better have some lunch beforehand." A table was spread in the cool of a grove of trees, and as we munched at a delightful repast we discussed everything but the Valotta case. After dessert we moved to a comfortable bench and chairs overlooking an expansive rolling lawn which dropped to a deep wood whose crest touched the blue horizon beyond. On a small table close by rested papers, a pitcher of water, and a glass.

I was happy that Mrs. Pinchot intended to listen to my argument with her husband. I felt that, if I convinced either the governor or his wife, Valotta would be saved because, while the responsibility was solely the governor's, it was inconceivable to me that he would allow Valotta to be executed if his wife believed him innocent of murderous intent. I knew also that Mrs. Pinchot would listen as a man intent on justice and fair argument. Of course in my argument I addressed only the governor:

"Governor Pinchot, I am grateful for the opportunity you are here affording me in this open courtroom, as it were, and in this open-hearted manner, to present my case apparently without limit or reserve."

"You are right, Mr. Musmanno," he replied, "you are not limited in any way at all. Speak as you will and as you wish, and cover whatever phase of the case you deem it important to cover."

"Thank you, Governor." I rose to address him.

"Your Excellency, you cannot allow Joe Valotta to go to his death unless you are absolutely satisfied that he laid in wait and willfully, deliberately, and premeditatedly killed Couch, the policeman. Can it possibly be said from the known facts that Valotta laid in wait for Edward C. Couch, when we know that the entire tragic episode came and went like the flash of a dreadful dream?

"Did Valotta know who Couch was? If Valotta knew Couch was an officer of the law before he pulled the trigger, then he must have been insane and thus incapable of harboring criminal intent, because if there was sufficient time in which to analyze Couch's appearance in the darkness and recognize in him a representative of law and order, then there was sufficient time for him to conclude that here was a force which would rescue him from the ruffians who had just attacked him. If, on the other hand, he shot, knowing that Couch was a policeman, but under such a paralyzed state of fear that it was impossible for him to appreciate the significance of his act, the killing could not rise higher than second-degree murder, which in itself would bar the death penalty.

"But this type of argument is academic because there can be no doubt that Valotta did not know Couch was a policeman. It was testified at the trial that powder marks were distinguishable on Couch's face. This would establish that the shot which caused these powder marks was fired at close range. Admitting the close-range firing, it has then been argued that this brought Couch within Valotta's distinguishing vision. But the bullet which produced the powder marks was the one which was fired *last*, and it was the only one which resulted in powder burns. Thus the first three shots were fired while Couch was beyond powder-marking range, and the fourth one was fired after he entered that range.

"All the witnesses agree that the four shots were fired with convulsive rapidity. Considering the speed with which Couch was pursuing Valotta, it is obvious that by the time he received the fourth bullet (no matter how rapidly they were all fired) he had progressed —because of his momentum—some several feet beyond the spot where he received the first bullet.

"Whatever thoughts you assume Valotta had in his mind when he fired the four shots, you must agree that he had these thoughts before he fired the first shot, because certainly he could not have formulated a plan or put together any thought or idea in the chaotic moments which followed that first shot.

"Albert Brady, eyewitness, testified at the trial that Couch was ten feet away when Valotta fired the first shot, and he also testified that at ten feet the policeman was not distinguishable as a policeman. I have a statement here from Dr. F. H. Frederick, a very reputable physician in Pittsburgh, in which he says that on the night of the shooting he was driving by Irwin Avenue and Freedmore Street between 12:30 and 1 A.M., and that the fog at this point was so dense it was utterly impossible for him to recognize anyone within the distance of four feet."

Here Governor Pinchot interrupted with : "Mr. Musmanno, the only real question in this case is: What was Valotta's intention as he fired the shots which killed the policeman? If he realized that he had killed a man and that the policeman was about to arrest him for that, and he shot to avoid arrest, would not that make out first-degree murder?"

"Yes, Your Excellency, what you say is true, if Valotta had time in which to reason in that manner. Let us test the time element, Governor."

Here we took up the printed record of the trial, and by following the testimony we re-enacted, so far as the time element was concerned, the whole scene. In this re-enactment Mrs. Pinchot held a stop watch. We found that, from the moment Valotta appeared at the corner of Irwin Avenue and Freedmore Street (where he was first attacked) until the last shot was fired, only thirty-two seconds expired.

Continuing the argument, I now said: "Everybody—and this without exception—has agreed that up to the moment Valotta reached Irwin and Freedmore Street he had no criminal intention of any kind. Could he, in thirty-two seconds' time, change from a peaceful, law-abiding citizen into a first-degree murderer? And for what reason? What did he have to gain by shooting anyone? Has anyone suggested the slightest ulterior motive for this shooting? Did he have any purpose other than the one to save his life? And who would deny him the right of self-defense?

"A man cannot be a harmless, humble human being for forty years and then suddenly, in thirty-two seconds, become a stonehearted murderer. The judge who presided over the trial in the state courts and the judge who heard the case in the United States courts have

both stated officially that they believe Valotta entertained no homicidal intention when he arrived at the corner of Irwin and Freedmore
Street that night. Could this father of five children, this home-loving
man, this peace-loving citizen, become, in thirty-two seconds, a vicious
killer?

"But, Your Excellency, the first-degree murder conviction in this
case is even more unreasonable than that. The death penalty has
been imposed here because of what happened between the time Hopkins fell and the time Couch fell. Let us see how much time elapsed
between those two occurrences."

On the lawn we now marked out an imaginary Freedmore Street
and paced off on it seventy feet. Mrs. Pinchot again held the stop
watch. I ran seventy feet, simulated Valotta's movements as taken
from the record of the testimony, pulled the imaginary trigger four
times, and then said: "Stop!" Mrs. Pinchot said: "Six seconds."

Puffing somewhat from my exertions, I returned to where the
governor and Mrs. Pinchot were sitting, caught my breath, and resumed: "Governor, this whole episode consumed six seconds. Is that
sufficient time in which to premeditate and deliberate first-degree
murder as it is defined in the lawbooks? I believe I react as the normal
person reacts, but I must in all candor say to you that as I ran those
seventy feet I did not feel capable of doing much thinking at all;
and if I had not done my thinking *before* I started on that race, my
mind might have been a blank as to the purpose of it all. With all
our training and education, I wonder how many of us, placed
in the same situation Valotta found himself in, might not have done
exactly the same thing.

"Governor Pinchot," I said slowly and with great deliberation,
"Couch was a good police officer, an officer with considerable experience. I believe that as he pursued Valotta he realized that Valotta was
panic-stricken and that he was fleeing from what he believed to be
deadly peril. Couch could have shot Valotta as he ran, but he did not.
If Couch believed that Valotta had killed Hopkins in cold blood and
was fleeing to escape arrest, Couch would have shot him as he fled. He
had not only the right but the duty to shoot a fleeing felon. The fact
that he withheld his fire is almost conclusive proof that he did not
believe Valotta was an escaping felon. Perhaps if Couch could appear
before you today he would ask you to spare Valotta's life as he spared
it on the night of October 29, 1922, and for the same reason. Your
Excellency, I respectfully ask that you do not allow this unjust sentence
to be executed. I ask that you save the life of this humble worker,

this husband, this father, this citizen, this good man whose only crime is that, attacked without provocation, he attempted to save himself from a certain death, for the benefit of his wife and his children, whose very lives depended on his own."

As I finished, Governor Pinchot's expression betrayed no suggestion of his thoughts. "I am very grateful to you, Mr. Musmanno," he said, "for your trouble in coming to Milford to give us your views on this most interesting case."

"Thank you, Governor, I appreciate the opportunity you have afforded me to make the final presentation in this tragic affair." I gathered up my straw hat and brief case and bade Mrs. Pinchot and the Sage of Milford good-by. I got into the taxicab which was to take me to Jervis City, where I would board the train for the trip back to Pittsburgh. I felt somewhat pessimistic, but as the car rolled on toward the station I became downright gloomy. It was evident that I had failed and Valotta was fated to die at last. While it was only reasonable that the Governor should want time to reflect on what I had presented, and perhaps also time to review the printed record, it seemed to me that if he had been at all impressed with what I had said he would have so indicated, no matter how circumspectly and gently, even though holding his eventual decision in abeyance.

The execution date was only four days away. If the governor refused to intervene, his refusal would be the end of the line—and the end of Joe Valotta. There could be no more reprieves. Four years had already passed since the night of the shooting.

As the cab swung into the driveway of the Jervis railroad station, a station attendant came running up to ask of the driver: "Is Mr. Musmanno in this car?" Startled, I spoke up: "I am Mr. Musmanno." He said: "You are wanted on the telephone."

Who could want to telephone me here? Who knew I was here? Only the Pinchots. My heart tumbled like a concrete mixer. I ran into the station, and the attendant pointed to a telephone with its receiver off the hook.

With nervous hands I seized it and in a foggy voice said: "This is Mr. Musmanno."

"Oh, hello, Mr. Musmanno," a fine clear, resonant woman's voice was at the other end. "This is Mrs. Pinchot."

"Oh, thank you, Mrs. Pinchot. I am very much worried."

"I imagined you would be worrying, so I called you. I know you will better enjoy your trip back to Pittsburgh if you know that the governor has decided to save Valotta's life."

"Oh, t-t-th-thank you, Mrs. Pinchot. And pl-please thank the governor for me. I think you are both wonderful."

"Good-by, Mr. Musmanno," and I heard a gentle click at the other end. I stood there holding the receiver, trying to readjust myself to this new world, a world without the thousand-pound weight it seemed I had been carrying on my back for a thousand years. Joe Valotta, the obscure worker, the humble citizen, had at last achieved the right to live, a right which for four years had been cruelly menaced. Justice, which had been buffeted around in courtrooms and other tribunals, now smiled in victory from the greensward of Grey Towers. I felt a desire to shout at the top of my lungs and to throw my hat in the air. But the train chugged in to the station at that moment— and I started for home. However, when I arrived in Pittsburgh and boarded the streetcar for Stowe Township, I took off my straw hat and held it poised for action. Then, as we reached the Ohio River, I drew it back like an Olympic athlete about to hurl a discus. In the middle of Point Bridge, working up greater enthusiasm with each revolution of the car wheels, I let it go. It was a beautiful sight, that plate of straw sailing through the air and gracefully gliding into the gloaming surface of the river, taking with it all the cares of the now happily ended Valotta case.

Chapter XXII

MARY ROBERTS RINEHART'S GARDENER

WHEN a merchant quests for patrons he rents a building on a prominent thoroughfare, erects conspicuous signs, and arranges his wares enticingly in the windows. People stop, survey the alluring display, and enter the establishment. The merchant goes further: he advertises in the newspapers. Then he may also hire time on radio and television and, to the accompaniment of a fifty-piece orchestra, a crooning voice will infiltrate itself into your pocketbook for the purchase of Double Q furniture, soap, tooth paste, sports goods, etc., etc. And lo! a business is established.

But neither the ethics nor the nature of the lawyer's profession permits him to do this. He may not display in plate-glass windows (with smiling mannequin and resplendent wardrobe) the types of wonderful divorces he can procure for his patrons; he may not proclaim in newspapers that his breach of promise suits surpass, in fashion and fabric, the suits of any other lawyer in town; he cannot over the air waves announce that the key of his eloquence will unlock the jail doors holding prospective clients in durance vile.

How, then, does a lawyer establish himself? How does a reputable doctor acquire an overfilled waiting room? As a good wine needs no bush, so also a doctor or lawyer needs no paid trumpeting. Despite the millions of dollars expended yearly for advertising in every field of endeavor, there is no advertisement which can surpass that of a pleased customer, a satisfied client, or the encomiums of an enthusiastic spectator. A lawyer will never get to know all those who praise his name and boost his stock. Therefore, he should from time to time offer a little prayer of gratitude to the unknown boosters and the anonymous benefactors who invisibly hold a supporting hand to the ladder as he climbs from rung to rung toward an honored and evermore honored height in his profession.

I had such an Abou ben Adhem in the late Judge W. H. S. Thomson of the United States District Court of Western Pennsylvania. Before elevation to the federal bench, he had been defense counsel in the case of Commonwealth versus Angelo Jackson, colored gardener in the employ of the dean of murder-mystery writers, Mary Roberts Rinehart.

One can imagine Mrs. Rinehart's astonishment when she learned that murder, with which she supplied so much entertainment to her world of fiction readers, had become a gory reality, stalking into her very home. The man who daily brought her fresh roses from her own garden suddenly killed his girl friend and quickly found himself tried, convicted, and sentenced to hang. As Mrs. Rinehart had often fought through chapter after chapter for the life of an embattled fancy-created defendant, so also did she breathlessly follow Angelo Jackson's lawyer through the various courts of appeal and finally rejoice to see the faithful lawyer save a real human being—her own employee—on the last page just before the trap was to be sprung. Jackson's death sentence was commuted to life imprisonment.

Five, ten, fifteen years rolled by and the name of Mrs. Rinehart had become familiar to every playgoer and reader of mystery stories in the land. As she wove and unwove her gripping tales of crime, mystery, detection, trials, conviction, and expiation, her thoughts at times reverted to the unfictionized tragic story of her gardener who was immured in the Western Pennsylvania Penitentiary for life. Could not his case be reopened, even as she could with a pen cross out any chapter and rewrite it? Mr. Thomson was by now a United States judge and he prevailed upon a lawyer friend to seek the release of his aging client, but the effort failed.

Five more years passed and Mrs. Rinehart, with her husband, Dr. S. M. Rinehart, was vacationing in Hawaii, happy in this distant retreat where the lush vegetation, lung-filling breezes from the limitless expanses of the Pacific, and the soft, lilting music wafted to them on those breezes bespoke the contentment of peace, love, and freedom. Dr. Rinehart turned to his wife: "Mary, I could enjoy this earthly paradise with more of a feeling of abandon if we made one more attempt for Jackson's freedom." A letter went off that day to Judge Thomson, and within a month's time I was reading it in his chambers, to which he had called me, much to my surprise. "Mr. Musmanno, I'm writing to Mrs. Rinehart that I've recommended you for Jackson's attorney," he said.

Several weeks later I received a letter from Mrs. Rinehart in which she said that Judge Thomson had recommended me to her as "an able, energetic, and persevering young lawyer," and she wished me to take up the case of her former gardener, hoping that I might be able to free him from his life term in the penitentiary.

I plunged into an investigation of the case and was amazed to find that although the cooling rains of twenty years had fallen on the world since Jackson's crime, in Ross Township (the locale of the murder) the passions which had been stirred at the time of the original tragedy still flamed. In the community which had known the murder at close hand people spoke with excitement, rage, or compassion of events over which the grass of time had been growing for two decades. The friends of Gertrude Nichollis, the girl who had been killed by Angelo Jackson, still reviled Jackson and believed that for him the gates of the penitentiary should not swing open until the angel Gabriel blew his horn. Those who had testified in Jackson's behalf beat their breasts in asserting that a great injustice had been done an innocent man.

From the people I interviewed I reconstructed the story of that violent happening whose shadows still flickered in the light of today. Angelo Jackson was a big, strapping Negro who had had two jealous sweethearts, which fact in itself would suggest difficulties at the very outset. One of these, Gertrude Nichollis, warned Jackson that if he did not cease his attentions to the other woman, Lizzie Gans, she would kill them both. One day as Angelo Jackson was walking through the countryside enjoying an afternoon off from his duties, he met Gertrude, who was in a belligerent frame of mind. As they discussed the cause of her belligerency, which was the inevitable jealousy of a woman who enjoys only an estate in common in the property of a man's heart, Gertrude demanded from Angelo a promise that he cease paying attention to Lizzie. Jackson laughed. "Gertrude, I wants to tell you sumpin'—dis jealousy stuff nevah got nobody nothin' but heaps o' trouble. Ah's cravin dat you please stop talkin' dat foolish stuff."

"Dat's not foolish stuff I'm talkin'. Dat's de truf'."

"Gertrude, please go away."

"Lissen, man, is dat de way you all talks to yo' sweetheart—tellin' her to go away?"

"Ah don't mean fo' you to go away from mah life forevah. Ah just means, woman, dat you go away so Ah can get on home, get mah fancy clothes on, and den Ah'll come right back and calls on you all formal-like."

"Angelo, lemme tell you. You ain't gonna call on dis woman widout you fust tell me dat Lizzie is a dead pigeon so far as you is concerned."

"Dawggone it, woman, when you all talk datta way, you sho talks plenty of foolishment, yassah—and dat's a fact."

"Yes, man, but not so foolish as you's gonna look when Ah gits through with you."

At this point, from what I was able to see as the curtain lifted on that ingenuous dialogue of twenty years ago, Gertrude thrust her hand into the pocket of her jacket in a manner which suggested she carried a concealed weapon. Jackson whipped out a revolver and fired a shot, as he believed and intended, above her head. She was walking ahead of him and had reached a slight ascent in the ground at the moment the shot was fired and she now disappeared over the crest of that elevation. Jackson, according to his story, thought he had frightened her away and returned home. At midnight the police called at the Rineharts' to take away their gardener to book him on a charge of murder. The shot he had fired had inflicted a wound from which Gertrude Nichollis died several hours later. People who had lived in the neighborhood for decades told me, in answer to my questions, that the topography of the land had not changed during the last twenty years.

Dr. Rinehart came on from Hawaii to add personally his and Mrs. Rinehart's recommendations to my plea before the Pardon Board for Jackson's liberation. In my speech I pointed out that, while I did not minimize the seriousness of Jackson's act, I yet hoped the Board would consider the facts from Jackson's point of view. If he did believe, no matter how erroneously, that his life was in jeopardy, he had the right to act as he thought necessary to save himself. I unfolded the blueprint prepared by a civil engineer and demonstrated that because of the peculiar sloping of the land Miss Nichollis' death may well have been the result of an accident. When Jackson raised his arm he failed to take into consideration the imperceptible rise in the ground which brought the girl within the trajectory of his loose aim.

But over and above all that, I presented an argument which was unanswerable. Since there was no evidence whatsoever in the record to show homicidal premeditation on the part of Jackson, the crime of which he was convicted should not have risen higher than second-degree murder. And since the maximum punishment for second-degree murder was twenty years' imprisonment, which Angelo had already served, he was entitled to a pardon and immediate release.

As I pressed this point, the lieutenant governor, who was presiding, leaned over to talk to the secretary of the Commonwealth, and then to the attorney general and secretary of internal affairs. I paused while they held their impromptu conference, and then, noting that they seemed to be in agreement with what I had said, I quickly brought my argument to a close.

A week or two later I received the pardon for Angelo Jackson. With the awesome document carefully stowed away in my brief case I got into a car and drove to that rambling gray stone pile on the banks of the Ohio known as the Western Penitentiary. I told the warden the nature of my visit. He smiled and said that it would come as a great surprise to Jackson, who seemed to have abandoned all hope. The warden sent a guard for the prisoner, and Jackson appeared, swathed in heavy clothing and burlap bags to protect him from the sub-zero temperature of the penitentiary refrigerating room in which he was working. Already a huge man to begin with, the extra garments he wore made him a veritable super-giant. "Hello, Jackson," I said, extending my hand and maintaining at the same time a completely impassive reserve.

Jackson took my hand silently, and intently studied my features, trying to read what tidings I was bringing him. Were they good or were they bad? Huge drops of perspiration rolled down his massive countenance as he shook like an elephant approaching a frail bridge of whose security there was grave doubt. Suddenly he broke down sobbing. He could stand the suspense no longer. "Tell me, Mistah Lawyah, has you done brought me libahty? Ah sho would like to taste dat sweet taste o' libahty——"

There are but few joys in the life of a lawyer which can surpass the gratification of carrying into the mausoleum of a prison a piece of paper which will dissolve steel, move huge stone blocks, melt iron doors, and unseal the doom of one entombed for life. I rested my hand on Jackson's shoulder and assured him: "Yes, Jackson, it is my great pleasure to inform you that I have brought you liberty."

"Oh, de Lawd be praised," he sobbed over and over, unable to handle the immensity of the relief which was now his to enjoy.

Unclasping my brief case, I withdrew from it the pardon and read its contents to him in ponderous voice. When I came to the words, "and the said Angelo Jackson is hereby fully pardoned by the Commonwealth of Pennsylvania," the Goliathan prisoner broke into unrestrained weeping. His face swimming tears, he exclaimed: "Gawd bless you, Mistah Musmanno. Gawd bless Doctah Rinehart and his missus. Gawd bless ev'ybody. De Lawd is sho good. Hallelujah."

It took him several moments to compose himself, and then, his teeth shining with ivory brightness, he grinned. "Mistah Musmanno,

Ah's been waitin' a powahful long time for dis heah papah. You all knows dat when Ah fust come down heah, you all was jus' a little kid in shawt pants. Yessah—Ah done had to wait until you all growed up and went to school—den to high school and college, den to war, den to Philadelphy and away 'cross de ocean to Italy—yuh see, de Rineharts done told me all about you." He paused for a happy sigh and added: "But you all is here now, and I sho do 'preciate it."

"Jackson, I want you to know that I rejoice with you in your good fortune, and I can assure you that Dr. and Mrs. Rinehart are equally glad. Tell me, Jackson, now that you are free, what do you intend to do?"

"Well, Mistah Musmanno, Ah's gwine to do two things."

"What are they?"

"Fust, Ah's gwine to go back to good old South Carolin' on de ole plantation—and den, Ah's gwine to stay dere."

Chapter XXIII •

CLARENCE DARROW

AT THIS point, in illustration of the episode to be related in this chapter, I will project my narrative a year beyond the ending of the period covered by the story of the young lawyer. In December 1932 I debated the famous and grizzled veteran of the Bar, Clarence Darrow, at the Carnegie Music Hall in Pittsburgh. I opened my affirmative speech with the words:

> "What Webster was to the Senate, Disraeli to Parliament, Henry Ward Beecher to the pulpit, and Ingersoll to the lecture hall, that is what Clarence Darrow was and is to the courtroom. It is a privilege to be selected as his opponent in debate, and it will be a privilege for you to listen to him, because there will never be another Clarence Darrow."

The hall resounded with the applause of two thousand people who filled every available seat and spilled over into standing room. They all agreed there would never be another Clarence Darrow. As I look back upon that event in my life I wonder, considering the awe with which I regarded this triumphant warrior and the spell he almost cast over me by his presence, that I was able to emerge from the arena in which we battled with no greater emotional upset than the one about to be related.

The subject of our debate was: "Does Man Live Again?" with me upholding the affirmative. In the course of my main speech I declared: "Voltaire said: 'If God did not exist, it would be necessary to invent Him.' "

In his negative rebuttal, Clarence Darrow challenged the accuracy of this quotation and scornfully remarked: "Now it is strange how these wild myths get around about what some good agnostic believed or did not believe. Voltaire never said: 'If we did not have a God it would be necessary to create one.' What Voltaire said was, 'If we did not have a God, man would create one.' Which is entirely different."

Over one half of the audience vigorously applauded this refutation, and horror galloped up my spine. As the debate was extemporaneous and I had quoted Voltaire from memory, I shuddered at the thought I might have erred. Darrow's derisive accusation threw me into an intolerable dilemma. The celebrated lawyer was in effect charging me with misrepresentation. I was quite certain I had quoted correctly, but how could I prove this? It would not be enough for me merely to insist I was right. Darrow was an international celebrity. His fame clothed him with an impeccability which imparted immediate authenticity to his factual utterances. And then he was venerable with age, a fact which adds considerable to hero worship and respect. The larger part of the audience, without being disrespectful to me, would accept Darrow's version of the Voltairian quotation without bothering later to look it up to see what it actually was. It was imperative that I produce the quotation right there on the stage if I wished to avoid the imputation that I had innocently or purposely misquoted the French author.

Quickly leaving the stage, I called the Carnegie Library, which was only a block away, and asked the lady attendant who answered the telephone to send me at once any book containing the better-known Voltairian quotations. I hurried back to the stage at the moment Darrow was saying to the audience, which he was molding to his will as he had molded many a jury in his lifetime: "The first question my friend asked me was: 'There must have been a first cause, don't you believe that, Mr. Darrow?' I will say I don't know a blooming thing about it." He then shot a penetrating glance at me and asked: "Do you?" Startled, I nonetheless had sufficient command over my wits to reply: "I do!" But my thoughts were on that Voltairian book. Would it arrive in time, and when it arrived, would I be able to locate the embattled quotation?

Then, as Darrow continued with his scathing rebuttal, I caught sight in the wings of the stage of a young man advancing toward me with a book. I hastened toward him and took from his extended hand the desperately awaited volume. With heart in mouth, oblivious to what Darrow was saying or that two thousand people were watching me, I riffled the pages of the book and drew up, exultant, at page 77. There was the quotation! Exactly as I had delivered it. If someone had offered me ten thousand dollars for that book at that moment, I would have refused it. No one could place a monetary value on the sweetness of the moment which I anticipated, when, with the quotation in hand, I would be able to prove the integrity of my memory and at the same time pull the great Clarence Darrow down a peg or two.

When the time for my affirmative refutation arrived I strode to the rostrum with the assurance of a matador and slammed the book down on the lectern, opened at page 77. Then, like a blacksmith with all the strength he can muster when he is sure of both hammer and anvil, I struck hard:

> "Mr. Darrow has misquoted and garbled my words throughout this entire debate, and now he questions my quotation from Voltaire. Well, I can usually substantiate my quotations. In my first speech, I quoted from Voltaire, who said: 'If God did not exist, it would be necessary to invent Him.' Here is a book, published by the reputable firm of Macmillan Company, with which Mr. Darrow is familiar, and on page 77 we find this quotation from Voltaire: 'If God did not exist, it would be necessary to invent Him.' "

Even those who were Darrow die-hards joined heartily in the applause of those who favored my views, and as the music of approval flooded my ears and soul, I crossed over to Darrow's side of the stage and thrust the book before his eyes. His courtroom aplomb did not desert him. He glanced at the open page, shrugged his shoulders, and grinned. The audience broke into good-natured laughter and further applause.

Following the debate my opponent and I were invited by some civic leaders to the famous Duquesne Club for refreshments, and there, while I munched at a sandwich washed down with ginger ale and Darrow munched at a sandwich lubricated with draughts of straight bourbon, he held us enthralled with his views on the world in general and stories on courtroom experiences in his illustrious, dramatic career. Commenting on our debate of the evening, he had a word of praise for my holding onto the Voltaire quotation with "an iron-vise memory." He expatiated on the subject: "No lawyer can be an effective trial lawyer unless he naturally possesses or develops a retentive memory. The successful lawyer is one who in cross-examination can recall everything that the witness testified to in the direct examination so that he can trip him up on contradictions and inconsistencies. A good trial lawyer, when he rises to address the jury, must have the evidence stored in his brain like goods in a show window so that as he speaks he can select what he needs, to support and emphasize points in his argument."

The Darrow-Musmanno debate did not occur until several years subsequent to the episode which is the subject of this chapter, but, as already stated, I have anticipated it for the purpose of preparing the way for the story on how memory beat the district attorney.

It is a general rule of trial procedure, and particularly so in Pennsylvania, that in summing up his case a lawyer may not read aloud to the jury from the stenographic record of the trial, the theory being that the reading of any page might offer documentary importance to one phase of the case as against all other phases. I doubt the wisdom of the rule, but it exists and all lawyers are bound by it.

I was trying a case in which my client, Frank Woods, stood accused of bank robbery. One of the Commonwealth witnesses, a certain Maude Weaver, had testified about the defendant, but a dispute arose between the prosecuting attorney and myself as to what precisely she had said. He insisted that she had testified she saw the defendant the morning of the crime. I was positive she had not so testified and I determined to disprove my adversary's assertion in the most effective manner possible.

I obtained a copy of the stenographic transcript and took it home the night before the summations. I memorized all of Maude Weaver's testimony *ipsissimis verbis*.

The next day in my final speech to the jury I picked up the stenographic transcript, held it conspicuously before me, and said: "Members of the jury, Mr. Jones, assistant district attorney, has sought to have you believe that Maude Weaver said she saw the defendant on the morning of the crime, but I tell you she said nothing of the kind. I have her testimony here and I will read it to you."

"I object! Mr. Musmanno knows he is not permitted to read from the record," Mr. Jones ejaculated.

Of course I knew this, but I was merely preparing the stage. The judge affirmed: "Objection sustained."

"Very well," I said with an aggrieved air. "I will give the jury her testimony from memory."

Flinging the typewritten transcript along the table until it came to rest before Mr. Jones's eyes, I began to recite from memory the testimony of Maude Weaver, beginning at page 37, to which I specifically directed the assistant district attorney's attention.

With phonographic intonation I began:

"What is your name?"

"Maude Wilson."

"Where do you live?"

"167 Walston Street, Fair Oak."

"Do you know the defendant, Frank Woods?"

"I do, that is, I would say—I do——Of course, I don't know him personally but . . . that is, I don't know him personally, I only know him because of the trial, but if you mean——"

This is exactly the way the answer appeared in the transcript. I knew this because I had mentally photographed the answer as if it were a picture. Thus, as I recited the hesitations and the repetitions, mimicking the peculiarities of the witness, the jury recalled that that was precisely the manner in which the witness had testified. As if what I was doing required no effort at all, I went on:

"Well, tell us just what you do mean."

"Well, I mean that this man meant absolutely nothing to me. I saw him in the neighborhood but had never spoken to him."

"Did you speak to him that morning?"

"I never spoke to him."

"Well, what do you know about the case?"

I paused and explained: "At this point, members of the jury, you will recall that I objected, and the transcript will show it as follows," and I went on, continuing to quote from memory:

"Mr. Musmanno: If the Court please. I object to the questioning of the district attorney. His question should be more specific."

The Court: "Objection sustained."

"All right, tell us specifically what you know about Frank Woods."

Mr. Jones was following with incredible finger each word and line as I pronounced them. Without turning my head I lifted my voice to him: "Mr. Assistant District Attorney, you may now turn the page." I heard the angry flip of a page and a muttered: "Well, I'm a son of a gun——"

I continued from memory:

"I know this. That on the morning of the robbery his brother came down Violet Street looking very worried."

Leaning over the jury rail, I said to the jury: "Here I objected again, as the record will show:

"Mr. Musmanno: I object! What does his worrying have to do with the Court?"

The Court: "Objection sustained."

"Well, did Frank Woods ever talk to you about the case?"

"*Yes.*"

By this time the judge had obtained a copy of the transcript and was following my words with scarcely concealed amazement. The jury was now probably marveling more at what I was doing than at what I was saying. The courtroom audience looked on, astonished. I pretended that what I was doing was something that had to be expected in this kind of case. I continued from memory:

"*Yes, he did talk to me and he said that on the morning of the robbery he had passed the bank and had seen nothing unusual.*"

"*Was that on the morning of the crime that he said this?*"

Without looking around at the counsel table I said: "Now, Mr. Jones, will you please read to me what you see at the top of the next page?" The assistant district attorney exploded with: "I'll do nothing of the kind!" and banged the transcript down on the table.

"Very well, Mr. Jones, you don't need to be so unpleasant about it. I'll give it to you. Does it not say:

'*No, it was the morning after the crime. I didn't see him on the morning of the robbery*'?"

Now looking directly at my opponent, I asked: "Mr. Jones, does not that transcript before you show Miss Weaver saying: '*I don't believe that Frank Woods had anything to do with the robbery*'?"

Jones fulminated: "Mr. Musmanno, don't talk to me, talk to the jury!"

"I will talk to the jury, but won't you please look at the record before you? Did you not say: '*I move, Your Honor, to have her answer stricken from the record*'? And did not the Court reply: '*Motion refused*'?"

And now, once more facing the jury, I concluded:

"That, members of the jury, is what is stated in the book of testimony, but it was not necessary for me to recite it to you because I know that it is recorded in your memory as well as it is in mine. I ask for an acquittal of the defendant at the bar."

The jury obliged. I believe he was entitled to an acquittal, but even though innocent he may well have been convicted if I had not been able to demonstrate in a conclusive manner that the prosecution was seeking to send him to prison on a vehicle, a wheel of which was unreliable because of a defective memory.

Chapter XXIV

CORN MUFFINS!

IN EVERY group conversation which lasts for an hour or more, when the range of subjects is limited only by imagination and whim, two questions, without ceremony or introductions, always draw up chairs at the table of discussion; namely, (1) Which came first: the chicken or the egg? and (2) Is circumstantial evidence reliable? If a lawyer or judge happens to be in the talkfest, the second question is always addressed to him for authoritative answering. If I chance to be the person so interrogated, I sometimes relate an experience which happened to me during my student days in Washington.

I was breakfasting one morning in a cafeteria equipped with one-armed chairs. The right arm of such chairs is in effect a small table, and it is on this widened arm that one places his food. There is no left arm to this piece of furniture because the space which would be required for a left arm is given over to the right arm of the adjacent chair. For one who is alone, such an arrangement makes for pleasant and comfortable eating, because it allows freedom and space for one to enjoy his newspaper while at the same time partaking of his ham and eggs.

On this particular morning I had my newspaper unfolded—projecting diagonally toward my left—while I plied my knife and fork on the right. At one and the same time, in accordance with the good old American custom, I devoured newsprint and victuals. Suddenly, while lifting the coffee cup to my lips, I felt a sharp tap on my left shoulder. I turned and faced in the chair adjoining mine a rather large scowling gentleman who asked accusingly: "What did you do with my muffins?"

"Your muffins!" I exclaimed flabbergasted. "What do I know about your muffins?"

"Listen, young man, you are the only one who could have taken my muffins. They were here on the arm of my chair. I turned around only for a second, and when I looked again, they were gone!"

"Well, of all the nerve! Do you mean to calmly sit there and insinuate that I took your muffins?"

"I'm not calm, I assure you."

"Well, calmly or heatedly—it doesn't matter to me, you must be mad. I've a good notion to call the manager. Things have come to a pretty pass when one can't eat one's food in peace. Who are you, anyway, to make such an insane accusation?"

The spiritedness, not to say aggressiveness, of my reply must have confused or cowed the irritated and muffinless breakfaster, for he now said in a restrained tone: "Well, I may have been mistaken," but then, his astonishment and indignation flooding back, he added with acerbity: "Mistakes like that just don't happen. You were the only one around."

"Well, it's immaterial to me what you think. You certainly *are* mistaken. Why should I want your muffins? I have my own breakfast, haven't I?"

He glared back speechlessly and I went on to finish, with not too much enjoyment, the remainder of my meal. I paid my check at the cashier's desk and started up Pennsylvania Avenue, nettled and even angry over the amazing fusillade of which I had been the target. But as I walked along I began to see the humor of what had happened and even half laughed at the antics of the silly man who had sat next to me.

As I continued walking, consciously wiping away the annoying episode with the philosophical observation: "Well, it takes all kinds of people to make all kinds of people," I became aware of something bumping against my side. It was summertime and I was wearing a loose, lightweight patch-pocket coat. I felt a weight in my left pocket which I had not sensed prior to entering the restaurant. I stopped dead in my tracks, the blood freezing in my veins. Mentally I exclaimed: "No, it can't be!" Slowly I lowered my hand to my side and into the depths of my pocket. My hand came in contact with objects I had not known before. My fingers automatically clutched at them. Measuredly I brought them up like a deep-sea diver lifting treasure from the bottom of the ocean. In the convulsive clutch of my hand there stared at me two corn muffins!

I gasped in fear that at that very moment I would hear a condemning voice rasp: "So you didn't have my muffins, eh?" If my restaurant neighbor should appear, how could I possibly defend myself? Here was circumstantial evidence which was practically conclusive. Although innocent, I bore every evidence of guilt. Ceasing to breathe, my head swiveled on my shoulders as I looked around for my accuser. He was not in sight. I resumed the process of breathing.

But how did those wretched muffins, which I now wrathfully flung into the first trash can, get into my pocket? I mentally reconstructed the entire scene in the restaurant, and then the only possible solution of the enigmatic situation dawned. Evidently the newspaper which I had been reading during breakfast had become the unintending purveyor of the corn products to my pocket. In some unexplainable manner the upper edge of the paper had wedged itself under the muffins on my neighbor's plate, and in a moment of movement owing to some sudden twist of my body they had slid from the plate onto the inclined paper and coasted down the chute (made by the paper) into my patch pocket, at that instant wide open. Would such an explanation be believed in court?

Would the jury believe Philip Gabrielle when, despite the circumstantial evidence which avalanched him, he was in fact innocent?

Lucille Gabrielle lifted her eyes from her darning needles and looked up at her husband laboring at the dining-room table over long rows of figures. "Philip," she said, "have you not worked long enough? It is eleven o'clock. Don't you think you had better rest? You look so tired."

"I'm not tired at all," he returned, a smile, like the sun passing over a freshly plowed field, emphasizing the lines of care and exhaustion on his face. "Lucille"—and he rose from the table to kiss his wife affectionately— "we are at last successful. After ten years of hard luck, good luck is with us, I think to stay. We have paid off every indebtedness, we have liquidated the mortgage, and now for the last five months the store has been showing a net profit of three-hundred dollars per month, with every indication that it will increase."

"Oh, Philip, that's wonderful. Now we can let Adela take the art course, and we can enroll Sonny in the auto mechanics school at Armstrong's."

At this moment the telephone rang, as if a stranger were seeking to project an ear into the privacy of their conversation. "Philip," she remarked, nettled that an eavesdropping voice should even for a moment veil the picture of prosperity and promise which her husband had just revealed to her, "I believe that all telephone service should be shut off at the latest by ten o'clock, don't you?"

"Yes, that would be quite desirable, but you can never tell about an emergency," Philip replied as he picked up the receiver in the little alcove of their sitting room.

"Yes, this is the Gabrielle residence," Mrs. Gabrielle heard her husband say. Then from resentment at the invasion of their privacy, her sensations passed from curiosity as to who the caller might be, to incipient fright as she detected alarm in her husband's voice, and then to terror as she heard the one-sided conversation crescendo in excitement.

"What? . . . Who is this? . . . Are you sure? . . . The store is really on fire! . . . Have you called the fire department? . . . They are there now? . . . I'll be right over!"

The next day Mrs. Lucille Gabrielle, whom I had known from boyhood, came to my office and related with handkerchief to her eyes what had happened the night before—how an idyllic evening had suddenly smashed into catastrophic nightmare. Not only had their store building been wrecked and the whole stock with furnishings and equipment destroyed but—and at this part of her recital my visitor broke down into uncontrolled sobbing—her husband had been arrested and charged with starting the fire!

"Michael," she said, "I never thought I would have to come to see you for help like this. You must save Philip! He didn't do anything! He was at home when the fire started. Oh, how can they say he did this? Please save him, Michael!"

At the magistrate's hearing which followed three days later, the battalion chief, who had directed the fire fighters at the store, testified to finding gasoline cans in the basement of the building. (Gabrielle did not sell gasoline.) The agent of the insurance company which had insured the store and its stock of wholesale groceries, testified that Gabrielle had purchased insurance only three months before the fire and that the stock did not measure up to the monetary value set forth in the application. Counsel for the insurance company maintained that Gabrielle had kindled the fire so as to collect money on his policy.

Gabrielle was held for court and subsequently indicted by the grand jury. Because of this, Adela postponed entering the art school, Philip, Jr., delayed his mechanics course, and the both of them, with pale, drawn faces, sat in the courtroom with their distraught mother as I faced a jury of ten men and two women and said:

"Ladies and gentlemen of the jury: Two months ago Philip Gabrielle stood at the mountaintop of domestic felicity and business success; today he languishes in the valley of despair, his business ruined, his domestic plans awry, his future dark—he himself in court charged with felony.

"There he is, members of the jury, broken in spirit, staring unmitigated disaster in the face, but I would say to him: 'Let your heart lift with courage, let your soul take strength, because there are two barriers which yet intervene before you can fall into the bottomless abyss. One is the love and devotion of your family, a barrier which will never dissolve, and the other is this jury, whose intelligence and sense of fairness will see to it that justice is done.' "

The law proclaims that every defendant is presumed innocent until proved guilty, and reason supports the precept. Anyone can be charged with crime. One may be taken into legal custody on the slightest suspicion or even as the result of another's spite or desire for revenge. Once arrested, the accused is brought before a committing magistrate, who may hold him for court. Later his case is considered by the grand jury, where he may not testify or even be present; nor may he there be represented by counsel. If indicted, he eventually appears before a jury of twelve persons, where for the first time he has opportunity to combat the phases of accusation which, like the tentacles of an octopus, have fastened themselves to him. Hence the presumption of innocence in our courts—a presumption which remains with the defendant unless and until he is proved guilty beyond a reasonable doubt. "And the proof of that guilt," I said to the jury in the Gabrielle case, "must be so convincing that upon it you would condemn your own son, your own father, and that is how you should regard the defendant here—as a father, because he is a father—a father of five children, two of whom with their mother sit here with anxious hearts while the others at home speak in frightened whispers about their daddy who is away.

"Members of the jury, why is Philip Gabrielle a defendant? The official title of this case is Commonwealth versus Philip Gabrielle, but the real prosecutor is the Apexe Fire Insurance Company."

In the first row of seats sat four men who had testified for the prosecution. As witnesses, their presence was no longer required, but they remained in the courtroom. So intense was their interest that they could not take themselves away from the man hunt. I wanted the jury to know about these men. I swept an arm in their direction.

"Who are these men lined up here in front? They are agents and officers of the Apexe Fire Insurance Company. Why are they here? They have testified, the trial for them is ended, but they remain. Eager and impatient, like wolves on——"

The prosecuting attorney interrupted. "If the Court please, I object to Mr. Musmanno's calling these witnesses wolves."

The judge agreed: "Yes, Mr. Musmanno, your language is rather strong there."

I turned to the bench. "I'm sorry if I have offended, but daily we read, in figurative language, of wolves of the stock market and wolves of the financial world, and it seemed to me that wolves might not be an inappropriate characterization here. However, I will withdraw the characterization of wolves. Let us call these men lambs. If Gabrielle is convicted, the ones who stand to gain are the Apexe Insurance Company and *these lambs here!*"

"I object to Mr. Musmanno's calling these witnesses lambs," the prosecuting attorney now said.

"Mr. Harrison," I said as I turned to address my interrupter, "first you objected to my calling them wolves, and now you don't want me to call them lambs. What do you want me to call them?"

"I don't want you to call them at all," he said.

"I didn't call them," I replied. "You called them, and it seems to me that now they have finished their assignment here you can tell them it is no longer necessary they remain. They may go about their other affairs."

The fire department presented a strong case of circumstantial evidence against Gabrielle. There were two windows in the cellar of Gabrielle's store through which the arsonist could well have entered, but the fire department officials would not admit the existence of these openings.

When I cross-examined Battalion Chief Morgan on the subject, he said that he did not remember whether there was an opening in the cellar or not. Reminding the jury of this, I asked: "Is that not absurd? Morgan remembered everything else: remembered the exact number of steps leading to the basement, remembered the course of the water, remembered the elevator, but did not remember whether there was an opening in the cellar. He did not remember that which he had to know in order to make an escape in the event the ceiling fell or the walls collapsed. The fact of the matter is that Chief Morgan had to know about those windows. But to admit their existence would be evidence in favor of Gabrielle's innocence, and since Morgan believes Gabrielle should be convicted, he will not concede anything which might favor the accused. But is that just? Some witnesses assume that when they mount the witness stand they mount a horse which must trample down everything which does not agree with their views and con-

clusions. But such an assumption is unjust. The witness's only province
is to tell what he knows, uninfluenced by bias of any kind."

Of course Morgan was motivated by no ulterior purpose in wiping
out the windows in the basement. He had simply allowed his enthusiasm to gallop away with his sense of fairness and he was laboring
to destroy a man whose ruin would bring him no material advantage
whatsoever. It was different, however, with the men testifying for
the Apexe Insurance Company. "If Gabrielle is convicted," and I
again pointed to the four men still in the front row, "these men will
refuse payment of the insurance for which Philip Gabrielle has paid
his care-laden money in premiums. Thus they have a direct, selfish
interest in seeing Gabrielle convicted. They are concerned about the
profit which can come out of this case—not the justice—and I tell
you, members of the jury, that it is nothing short of contemptible
that Philip Gabrielle should be dragged through the terror and disgrace of a criminal trial because of the avarice and greed of the
Apexe Insurance Company."

And now, taking up the circumstantial evidence in the case, I
impressed on the jury the imperative need for lingering hesitation before convicting on evidence of that character. "Circumstantial evidence,
in order to be convincing and complete, must form one continuous
chain of events with no links absent. If one link is missing, the case
fails entirely.

"Do you have all the links in the circumstantial-evidence chain
here?"

At this point I picked up a box of paper clips from the court clerk's
desk and held it in my hand.

"Members of the jury, let us regard these clips as links in the chain
of circumstantial evidence necessary to convict Gabrielle. First we
will put them down loosely and then we will connect them later.
You have the fact that there was a fire—we will call that a link."
I removed one clip from the box and laid it on the ledge of the jury
box. "Then there is the fact that gasoline was found on the premises—
we will call that a link." And I set down another clip. "Then we
have the fact that the defendant did not deal in gasoline and therefore
offers no explanation as to the presence of the gasoline cans. That's
another link." One more clip. "We will join these three links into
a small chain and put them to one side."

Then, picking up a fourth clip, I said: "We have the fact that the
defendant had insurance. That's a link. Then the fact that he had full
control of the premises is another link, and the fact that he claimed

the insurance is still one more link." I now joined these other three clips together.

"We now have two small chains of three links each," and I carefully laid down to my left the short chain of three clips and to my right the other short chain of three clips. Then, lengthwise, I had them approach each other until there was just enough space for one clip between them. A clip in the intervening space would have caused them to join into one continuous chain of seven links.

"Members of the jury," I asked with deep feeling, "where is that other link? The link which connects these two sets of suspicious circumstance into one unbreakable chain of guilt fastening itself around the defendant? We have this section"—pointing to the three links on the left—"which establishes an incendiary fire, and then we have this section"—pointing to the three links on the right—"which indicates the possibility—not the certainty, mind you, but only the possibility—that the defendant might have, because of the insurance, profited by the fire; but where is the link that joins these two sets of circumstances and forms the chain which fetters the defendant?

"What could that missing link be? It could be an overheard remark made by the defendant before the fire that he intended to benefit from his insurance soon; or a statement made after the fire that he had put something over on the insurance company; or testimony to the effect that the defendant had been seen in the cellar the day of the fire with gasoline cans; or testimony that he had been seen purchasing gasoline. But there is no evidence of any such character in the whole case."

Turning now to Mr. Harrison, the assistant district attorney, I addressed him with some vehemence: "Mr. Assistant District Attorney, until you find that link, you cannot on your conscience declare that you have established *with evidence* that this defendant is guilty of arson. Where is that missing link?

"Members of the jury, that missing link must come through those two windows in the cellar. Those two windows open to the world. Who entered through those windows? Let the prosecuting attorney answer that.

"We want that missing link!" I now picked up the left section in my left hand and the right section in my right hand and held them apart, and as I spoke I kept drawing them farther and farther apart. "Members of the jury, the more you reflect, the more these fragments separate. Unless and until the Commonwealth produces that missing link, the defendant is an innocent man, which indeed he is, and is entitled to an acquittal."

I then showed that we had gone farther than merely disproving the Commonwealth's case. We had established that it was impossible for Gabrielle to have committed the crime. There was no evidence that the fire had been started by means of any mechanical device. It was simply a fire caused by gasoline which had to be ignited by a human being.

On the night of the fire Gabrielle left the store at 6 P.M. and arrived home at 7. The fire alarm was turned in at 11 P.M. To charge Gabrielle with responsibility for the blaze when he was four to five hours removed from it was not only unfair but absurd, I told the jury.

I then talked about Gabrielle's home life. Twenty-five character witnesses testified to Gabrielle's good name. "A man's good name is his greatest treasure. It is the shield which he lifts to ward off the poisoned arrows of false accusation and scandal. A good name is not acquired overnight. A man may become wealthy in a day, but a good name is achieved only after years of honest, decent, and legal living. That good name must and will protect Philip Gabrielle."

After two hours' deliberation the jury returned with a verdict of not guilty.

Chapter XXV

CAMPAIGN CARDS

ON THE day after the Gabrielle acquittal I received the following letter:

> Dear Michael:
>
> Our hearts are filled with gratitude for helping us in our hour of great need. I see you are a candidate for the legislature and I hope that you will be elected and that this election will be another clip in the long chain of success which will never end until you reach the goal of your heart's desire.
>
> Yours gratefully,
> *Lucille Gabrielle*

Yes, I was a candidate. It was inevitable that sooner or later I would seek public office, for law and politics are Siamesen. It may be possible to find lawyers who are uninterested in the governmental aspect of public life, but then it is not outside the realm of possibility to find a duck that does not swim. Once a young lawyer feels the lure of a public career, the first star to which he would like to hitch the wagon of his ambition is the state legislature. It was the star which led political efforts across the sky of success for Abraham Lincoln, Henry Clay, John Calhoun, Patrick Henry, Stephen Douglas, and innumerable other American statesmen.

I announced my candidacy for the Pennsylvania General Assembly from the 12th Legislative District in which I lived.

Steeped in the literature of the pre-Civil War period when sheer determination and public-speaking enterprise took young men into state legislatures and eventually made them leaders in their respective states and the nation, I felt confident that with a rousing stump-speaking campaign I could ride to my first office on the horseback of oratory and energy. I was to learn that campaigning in the twentieth century had changed somewhat from what it was in the earlier days of the Republic, when political meetings often were public festivals, with all candidates, regardless of party, faction, or platform, eagerly awaited and welcomed for speechmaking.

My first attempt to acquaint the population with my legislative candidacy was something less than a Patrick Henry triumph. In the borough of Carnegie one evening I saw men and women pouring into a large building which carried on its façade an enormous banner inviting the outside world to "COME AND HEAR THE CANDIDATES!" Since I was a candidate I certainly qualified to appear before that crowd, and my pulse quickened as I visualized myself delivering a spellbinding address which would win the votes of these prospective listeners who were now pushing forward through the doors with the enthusiastic eagerness of political picnickers going after free beer. (I found out later that *that* was actually the attraction.) I committed myself to the millrace, and although somewhat jostled and mauled, I entered the hall unhurt. Once across the threshold, I immediately headed for the stage at the front end of the hall, on which several candidates had already gathered. Halfway to the platform, a tubby man with a swollen left cheek, sitting in the middle of the aisle, thrust out his foot and blocked my advance. "Where do you think *you're* going?" he asked with an intonation which plainly said I would not reach whatever point I was headed for.

"To the platform," I replied.

"Why?"

"To make a speech."

His left cheek deflated and his right cheek expanded. "Who are you?" he asked as he finished shifting his quid of tobacco.

"Michael A. Musmanno, candidate for the legislature."

"Never heard o' you. You'd better find some other place to do your speechifying." Without averting his head he spat at a cuspidor ten feet away against the wall. Clang! He scored a perfect bull's-eye, but I caught some of the accompanying spray. He then authoritatively pointed a pudgy forefinger in the direction of the door. Although mollified, I departed hurriedly, rather relieved to get beyond the range of his unerring sharpshooting.

Four House members were to be elected from the 12th Legislative District, which embraced twenty boroughs, three Pittsburgh wards, and seventeen townships. The dominant political organization in the district had already endorsed its preferred candidates. I was not one of them. I appeared at advertised meetings in Coraopolis, Dormont, and Mount Oliver, but even without tobacco-juice barriers I was never able to reach the rostrum. And in all fairness I must say that those who prevented me from speaking were entirely justified in doing so. Free speech does not mean speech free of expense. It costs money to carry on a political campaign. Halls must be rented, signs must be painted, refreshments must be purchased. And naturally the organization making these financial outlays has nothing to gain by allowing outsiders to attend its gatherings to make speeches which could well be in opposition to its own interests and to its own candidates.

Since it was, of course, impossible for me to finance any meetings of my own, I had to devise some method other than oratorical to get my candidacy before the electorate. I had it! Although I was enjoined from addressing organization affairs, no one could object to my handing out campaign cards to the people as they entered the meeting halls. This type of campaigning might, in fact, be even more effective than talking to people who were more concerned about the beer awaiting them at the end of the speech than the subject of the discourse they were not listening to. I reasoned also that each person receiving a card would take it home, read it, and exhibit it to other members of his family, saying: "Look, here's a young man with an honest face. And he's not bound hand and foot to any political organization either. He will speak for the people and the people alone. And he wasn't born with a silver spoon in his mouth. He had to work to get his education. Believe me, I'm voting for him." The children listening to their father speaking in this enthusiastic manner would be impressed and they would talk about Musmanno to other children, and these children in turn would acquaint their own parents with the virtues of the young candidate. There was no end to the fruitful possibilities of this kind of campaign. I felt confident it would gather size and momentum like a snowball charging down a wintry hillside.

Aglow with the idea, I designed a card carrying my picture flanked by the bold pronouncement: "Vote for Michael A. Musmanno —A True Representative of the People!" On the reverse side of the card appeared a modest, but not too modest, account of my qualifications.

I had five thousand of these cards printed and I at once began to picture myself in Harrisburg taking the oath of office in the House of Representatives. I calculated that if each card brought me only two votes, that alone would net me ten thousand votes; and it was conceded that nine thousand votes would clinch the election.

Thus, stuffing my pockets with these campaign weapons, I set out for a large organization meeting scheduled in Brentwood. I arrived at the meeting place a half hour ahead of time and took up a position of vantage at the entrance to the hall. The first person to put in an appearance was a well-dressed middle-aged gentleman, undoubtedly one of the civic pillars of the town who had come early so as not to miss anything. I stepped forward with a big smile to greet him, my voice almost going into a shrill with the good cheer I was pumping into it. "Good evening, my dear sir, won't you take one of my cards? I'm a candidate for the legislature." And I proffered the glossy, handsome pasteboard.

"Why waste a card on me?" he returned. "I don't live in this district. I'm the custodian of this place and I've come to open it up for the meeting."

"Well, take a card anyway."

"Oh no, thank you. I never carry cards from candidates not in my district."

During the next ten minutes no one showed up. Then a very pleasant-faced lady amiably approached the building. "Good evening, madam." I smiled eagerly. "It's a wonderful evening, isn't it? I'm Michael A. Musmanno, candidate for the legislature. Won't you please take one of my cards?"

"I'm very sorry," she replied, "but I work for the organization and you are not one of the endorsed candidates. If I were to be seen with one of your cards I would be charged with disloyalty, and you wouldn't want that, would you?"

"Oh no, madam, not at all, but it was nice to see you—very nice indeed, madam. Good evening."

Five minutes later I espied a young man light-footedly turning in from the street and blithely starting up the gravel path toward the building. This fellow would be attracted to my candidacy, I reasoned, if only for the fact that we were about the same age. I sallied forward to greet him and sang out: "Hello, young fellow! How about a card?"

"Oh, sure," he replied jauntily. He took it in his hand, gingerly glanced at it, and twirlingly tossed it away so that it fluttered like a wounded bird and then slowly but gracefully descended to the ground. I felt a sliver of pain in my chest.

I quickly regained my composure, however, determined not to allow a little embarrassment to cut too deep. I gulped and built up another smile.

The card had fallen face upward. It was a perfectly good card and I did not like to see it lying on the ground. Its neglected presence could suggest an abandoned candidacy and thus work a bad psychological effect on those I wished to impress. I quickly bent over to rescue it from the dust of the earth in which it uncomfortably rested, but just as my fingers extended to retrieve it, the shadow of a falling foot fell across my hand. Rapidly it descended and tramped down flatly on my campaign masterpiece before I could reach it. The big foot lifted and passed on. The face of the card looked up pathetically through a deep smear. Humiliated, I stepped back. As I did so, another shoe dropped through space and tramped down squarely on the grieving countenance. This second shoe bore projecting nailheads and left perforations across my chin and mouth. I almost expected to feel my mouth bleeding. I wanted to run away and hide.

But then I seized hold of my nerves and resolved I must not let myself be so thin-skinned. After all, it was only my card they were trampling on, not me. I braced up, forced a grin, and stepped up to the now more numerous and rapidly moving line of people entering the hall.

"Good evening," I said through an emotion-strained voice, "have a card."

"Good evening, it's a nice evening, have a card."

"Good evening, my friend, won't you take a card, please?"

"Good evening, glad to see you, won't you take this card and put it in your pocket, please?"

And so one by one I handed out the pasteboards, courteously, persuadingly, coaxingly—and one by one they were thrown away. The ground was alive with appeals of Vote for Musmanno!

The stream of people entering the building had ceased. The meeting was about to begin. The doors banged shut and I stood outside alone.

The portals of the day were also closing, but night had not yet fully taken over. Through the narrowing doorway of the horizon a beam of light fell through infinity and allowed me to sum up the results of my evening's endeavors. From what was left in my hands and pockets I could compute that I had handed out about three hundred fifty cards. Of that number, at least three hundred whitened the ground in and about the entrance to the meeting hall. I sensed a tightening sensation in my throat. I seemed to be standing under a spreading tree of melancholy which was shedding blossoms of regret.

Among the three hundred abandoned greetings, one card stood out more prominently than the others. It was the first one which had been cast to the earth. I had kept my eyes on it throughout the entire heart-wrenching experience. It seemed part of myself. Its face was crossed and crisscrossed with marks of shoe nails, sharp tack heads, rugged macerating heels. I recovered it from the mud into which it had been driven by that infantry of indifferent boots, and I took it home. And among my souvenirs it remains as a memento of that harrowing night when it seemed the world was divided into two groups: the young lawyer on one side, and on the other side the rest of the universe.

I now concluded that, cost what it might, if I intended to address any sizable number of voters or even distribute campaign literature effectively I had to have meetings of my own. I located a hall in Carrick which I could rent for one evening for ten dollars. I then had a hundred large advertising placards printed which I personally placed in store windows or nailed to fences and old barns in the area. It was inevitable that many hundreds of the countless thousands who would see these placards would become curious and have enough free time to go to see and hear what this candidate Musmanno had to offer. I exulted over this, my first political rally. I took around to the newspaper offices in Pittsburgh a notice of the great event and I was quite gratified to see it listed in the daily papers with the other political news of the day. The Pittsburgh *Sun* referred to me as the "Stowe Township Boy."

On the evening of the memorable occasion, while riding out to Carrick in the car of my long-time friend, Frank Parco, I wondered if I had not erred in holding my meeting in a strange community. However, replying to my own query, I reasoned that it was more important I appear where I was not well known so as to win the votes of the people living in that community than to address my own townspeople, of whose vote I could with some assurance be certain. Carrick was a good choice after all.

My brother Sam, who had become my campaign manager, said that for dramatic effect I should not make my appearance until the crowd had fully gathered. In fact, he urged, I would make a better impression if I arrived a little late. This would convey the idea, he said, that I had many other meetings besides this one.

At eight-fifteen we stopped a block away from the hall. The meeting was scheduled for 8 P.M. I of course could not hope for an overflow crowd. If the hall, which would hold about five hundred people, was just comfortably filled I would be entirely satisfied. Sam went ahead to notify the audience that the candidate had arrived. A few minutes later he returned with an enigmatic expression on his face. I asked: "Are they ready?"

He replied: "Yes, they are ready."

We drove the extra block, Parco throwing on his brakes loudly so that the audience might know we had arrived. I decided to emulate the technique of such veteran political campaigners as Teddy Roosevelt and William Jennings Bryan, whom I had seen as they made their way into meeting places where thousands of enthusiastic admirers shouted and cheered boisterous welcome. I leaped out of the car, held my hat aloft dramatically, and strode into the hall. Nothing happened.

In the hall were six people.

I coughed and said to Sam: "There must be something wrong."

"There certainly is," he replied heatedly. "I'd kick out three of those guys. They're opposition candidates trying to horn in on your meeting. Each one of them expects to make a speech to your crowd."

"Who are the other three persons?" I asked, my voice just a little tremulous.

"Well, one of them is the janitor and the other two live next door. They came in just to see what was going on. I told you, you should have waited. In an hour's time this place will be jammed."

"Well, we can wait. I have no other place to go."

We waited. In the next half hour the two neighbors went home, so that when we finally got the meeting under way I spoke to the janitor, three rival candidates, my brother Sam, and Frank Parco.

On our way home Sam complained to me: "You are entirely too generous. You shouldn't have allowed those three other candidates to talk."

"Why?"

"Well, they may have taken that janitor's vote away from you!"

It was now obvious that the wine of victory was not to be squeezed from the grapes of meetings; that is, meetings planted in my own vineyard. I had to search out the voters and talk to them directly. I went from house to house. No itinerant salesman selling vacuum cleaners could have been more assiduous than I as I sought to convince the housewives and their husbands how much they needed me in Harrisburg.

Nor did I always receive an encouraging reception as I rang the doorbell or banged my knuckles against unyielding panels. At some of the residences a window would fly open, a head emerge, and a voice yell down: "We don't want nothing today."

"I'm not selling anything," I'd reply.

"Who are you?"

"A candidate for the legislature."

"Oh, that's worse!" not a few would acidulously comment. Others would good-naturedly reply: "All right, I'll vote for you. Leave your card." When I got an invitation of that kind I always left a nice package of cards, with placards too.

I was canvassing Crafton one evening and entered a drugstore to persuade the proprietor to brighten up his window with my placard. Before I could describe the purpose of my visit the druggist asked: "Aren't you the lawyer who represented Joey Mackintoshe in a damage case?"

"Yes, I replied, pleased for what I thought was a friendly reception. And it was. He shook my hand warmly and said: "I was one of the jurors in that case and I liked the way you tried it." He closed up his drugstore and took me through the neighborhood asking people to vote for me.

In Carrick a kindhearted contractor, D. Carapellucci, enthusiastically endorsed my candidacy and introduced me to his employees on various construction jobs throughout the legislative district. In Brentwood a businessman active in civic affairs, Albert G. Kaufmann, announced he would give me political support.

In the coal regions my candidacy was also being received in a kindly manner because of the battle I had been waging against the Coal and Iron Police. I was further encouraged by the fact that now more and more of my cards were being received and less of them were being thrown away; that is, in my presence anyway.

Philip Murray, vice-president of the United Mine Workers of America, who lived only six miles from my home, volunteered his support. And so did Patrick T. Fagan, president of District No. 5 of the miners' union. Both Mr. Murray and Pat Fagan arranged meetings for me in the headquarters of various local unions, and at last I got a chance to make political speeches to more than the groups of three to five persons I would corral on the sidewalks and at gasoline stations. I was invited to address other labor organization meetings. Fraternal clubs, lodges, and societies allowed me to speak at their clambakes, picnics, and social gatherings.

Although it might seem bizarre to mention such a subject today, it is true that in the early '20's a strange notion persisted in parts of Pennsylvania, and perhaps in some other states as well, that a person bearing a name with an unusual spelling must be a recently arrived immigrant who had to speak with a foreign accent. Italian names particularly seemed to fall within that classification. Thus I heard that in certain sections of the 12th Legislative District I could not expect much of a vote because, aside from the fact that I was generally unknown, what was known about me was that I was not an "American" but a "foreigner."

This idea seemed to prevail to a degree worthy of note and concern in Mount Lebanon Township, where one evening I attended what was known as an "open meeting"—a meeting open to all candidates, regardless of the office sought. Entering the hall, I said to the chairman, who did not know me, that I would prefer to be introduced merely as "another speaker." He had no objection to doing this, and accordingly, after seven or eight candidates had addressed the audience of some 350 people, I appeared before them with no other designation than "another speaker." I plunged immediately into my speech:

"Ladies and gentlemen, I come to speak to you in behalf of a legislative candidate I know well. He was born in Stowe Township on the banks of the Ohio River; he attended and graduated from our local public schools and then attended and graduated from the following universities, all in Washington, D.C.: Georgetown, George Washington, National and American, where he obtained the degrees of Bachelor of Arts, Master of Arts, Bachelor of Laws, Master of Laws, Master of Patent Laws, and Doctor of Juristic Science. He served in the United States Army with three other brothers, one of whom gave his life for our beloved America on the battlefields of France. The candidate for whom I speak is a lawyer and has written on legal subjects. Articles of his have been published in the American Bar Association *Journal,* the *American Law Review,* and the New York *Times.* This young man is a candidate for the Pennsylvania legislature—and his name is—Michael Angelo Musmanno."

For a moment there was a gasp of silence. I could feel in the air the sense of general incredulity that a person with such a name could be an "American." An elderly gentleman sitting in the third or fourth row rose and asked: "Why doesn't this Michael Angelo fellow come here to speak for himself?"

I replied: "He is here."

"Where?"

"I am he."

There was another pause of startled silence, and then generous applause followed, my interrogator joining in it most genuinely.

I felt I was now making headway. The blossom of optimism flowered in my breast. My brother Sam and Frank Parco were sure I would win, but I did not allow overconfidence to impede my continuing efforts. On the contrary, the more hopeful the outlook, the more determined I toiled for victory. Night and day I traveled through the vast Ohio River and Chartiers Creek valleys seeking votes. I had now distributed some twenty-five thousand cards.

My fellow townsmen in Stowe Township recruited car owners for an auto parade in my honor. Sitting high on the hook-and-ladder truck of our local fire department, I waved my great fire helmet as with siren sounding we roared through the various municipalities of the 12th Legislative District, while huge banners flapped in the wind trumpeting in large letters: "VOTE FOR MUSMANNO—A REAL MANNO!"

Came the day of the elections—and I lost.

Chapter XXVI

THE HIGHEST PEAK

THE defeat was not as devastating as it might have been. I received over seven thousand votes. Nine thousand would have elected me. There were those who said that I *was* elected but that I had been "counted out." This was in the days when election cheating was not a rare phenomenon. Political bosses who controlled election boards were often able to manipulate the count so as to make losers winners and winners losers.

To be assured an honest count in many municipalities represented a triumph in itself. During the campaign I called on a political leader in Mount Oliver to complain that he had "influenced" business establishments in the town not to display my placards. He said: "Musmanno, I got a lot of admiration for you because you got fire and courage, but I can't support you because you don't stand in with the bosses—and I'm a strict organization man. But I'll tell you what I'll do. I like you and I'll do you a favor. I'll see to it that on election day all votes marked for you here will be counted for you."

Although disappointed with the over-all result, I was highly gratified that in my home town of Stowe Township I snowed under my immediate opponent by a vote of 1333 to 269. I recalled that Lincoln had fared somewhat similarly in his first candidacy for the Illinois legislature. He was defeated in his legislative district but he carried his home town handsomely. And then he won in his second attempt. So I took down Carl Sandburg's *Prairie Years* and hoped for more favorable weather should I launch a second endeavor.

Although this was the first time I had been wounded in politics it was not the first time I wore about my head the bandage of election defeat. In 1921, while I was a student at George Washington University, I lost by six votes in my campaign for presidency of our debating society. I was inconsolable. How foolish in retrospect are the sighs and tears of our youth, but only one who has reached for a beautiful flower and had it turn to a prickly burr in his hand can understand the sadness and bitter disillusionment of a rejected plea. I longed for consolation and assurance that life would still be sweet even though I would not be president of the George Washington University Debating Society. But I wanted consolation from someone who had dared the fates in some enterprise of breath-taking grandeur. The captain who has lost his ship spurns the solace of a land turtle. Thus I looked around for someone whose frigate of war, too, had been smashed on the rocks of electoral ambition. I thought of William Jennings Bryan, who, after having been sunk three times in presidential oceanic storms, should know more about the spiritual aftermath of political disaster than any other person alive. I wrote to him:

> My dear Colonel Bryan:
>
> What formula or method do you use to regain your poise and spiritual equilibrium after you have been worsted in an election? I recently participated as a candidate in a contest, and was defeated only by half a dozen votes. I feel the disappointment keenly and nothing tastes good any more. Your equanimity has apparently never been shaken, and although horse after horse has been shot from under you, you still ride on full of cheerfulness and dare. In the words of the modernist, "How do you do it?"

The silver-tongued orator was not too parsimonious with his golden words not to share a few with his unknown correspondent. He wrote:

> Your question is easily answered. A man never suffers a severe disappointment except when he loses something upon which his heart is set. The way to keep from being disappointed by political defeat is not to set your heart on an office. Offices, in a country like ours, are simply opportunities for service. While it is perfectly proper for one to be willing to serve, his candidacy ought to be merely an offer, and he should not feel disappointed if the people choose someone else. Have they not the right to choose whom they please? And suppose they make a mistake; have they not the right to make mistakes? If they make a mistake, they suffer for it, and will correct it when they find out. Do not

allow yourself to worry a moment about defeat. . . .

Very truly yours,

W. J. Bryan

A week later he arrived in Washington on a lecture tour, and only the brashness of college youth could excuse the temerity of my calling the great man and informing him that I was the defeated candidate to whom he had written his comforting letter. And then, accepting his invitation to call on him, I appeared at his hotel. When he got over the shock of beholding a young lad in peg-bottomed trousers and a flowing student's tie instead of the doleful, scarred man my letter had persuaded him to believe I would be, he invited me to take a walk with him. Although given to corpulence, he walked with a vigorous stride, and when we got to Lafayette Square he suggested we rest. We sat down on a bench close to the statue of Andrew Jackson, the first fighting Democrat, who, astride a prancing bronze horse, seemed to epitomize Bryan's valiant spirit on the battlefield of politics. Across Pennsylvania Avenue our eyes fell on the beautiful White House, its shapely pillars glistening silver in the light of the massive lantern suspended in the classic portico. "It's a magnificent sight, isn't it?" Bryan observed as his range of view then swept down historic Pennsylvania Avenue on which abutted the Corinthian columns of the Treasury Building and the battle-flagged architecture of the State, War and Navy Building. His face continued to light up like succeeding candles on a Christmas tree as he presently lifted his gaze to the tip of the Washington Monument, the centerpiece of the realm which could have been his.

I remarked: "How thrilling that scene must be to a President of the United States."

No sooner had these words left my lips than I realized their tactlessness and I hastened to add: "I'm sorry."

He laughed. "Why be sorry? One can be happy without being President. After all, only a very small number of men can become President in a generation. If contentment depended upon our ability to win it at the polls, but few would ever be content, and it would be unjust and contrary to all teachings of Christ that peace and contentment should be limited to a few. Happiness is within reach of all, and it does not depend on money, society, or office. It comes from an overflowing faith in God and a trust in Providence."

For half an hour we sat in the park within an easy stone's throw of his life's goal, but never once did he suggest by word, tone, or gesture that he was sorry for himself or angry at anyone for having wrecked the ship of his fondest dreams. And here he confirmed his prescription, one which every candidate should carry in his pocket when he enters the lists of political contest:

> Make service of the public in any capacity that falls to your lot your highest political purpose and let holding office be merely incidental—a thing to be enjoyed when the people want you to hold office and not to be mourned when they prefer someone else.

It is a good prescription—a homemade remedy by an American—for all Americans.

Nothing can be less beneficial or more destructive to one's self-reliance than rumination over political defeat. Thus, after 1926, if Self-Pity ever took me by the coat lapels to discuss what might have been, I always shook him off by recalling the cheerful and healthy conversation I had had with presidential candidate William Jennings Bryan. Moreover, I determined that, while always maintaining a vigorous interest in the public affairs of community, state, and nation, I would not permit political boulders to hold up traffic on the main track to legal success.

And so I dwelt wholly in the mansion of the Law, within whose curtilage there were no houses devoted to hobbies or "escape." I even surrendered my violin. This was one sacrifice I laid on the altar of my profession with genuine infelicity.

There had been a time in my early teens when I entertained fantastic ideas of becoming a Kreisler or even the echo of a Paganini. But when I fell under the spell of Blackstone I became aware that I had to choose between the fond yearning of capturing an audience of five thousand with the magic of my violin and the ambition of convincing an audience of twelve people of the justice of my cause. If I could have combined the fulfillment of both desires I would have known the meaning of the refrain popular at the time: "All this and heaven too?" To have witnesses tell their story from the witness stand, while I later summed up to the jury on my violin! What eloquence would speak from those strings so rich with feeling, so deep with sentiment, so vibrant with emotion. To what heights of human understanding would I soar in rapidly executed cadenzas and variations. With that violin I would speak so that no one could fail to understand the most subtle argument of the intellect, the tenderest appeal of the heart, the most ethereal supplication of the soul—for music is the universal language of mankind. It is, as Carlyle said, the speech of angels. But alas, no concert can substitute for cross-examination, no rondo can take the place of a refutation, no pizzicato can do the work of a peroration, and so, with a sigh which was a solfeggio of broken dreams, I folded up my music stand, affectionately laid away my violin, and bade farewell to the world of music.

In 1925, for a brief day, my violin took the spotlight in our home. When I returned from Europe to a law practice which lacked practice, office, and prospective clients, I thought I might earn money for carfare and other immediate necessities by giving lessons to children. I hung up a sign in the window of our parlor: "Violin Lessons Taught at Reasonable Rates." To my surprise, and even consternation, I got three or four pupils. They were fine little lads and I spent most of the time telling them stories, which they frankly said they enjoyed more than the violin instruction.

I was aware, of course, that when the courtroom hopefully again became my arena the doors of my music school would automatically close, but one day an event occurred which accelerated the closing more effectively than a sheriff's eviction. Ten-year-old Bobby Massey was performing an exercise which I had assigned to him as I stepped into the kitchen to get a tray of tea and cakes. (I always fed my pupils *and their teacher*.) Suddenly there fell upon my ears a cry of alarm. I dashed back to the parlor to find Bobby crying over his violin—he had thrust the bow between the strings and could not loosen it. The horsehair stick had passed under the A and D strings and over the E and G strings, and in that position it remained entangled while the lad howled. My first impulse was to laugh; never had I seen anyone try to embroider or knit a violin, but Bobby's terror was too genuine to treat as a laughing matter. "Don't cry," I said, trying to tranquillize his fears, "we'll have this attended to quickly and it won't hurt you a bit." Then, taking hold of one end of the bow and gently pulling, I extracted it with the care, trepidation, and eventual success employed by Androcles when he performed the storied feat of removing the thorn from the lion's paw. "There," I said, "don't you see, it was nothing." I handed the violin and bow back to the boy, but he recoiled as if from an evil spirit. He was afraid, especially of the bow, and set up a yelling which brought my brother Sam bounding into the room. "You ought to be ashamed of yourself," he scolded, "for beating a child just because he makes a mistake in his lesson!"

"I didn't beat him," I hotly rejoined.

"Certainly you beat him. For what other reason would he be crying like that? I don't remember that you were so hot when you first took lessons either. Oh, how many times I had to stuff a towel in my ears not to hear your wheezing and scratching."

He continued to insist that I had struck the pupil, until the boy himself spoke up: "No, he didn't hit me. Professor Musmanno is very kind to me. I think he's the grandest professor, the nicest man, and the most wonderful violinist in the world."

I knew at that moment that my musical career was ended, for on the wings of the sincerity and simplicity rising from the goodness of this little boy's heart I had been carried to the highest possible peak of eulogy and praise; so I kissed my beloved Stradivarius (only it was not a Stradivarius), placed it in the case, and there it remains today.

I did not, however, relinquish the delightful prospect that when I should become renowned in the legal world I could always achieve comfort and consolation—in the event I lost an important case—by playing a sweet and comforting melody on the violin—a nocturne which would drain my melancholy and let it flow away into the streams of forgetfulness and oblivion. But one day when I picked up my beloved fiddle which I had not held to my chin for years, and drew the bow, as I thought, with a rich melancholic sweep across the strings, the unearthly sounds which eeried forth from the tortured instrument convinced me that hereafter I would need to obtain solace from my musing and not my music.

I never gave up my passion for the theater. Two forms of theatrical entertainment have always entranced me. Like the postman who on his day off takes a walk for leisure, I always eagerly responded to any dramatic presentation with a courtroom setting. The reason for this predilection was a perfectly natural one: I liked the courtroom. Though it produced more problems and headaches than a broken fence in a zoo, it was always an arena in which, after winning a decision in a bitterly contested conflict, I experienced a thrill of ecstasy which would make even the bagging of a lion in the jungle a mediocre accomplishment in comparison.

The other type of performance which attracted me like a magnet was any play which came from the most miraculous pen "in the tide of times." This was a love which reached back to school days in Washington, when I was actually a Shakespearean actor—as a spearbearer and costume-wearer. When road companies needed supernumeraries I always volunteered and, in consequence, I appeared on the stage with the greatest Shakespearean interpreters of the age. As a lance-carrier, non-talking senator, soldier, courtier, sailor, page boy, "shout outside," and walking ghost, I shared the footlights with such immortals as E. H. Sothern, Julia Marlowe, Walter Hampden, David Warfield, Otis Skinner, and Robert Bruce Mantell.

Mere proximity to these immortals of the theater was adequate compensation in itself, but I received, in addition, the practical stipend of seventy-five cents per performance, plus training in poise, self-possession, and audience conquest, all of inestimable value to a lawyer or anyone who has to appear before the public. This was highly gratifying. But, as is true in all things in this counterbalancing world, there was a debit side as well to this glamorous occupation. A supernumerary always took the chance of losing his shoes or some other item of wearing apparel to some sharp-fingered intruder while he was occupying the stage. This had happened to me one evening while I was performing in *Macbeth*. I wore in that play, as one of Macduff's soldiers, a pair of elegant, richly engrained, soft leather boots, but when the curtain came down on what I regarded as a rather inspired characterization on my part, I was missing my civilian footgear. Someone, apparently less enthusiastic about my stage performance than my civilian shoes, had walked off with them from my unguarded locker. I had to race home partly accoutered as a Scotsman, put on other shoes, and return the boots before the property custodian discovered their absence.

One evening I hit upon what I thought to be an ingenious plan to safeguard my shoes. That week I was playing (without billing) with Robert Bruce Mantell in *Julius Caesar*. I was a Roman senator and postured about the stage looking very senatorial. Of course, what I really was, was walking scenery, but I never doubted that I was rather eloquent scenery. My feet were encased in sandals, but, latched to my belt beneath my toga, hung my walking shoes, one on each side. Since the senatorial robe with its ample folds hung loosely about my form, I felt confident that the little bulge on my flanks would not be noticeable. It did not occur to me that this protuberance, no matter how slight, could impart to my movements the rolling swing of a veteran sailor rather than the majestic stride of a Ciceronian representative of Eternal Rome.

Thus, on that unforgettable night, I stepped out in my openwork sandals in the momentous scene (Act III, Scene I) where the imperious Julius falls beneath the daggers of the conspirators. My part in the grisly affair was to register first unconcern, then interest, then intense curiosity, followed by fright, and finally horror, the horror crescendoing as dagger after dagger fell upon the hapless author of *Caesar's Commentaries*. The apogee of my terror was to be attained when the slipping Julius, as his heart burst, cried out, "*Et tu, Brute*," but I began to register consternation at the very beginning of the scene where Artemidorus implores Caesar to heed his warning about the Ides of March. I knew what Caesar was in for: I had seen him get it the night before, so that my horror was not entirely manufactured.

By the time I reached the "*Et tu, Brute*" sequence, my eyes were protruding from their sockets like electric light bulbs. I knew I was doing my part very well, perhaps overdoing it a little, but in performing Shakespeare, overacting is really underacting. At this moment I noted that the stage director in the wings of the stage was watching me with orbs that were hanging out even farther than mine, and he was excitedly beckoning with crooked finger for me to come to him. For a long time I had been besieging him for a speaking part and he probably wanted to inform me that he had such an assignment for me. I wondered why he did not wait until the end of the evening or at least until the curtain fell on the present scene to tell me. Was I that good? However, just as Cassius and Trebonius fell into a dialogue as to the whereabouts of Antony I softly sandaled off the stage to the director, who at close range seemed to be wearing more a mantle of rage than one of commendation. What had happened? Leading me more deeply into the wings of the stage so that his voice could not be heard in the orchestra pit, he asked with a quite obvious herculean effort to restrain himself: "What in the name of the eleven thousand virgins of Cologne do you have on your hips?"

"My shoes."

"Your shoes?"

"Yes, my shoes."

"What do you mean, your shoes? Let me see."

I unwound the bed sheet I was wearing and there, on either hip, dangled my $3.50 pair of Excelsior-special-sole-reinforced-rubber-heeled brogans. I thought at the moment that the director would fall into an epileptic fit such as the one Julius Caesar threw when he learned that the people of Rome were not as happy as he thought they would be, and should be, upon being informed that the mighty Caesar was angling for a crown. My director turned red, yellow, green, and then deathly pale as the veins in his face bulged like mountain ranges on a bas-relief map. There comes a time in every person's life when no words, no matter how piercing, explosive, and profane, can adequately meet an exasperating situation. That time had come to the director. He sputtered, stammered, and then broke into weeping. "Will you please," he sobbed, "take those damn shoes off your hips? Who ever heard"—sob—"of a senator"—sob—"wearing shoes on his hips?"

Appearing in Shakespearean plays offers unexcelled training for a lawyer, whether he wears shoes on his feet or on his hips. The matchless language, the dramatic sequences, the heroic characterizations, the tragic plots, the majestic march of human emotions from the profoundest griefs to the most exalting ecstasies and from soul-tearing doubt to element-defying boldness—all this offers a tutelage which cannot be found in any school, book, or library of reading. Shakespeare knew the courts and what went into them; he knew lawyers and judges as no other human being has ever known them.

To be a lawyer without knowing Shakespeare would be like being a musician without burning a candle to Beethoven. Let cynics mutter that the race of man is weak, let the rubber-kneed defeatist bewail his fate—and then look upon Ludwig van Beethoven, piano virtuoso and symphonic composer—deaf. With faith in Providence and in his indomitable self he overcame the cruelest handicap which could ever afflict a man of music, and achieved the most exalted heights to which mortal man can climb.

Chapter XXVII

BABETTE

ON NOVEMBER 11, 1921, as the Unknown Soldier moved up Pennsylvania Avenue in Washington on an artillery caisson, I marched as a flag-bearer in the great military parade which accompanied the returning hero. In my immediate vicinity an army band, with singing trumpets, melodious basses, happy trombones, and resounding drums, put wings on my feet, while the flag at the top of the staff, held firmly in my grasp, billowed and danced like the sails of a caravel on the high seas of joyous animation. "There's a Long, Long Trail A-Winding," the cornets said, and then, with an intervening rat-a-tat-tat of the sonorous drums, the baritones took up the lead in "Over There! Over There!" But the flag fairly capered when, with every brass horn shouting and every clarinet sweetly warbling, the band proclaimed "The Stars and Stripes Forever"! All along the parade route the enthusiastic spectators applauded and cheered and removed their hats as the colors sailed by. Now and then a viewer, overawed by the beauty of the procession and the solemnity of the rumbling caisson being drawn by eight black caparisoned horses, forgot or delayed removing his headgear, whereupon a heavy, hardboiled voice at my left barked: "Remove your hat. Where do you think you are? At home?"

The voice belonged to Sergeant Andrew Gilmore, color guard marching at my side. At Arlington we stood together and listened reverently to President Harding's tribute to the Unknown Soldier, which began with: "We know not whence he came, but only that his death marks him with the everlasting glory of an American dying for his country," and ended with the Lord's Prayer.

And then, as a silver bugle sounded taps, its echoes rolling over the Virginia hills, the Potomac River, the Washington Monument, and the Lincoln Memorial, the Unknown Soldier was lowered into his marble tomb with its imperishable inscription: "Here Rests in Honored Glory an American Soldier Known but to God."

I did not see Sergeant Andrew Gilmore again until seven years later, when as an army reserve officer I was in training at the field artillery post, Fort Hoyle, Maryland. My activities in the Officers' Reserve Corps constituted the only physical relaxation I allowed myself from the law.

My brother Pasquale, an ex-cavalryman who had served in Cuba in Colonel Teddy Roosevelt's famed Rough Rider regiment, had inspired me with a longing to see the world from a horse's back. At Fort Hoyle I had the opportunity to satisfy that desire to the hilt. Horses here were as plentiful as at a Wild West circus, so that daily I cantered and galloped over the parade grounds and through the adjacent woods until I concluded I had now become sufficiently expert to ride something more spirited than an artillery Percheron.

The post swarmed with polo teams, so one day I mounted Tommy, a polo pony, to get the feel of a speedy steed. However, no sooner had I thrust my feet into the stirrups than the lean racer shot forward like a streak of lightning. I lurched backward but did not topple off as in that first appalling moment I feared. With herculean effort I regained a vertical position and then bent forward as Tommy stretched his neck and sped across the polo field like a comet.

To my consternation I noted that he was heading for the highway which bordered the camp, and I tried to rein him in or slow him up, but he ignored all my efforts and commands. I knew that if he reached the highway, serious trouble awaited me. It was imperative I head him off. With both hands I seized the left rein and pulled like the strong man in a tug of war, but his arrow swiftness continued unabated for the glistening stretch of concrete. I turned to the right rein, but a flea could not have disturbed him less. I recalled one of our equitation instructors having warned us that aboard a runaway horse one must maintain absolute calm. He had failed, however, to explain how one remains calm with nine hundred pounds of dynamite exploding beneath him.

We had left the greensward of the polo field, flashed over the yellow clay of the marginal berm, and now all that was left to receive me as I parted company with that plunging equine (because I knew sooner or later it was coming to pass) was the hard cement. He cleared the embankment like a greyhound. We were out on the dreaded highway.

Apparently Tommy had never touched an unyielding surface before. The sound of his hoofs striking the pavement convulsed him with terror and he accelerated speed in a frantic endeavor to get away from the nerve-splitting torment, but the faster he advanced, the louder and closer on his ears fell the reverberations of his clacking feet. He became a cyclone of detonating cannon crackers.

Up to this point my boots held firmly to the stirrups, but as Tommy executed a sharp turn in the road I lost anchorage and my legs went dangling against his bounding sides. With frantic toes I tried to relocate the iron foot supports, but they were bouncing, flying, and goading the pony into even greater frenzy. As I clung astride that thunderbolt I could understand why the infantry still remained the most popular branch of the military services.

I was now at the complete mercy of the fright-crazed animal. If he stopped in his tracks, nothing could prevent my flying over his head; if he swerved, nothing could save me from catapulting over his side. In either event, a broken leg, a cracked shoulder, or worse was inevitable. Suddenly he violently shook his head like a dog emerging from a pond, and I lost the reins. I was forced into the horseman's unpardonable sin of "pulling leather"; that is, holding onto the saddle pommel with both hands. But as I did this I felt myself losing balance. The end of the journey would be worse than merely being thrown. I could almost feel the horse's macerating hoofs passing over me.

At this moment I heard the thudding of other hoofs, and from the corner of my eye I detected a meteoric shadow shooting into full view from the paralleling countryside. It crossed the margin and was now on the road, it was at our heels, it was at our flank; a strong arm reached out from the back of another horse, seized me around the waist and steadied me. "Grab your reins," a voice called. I took the flying reins. "Get into your stirrups, I'll hold you." I found one stirrup and then the other. "Hold tight." I obeyed. A hand reached out for my horse's check rein. The unknown rider now threw his weight and strength against mad Tommy, who gradually slackened speed and finally came to a halt.

I slid to the pavement and hobbled to the side of the road, where I collapsed on the grass, puffing and rejoicing over the narrow escape. Suddenly a voice boomed out: "Remove your hat. Where do you think you are? At home?" It was Sergeant Andrew Gilmore. He was a member of a visiting polo team which had come to play at Fort Hoyle.

How delightful can be life's coincidences. I had been with Gilmore for but a day. We had together witnessed one of the most solemn and beautiful ceremonies in the history of our country and we had become friends, but it seemed a friendship of but a day's duration, for after the ceremony we each took to our own separate paths and were separately swallowed up in our own individual worlds. Then seven years later I am on a horse galloping toward a precipice of disaster. Over the highway of time, like a guardian angel, speeds Sergeant Gilmore. Although our lives had known wholly different highways, the events of the intervening years had plotted their merging in such a manner that at the supreme moment of crisis they were as one. Gilmore had been on the polo grounds only five minutes when he recognized me; he had just started across the field to greet me when my horse plunged. Had he not made the recognition at that moment and had he not been coming toward me at the crucial instant of the runaway, he could never have caught up with me, and the career of the young lawyer might have been considerably different.

We dined together that evening and then went our respective ways once more. I did not see him for another year. This time *he* was riding a "runaway horse," a horse as panicky and as ungovernable as the one which had carried me to near destruction at Fort Hoyle. Gilmore was ready to commit murder, mayhem, bigamy, suicide.

He had married a girl in France and had brought her back to America to live with her in perpetual honeymoon. For ten years this honeymoon was uninterrupted. One evening, however, Gilmore returned home to find her entertaining a Frenchman he had never seen before. But let him tell the story as he impetuously related it to me in my office in Pittsburgh: "Musmanno, there are many lawyers in New York, but I came to you because this case of mine needs more than professional advice; it needs human understanding and sympathetic appreciation, both of which I know you possess."

I thanked him for his generous appraisal and assured him I would be happy to aid him to the extent of my capabilities. "My wife is in love with this Frenchman. His name is Julian Guerette," he went on. "They were born and reared in the same little town, they went to school together as children, and as children they became engaged to each other. Then he went away to war and my outfit came to this town. One day I met Babette at the village fountain. I carried home a bucket of water for her, and when we drank from the same dipper I knew we could never drink separately again. Soon after that I married her. Babette put Julian Guerette out of her mind, or rather he just fell out of her mind. However, ten years later he came to

America, found her, and the love of their childhood, all those years buried in obliterating sands, now, with this reunion, burst into renewed life. It is hard for me to believe it, but it is true! She loves him and my honeymoon has come to an end—and I don't know what to do with myself. I must either shoot Guerette, shoot myself, marry another woman to forget Babette, or get a divorce."

"Well," I laughed, "you have inverted the order of the last two items. You must get a divorce before you can marry someone else. But don't you think you may be a little hasty? Are you sure she does not love you? The fact that your wife greeted her childhood friend does not mean she has ceased loving you, does it?"

"No, but her attitude has changed. She has withdrawn to a room of her own. She no longer talks to me. It is an awful situation. Often I think I will forget her in a wild orgy of drink, but even in those moments I think how wonderful and exciting it would be if Babette were with me."

"I can understand your emotions, Sergeant, but where is this man? Does your wife see him?"

Gilmore nervously lighted a cigarette and proceeded to relate that he did not know whether the visiting Frenchman was calling on his wife or not, but that his wife had confessed to him she went out with him one evening.

I asked: "Are you sure, Andy?"

Puffing at his cigarette as if his very life depended on getting as much smoke as possible into his lungs, he said: "Well, I have accused her of going out with Guerette and she has not denied it."

"But do you know of your own personal knowledge that she cares for him?"

"Well, when I came home that first night he was there, and when he left her he kissed her. It was a gentlemanly kiss, I suppose, but I didn't like the idea at all, so I hit him and knocked him down the stairs."

"What did your wife do?"

"She made a scene."

"And what did you do to her?"

"Oh, I didn't do anything to her except scold her a little bit and say I didn't want her to try any of her French tricks out on me."

I started at this and suspected that here lay the source of the unfortunate difference between the lovers. "What happened next?"

"The following day I came home and she was not there. She didn't return until midnight and she said she had gone to dinner with Guerette."

"And then what happened?"

"Well, then we stopped speaking to each other."

"And how long has this been going on?"

"For about a week."

As Gilmore lighted the last cigarette from the crumpled package which he threw into the wastebasket with needless energy, I expressed my satisfaction that he had not allowed the situation to drift into irremediable disaster.

"Oh, you don't think the situation is hopeless, Musmanno?" he queried eagerly as he tore loose a fresh package of cigarettes.

"Of course not. Now listen to me, Andy. I'm going to cross-examine you as if you were a witness in court, or as perhaps Sherlock Holmes might question one who came to him for advice, and from your answers I am confident we will derive a solution to your problem."

"Shoot, Musmanno, I'm ready."

"Well, Sergeant, it's a very simple case. Or should I say, 'Elementary, Watson, elementary.' Employing the deductive methods of the seer of 21 Baker Street, who is a great favorite of mine, I would say that Babette is profoundly in love with you."

"What? After the way she treated me, you say she loves me?"

"Devotedly."

"I don't understand."

"You have just told me that *you* love her madly, and yet you say you berated her, insulted her, ceased to speak to her."

"Yes, but what else could I do?"

"You could spare her feelings, you could reason with her, you could understand her."

"What is there to understand?"

"When she made the scene you describe, what did you do?"

"I scolded her."

"But what did you say?"

"I said she shouldn't try any of her French tricks out on me."

"Do you think that was the language to employ in the circumstances?"

"What was wrong with it?"

"France is the girl's home country, is it not? Did it not occur to you that when you cast aspersions on her motherland you may have offended her deeply, hurt her, in fact, to the extent that she does not know if you really love her or not? Words are little things, but they sometimes cut deeper than bayonets. She may have thought that when you generalized on a whole nation you could not have much respect for her."

"Oh, I didn't know she was so sensitive about France."

"Suppose in the discussion she had said: 'Don't you try out any of your American tricks on me,' what would you have said?"

"I probably would have been very mad about it."

"Do you begin to understand now?"

"I do, and I admit I should not have brought France into the quarrel."

"But why should there have been any quarrel? There should have been an attempt at understanding before a quarrel. However, I'm not attempting to lecture to you. I'm only endeavoring to show you why I am confident Babette loves you."

"If you can prove that, I'll be indebted to you for life."

"You do not need to be indebted to me. I'm merely revealing what exists. In the ten years of your marriage have you and your wife ever seriously disagreed—that is, prior to this time?"

"No."

"Had your love been a profound and confiding one?"

"It had."

"There's your answer."

"How?"

"If your love had been a shallow one, subject to frequent differences and incompatible positions, an argument would have meant little. She would have spoken to you the very next day. There would have been a perfunctory kiss, and life would have gone on in its uneventful, superficial way. But the fact that Babette has given every indication of being greatly hurt is almost conclusive evidence that she loves you deeply or, if you prefer, is madly in love with you."

"It sounds good."

"Now, you have told me that at one time Babette was in love with Julian Guerette, that they went to the same school, that they played together, that they promised to marry each other. Then you entered the picture, and she married you instead."

"Yes, that is true, and she married me because she loved me."

"Yes, she loved you, but when you married Babette you did not liquidate Guerette's love for her, and Babette was always aware of the fact that she gave to you a troth which she had already plighted to another. She loved you, there's no doubt about that, but there still lingered in her mind and soul the unhappy recollection of a broken word. When Guerette appeared, the opportunity arrived for her to ease her conscience, to tell him she could never marry him, and to ask him to restore to her the promise she had made. Circumstances dictated he would have to comply with her request because she was already married to another. Still, ceremony and appearances had to be preserved. She was perhaps asking for the return of her promise when you appeared. Perhaps she had already received it when you came upon the scene and kicked him down the steps."

"Yes, I'm ashamed of that. But if she loved me, why did she go out with Guerette?"

"I don't think she did."

"But she admitted she did."

"That may have been only a ruse to find out whether you really loved her. And you certainly have proved that you do. It was cruel for her to have told you an untruth, but you also were cruel. You have both been cruel to each other, all so unnecessarily——"

"Musmanno, what can I do? What must I do?"

"Is your action not obvious? Here's the telephone. Call your wife and tell her you are coming back on the next train to resume your honeymoon."

He seized the telephone and in three minutes was excitedly saying: "Babette, I hope you forgive me. . . . He has left? . . . He left the first day? . . . Well, why didn't you tell me? . . . I know *I* was unreasonable. And you did not speak to me because you thought I had ceased loving you? . . . Babette, when I stop loving you, they can stop handing out air for me to breathe. *Ma chérie, dites-moi*—how about a little trip to our beloved France? You would like that, *non?* To visit the country of your childhood—a second honeymoon, *n'est-ce pas?*—which will—last a long time—*pour toujours et toujours*— *dites-moi, chérie,* okay? . . . Okay . . ."

Chapter XXVIII

EXTRA STITCHING

IS IT possible for one to be right and still lose in court? It is this type of question which causes Satan to reinforce his sides with extra stitching to avoid bursting as he laughs the laugh that shakes the walls of hell.

On July 6, 1927, Casper Geislerr hummed a merry tune as he sank his pick into a black mineral vein three hundred feet below the surface and brought down a sizable avalanche of coal. Then, seizing his No. 2 shovel, he scooped it full and, with practiced arm and eye, heaved the contents into a coal car fifteen feet away. It was a study in poetry of motion to watch the shovel, in an even-tempered r-a-s-p, bury itself in the coal, rise to the surface symmetrically heaped with its black cargo, draw back and down, and then swiftly ascend in a graceful parabola. Suddenly the shovel would stop in mid-air as kling! its contents, in a puff of dust, left the wide-mouthed carrier and sailed cohesively through the air to the waiting mine car, where clack! it fell with controlled clatter.

R-a-s-p . . . kling . . . clack . . . clatter . . . Perfect tempo, perfect rhythm.

Geislerr accompanied each movement with a smile which cracked the cake of black dust constantly forming on his intent face. He was recalling his conversation the night before with Nellie Novalk, who promised to marry him as soon as she obtained a divorce from her absconding husband who had left her with four children, now being cared for by Geislerr. He had taken them into his home and fed them; he bought them clothing, books, and toys; he provided them with entertainment—and they returned his love and devotion in the fullest measure. It was Geislerr's intention after his marriage to Mrs. Novalk to adopt her offspring, who ranged in age from four to fourteen years. As he daydreamed on this happy moment of the happy future, his foot resting on his shovel, the main timber support above his head hissed menacingly. His practiced ear told him the ceiling was weakening. He leaped for the entry, but it was too late. When they dug him out of the slate and earth which engulfed him he lived only long enough to relate what had happened.

Mrs. Novalk came to me for counsel. It was obvious from the uncontested facts that the deceased Geislerr stood in the status of *loco parentis* to her children and that therefore they were entitled to workman's compensation the same as if Geislerr had been their father—natural or adoptive. As the accident occurred in——County, although Mrs. Novalk and her brood were now living in Allegheny County, we filed claim for compensation in the former county, and the workmen's compensation referee who heard the case awarded full compensation to the children.

The coal company appealed the referee's decision and the case was heard in the Court of Common Pleas of——County before President Judge Stanley and Judges Ferguson and Jones. I assured Mrs. Novalk after the hearing that our case was impregnable and that, it now being the month of April, we could expect good news before the summer holidays began. However, the summer came and passed, the autumn leaves fell, and now snowflakes were swirling about the courthouse, which, however, so far as our case was concerned, was as silent as the grave in which poor Geislerr lay buried.

As the new year began, I concluded that fidelity to my client required that I make some discreet inquiry of the judges as to the reason for the unusual delay, even though it might be embarrassing to do so. Toward the middle of January I telephoned President Judge Stanley and tactfully asked when we might expect judgment in the Novalk case, since the children were very much in need. The jurist replied that on account of a heavy calendar the court was a little in arrears in its work but that a decision could now be expected in the "very near future."

But January ran its icy course and so did February, and the mails were still as empty of news from——County as the Novalk family larder was empty of food. From time to time I visited the Novalks in their tiny two-room home (Mrs. Novalk did not always have the carfare to come to my office) and bade them be of good cheer, explaining that while the machinery of the law might move slowly it inevitably produced justice, and that when compensation for the children was finally authorized it would revert back to the date of Mr. Geislerr's death. Thus, excepting their present discomfort, they had nothing to worry about.

On one of my visits I was surprised to find on a wall of the Novalk abode an old campaign placard of mine mounted in a silver frame. I asked six-year-old Tessie where they had obtained the money to purchase the silver adornment. She related that her mother and two elder sisters (Marian, fourteen, and Sylvia, ten had done a house-cleaning job in a neighbor's home and had received several dollars in payment, and with this money they were able to decorate my picture. "Isn't it a pretty frame?" she asked.

"It's wonderful," I replied as I went on talking about the case but sadly reflecting on the sacrifice this family made by spending money for a tribute to their attorney, when that money could have been better used for buying food. As I reached for a handkerchief Tessie asked: "What's the matter?"

"Oh, nothing," I replied, "I got a particle of dust in my eye." Then, pressing a bill into her hand, I dashed away before my little lie about the dust became too apparent.

What faith poor people have in their lawyer! He stands between them and the dread, mysterious thing known as the law. The court-house to them is a forbidding structure, stern, cold, perhaps even cruel—certainly unsympathetic. The judges live in another world and often cannot understand these people beyond the pale. But the attorney speaks their language. He visits at their home, he fights their cause. He is brave, wise, aggressive. No one can intimidate him; no one can deceive him; no one can thwart him. Thus the lawyer be-comes in the eyes of these helpless and confiding folk a protector—aye, a knight on a white horse, a Galahad! They expect him to save them from all evil forces and to bring to them their just due, even as the knights of old rescued the imprisoned ragged princess and restored her to her rightful place in the shining castle.

March and April of the new year having now fallen into the abyss of profitless time, I engaged Attorney Harry Hixon in——County to check the docket in the prothonotary's office from time to time so as to protect myself against the rare possibility that a decision might be filed without my being apprised of it by the court officials. I also asked this fellow lawyer, considering that a whole year had now ex-pired since the date of the hearing and argument, to visit President Judge Stanley at his chambers and, as diplomatically as possible, obtain some information on the status of our case. We realized that it was a very delicate matter to visit a judge and, in effect, suggest that he no longer delay in attending to his duties, but the emptiness of the Novalk pantry impelled us to encroach a little bit perhaps on Emily Post etiquette.

Hixon followed my suggestion and later reported to me that he experienced no embarrassment whatsoever in talking to President Judge Stanley, who cordially explained to him that if there was any delay in disposing of the Novalk case the fault was not his. He had assigned the case to Judge Ferguson to write the opinion. Hixon called on Judge Ferguson, who, in his turn, was as gracious as Lord Chesterfield, and expressed his regrets about the delay in the Novalk decision but promised that he would now write the opinion at once.

One more month disappeared from the face of the earth and the opinion was still a phantom in the courts. I decided to telephone Judge Ferguson myself, making, of course, due apology for disturbing him. He was as cordial as a restaurant manager expressing regrets to a patron whose suit had been ruined by a waiter's carelessness with the soup. He promised me, as he had promised Attorney Hixon, that nothing would keep him from getting to the opinion-writing "at once."

Still another month later, on a visit to Philadelphia, I met Judge Ferguson, entirely by coincidence, in the lobby of the hotel where we both were staying. I inquired about his health and whether he was enjoying his trip. I commented on the baseball games of the day, and then, treading as gently as if I were on stilts making my way through a barnyard of eggs, I brought up the Novalk case. My precautions seemed entirely superfluous, because the judge was not annoyed at all. "Musmanno," he said, "I'm glad you brought that up. I will be back at my desk in a week's time, and the first order of business will be the writing of the opinion in that case."

But presently summer with its languid vacation days had moved in—the second time. July and August closed up shop, and we now would have to wait for the courts to reopen and for September, suntanned and refreshed, to return to take up the flagging burdens of justice. My colleague Hixon, again exercising diplomatic restraint, waited until several days after Labor Day to assure himself that Judge Ferguson had accustomed his vacation feet to the comfortable hassock beneath his desk and then he called to ask about the Novalk affair. Of course Hixon first inquired of the judge if he had had a nice vacation. The judge replied that he had had a "corking good time" and it was very nice of Hixon to inquire. However, he added, "If you have come to see me about the Novalk case, I don't know why you keep asking me about it. I don't have that case. Judge Stanley has it." Flabbergasted, Hixon blurted out: "But, Judge Ferguson, you told Mr. Musmanno three months ago that the case was on your desk and that you were about to write the opinion."

Judge Ferguson now leaned back in his swivel chair. Laughing aloud, as if it were a rather droll tale, he explained: "Yes, I did tell Musmanno that, but I was in error. It's strange how these things get mixed up. The case is really in the hands of President Judge Stanley. You might inquire of him." Perplexed and worried, Hixon now went to President Judge Stanley, who received him with good temper and affability. Again Hixon began with the vacation routine. He hoped Judge Stanley had had a nice summer. The judge replied that he had had a "bully time" and hoped that Hixon had had one too. "And now, what can I do for you, because I know you must have called about something specific."

Hixon coughed apologetically and said: "I'm terribly sorry to keep bothering you about the Novalk case, but there seems to be some grievous misunderstanding. You told me you had assigned that case to Judge Ferguson and he now tells me that Your Honor has the case. Of course there is no way for me to know which one of you is writing the opinion, but I would certainly appreciate knowing when we may expect a decision. Seventeen months have passed since we argued the case."

The judge, who had met Hixon at the door, now walked back to his desk, sat down, and leaned back in his heavily upholstered chair. Almost in a hurt tone he observed: "I don't know why you are making so much fuss about that case. We decided the Novalk case last April."

Hixon lifted an incredulous hand to his forehead. "Why, Judge Stanley, you told me last April that you had assigned the Novalk case to Judge Ferguson."

"Yes, but there was some mix-up."

"And how did Your Honor decide the case?"

"We decided it in favor of the coal company and against the Novalks."

When Hixon telephoned me this news I had difficulty holding the receiver to my ear. The Workmen's Compensation Act specifically says that compensation shall be paid to "children to whom the deceased stood *in loco parentis,* if members of the decedent's household at the time of his death." At the referee's hearing the coal company did not even present any evidence to dispute the generally accepted fact that Geislerr occupied the status of *loco parentis* to the Novalk children.

What had happened? Why had Judge Ferguson told me in May

and June that he was about to write the opinion in the Novalk case when, as it now turned out, the case had already been decided in April? And why had President Judge Stanley said that he had assigned the case to Judge Ferguson when in point of fact he had retained the case himself? What was wrong? Who was playing at ducks and drakes with the law? And what was behind the game?

However, there was no time to moralize. Since the Court, no matter how tardily, had now spoken, and spoken against us, our only recourse was to appeal to the next higher Court, the Superior Court of Pennsylvania. I filed or attempted to file an appeal at once, but a grave obstacle intervened. The Workmen's Compensation Act provides that appeals must be entered in the Superior Court not more than thirty days following the decision in the lower Court. But through no fault of ours, 135 days had now expired since Stanley's decision. I explained to the president judge of the Superior Court that the delay in filing the appeal was due to the fact that we had not been notified of the Common Pleas decision until 135 days after it was rendered. In fact, at the very time that the decision was being filed we were being told that the decision had not yet been made. The president judge of the Superior Court was very sorry, but it was beyond his jurisdiction to extend the statutory time in which to file an appeal. Our only relief was in the Common Pleas Court.

I returned to——County and asked for another hearing, which was granted, and a few days later I appeared before the original Court, composed of President Judge Stanley, Judge Ferguson, and Judge Jones. I read to them the section of the Workmen's Compensation Law which was involved; I cited the many decisions of our appellate courts and precedents from other courts, all of which authorized workmen's compensation to children who had been accepted into the household of a deceased workman who had cared for them as his children. After I had spoken for about ten minutes President Judge Stanley interrupted somewhat irritably: "Mr. Musmanno, you are arguing about something which is already behind us. How can we consider your case when you know that more than thirty days have expired since we rendered our decision?"

"If the Court please, I am endeavoring to have you change the decision you made denying compensation, but, if you will not change that decision, then I am asking that you allow us to appeal to the Superior Court, since it was due to your failure to notify us of the rendering of your decision that more than thirty days expired before we could knock at the doors of the Superior Court."

"But how can we authorize what the statute prohibits?" Judge Stanley asked with an air of finality.

"You can authorize the appeal by simply relating what occurred. I am certain that the Superior Court will entertain our appeal if it is informed by you that the delay in applying to that Court was due to the inadvertence, mistake, or miscalculation of this Court."

"But there was no inadvertence, mistake, or miscalculation on the part of this Court."

"Whose, then, was the inadvertence, mistake, or miscalculation?" I asked, my voice rising.

Judge Ferguson now intervened: "If there was any inadvertence, mistake, or miscalculation, it was simply because you waited too long to file your appeal."

"If Your Honors please, I wish to be very respectful to this Court, but I want to say, with no equivocation whatsoever, that if thirty days for appeal have expired, the fault is that of this Court. Let me call to this Court's attention some of the statistics in this case: One year and twenty-seven days elapsed between the time we first appeared in this court and the date you finally rendered your decision. Ten months expired between the time we filed our briefs and the date of your decision. Four and one half months—135 days—passed after you had made your decision before we were notified of it, although we were constantly asking about that decision. Nearly three years have passed since Casper Geislerr was killed, and the Novalk children are still denied the bread which the laws of this Commonwealth allow them. While this case has been pending before this Honorable Court, Mr. Hixon and myself have made ourselves obnoxious in asking, asking, asking, always courteously but insistently, when you would render your decision—and now to be told that we are late in appealing, when the information which would have guaranteed our appeal was withheld from us by this very Court, represents to me the very apogee of injustice. I have not yet heard an explanation by this Court as to why Mr. Hixon and I were deceived not once but many times——"

"Mr. Musmanno, you were not deceived, and I don't want you to say that this Court practiced any deception on you," Judge Ferguson heatedly declared.

"I will withdraw the word 'deceive,' but I believe the world is entitled to know why we were being told one thing when the facts were not in accord with what we were being told."

Judge Stanley straightened up in his high-backed chair. "Mr. Musmanno," he said, "I agree with Judge Ferguson that you are wrong in saying you were deceived, but I will gladly explain just what happened. I wrote the opinion in the Novalk case many months ago and I sent it over to Judge Ferguson, with the record, for his examination, since he had sat with me at the original argument. I could not file the decision without his concurrence, Judge Jones being absent at the time. The papers were placed on Judge Ferguson's desk. Sometime later some renovation work was done in his chambers and the papers became misplaced. Last April when you asked Judge Ferguson about the Novalk case he had forgotten entirely about it. Later on he came across a bundle of papers on his desk and he assumed, without opening the bundle, that they were cases which had been assigned to him from this last January's argument list, and he assumed further that you and Mr. Hixon were asking him about one of the cases which had been heard on that list. That is why he said to you that he would prepare the opinion at an early date. During the week ending April 26, Judge Ferguson then took up the bundle of papers on his desk and, upon looking at them, discovered that he had been mistaken in his previous assumption; namely, that the Novalk case had been assigned to him. He then found out that the case was not his at all but that the opinion had been written by the president judge and had been submitted to him only for his examination. He then examined it, approved it, and returned it to me, along with the record papers, so that it could be filed. Since you are insistent on knowing what happened, I now have told you what happened."

I could scarcely believe my ears as I listened to a judge explaining that four helpless children should be denied their day in court because a judge failed to open a bundle of papers on his desk to ascertain what it contained; because a judge's papers had been disarranged in the renovation of his chambers; and because a judge assumed what was not fact. I bit my lips to curb the expression of wrath boiling within me. I remained silent for a few seconds and then, looking at Judge Ferguson, asked: "Judge Ferguson, will you please tell me and the world why, when I asked you in May and June—after the decision had already been rendered—why you did not tell me you did not have the opinion to write and that the decision had been handed down?"

"Mr. Musmanno," Ferguson replied, "the president judge has made explanation of what has occurred and we are not required to answer questions put by counsel."

"Very well, Judge Ferguson," and I turned again to the three judges. "If the Court please, I am told that you are not required to answer questions put by me. Nonetheless I ask: Is bread to be taken from the mouths of four innocent children because Judge Ferguson failed to examine a bundle of papers on his desk—failed to open them and find out what they were? Is the world to assume that that is the way judges attend to their work and that is the way justice is administered? Is justice to be denied because over the period of a whole year two judges cruelly misled counsel?"

Judge Jones now stepped into the breach, his face reddening. "Mr. Musmanno, I will not allow you to cast reflection on my colleagues. And I would like to say that you are adopting a very improper attitude in this whole matter. You are making justice personal."

"Of course I am making it personal. True justice is always personal, it is never abstract, it is never theoretical, it is never academic. Justice means bread and milk and clothing—and decency and fair dealing, that's what justice is."

"Mr. Musmanno," the president judge now took over again, "this argument is being prolonged far beyond what the merits of the case deserve. We have rendered our decision, and if you wish to appeal, your appeal is to the Superior Court."

I returned to the Superior Court and was there informed that they were powerless to act. The thirty-day period had expired and it was up to me to get the lower Court to make whatever correction was required. I came back to the——County court, but just as Judge Ferguson had failed to look into the papers on his desk, so did the Court refuse to look further into the bundle of injustice.

Coal Miner Casper Geislerr had blasted a competence out of a mountain of coal for the four children he had accepted as his own, but the children were denied that treasure because someone in the courthouse chose the wrong time to paint the chambers of the judge in which the destiny of the Novalk children had been placed for safekeeping.

Ask these children and their mother as they recall their years of want and destitution if it is possible to be right and still lose in court.

Chapter XXIX

EUREKA!

THE winning party in the Novalk case was a coal company. As a matter of moral justice, why didn't it pay the referee-awarded compensation to the Novalk children? Why did it avail itself of a technicality to prevent the children from appealing to the Superior Court? The answer to that question is that the coal company is in business to make money, and it disburses funds only when required to do so by law. And even where the law requires payment, the company will not pay if, through astute court procedure, it can circumvent that legal duty. The corporation retains an attorney to protect its interests, and when the Court agrees with the attorney's position, who can deny that the company is right?

But what about the attorney in the case? Does he not have a conscience? Indeed he does when his own personal obligations are concerned: he pays his taxes, supports his wife and children, and behaves like the good neighbor he undoubtedly is. However, putting aside for the moment the merits of the legal controversy, does the attorney believe he is engaging in fair dealing when he avails himself of a cold technicality, knowing that it was a judge's oversight or neglect which deprived four fatherless children of their rights in an appellate court? His reply to that question would indubitably be: "But who am I to attack the integrity of the courts? The judges have spoken and I will abide by their decision. If they had decided against us, the coal company would have paid the money. And that's an end to it."

It sometimes seems quite complicated, this machinery of justice—wheels within wheels, and wheels within them. You are struck by an automobile and sustain injuries. The automobilist is insured. Good, you say. The insurance company will send its agent to compute your damages and pay you at once. Why not? You are without fault; if you take the motorist into court you will probably obtain a larger sum of money than the amount you are willing now to accept in settlement. It behooves the insurance company to make a settlement, but the insurance company won't pay. Why? The motorist denies he struck you.

Why has he denied this? Because cowardice was at the wheel. He struck you down, ran over you, and fled like a thief in the night. He knew you were lying on the ground injured and helpless; he knew that the laws of the state, of humanity and elementary decency, required he stop to render aid; but fear, like a narcotizing drug, was in his veins. The coward's fear is selfishness. At the root of every act of poltroonery, at the base of every white feather, is the venal regard for self as against the cry of humanity in distress. It would have been an annoyance for the motorist to stop, to pick up a messy, bleeding person, to get his well-pressed suit streaked with blood, to take the unknown person to a hospital and then be required to answer so many questions. All this would delay the motorist. It was 3:30 A.M.; he wished to get to bed as soon as possible. Anyway, a man who would work in the middle of the street where he knew automobiles would pass could not be very bright and should not annoy good citizens who have other things to do. . . . And so the motorist, like a midnight prowler, melts into the night. . . .

Ralph Stevenson was laying paving blocks in the middle of the street. This work had to be done at night so that streetcars could travel unimpeded during the day. He felt himself safe, since barriers, safety lanterns, and signs barricaded the passage of all vehicles. Even so, he suddenly finds himself ascending amid a clatter of flying missiles, and on the gray wings of bewildering pain he lands in a whitewashed world: he is surrounded by white walls, about him are white sheets, his arms are swathed in white bandages, a white-clad lady stands at his side. "What has happened?" he gasps.

The white-clad lady replies: "You have been in an automobile accident."

The next day the bandaged man's wife came to seek my help. She did not know who or what had sent her husband to the hospital. Dropping everything, I hurried out to the corner of Penn and Negley avenues, the scene of the accident. My inquiries disclosed that two gasoline-station attendants had obtained the license number of the offending automobile—that is, between them they had lassoed the number. Jack Kirkpatrick had caught the first three digits—642— as the car, in a cloud of scattering debris and the cries of several street repairers, flashed by. On the other side of the street, Robert

Higbee, the attendant at another gasoline station, had caught the four right-hand digits—2357. The fact that Higbee bagged one of the digits also taken by Kirkpatrick reassured both of them that they had captured the right number.

The police had not been slow in following up clues. Officer John Campbell, after ascertaining that the owner of the license number was Clark Crandale, hurried to Crandale's home, where he found a car bearing the telltale license number. It was splashed with mud (there were puddles of water at Penn and Negley). Crandale, who was just getting into pajamas, denied knowing anything about the accident but admitted he had passed the corner of Penn and Negley at 1 A.M., going north on Negley. The car which had struck Stevenson was traveling *south* on Negley. Where was he going when he passed the intersection at 1 A.M.? He was taking a Miss Dorothy Dickson home. Where did she live? On Foxchapel Road. Returning, did he take the same route over Negley Avenue? No, he had returned by way of Washington Road.

When the case came to trial three years later, the gasoline-station attendants knocked the bottom out of my case. They said they did not remember the license number and had lost the paper on which they had written it. My knees buckled.

"But didn't you make some other notation?" I appealed to Higbee.

"Yes," he replied a little awkwardly, "but you couldn't use that in court."

"Why?"

"Well, when I got home that morning and went to bed I kept thinking of the accident and especially the number. Those figures kept chasing through my mind—and they were getting larger—and I couldn't get to sleep. I thought if I could write them down I would feel better. I got up and wrote them on the wall and then I slept fine."

"Did you ever check those figures with the slip of paper on which you and Kirkpatrick had written the number?"

"Yes, the next morning I found the slip in my pocket and checked it with the figures on the wall and they were both the same."

"Eureka!" I exclaimed.

"What do you mean by 'Eureka'?" Higbee asked.

"That means we have found it."

"Well, that's a good word to know, but I don't know that you have found anything yet. I don't live there any more and I think that they have torn down the house since I left."

My heart plummeted. "Well, let's go see." When we drove to Milton Street, Higbee yelled: "Eureka!"

We took the steps three at a time to Higbee's former room, and there on the time-stained wall appeared the inscription that meant more to me than all the bronze plaques in the city—6 4 2 3 5 7 in bold, plain, indelible penciling. Higbee transferred the number to his notebook and testified in court that those were the figures on the license plate as taken down by himself and Kirkpatrick.

The defendant's attorney sought to discredit Kirkpatrick and Higbee because they could not recall the exact color of the machine. Both witnesses explained that in the short time the car was within their view they were concerned only with getting the license number. This line of questioning on the part of my opponent opened a vista of cross-examination for me. The defendant had brought into court five of his immediate friends to testify that they were with him the night of the accident, that they knew the car, and that at the exact time of the accident it was nowhere near Penn and Negley. At each one of these witnesses I hurled the question, "What was the color of the car?" Each one recalled a different color. In my summation to the jury I said:

"If these people, who were so intimately associated with the car for over a year, were unable to agree on its color, how could you expect Kirkpatrick and Higbee to know its exact tint when they saw it for only the matter of seconds as it whizzed by—at night? Mr. Williams complains because they cannot tell you the machine's precise color. He would have been more satisfied—oh, so much more satisfied—if these two good men had overlooked the license number and noted the color. And then how Williams would have stormed: 'Oh, how can you identify a car by giving us only its color!' "

Attorney Williams objected to my line of argument and we fell into a bitter altercation. In this connection I should like to say something about the attitude of lawyers toward each other during a trial. Throughout the period of my practicing career I maintained a good and friendly relationship with all members of the Bar, but I could never do what I have seen so many opposing lawyers do; that is, joke and exchange meaningless banter across the counsel table during a trial and then often leave the courtroom arm in arm. I was always deadly in earnest in the courtroom. To the extent that my lawyer-antagonist was trying to worst me, he was trying to take from my client what I believed was justly his, whether it happened to be his life, liberty, property, or damages due him because of personal injuries.

I have been annoyed at times to hear contending lawyers pay insincere compliments to each other while arguing before a jury, even going so far as to say that their antagonism was only of the present trial and that once it was ended they would probably be having dinner together. All that might be true, but it seems to me that such observations suggest that trials are only games and that it does not really matter who wins. It meant a great deal to me who won this case. Stevenson was entitled to a verdict, and to the extent that Williams was trying to deprive him of it, I resented it and I wasn't thinking of having any dinner with him after the trial, either.

I do not suggest that all the cases tried by the young lawyer (of which only a small percentage are referred to in these nostalgic reminiscences) were spectacular, but I have attempted, by lifting a corner of the curtain covering the human heart beating in the courtroom, to reveal mainsprings which sometimes control little things in life which, in turn, govern big things. Cross-examining Crandale, I asked him why he did not return to his home via Negley Avenue since he had used that route on his way out to Foxchapel Road and it was admitted that this was a shorter route between the two points involved. He replied that he had returned via Washington Street in order to avoid the traffic. Here was a little mainspring gone awry. "Crandale says he did not come back via Negley Avenue because of traffic—because of traffic, members of the jury—at three-thirty in the morning! Oh, what absurd things people say when they are trying to support a lie that refuses to stand up. Oh, how they try to bolster it up and oh, how it falls and falls again. Avoiding traffic at three-thirty in the morning! Members of the jury, on this statement alone Crandale displays his falseness. And as he falsifies on these subsidiary matters, he perjures himself on the main issue.

"You heard him say on the witness stand that on the night of the accident he had been to the theater, but only two hours after the accident he told Police Officer Campbell that he had attended a party. One who seeks to deny the crucial fact in the case will deny the little facts as well. What difference did it make whether he had been to a theater or a party? Crandale feared, when Officer Campbell questioned him, that if he said he had taken in a show that evening the police would have been able to trace his movements from that point. A guilty man is suspicious of all circumstances."

The most important item in a personal injury case is the amount of the verdict. Once the jury decides for the plaintiff, it must calculate the damages to which he is entitled. It awards an amount which will reimburse the plaintiff for his medical expenses, loss of wages, and impairment of earning power, and then allows an amount to compensate him for his pain and suffering. This last item of compensation cannot be computed with mathematical accuracy. How do you compensate for physical pain—nerve-shattering, soul-searing pain? Upon the jury the law places the responsibility of compensating the plaintiff for what he has endured in physical agony.

"You have heard how Ralph Stevenson has been suffering unceasing, skull-splitting headaches for three years, with the prospect they will continue into the indefinite future. Everyone at some time or another experiences a headache, an annoyance, a slight throbbing at the temples, a languidness which is easily overcome by ingesting a pill, by taking a walk in the fresh air—and then the music of life again thrills your soul. But what do you do when pills fail, fresh air does not help, and doctors cannot lighten the heavy weight pressing down on your brain? What do you do when science trips, philosophy falters, and the torment goes on and on in your cranium? What do you think such a torment would mean in money damages?

"Before the accident Ralph Stevenson slept well. Now sleep to him is a stranger. He is chained to the ogre of insomnia. Have you ever wanted to sleep, to lose consciousness, to go floating along on the river's bosom of restful abandon; to know no worries, no cares, but sleep eludes you because of the very thing you wanted to forget— your pains? What would you give in the way of money to find the balsam of sleep?

"One of the cruelest of punishments administered in the third degree where that loathsome relic of barbarism still lingers is to forcibly deprive the prisoner of sleep until he is ready to confess to anything—murder, treason, betrayal, anything—only so that he may drink of that rarest of wines and breathe of that sweetest of fragrances—sleep.

"What would be your sensations if you tossed on a bed of spikes and kept recalling that this was your lot because you were struck down in the road while you were working—working to place bread on the table for your wife and your children? Consider all that in your verdict. The law requires you to do so.

"My friends, you have heard Stevenson describe the incessant ringing in his head. No disharmony the defendant may hear because of money he must pay can outdo the discordant clanging and tolling of bells the plaintiff has endured for the last three long years."

In Williams' closing speech to the jury he agreed with me that the man who struck down Ralph Stevenson was a beast and was not entitled to any mercy or sympathy from the jury. It was quite evident he believed that the jury would never return a verdict against his polished and cultured client, Clark Crandale, so he made bold to say, with a smirk on his lips: "Why, if Clark Crandale is guilty of this inhuman deed you should soak him." And the jury did just that— they returned a verdict for Stevenson in the sum of ten thousand dollars.

Chapter XXX

WHEN JUSTICE BECOMES COMPLICATED

THE appeal to the jury is the climactic third act of court-room drama. In cases which attract public attention it is on the day that the lawyers make their final speeches that space in the courtroom is at a premium and the S.R.O. sign is figuratively displayed. And this is only natural, because this is when a trial most resembles the spectacle of a pitched battle. On this day the lawyer fires his artillery of facts, gallops his cavalry of logic over the sunken road of the opposition's theories, and then advances with the bayonets of rationalization to the battlefield of argumentation swept by the enfilading fire of his opponent. From it all rises the spirit of rivalry with its expectant thrill of victory, all vicariously felt by the spellbound audience looking on.

In his final speech the lawyer calls into play his entire forensic armory. He appeals to the jury's common sense, their emotions, their love of God, home, and country—he fires every argument which may help him win his case. A tendency has developed in recent years in the institutions of higher learning and in certain intellectual circles to look with disfavor upon demonstrative oratory, and yet I would say to young lawyers that they must learn to feel as well as to reason. More people "feel" their way than think their way through life. The basic emotions can never be obliterated or submerged, and to ignore them in a speech to the jury is to display an unawareness of reality; for every case is a slice of raw life boiled, broiled, and roasted over the fires which generate from the friction and clash between human hates and human loves.

One of the most successful lawyers at the Pittsburgh Bar during the past generation was the late William H. Coleman, who in his closing arguments to the jury would put on a show that could out-rival Billy Sunday, William J. Bryan, John Barrymore, and James Cagney, all welded together into one speaking phenomenon. Standing at the jury rail, he would thunder, cry, whisper, and gesture. He played on the keyboard of human feelings and emotions as an organist performs at the console. He had the blazing sincerity which seemed to say that he would give his life to prove his client's innocence— and I believe he would have. Coleman lost very few cases. Of course he was by nature a demonstrative orator. He had what is known as a "tear in his voice." Others lacking that natural aptitude might find themselves an object of ridicule if they attempted to ape his style. Nonetheless, his manner of speaking proves that, when applied without artifice or guile, demonstrativeness has its place before a jury, as it has its place in everyday life. Do people become angry? Of course they do. Do they fall into confusion? No one can doubt it. Do they succumb to their emotions? Every day we see it. It is of this stuff that life is made. And the more directly and simply this is brought to the jury's attention, the more directly and simply they can arrive at a just decision.

Life is expression. Music, sculpture, painting, embroidery, literature are all forms of expression. Expression is the transmission of sunbeams from the sky to the earth and of moisture from the earth to the clouds. Expression is an exchange which benefits both the giver and the taker. And in all the media of exchange, none is more universal or more effective than speech.

The thoroughly alive lawyer vibrates with the righteousness of his client's cause: the client has been maltreated, injured, damaged, and the lawyer must obtain justice for him. He presents his case—to whom? To a body of unfeeling technicians? To a Univac of nuts and bolts? No, he makes his appeal to twelve men and women, people you see every day on the street, in the stores, fields, shops, and at the baseball park, people who understand justice in its elementary forms—and justice should always be elementary. Once justice becomes complicated, it loses the rich essence which is the very attribute of justice.

I was representing a twenty-two-year-old girl who had been hurled through the windshield of the automobile in which she was riding when it was hit by a truck traveling on the wrong side of the road. Prior to the accident, Mary Walker had been a vision of superlative beauty, now she was tragically disfigured.

Nothing complicated about that: "Members of the jury, Mary Walker comes into court for justice. One year ago on April 15 she could not appear in public without becoming the cynosure of every eye. Her loveliness was so extraordinary that it attracted like a shaft of gold from the sky breaking through a dark and foggy day. Now she cannot appear in public without attracting the attention which no one desires.

"Prior to this horrible accident Mary Walker was a ravishingly beautiful girl. She evoked thoughts of Venus, Mona Lisa, Helen of Troy, and all that entrancing parade of beauty gracefully treading the flower-strewn path of history's charming womanhood. Here is her picture"—proffering photograph—"taken a month before the accident. Breath-taking, isn't it? Look upon those features fit for a Greek goddess, perceive the coral lips, the capturing smile, the perfect blending of harmonious lines. Even this untouched photograph tells of the roses and cream in her complexion, of the glorious health in her sparkling eye, of the wondrous luster of her hair. You heard witness after witness describe with a sigh the gorgeous beauty of this once happy girl.

"Beauty. Ah, beauty, the dream of every girl, the yearning of every maiden, the longing and aspiration of every lass as she appears on the stage of life.

"This girl had beauty, but now it has disappeared behind the curtain of the past. Never to have been beautiful is not so piercing a tragedy as to have possessed this most priceless gift of the gods and then lose it. That merciless gasoline truck cut beauty out of the face of Mary Walker as the vandals once ripped Mona Lisa from her frame and left an empty quadrangle of wood.

"This is an age of beauty. On comeliness of form and harmony of feature are today conferred rewards never even imagined in the past. With motion picture directors, stage producers, and commercial artists constantly seeking girls of facial splendor, blemishless skin, and perfect teeth, every pretty girl has become a potential financial treasure. We do not know whether Mary Walker aspired to the stage or screen, but we do know that with her sheer enchantment of grace she possessed the potentialities of riches founded on sheer pulchritude.

"But the bloom and radiance which were hers have been scraped away by the broken glass cruelly dashed into her face by that monster truck. She is no longer beautiful. That rosebud mouth of hers is deformed, the coral lips are jagged, her smile turns into an unwanted leer. That matchless skin with its rose-petal texture has been roughened with merciless scars. Her dainty chin, which she had so joyously tossed in girlish abandon, is branded. As long as she lives Mary Walker will bear these ugly slashes which disqualify her at once in the ever-present contest for faultless beauty. Miss Walker can and will be referred to as 'the girl with the scarred face.' "

I stopped speaking. The heart-stricken maiden had broken into unrestrained sobbing which mounted to frenzy. Even against what the candid mirror told her, she still hoped she might once again be beautiful. "Perhaps it was unkind of me to say what I have said," I went on after a pause, "but my expression was the creation of pity. Many will voice it out of malice."

There was never any doubt about the liability of the truck owner. The only question the jury had to decide was the amount of the verdict they should award the plaintiff. I hoped it would be a large verdict, because there always lingered the hope that with plastic surgery something might be done, if not to restore the girl's original flowerlike delicacy of feature, at least to remove scars which made hideous to her every mirror, every windowpane, every shining metal surface which would catch and send back to her affirmation of the unsightliness which she hoped might still not be true.

Never did I plead with more feeling and fervor for a sister human being. "Members of the jury, Mary Walker is a young girl with her whole life ahead of her. She was struck down by a merciless fate traveling in a truck on the wrong side of the highway. Award her such a verdict as you would expect another jury to assign to your own daughter if she were similarly afflicted and similarly disfigured. My friends, render such a verdict that when you yourselves stand before the Great White Throne on Judgment Day you will be satisfied with the justice you rendered unto this little girl with her poor scarred face and her pain-racked form."

When I ended my speech, a dead silence, interrupted only intermittently by the stifled sobs of Mary Walker, had settled on the courtroom. Two or three of the women jurors were dabbing at their eyes with handkerchiefs as they looked on the hapless little girl who had come into their lives. Would they ever be able to forget that pathetic countenance? What could they do for her? Although they could never restore to Mary the bloom of beauty which was once hers, they could plant a lilac bush or two in the bleak garden which had at one time been a riot of roses and dreams.

But suddenly another truck rumbled into the picture—and it seemed to be traveling on the wrong side of the road too. My opponent, the attorney for the truck company, rose and addressed Judge Moore on the bench: "May it please the Court, I ask for a mistrial on the ground that Mr. Musmanno has inflamed the jury. In the present state of their excitement to which his speech has brought them, they will be incapable of rendering a verdict which will be just to both sides."

"Your Honor," I replied, "Mr. Pierce's motion is absurd. I have said nothing which is not supported by the evidence. Your Honor has the right in his charge to make any reference to my speech which he deems necessary. I see no reason why, after a week in court, Mary Walker should again be required to undergo the ordeal of another trial, which in itself will leave another scar on her sensibilities and on her soul."

But Judge Moore heeded not my protest or the beseeching eyes of my client. As the jury gasped in astonishment, the black-robed arbiter of justice declared: "The motion of Attorney Pierce is granted, and I declare a mistrial."

Spectators in the courtroom looked at one another in helpless inquiry. Can a judge do this? Can he take the decision away from the jury? And why should there be attorneys if they may not plead the cause of their clients to the full extent of its demands for justice?

The judge's decision was even more unjust than it appeared. Miss Walker simply could not come into court again. The torture of another trial, listening to the doctors say she would never again be beautiful, and feeling the world sink beneath her feet at pronouncement of the word "ugly" went beyond what she could endure. She preferred anything but another trial. Thus we were compelled to accept from the truck company a settlement which was not even a beauty patch on the face of loveliness. . . .

When justice becomes complicated, it loses the rich essence which is the very attribute of justice.

Occasionally the lawyer can simplify the complications of the law. I was in Criminal Court defending Pete Mardik, an unschooled vegetable huckster indicted on a charge of perjury. He was accused of swearing falsely to an affidavit filed in an action for divorce he had brought against his wife, who, among other things, had once attempted to shoot him. When Mrs. Mardik was brought before a judge on the criminal charge which had followed this attempt, she was paroled on condition that she leave town, whereupon she took up residence in Chicago with a brother. Her husband, however, was required to support her, so that each week he paid into the Non-Support Court a sum of money which was forwarded to her through court channels.

A couple of years later Mardik began his divorce action, and at the request of his attorney (not I) he went to the courthouse to obtain his wife's address so that notice of the divorce proceedings might be served on her. In the courthouse Mardik became bewildered as he wandered through the corridors, courts, and offices in that vast building and he reported to his attorney that he had been unable to obtain the desired information. Later he made the affidavit in which he stated he was ignorant of his wife's whereabouts. His wife's brother in Chicago, learning of this affidavit, came on to Pittsburgh, appeared before a committing magistrate, and charged Mardik with attempting to obtain a divorce fraudulently. The charge of perjury followed, and I was retained to defend Mardik.

I realized the difficulties of my case. Since Mardik's wife's address appeared in the records of the Non-Support Court, the Commonwealth would maintain that all Mardik had to do to get it was to ask for it, and particularly would this be true since he was contributing to her support in that very court every week. Still I believed Mardik was innocent of any intentional wrongdoing.

The only reason he had come away without his wife's address was that, like a sheep in the woods, he could not find his way around in the forest of rooms in the courthouse, but how could I prove that fact to the jury? Merely to assert it was not enough.

I outlined in my mind a plan of defense which was really in the nature of an offense. At the opening of the trial I casually asked Hiram Wilson, the trial assistant district attorney, where I could obtain the records in the divorce proceedings between Mr. and Mrs. Mardik. He replied that he did not know. Later on I asked him if he would be so kind as to locate for me the indictment which had charged Mrs. Mardik with an attempt to shoot her husband. Petulantly he replied: "Find it yourself. I don't know where it is."

Mr. Wilson's first witness was the chief clerk of the Disbursement Section of the Non-Support Court, who testified that Mrs. Mardik's address was on file in his office and that if Mr. Mardik had called for it, it would have been given to him. Cross-examining the clerk, I asked: "Do you receive the money which is paid by husbands for their wives?"

"No, I only disperse it."

"Where is the money received?"

"In the Acceptance Section."

"And where does the money then go?"

"To the Bookkeeping Section."

"And from there where does it go?"

"To the Disbursement Section."

"And that is your section?"

"Yes."

"And you send the money to the wife?"

"Yes."

Wilson then put on the witness stand a clerk from the Acceptance Section, who testified that Mr. Mardik came once a week to pay his support money, and he recalled that on one occasion Mardik asked for his wife's address and he was sent to the Disbursement Division.

In my cross-examination I asked:

"Did you give him the number of the room?"

"No."

"Did it not occur to you that he might lose his way in this big building?"

"No, that did not occur to me."

"Did you give him any instructions on how to get to the Disbursement Section?"

"No, I just told him to go to the Disbursement Section."

"Do you think he understood you?"

"I object," Wilson interjected. "How does he know if the defendant understood?"

The judge sustained the objection.

In his opening statement to the jury Wilson had made a vigorous demand for conviction and he had followed it with documentary and record evidence which seemed incontrovertible. He now rested his case.

I called the defendant to the stand and he testified that he truly did not know where his wife lived, that he had applied for that information at the office where he deposited his weekly support money, that there they had referred him to another office, and from that point he went to still another office, and finally he became lost. He tried unsuccessfully on several other occasions to ascertain his wife's address and at last concluded that he was not supposed to know her whereabouts. He feared the authorities might think he wanted to do her some harm, so he ceased trying to locate her. When he signed the affidavit in which he said that he did not know where his wife lived, he was telling the truth.

At this point in the proceedings I picked up a sheet of paper and, scribbling something on it, I turned to the tipstaff and said: "Mr. Tipstaff, please deliver this paper to the Disbursement Section."

"What is the room number, Mr. Musmanno?"

"I don't know, Mr. Tipstaff, but certainly you ought to know. How long have you been an officer of this court?"

"Ten years."

"And you don't know where the Disbursement Section of the Non-Support Court is?"

"No."

Wilson angrily interposed: "If the Court please, I object to Mr. Musmanno interrogating the tipstaff in open court. The tipstaff is neither a witness, nor is he on trial."

"Well, Mr. District Attorney, perhaps you can tell me where the Disbursement Section is."

"It's in the courthouse somewhere," he replied with a sneer, "and your client could have found it if he really wanted to."

"Really? All right, Mr. District Attorney, I'll ask Court to recess for a few minutes while you direct me the the Disbursement Section."

"If the Court please, I refuse to be annoyed in this manner by defense counsel."

"If the Court please, I rest my case."

I advanced to the jury box and asked: "Members of the jury, do any of you know where the Disbursement Section is? The district attorney does not know, the tipstaff does not know, and they have been in this courthouse for many years, and yet they expect this poor, ignorant huckster to know.

"The machinery of the courts is a complicated one, and it is not given to every person who is caught in its crushing gears to know how it operates. Even many who have a hand in the operation of that machinery do not know the location of the various levers and controls. You will recall that I asked the district attorney at the very outset of the trial how I could obtain the records in the Mardik divorce proceedings and he said he did not know. I later asked him to get for me a copy of the indictment against Mrs. Mardik in the felonious shooting case and he indignantly replied: 'Find it yourself. I don't know where it is.'

"And yet they expect this illiterate, dumb potato peddler to find his way through the labyrinthine passages of this enormous edifice seeking a card among tens of thousands of cards, seeking an address among tens of thousands of addresses, seeking what no one wanted to give him because it might mean a little inconvenience to them. Members of the jury, Pete Mardik did not know the location of the Disbursement Section, but he does know the location of justice. It is right here in this box. I ask you to acquit him of this heinous charge which should never have been brought. I ask you to acquit him and to place the costs of the prosecution on the one responsible for it."

And that is what the jury did. They acquitted Mardik and assessed the costs against the itinerant brother-in-law from Chicago.

Chapter XXXI

CRUTCHES

MRS. EVALINE BARTLEY, white-haired and gentle-mannered, came to see me about her intended son-in-law, Emery Gordon. He was in a little trouble. Prospective clients never tell you they are in a great deal of trouble. It is always only a *little* trouble. Emery Gordon's little trouble was that he had been indicted on a charge of armed robbery and burglary!

Mrs. Bartley, however, assured me he was innocent. And if what she related was true, he had to be innocent. She said that on the night he was supposed to be breaking into Miller's Jewelry Store he was at her home courting her daughter, whom he intended soon to marry. Moreover, she explained, it was impossible for him to have committed the crime because his legs were paralyzed; he could never have climbed in through Miller's store window and then driven the bandit car, as asserted by the police.

The next day I rang the bell at the entrance to the Allegheny County Jail. A barred door swung open. I passed into the prison office. Then another door glided away on well-oiled hinges and I entered the rotunda of the prison from which radiate the tiers of cells. Here lawyers talk with their clients. I asked the head guard to call Emery Gordon and waited.

I sat at a table and studied the steel cages housing the human poultry beating their wings against the bars of Lachesis. Some were innocent, some were guilty. What force is it that mingles the guilty and the innocent in one undiscriminating collectivity? And is the law always able to distinguish between the innocent robin and the predatory hawk?

As I pondered these imponderables there fell upon my ears a tapping sound on stone floors. I turned and beheld a young man approaching on two crutches, his body swinging between the supports like a bell on its axis. I rose to help him to a chair. "Thank you," he said as he sat down and rested his crutches against the table. "I've been expecting you, Mr. Musmanno. Mrs. Bartley told me about you."

"How long have you been disabled?" I asked.

"Three years."

"What's wrong with your legs?"

"They're paralyzed, and I don't see how the police have the nerve to say I could be mixed up with a burglary."

At the magistrate's hearing a Tim Dennis had testified that Gordon had planned the burglary with him and two others, that Gordon was not crippled, and that his crutches were only a ruse. One apparently disinterested witness testified that he had seen Gordon in Dennis' company the day prior to the attempted burglary. Gordon explained to me that it was true he had been with Dennis, but there was nothing strange about this since they had been friends since boyhood. He said that on the occasion of the meeting prior to the attempted burglary Dennis had wanted Gordon to join him in the proposed crime and that when he refused to do so Dennis asked him to concoct an alibi for him if he, Dennis, got caught. Gordon declined to do so, and Dennis then threatened that in the event the venture misfired and Dennis did not escape he would involve Gordon.

The venture did misfire. Dennis was apprehended at the very scene of the crime when the sounding of a burglar alarm brought police to the jewelry store just as an automobile carrying the accomplices raced away. Dennis told the police that Gordon was the driver of the escaping car.

At my request the prison doctor examined Gordon and declared after searching tests that Gordon had no motor control over his legs.

At the trial Dennis related in considerable detail how Gordon had planned the burglary with him and the gang and had played his part so well that he, with the others, got away while Dennis was left to face the music. On cross-examination I exposed Dennis' long criminal record but could not break his story that Gordon had helped to plan and execute the crime.

In addition to Dennis, the Commonwealth produced the witness who said he had seen Gordon and Dennis conferring the day before the crime. I called the jail physician, who testified to Gordon's paralytic condition. Although Mrs. Bartley testified that Gordon was at her home the night of the burglary, the prosecuting attorney argued that she was taking Gordon's part because Gordon was betrothed to her daughter. It became evident that if Gordon was to walk out free he could do so only on his crutches.

At the beginning of each day's session Gordon entered the courtroom on his wooden staffs, the metal-bound tips striking hard against the cement floor, producing an awesome clatter. Between them, Gordon advanced with the pathetic jerky movement of a large clumsy toy.

When Gordon finally got to the counsel table where he was to sit beside me, he would hand me the crutches, which I would take and proceed to place under the table. Occasionally one of them would slip from my grasp and go rattling to the floor. At each recess time and at adjournment, when Gordon was to return to jail, I unostentatiously made a ceremony of reaching for the crutches, standing them on end and placing the padded arm rests under Gordon's arms. The sight of this otherwise perfectly healthy and good-looking young man depending on wooden props for locomotion excited the sympathy of the five women on the jury. If a crutch slipped and banged to the floor, I always gasped and begged the pardon of the Court.

The issue of fact for the jury to decide finally narrowed down to one of credibility between Tim Dennis and the silver-haired Mrs. Bartley. "Whom will you believe?" I asked the jury. "Mrs. Bartley, upon whose head the snows of age are beginning to gather and to whom testimony in court is sacred, or Tim Dennis, to whom honor is a stranger and sworn oath a mere superfluity? To convict Emery Gordon you must make of this admitted burglar a paragon of veracity and you must transform Mrs. Bartley into a perjurer. Will you do this?

"Members of the jury, I implore you not to make any mistake in this case. There are twelve of you; each one of you must concur in the verdict, whatever it may be. Why does the law require a unanimous verdict? It requires unanimity because once your verdict is rendered you may not come back to change it. It will be recorded as if on tablets of imperishable bronze. You may not alter it tomorrow, the next day, or any other day.

"If you are convinced of Emery Gordon's innocence, now is the time to say so. Do not delay until you have been dismissed to declare it; do not tarry until you have returned to your homes to pronounce it; do not wait until some mist-heavy day in the future to reflect and then say: 'If I had to do it over again I would stay there until Doomsday before I would vote guilty.' It will be too late then."

During my speech a rainstorm broke. The courtroom darkened; furious sheets of water lashed at the large windows, throwing fitful shadows over the floor. In this somber setting, made dramatic by the driving elements, I went on: "If you permit yourself to vote guilty, although you believe this young man innocent, and he is sent to that living tomb down the river, some night you may waken to an ominous sound—a tap-tap-tapping through your consciousness. You will wonder the cause of that disturbance and whence it comes. Then before your startled vision will appear a pair of crutches and a thin, saddened face between. As you sit bolt upright in bed, those crutches will go tap-tap-tapping down the corridors of your vivid and painful memory."

As I spoke these lines I seized Gordon's crutches, placed them under my armpits, and swung between them as Gordon had so often done in the courtroom. Struggling to maintain my equilibrium on the wobbling sticks as I awkwardly and in unrhythmic staccato forced myself over the floor before the jury box, I went on: "Yes, you will then think of Emery Gordon between these crutches, behind those grim and dirty walls on the dark river. Your nerves will jump to those metallic feet hitting the desolate stone pavement: tap-tap-tapping. Your flesh will creep, your blood will run cold, and you will want to change your verdict, but it will then be too late, too late.

"Members of the jury, render such a verdict so that no matter how black the night or violent the storm there will shine through it all the white light of your chastened hearts in the realization that you have adjudged according to your conscience."

In his summation the trial assistant district attorney took bitter issue with me on the subject of what could happen after the verdict was rendered. He said that the jury had no jurisdiction once the verdict was arrived at. The trial judge in his charge to the jury affirmed what the prosecuting attorney had said in that respect and instructed them to ignore all references to post-verdict developments. One hour after the jury received the case for their decision, they returned with a verdict of not guilty.

Chapter XXXII

TUNNEL WITHOUT END

SUPPOSE an attorney represents someone who has lost a leg in an accident. He is disabled for life, and if he does not win his lawsuit he may hold his lawyer morally responsible for all his succeeding misery. The attorney also may feel uncomfortable every time he sees a one-legged man.

On Christmas night while George McCarthey, twenty-five years of age, was boarding a streetcar, the motorman closed the door and McCarthey slipped, falling under the wheels, which crushed his right foot. Gangrene later set in, and over a course of four operations, at each one of which a further segment of his leg was amputated, he finally lost the entire leg.

He engaged me as his attorney and we entered suit against the Pittsburgh Transit Company, which denied responsibility under three heads: (1). That McCarthey had attempted to board the car at a point not designated as a car stop. (2). He was drunk at the time the accident happened. (3). He had collided with the car while it was in motion.

At the trial the transit company introduced considerable evidence as to McCarthey's drinking habits. We admitted that he had in the spirit of the holiday taken several drinks that day but denied that he was intoxicated. Two or three persons on the jury frowned each time alcohol was mentioned. I realized that here I confronted grave difficulties: Might they not unconsciously develop a prejudice against my client and deny him recovery on the theory that his misfortune was the bitter fruit of a tree he had himself planted?

The issue had to be met directly. I could not dodge it: "Members of the jury, the transit company has endeavored—by every means possible within the scope of its resourceful ingenuity—to convey to you the idea that McCarthey is a drunkard. It is an unjust accusation. It is not true that he was drunk on the night of the accident, but even if he were, that unfortunate disablement would not give the motorman license to run him down. To whatever degree McCarthey has deviated from the strict path of sobriety, we ask for no mitigation of moral censure; for whatever his drinking habits may have been, we have no excuse; for any consequence directly attributable to alcohol, we ask for no sympathy—but for an able-bodied youth who was struck down in the street without remorse, without conscience, and without pity, we ask for justice!

"George McCarthey is entitled to justice even if he were the town sot, which he is not; he is entitled to justice, even assuming he were paralyzed drunk, which he was not; he is entitled to justice even though he occasionally took a drink out of sheer perversity and not as a way to forget the sorrows which came early to him in the death of his father, his mother, his young wife and child."

Attorney Frank Chapman, representing the transit company, said: "We do not attack McCarthey because of his drinking habits, but we do say that if a man is so drunk that he runs into the side of a street-car and injures himself, that is no reason why this transit company should be mulcted for damages."

And so, around the issue of intoxication the trial raged, with our side, I fear, getting a little the worst of it. Still, there were four witnesses who testified that McCarthey was not intoxicated when he stepped out to board the streetcar and that the motorman slammed the door shut in McCarthey's face. On the other hand, the streetcar company produced three witnesses who testified that McCarthey staggered out to the car just as the doors closed and fell beneath the wheels. Which set of witnesses would the jury believe?

One piece of evidence which the defendant company introduced and which it used as an unceasing pile driver throughout the trial was an admission allegedly made by McCarthey when he was shaking off the effects of the anesthesia following one of his operations. A nurse testified that McCarthey moaned: "If I hadn't been drunk this would never have happened."

Against this I fought: "Members of the jury, I call upon your sense of fairness to determine whether it is proper to present here a statement charged to McCarthey when he was suffering the torment of the damned, when the surgeons had lopped off another fourth of his leg, when he was alone, distraught, frantic, insane from pain. Oh, what this transit company will do to hold in its treasury the money which belongs to McCarthey, the man whom they have wrecked!

"Those of you who have undergone an operation know the sensations which assail you both before and after the scalpel and saw cut through living flesh and bone. Don't you recall that weary feeling of futility, the hard breathing as the either is forced upon you, the strangling sensation, the struggle against what seems to be death, the nightmare of abnormal sleep? Then the awakening with throbbing pain, unendurable headache, raging fever, torturing thirst, the despair of being alone?

"Four times George lay helplessly on the operating table, four times on the rack. No wonder his nerves finally snapped; no wonder his brain reeled under the tempest of ache and pain—and delirium followed. And while that delirium raged he cried out: 'If I hadn't been drunk this would never have happened.' The pain was more than he could stand. It was while he was suffering that blazing fire of torment, each flame cutting like a keen-edged sword—it was while he could neither reason nor reflect—that he said what he said. And if the destiny of an aggrieved person is to be decided in court by what he says when he is roasting in an oven of agony, then George McCarthey is not entitled to anything and you may as well turn him out.

"But before you do that, let us hear the rest of the story. On April 23, George left the hospital. The cutting had at last ceased; his leg, which had been three or four feet long, had now been whittled down to three or four inches. You would think that with this calamitous culmination there was nothing more to suffer. But there was—and is. George now feels weird sensations in a leg which no longer exists. What a ghastly experience that must be. You wince from a twinge in your knee; you clap your hand against it to massage away the pain, but there is no knee. Your shoes seem to be filled with bees stinging your toes and you stamp your foot to drive away the bees, but there is no foot—only empty air. Needles and nails jab at the whole length of your leg; they attack a limb which is invisible and intangible. In some improvised cemetery lie the fragments of what was once a living part of your anatomy, and the ghost of those fragments return to haunt you. If they must return, they should return to haunt the motorman, or rather the transit company which makes one man do the work of two, which jeopardizes life and limb, as in this case, for profit.

"Members of the jury, McCarthey is entitled to an award of compensation for a leg which has disappeared. What does the loss of a leg mean? It means what it reveals; it means what you see. It means first almost permanent unemployment. What chance does a one-legged man have? Who will employ a one-legged man when he can get all the two-legged men he may desire?

"McCarthey is not a college man; he has no profession, no business, no specialized training except that obtained in the produce yards where he worked and where no one-legged man would even be permitted. As a two-legged man he was able to make a fairly good living. Nothing pretentious, but a good substantial living. That wage has been taken away from him permanently.

"McCarthey is entitled to a recovery for the pleasures and joys which will no longer be his. He cannot in the springtime, as you can, hike through the sweet-smelling woods; he cannot in the summertime race up and down the beach before diving into the cooling waters; he cannot play baseball, football, tennis, or golf; he cannot of an evening dance with his sweetheart to the rhythm of captivating music. All this has been taken away from him.

"He has been deprived of his diversions, his pleasures, his life's work by the Pittsburgh Transit Company—and by your verdict they must pay for what they have done.

"My friends, until four days ago you did not know George McCarthey, he meant nothing in your life, but from now on his name will forevermore be associated with yours because you sit here today as his judges. And as his judges I ask you to return a verdict which will soften the hard and weary road he must travel for all the days ahead of him on his crippled journey through life."

The judge's charge to the jury gave us much to worry about. He discussed drunkenness in a way that seemed to impart authority to the defendant's lawyer's position as he had energetically presented it throughout the entire trial. Attorney Chapman was elated.

After the jury had retired he came to me and said: "Musmanno, I think I'm going to win this case. But of course there's the possibility I can lose it too, and that is why I'm willing to offer your client five thousand dollars in settlement. If the jury returns a verdict for the defendant, we lose five thousand dollars; if it returns a verdict in excess of five thousand dollars, your man loses the difference between five thousand and the amount of the verdict."

I related this to McCarthey and he spurned the offer. I was gratified and reassured by McCarthey's decision, and yet we had to acknowledge the possibility the jury might award him nothing. The two or three jurors who had registered stern disapproval each time alcohol was mentioned had smiled approving glances on Attorney Chapman as he finished his vehement argument in behalf of the transit company.

If the jury should decide in its favor, there could be no effectual appeal. The only issue in the case was one of fact, and the jury was the final arbiter of the facts.

After the jury had been deliberating for four hours, my habitual trepidations and anxiety about verdicts rose to a state of alarm. I of course never wanted to lose any courtroom battle, but to fail in a case which would leave a one-legged person hopping through life without the crutch of financial aid would inflict a poignancy all its own. Never would I be able again to look at a one-legged person without self-reproach and harrowing regret.

Once more I asked McCarthey whether he would accept five thousand dollars from the transit company as against the possibility of receiving nothing at the hands of the jury. His reply epitomized one of the highest types of moral courage. I do not recall his exact words, but substantially they were as follows: "If that jury wants to give me only one hundred dollars or ten cents or even nothing, that is their responsibility, but I see no reason to compromise. I would rather go through life with only the memory of having fought for my rights, even though I get only a goose egg, than to take their measly five thousand dollars, which would be a compromise with justice."

Five hours passed and the jurors still battled over the compensatory fate of McCarthey's missing leg. I asked the court clerk to call me when a verdict had been reached, and I gloomily trudged back to my office down Fourth Avenue, which seemed newly paved with sharply edged blocks of anguished foreboding. At my desk I waited as each moment, like a moth, rose and flew about the room on blacker wings than the one which preceded it. Although I was expecting the call, my whole being quivered with shock when the telephone finally jangled like a fire alarm and, with nerves trailing, I raced back to court. But when I arrived, the jury had already announced its verdict and dispersed. The court attendant who had called me had also left for the day. The courtroom, which for four days had resounded with the clash of conflict, was silent and deserted, offering no clue as to the decision which had now been chiseled into the granite tablets of time. Fearing the worst, I stepped out into the empty corridor while chords of misery vibrated in my breast. Suddenly a strange-looking man, grinning and chuckling peculiarly, sidled up to me, struck me on the back with affected familiarity, and snickered: "Well, that's one you dropped. The jury decided against you and in favor of the transit company."

I leaned against the wall, while the corridor became a black tunnel. In that dark passageway, ominous and endless, I could make out McCarthey hopping toward me on one leg. As he neared me he asked when he might expect to reach the end of the tunnel and the light of day. He added that he knew he could depend on me to help him find the light. Agony, like a hot iron, seared my vitals.

Presently I staggered to another blow on my back. I wheeled about. It was the laughing hyena again, he who had sunk my craft of hope into the sea of undredgable depths. He was grinning again, the grin degenerating into a sardonic and repellent laugh. "Say, can't you take a joke? I was only kiddin'."

If the whipping post is ever restored it could profitably be used for those who imagine themselves quite clever in essaying jokes at the moment the blade of destiny is falling. The hyena went on to say that the jury had returned a verdict for the plaintiff in the sum of fifteen thousand dollars. When he slapped me on the back again I thought my spine would snap in two. A court clerk presently appeared and verified the report.

It was ten o'clock at night as I left the courthouse, a bundle of frayed nerves. I turned my steps toward Fifth Avenue, looking in at all the entrancing shopwindows while the springs of tension and apprehension gradually uncoiled. Then, without any conscious decision to do so, I headed for a drugstore. A glow of happiness began to circulate through my system.

I was now on my third chocolate malted milk shake and it was wonderful. It bore a thick, creamy, delectable foam on its delicious surface. And there was reason for it, as there is reason for everything: the friendly waitress had whipped into it an extra dipperful of chocolate ice cream.

Chapter XXXIII

RESIDENCE IN SAMARIA

THE practice of the law may become a game. A lawyer often battles vigorously not only to win for his client but for the thrill of defeating his adversary. Practically every lawyer cherishes the ambition of becoming a "big lawyer," a lawyer whose name is pronounced with a certain awe, one who is summoned when giants of the law prepare to grapple, one who is sent for when others have failed or a cause seems hopeless. I was eager to try cases against lawyers with established reputations because the joy of outgeneraling them (if I could) in forensic battle kindled an ecstasy which scarcely finds a parallel in professional competition.

Mountain climbers exult in climbing a sky-piercing peak, swimmers rejoice in braving the waters of the Hellespont, ski enthusiasts leap joyfully from snowbanked crags, authors expand with the printing of their works, actors jubilate to the music of an applauding audience; but when a lawyer has fought for days and sometimes weeks in a thrill-packed courtroom, when he has crossed swords with a skillful opponent and the sparks illumine on one side the glorious heights of victory and on the other the calamitous steeps of defeat, and he goes to the jury and his voice pours like a cataract in behalf of his client who is the plaintiff, and the jury returns a verdict for the plaintiff, or if he represents the defendant and the foreman of the jury says, "We find for the defendant"—when that happens, the resulting sensation is one which can be described only as boundless ecstasy. He rides ethereal waves which splash and foam on the shores of an Arcadia where mere breathing is a felicity and thought alone is a joy.

But above the plans of the skyscraper of success I hoped to erect, there began to form a little cloud of doubt as to what constituted true success. I might finish the structure and find that it lacked adequate illumination. I might become a celebrated lawyer and yet lack something in the equipment for ideal citizenship in the commonwealth of humanity.

The lawyer with the "big name" is the one whom both sides would hope to retain in momentous cases. I have heard it said of some illustrious lawyers that they represented a certain interest in a controversy only because they were engaged by that side before the opposing party could employ them. I wondered about this. It is very well to say that an attorney defends to the best of his ability the case which his client unfolds to him, but it is not easy to understand, from a strictly moral point of view, how a partisan can, with clear conscience, say he could have represented just as well the adverse side, which he has so strenuously opposed.

If a lawyer can take either position and argue as ardently for one as for the other, his show of championing justice can only be a pose, for one of the litigants must in the end be proved wrong. Of course there are moot questions and legal problems which involve no strictly ethical consideration, and in such cases an attorney might fire from either rampart without self-censure. But if in his heart he knows his position is not sustainable in moral law he would do well to follow Abraham Lincoln, who said he would not represent a client in whom he had no confidence because he feared that during the trial he might say aloud to himself: "Lincoln, you're a liar."

I thought of the lawyer who asked the Master: "What shall I do to inherit eternal life?" And the Master answered with another question: "What is written in the law?" The lawyer replied: "Thou shalt love the Lord thy God with all thy heart, and with all thy soul, and with all thy strength, and with all thy mind; and thy neighbor as thyself."

Jesus said: "Thou hast answered right." The lawyer, willing to go further, asked Jesus: "Who is my neighbor?" And Christ related the story of the traveler who, going down from Jerusalem to Jericho, was assaulted, beaten, and left to his miserable fate on the road. Two passed him by, but along came a Samaritan who took compassion on his plight and helped him. Turning to the lawyer, Jesus now added: "Go, and do thou likewise."

The true lawyer must live in Samaria. His home must be open at all times to the wounded, the poor, the oppressed—not only those who can reward him with the material things of life.

The sincere lawyer is not the one who pleads any case regardless of the right or wrong of it. Such indiscriminate championing can only blunt one's appreciation of the important distinction between justice and injustice, and eventually it may deaden the moral sensibility of the heart.

The lawyer who accepts a case only because of expected high monetary gain, regardless of merit, or who turns away a litigant because of his inability to pay an attractive fee may become a big lawyer, but he still wears the clothes of a little man. By the same token, a lawyer who rejects a cause because it is unpopular, although he is intellectually and morally convinced it deserves support, may be tall in the eyes of the contemporary world but very short in the mirror of his own honest appraisal.

I was on the way to becoming a successful lawyer. My experience had now covered practically every phase of the law. As a general practitioner, particularly specializing in personal damage cases, I believe that—with a corps of investigators and assistants at my command—I could have developed a highly lucrative practice, eventually acquiring and maintaining a large suite of offices, riding around in a big car, and luxuriating in a palatial home. And after years of struggle there was something quite delightful about such a prospect, provided I could become more objective about fees. I could never argue with a client as to the amount I should charge for my services. There was the episode, in the early days of my practice, where I defended a property owner in a suit of ejectment. We won the case, and when we got back to my modest office he asked me how much I was charging him. The trial had lasted only one day, but I had devoted many hours to searching titles, checking documentary evidence, and interviewing witnesses in support of his claim. I said: "The work I did, Mr. Walson, is easily, I believe, worth one hundred dollars" —his face dropped—"but I'm not going to charge you that much. If you are satisfied, I shall be content with fifty dollars."

He said: "I think that's entirely too much."

"Very well," I said, "I never quarrel about a fee. Let's make it one half of that. Twenty-five dollars will square the bill."

In obvious irritation he grumbled: "I wish I had twenty-five dollars," and with a great show of resignation he reached into his pocket and withdrew two ten-dollar bills which he placed on my desk, adding: "That's all I have."

I took out my wallet. It contained a five-dollar bill. I placed it next to the two tens, picked up the three bills, and handed them to him with "Now you have twenty-five dollars." I accompanied him to the door and said: "Good afternoon." He stared at the three greenbacks in his hand, clutched them tightly, and walked away, adding as he proceeded down the corridor: "Good afternoon."

In 1927 there evolved an experience which revealed more than anything else in my professional life the eternal verity that he who would be content with himself must not set his sights on an easy living but must aim toward a fulfillment of the inherent yearning and craving for justice, even though his efforts might lead to what the world calls defeat. George McCarthey spoke more truth than perhaps he realized when he said: "I would rather go through life with only the memory of having fought for my rights, even though I get only a goose egg, than to take their measly five thousand dollars, which would be a compromise with justice."

I knew another man who refused to compromise with justice. He stood at the foot of the scaffold and pronounced these moving words:

"If it had not been for this thing, I might have lived out my life talking at street corners to scorning men. I might have died, unmarked, unknown, a failure. Now we are not a failure. This is our career, and our triumph. Never in our full life could we hope to do such work for tolerance, for justice, for man's understanding of man as now we do by accident. Our words—our pains—nothing. The taking of our lives—lives of a good shoemaker and a poor fish peddler—all. That last moment belongs to us—that is our triumph."

Chapter XXXIV

A SHOEMAKER AND A FISH PEDDLER*

I WAS still a student at college when on April 15, 1920, two men, Frederick A. Palmenter, paymaster, and Alessandro Berardelli, guard, fell on the main street of South Braintree, Massachusetts, under the gunfire of a gang of five bandits who escaped with a shoe-factory pay roll of over fifteen thousand dollars. Three weeks later a shoe-maker, Nicola Sacco, and a fish peddler, Bartolomeo Vanzetti, were arrested and charged with the crime. On July 14, 1921, after a trial lasting seven weeks, these two men were convicted of first-degree murder. This, however, was only the beginning of what shall live forever in the annals of the law and in the hearts of mankind as the Sacco-Vanzetti case.

On April 9, 1927, Judge Webster Thayer, in Norfolk County Courthouse at Dedham, Massachusetts, sentenced the convicted men to death in the electric chair. Rarely in the history of the criminal courts of our country had there been so long an interval between a jury's verdict of guilty and the imposition of sentence. There were good reasons for the delay. Evidence was constantly being uncovered, casting grave doubts on the correctness of the verdict and on the reliability of the manner in which it had been attained. It was revealed that the foreman of the jury had formed a partisan opinion on the merits of the case before taking up his duties as a juror. It was re-ported, under oath, that he had declared just before the trial began: "Damn them [the defendants], they ought to hang anyway!" It was additionally shown that he had taken into the jury room on his own account some cartridges (not connected with the case) for the purpose of demonstrating to his fellow jurors why he believed the defendants guilty. It was even claimed that the judge himself (Judge Webster Thayer) was partial to the prosecution and had made numerous state-

---

* I have related the whole story of the Sacco-Vanzetti case in my book, *After Twelve Years*, published by Alfred A. Knopf, New York, 1939.

ments outside the courtroom (and in the courthouse as well) manifesting a deep and abiding prejudice against the accused.

And then, as a crowning climax to the disclosures of a tainted conviction, a Portuguese youth by the name of Celestino F. Madeiros confessed to being one of the South Braintree robbers and, in his confession, absolved both Sacco and Vanzetti from any participation in the criminal venture.

During the trial and after the trial I followed the many momentous developments in the case, not only in the newspapers, periodicals, and law reviews, but through the printed briefs filed in the Supreme Court of Massachusetts, to which the case had twice been appealed. Thus, by the time the defendants were brought to the bar for final sentencing, I was quite disturbed over what was transpiring in Massachusetts in the name of Justice. Of course I had no responsibility in the matter. The shoemaker and fish peddler were not clients of mine—and yet in some way I felt they were. They were the clients of every lawyer devoted to the ideal of universal justice. The case had provoked debate, controversy, and even physical violence in every country where the sweat of toil had become an honored badge of the recently acquired dignity of the workingman. Utterly unknown at the time of their arrest outside the communities in which they lived, the names of Sacco and Vanzetti, by the time they were sentenced, had become household words on six continents. Labor organizations, university professors, famous authors, powerful newspapers, clergymen, scientists, and men in high office spoke, paraded, and demonstrated in behalf of the sentenced pair. The London *Herald* editorialized across the seas:

> The people of the United States should realize that in the opinion of millions of workers, lawyers and professional men, not only the lives of the two Italians are involved, but that the whole question of honest, honorable administration of justice in the most powerful republic of the world is at stake.

H. G. Wells and Arnold Bennett, world-celebrated authors, wrote:

> We, the undersigned, firm friends and admirers of America and American institutions, are deeply impressed by the weight of evidence against the conviction of Sacco and Vanzetti. We implore the Governor and

people of Massachusetts not to stain the history of their State with the blood of two innocent men.

Felix Frankfurter, then professor of law at Harvard, later to become a United States Supreme Court justice, wrote a long article for the *Atlantic Monthly** in which he demonstrated that into the Sacco and Vanzetti case had gone untrustworthy testimony, dishonest and equivocating prosecution methods, and unjudicial behavior on the part of the trial judge.

As the case dragged on month after month and year after year, with an ever-augmenting quantity of evidence supporting the defendants' insistence they were innocent and yet apparently ever-diminishing chances for their liberation, I worried as to what was happening to our whole system of jurisprudence. It was important for my peace of mind to find out. I decided I must get a firsthand view of the situation in Massachusetts. I boarded a train for Boston, where I called on William G. Thompson, chief counsel for Sacco and Vanzetti, and asked him to make arrangements, if he would, for me to see the prisoners. Graciously he did so.

As I approached the Norfolk County Jail in Dedham, Massachusetts, one beautiful morning in April I wondered what kind of men they were who had brought me here. The prison itself was not a forbidding-looking structure. Set amid closely cropped lawns and the friendliest of trees, one might almost expect to hear the voices of a college glee club rehearsing on the greensward. But as the gates swung open and I passed into the building proper, with its iron bars, cages, and armed guards, spring vanished and the leafy landscape blended into a memory of some distant excursion into the country. I heard the clanking of keys, the squeaking of ill-oiled hinges, and then far into the dimly lit corridors I could trace the outlines of three men approaching the space by a window where I waited. One of the figures walked in the rear with a sawed-off shotgun under his arm, while the other two preceded him with an obvious eagerness to enjoy a moment of semi-liberation from their Stygian isolation.

Considering the world-wide furor the two men in the lead had caused, the excitement they had stirred, the schisms in society they had provoked, I would not have been surprised to see before me a couple of giants whose footsteps set off thunderous echoes as they moved through the prison passageways. But I saw no supermen.

* Later published in book form, *The Case of Sacco and Vanzetti*, Little, Brown and Company, 1927.

As the guard moved back to supervise the interview from a respectable distance, I rubbed my eyes to look upon two smiling creatures of frail and slim build, medium height, and of the gentlest demeanor.

They had just been condemned to death; for seven years they had been stretched on the rack of the law—yet they were smiling. Instead of doomed prisoners, they seemed more like two genial laborers who had only recently completed a day's labor and now, on their way home, tarried to hail and converse with a friend met by chance. They shook my hand warmly.

Vanzetti's eyes sparkled with such good nature that he seemed to be playing a game, hiding behind a pair of walrus mustaches which all but placed the lower part of his face in humorous ambush. Apparently warmhearted and fond of amiable conversation, he was nonetheless a serious person quite capable of plumbing the depths of human despair while battling for liberation. When Judge Thayer condemned him to death he held the courtroom enthralled with a forty-five-minute speech which some listeners likened to the immortal discourse of Socrates as he prepared to take the hemlock. Vanzetti wanted to live but he was not afraid to die.

Sacco was less eloquent than his partner. The confinement of twenty-three hours a day for more than twenty-five hundred days had drawn tight lines about his eyes and had banished the color from his cheeks, but he was ready to thrust aside the painful recollection of those sunless and hopeless days. "Hello, Mr. Musmanno!" he exclaimed. "It was mighty fine of you to come see us."

Behind his facial foliage Vanzetti chimed in: "Yes, Mr. Musmanno, you have no idea how much we appreciate your coming from Pittsburgh to pay us a visit. And we are grateful for your offer of support." This was spoken with ease, cultural tone, and a picturesque Italian accent. From boyhood he had studied the classics; the prison library had added to his store of knowledge. Quite a lover of books, he was known in his home town of Plymouth as an itinerant philosopher ready at any moment to speak on the struggle of the human race down through the ages for an objective application of the Golden Rule.

Sacco was now grinning like a boy. "What do you think of our Massachusetts weather?" he asked. He liked weather and he made the most of the opportunity to drink it in through the open barred window. He was allowed only an hour of weather a day. So we talked abut the weather, the normalized beginning of conversations among people throughout the world. There was no precipitate plunging into a discussion of the *case*. From the weather we drifted somehow into ancient history, of which they both seemed to have an astonishing grasp. Ancient days were compared to the present, and then naturally there came to the fore the subject of justice through the ages.

"What do you think of justice, Mr. Vanzetti?" I asked.

Instead of speaking vehemently on this choice desideratum of life which had eluded him for seven years, Vanzetti chuckled and smiled. His white teeth glistened through the shrubbery of his mustaches as he reminisced: "Some years ago I saw a statue of Justice—a tall stone figure. In one hand it held lawbooks, the other hand pointed forward. Carved on the base of the statue appeared the words: 'The law of justice treats everybody alike.' And then I noted that the extended hand was pointing toward a cemetery!"

Vanzetti's smile widened hugely and then exploded into gargantuan laughter in which Sacco hilariously joined. This seemed a natural introduction to the subject of justice in the Sacco-Vanzetti case, and we were now, with easy transition, launched into a discussion of its present aspects.

From Pittsburgh I had written the men urging hope. Although the Supreme Court of Massachusetts had refused them a new trial, it fell within the province of the governor of the state not only to commute their death sentences to life imprisonment but to grant outright pardons. It was an odd and scarcely praiseworthy feature of Massachusetts judicial procedure that its highest court could not pass on the sufficiency or quality of the evidence which had convicted the defendants in the court below; it could only decide whether the trial judge had committed any errors in law. The governor, however, was not bound by any such limited review. He could weigh the substance of everything which had been presented in the case, he could consider the after-discovered evidence, the confession of Madeiros, the repudiation and discounting of prosecution witnesses; and, once satisfied that a reasonable doubt existed as to the men's guilt, he could exert executive clemency and free them. I felt certain he would do so.

Vanzetti, while willing to share my optimism, was disturbed over what he had heard regarding the governor of Massachusetts, Alvan T. Fuller. "I hope I may be wrong," he said, "but I fear Fuller is already prejudiced against us. Recently, without any provocation for it, he declared vehemently in favor of capital punishment, and I think he was serving warning that we could not expect clemency from him."

"I wouldn't take that gloomy interpretation of it," I replied. "If he believes in capital punishment, certainly he can advocate it only for those who are guilty. Even the most bloodthirsty champion of the death penalty must oppose execution of the wrong man. And as soon as he begins a review of the case Governor Fuller will see that you and Sacco are the wrong men."

"I hope you are right," Sacco commented in his turn, "but I think that Fuller is too rich to do justice to poor people. He is worth forty million dollars and he has always talked against the workingman."

These remarks raised in my chest a lump of discouragement which began to melt only when I called on Professor Felix Frankfurter, who received me most graciously at his home in Cambridge. Brilliantly and with feeling he reviewed the most recent disclosures in the case, and I left his home, again encouraged in my hope that, despite Fuller's harsh attitude toward convicted persons and his hostile feeling toward all liberals in economics and politics, the overwhelming proof of Sacco's and Vanzetti's innocence must bring about their ultimate exoneration and freedom.

I visited the home towns of the condemned men—Stoughton, a shoe-manufacturing town, and Plymouth of Pilgrim fame. In talking to people on the streets, in stores, and other public places about the case which had made their fellow townsmen objects of lively interest and concern around the world, I encountered the most extraordinary reaction. Surely, after a trial and conviction in a court of law, someone must say that Sacco and Vanzetti were evil characters. Among those who had had any contact with the men, I found not one. The only thing, apparently, that the two Dedham prisoners had robbed was the affection of those with whom they had had any immediate association. In this they were wholesale bandits capturing everywhere the friendship and esteem of those who came within the orbit of their lowly occupations and the circle of their humble social enjoyment. The accolade of admiration is not bestowed alone on giants of achievement and popularity. The appreciation we feel for the honesty, good nature, and trustworthiness of our grocer, druggist, newsboy, shoemaker, or fish merchant can generate as much warmth of good will as that which we feel for the sheriff or the leading citizen of the town.

In Plymouth I talked with Melvin Corl, a fisherman with whom Vanzetti often had had business dealings. He was mending a net, sitting on an overturned boat, when I approached and asked him about Vanzetti. This Yankee merchant of the sea paused to take a fresh hold of the net as well as of himself as he looked up at me and solemnly said: "If Vanzetti is guilty of murder, so am I, because I was with him on April 15, 1920, between three and four o'clock in the afternoon." (The murder occurred at 3:05 P.M.) "We were together on the beach right here discussing an arrangement whereby I was to turn over to him a catch of fish he was to retail." And as he spoke he cast his eyes over the vast waters as if trying to reconcile his open-eyed consciousness of fact with the mysterious processes of law which sought to make him believe that, in spite of his senses, Vanzetti's presence on the fatal afternoon had been merely a phantom visitation.

I visited the home of Vincenzo Brini, where Vanzetti, the bachelor, had lived for six years. Brini told me of a lady in the town who kept a framed newspaper picture of Vanzetti in her window, so moved had she been over an episode of kindness which she had witnessed. She had seen Vanzetti take off his shoes and give them to a tramp whose own footwear was so badly worn and torn that he walked with obvious pain and discomfort.

Mr. Brini and his family related many incidents touching on Vanzetti's gentleness and charitable spirit. Faye Brini (now Mrs. Wager) told me how one day Vanzetti brought home a weak and emaciated kitten he had found snuggling against a building for protection from the cold. "The kitten's eyes were practically glued shut," Mrs. Wager described, "with some sort of skin disease that covered its body with sores. Vanzetti bathed it, anointed it with a salve he had obtained at the drugstore, and with much care and attention cured it. The kitten grew into a lovely cat, and it became our dearest pet.

"Vanzetti was always counseling us," the young lady enthusiastically went on, "how we should comport ourselves with courtesy, respect, and strict honesty in all matters. He taught me to speak Italian and I helped him with his English."

In Stoughton I saw the modest home in which Sacco had lived with his wife and child (another child was born shortly after his arrest) and raised crops of luscious tomatoes which he distributed among his neighbors—hardly the figure of the vicious bandit described at the trial.

In all the seven years that the Sacco-Vanzetti case was the ceaseless subject of study, inquiry, and investigation, not one item of evidence was ever discovered or produced which even remotely suggested that these two men had ever associated with bandits or criminals. It seemed to me incontrovertibly opposed to every rule of reason and experience of mankind that two men who bore, without contradiction, the reputation of being considerate, generous, and gentle in their everyday dealing with their fellow men could suddenly become skilled, hardened robbers and conscienceless killers. Few crimes of violence have been successfully executed with the expertness which characterized the South Braintree robbery. The highwaymen had had to ascertain the exact hour that the pay-roll men would be on the street; they had to plan with perfect timing for three of the robbers to lie in ambush, awaiting the precise moment they were to shoot down the guards and seize the money, while the getaway car moved into place with another bandit at the wheel and one on the rear seat with poised shotgun ready to pour fire at police and other pursuers. The whole job was prepared with such meticulous attention to detail that the bandits had even supplied themselves with steel tacks to carpet the highway behind them so as to puncture the tires of pursuing cars. Obviously the philosophic fish peddler of Plymouth and the tomato-growing shoemaker of Stoughton had had no training which fitted them for so scientifically perfect a piece of ferocious brigandage.

William H. Proctor, captain of the Massachusetts State Police for sixteen years, with a distinguished record of twenty-three years of extensive police experience, declared after a long and thorough investigation into the South Braintree crime that it was the work of veteran criminals and that it was impossible for Sacco and Vanzetti to have taken part in it. As already stated, five men committed the robbery and murder. If Sacco and Vanzetti were members of this quintet, there had to be three more men to account for. Considering the dovetailing professionalism with which the crime had been enacted, the five men had to be a well-co-ordinated team. Thus it was opposed to all rationalization in criminal investigation that the supposed revealment of the operation of two fingers of a criminal hand would not in some way simultaneously offer a clue as to what the other three fingers were doing.

It is thus a startling fact, nonetheless, that in the seven long years that the Sacco-Vanzetti case ran its dramatic course, with the district attorney's office never backing down once from its position that Sacco and Vanzetti were guilty, not one person of the numerous prosecution staff ever explained or even attempted to offer any clue as to the whereabouts, fate, or activities of the other three men of this admittedly intimately integrated coterie of desperadoes. With state police, county detectives, private detectives, and personal investigators combing through every association which Sacco and Vanzetti had experienced in their respective vocations, their labor connections and social activities, it was impossible that, if they were really members of the guilty bandit gang, nothing would have turned up to point in some direction at least toward the identity of the other three bandits. Furthermore, on the basis of a Sacco-Vanzetti participation in a five-man pay-roll robbery of fifteen thousand dollars, it is extraordinary that not a penny of the money was ever traced to Sacco and Vanzetti or any of their friends or associates.

What was the evidence which convicted the fish peddler and the shoemaker? The Commonwealth's star witness against Sacco was a bookkeeper, Mary E. Splaine, who on the day of the robbery was working on the second floor of the Slater and Morrill shoe factory which set back seventy feet from Pearl Street, over which the murder car moved in its flight from the scene of the crime. Considering the speed at which the car traveled and the limited vision Miss Splaine had of it, her view of the bandit automobile did not exceed two seconds. At the trial, fourteen months after the robbery, Miss Splaine identified Sacco as one of the robbers and enumerated sixteen points of identification: height, weight, complexion, muscularity, size of hand, clothing, facial characteristics, etc., not excluding the color of the bandit's eyebrows!—all obtained in two seconds, amid the shooting, excitement, and turmoil of a double murder on the main thoroughfare of the town.

Was Miss Splaine's testimony reliable? On April 20, 1920, only five days after the robbery, she had identified a totally different person as the robber she saw—one Tony Palmisano, whose picture she selected out of a series of photographs exhibited to her. Then, forty days after her identification of Palmisano, she was taken to see Nicola Sacco in the police station in which he was being held. After studying him for some time from every angle of view, she said that her view of the robber on the day of the crime did not allow her to say that Sacco was the man she had seen. Yet a year subsequent to this nonidentification of Sacco she took the witness stand at the Dedham trial and testified that Sacco was the man she had seen in the murder car, enumerating, as already stated, sixteen points of identification—all this, of course, while looking directly at Sacco in the courtroom!

Another bookkeeper, Frances Devlin, whose view of the bandit car was limited to from one and a half to three seconds, testified at the preliminary hearing after Sacco's arrest that she could not say Sacco was the bandit she saw. She described the bandit in question as tall and big with long black hair. Sacco was neither tall nor big, and he did not have long black hair. Immediately after the murder she had also, like Miss Splaine, claimed that Tony Palmisano was the bandit she had seen. Yet at the trial Miss Devlin identified Sacco as that bandit.

Louis Pelser worked in the Rice and Hutchins shoe factory, which directly overlooked the immediate scene of the robbery-murder. At the time of the shooting, Pelser hid beneath a workbench, and then as the bandit car roared away he straightened up enough to take a peek at the license plates of the car and jotted down the number. When Sacco and Vanzetti were arrested, Pelser was taken to the police station to look at the prisoners for possible identification. Pelser said: "I did not see enough to be able to identify anybody." He lost his job. Later he was re-employed. His foreman talked to him about the case, and he now went on the witness stand and identified Sacco as the "dead image" of the man who did the shooting.

While it was the Slater and Morrill Company pay roll which had been robbed, the Rice and Hutchins Company had more than a neighborly interest in the case because, among other things, insurance rates are always based on the risk involved. It is not difficult to understand the zeal with which several shoe companies with factories in South Braintree urged the prosecution and conviction of Sacco and Vanzetti. A heinous murder had been committed on the streets of their municipality. Three weeks passed and the police were barren of any clue as to the identity of the bandits. Speculation and indignation mounted. Then suddenly two men were arrested, and it developed that they belonged to that class of persons who had been worrying factory owners throughout New England. The arrested men were labor organizers, said the millowners, men who were active in unionizing workers and complaining that wages were too low while hours were too long—men who caused strikes to occur, wages to soar, and competition to become keener—they were a pestilence!

Before Vanzetti became an itinerant and fish-peddling philosopher on the streets of Plymouth, he had been employed by the Plymouth Cordage Company, which, because of World War I, was reaping unprecedented profits. With the ever-increasing toll of ships sunk by submarines there was a constantly increasing demand for marine cordage. Almost every torpedo released by a submarine at a merchant ship carried with it an order to the Plymouth Cordage. The flood tide of the company's prosperity, however, did not touch the economic shores of their employees' needs. Male unskilled employees received in many instances as little as nine dollars a week and unskilled female workers even less. Vanzetti organized a strike. The company offered a 5 per cent increase. Vanzetti exhorted his fellow workers not to accept it. In a few days the company offered a 10 per cent increase and the strike ended. The workers returned to their jobs—all but Vanzetti. He was blacklisted, not only at the Plymouth Cordage, but at all other factories and shops around. He bought a handcart and a pair of scales and, wearing an open-necked shirt and a broad-brimmed sombrero, he dispensed philosophy with cod, mackerel, and eels to the fish-eating population of Plymouth town.

Sacco had also been active in the arena of labor controversy. When the woolen workers of Lawrence, Massachusetts, struck for higher wages (they were earning an average wage of eight and nine dollars a week), Sacco helped raise funds for the strikers. When the textile machinery workers in Hopedale laid down their tools in mass protest against working conditions and starvation wages, Sacco joined the picket line. Sacco's job was to construct shoes; the Hopedale workers manufactured machines. There was no occupational relationship between Sacco and the Hopedale employees, but for Sacco, as for Vanzetti, there was an affinity between all workingmen, regardless of their respective trades and calling.

Upon finding themselves enmeshed in the toils of the law, these two labor enthusiasts were amazed not only at the crushing gears of the prosecution machinery but at the furor their arrest had precipitated. Humble and obscure, they did not realize that they were energetic participants in an active labor movement which had become abhorrent to the financial hierarchy of Massachusetts. In labor-organizing activities, most of the millowners of the Bay State saw higher wages and greater production costs, all of which brought more determined and effective competition from the South, where the workers were then to a great extent unorganized.

Thus Sacco and Vanzetti became targets of an animosity apart from blame for alleged complicity in a criminal enterprise involving robbery and murder. Shoe-company officials read eagerly all the details in the newspapers about the arrest of these two disturbers and hoped audibly and ostentatiously that such undesirable persons would receive "what was coming to them." On May 13, 1920, eight days after the arrest of the two workers, a Pinkerton operative in the pay of the Slater and Morrill Company reported that he had talked to a certain witness of the South Braintree crime and that this witness had said, after looking at photos of Sacco and Vanzetti, that neither of them resembled any of the bandits he had seen. The Pinkerton operative then added this significant comment and recommendation to his report:

He [this witness] ought to be interviewed by someone
who can talk and understand Italian, as at present he,
if located by the attorneys for the defense of Sacco and
Vanzetti, would go on the stand and say they were not
the men who did the shooting.

Is it the duty of a detective investigating a crime to pick up every
stone of evidence so that the absolute truth may be ascertained,
or is he to gather up only the boulders which will bolster the scaffolding of his master's desires?

At the factory in which he was employed as a shoe "edger" Sacco
doubled as a night watchman and in this capacity bore a watchman's
pistol. Vanzetti, because of the money which came to him in his mer-
chandising of fish, also possessed a firearm in the form of a Harrington
and Richardson .38-caliber revolver. Unfortunately the defendants
had these weapons on their persons the night of their arrest, and the
district attorney, Frederick G. Katzmann, was to argue that both firearms had played a part in the robbery.

Sacco carried a .32-caliber Colt automatic. One of the four bullets
found in the body of Berardelli, paymaster guard, was also of .32
caliber. Katzmann turned Sacco's pistol over to State Police Captain
William H. Proctor to determine if it could have been the weapon
which had fired the .32-caliber bullet. After making exhaustive tests
Proctor reported that it was his opinion the Berardelli bullet had not
passed through Sacco's weapon. Dissatisfied with this report, District
Attorney Katzmann and Assistant District Attorney Williams sought
to have Proctor testify in such a way as to convey the impression that
the fatal projectile had been discharged from Sacco's pistol, without
actually making a statement to that effect. A suitable formula was
concocted so that at the trial when Williams asked Proctor if the
telltale piece of lead had actually been fired through Sacco's pistol
Proctor replied that it was "consistent with being fired through the
pistol." The strict literal interpretation of that answer meant, of course,
that the bullet *might* have passed through the muzzle of Sacco's gun.
But on that basis it *could* have been fired through any one of *two
hundred thousand* Colt .32's then in existence.

The ruse worked. The Court, jury, and even defense counsel believed that Proctor testified the mortal bullet had passed through the
muzzle of Sacco's weapon. So convinced were the defense counsel that
Proctor meant this, they were afraid to cross-examine him on the
subject. However, two years later Proctor acknowledged the deception

of which he, Katzmann, and Williams were the authors. He cried out: "I don't care. I have been too old in the game. I have been too long in the game, and I'm getting too old to want to see a couple of fellows go to the chair for something I don't think they did." A few months later he died, having first made a full confession.

The plan to connect Vanzetti's weapon with the robbery was even more grotesque than the Proctor plot. The prosecution contended that the revolver which Vanzetti had in his pocket on the night of his arrest was taken from the pay-roll guard, Berardelli, after he had been shot down. Putting aside for the moment the absurd notion that a murderer would carry around with him a revolver belonging to the man he had shot, the possession of which would automatically connect him with the crime, and shelving also the even more preposterous proposition that a bandit would plunge into so desperate and perilous a venture unarmed, depending only on the hope that he might obtain a gun from the man who was to be his victim, there are other more cogent reasons why Vanzetti's revolver could not be Berardelli's revolver. While it would be natural to assume that Berardelli himself would be armed, it so happened that on the day of the holdup he did not have his revolver with him. He had experienced trouble with the hammer of his Harrington and Richardson revolver and had left it at the Iver Johnson repair shop but failed to pick it up by April 15, 1920, when he needed it most. When his widow viewed his body at the funeral parlor she lamented:

> "Oh dear, if he had taken my advice and taken the
> revolver out of the shop he would not be, maybe he
> would not be in the same condition he is today."

The history of Vanzetti's revolver was traced back five years, with not a link in that chain of previous possession touching Berardelli in any way. It was also established that Vanzetti's revolver never had need of a new hammer. Despite this airtight, exclusionary evidence, Katzmann presented Vanzetti's revolver to the jury as the deceased Berardelli's revolver.

And then there was the matter of the so-called bandit's cap. After the South Braintree crime someone found a cap on Pearl Street. The prosecution claimed that this was Sacco's cap since Sacco wore a cap at his work and there was a hole in the lining of this cap which, the prosecution maintained, was caused by Sacco's daily hanging it on a nail above his workbench. However, no one testified to seeing a bandit wearing a cap on the day of the crime, and no one identified the cap as Sacco's. The superintendent of the factory in which Sacco worked testified that he did not believe it was Sacco's cap. Sacco denied that the cap ever belonged to him and at the trial put it on his head to show it did not fit. It turned out to be so small that it sat rather comically on the top of his skull, causing amusement among the spectators and inspiring a newspaper cartoonist to draw a sketch of the humorous scene, which appeared in the newspapers the next day. But the theory that this cap connected Sacco with the crime was so "good" that Katzmann insisted it be introduced as circumstantial evidence against Sacco, and the judge conveniently admitted it as evidence.

No matter how weak and frail might be any particular thread of evidence with which District Attorney Katzmann sought to tie Sacco and Vanzetti to the South Braintree crime, he was able to plait it in with strands of surmise, supposition, and dramatic show of earnestness in such a manner as to make of them all a powerful rope which was eventually to accomplish the hanging which the foreman of the jury had indicated he desired even before he heard a word of testimony.

Only one witness, a certain M. Levangie, watchman at the railroad crossing over which the murder car passed in its escape route, placed Vanzetti anywhere near the murder locale. He testified that he saw Vanzetti at the wheel of the car. There were many reasons why this could not be true. There was not the thinnest shadow of the remotest evidence that the fish-selling pedestrian philosopher had ever driven a car in his life. And then there was the fact that all of the other Commonwealth witnesses testified that the driver of the car was a light-haired, light-complexioned man—which Vanzetti certainly was not. Levangie's testimony thus put Katzmann in a dilemma. If he accepted it as true he would be compelled to repudiate other witnesses who had testified to other salient features of the prosecution's case. On the other hand, if he rejected Levangie's identification of Vanzetti, there would be no testimony left to place Vanzetti at the scene of the robbery. With diabolical ingenuity, of which he was more than capable, Katzmann proved himself equal to the occasion. He would say that Levangie was wrong and at the same time prove he was right! He asked the jury to accept Levangie's testimony so long as they were satisfied that he "honestly meant to tell the truth." In other words, Katzmann asked the jury to accept, not what Levangie said, but what Katzmann wanted the jury to believe that Levangie *meant* to say; namely:

> "And can't you reconcile it with the possibility, no, the
> likelihood or more than that, the probability that at
> that time Vanzetti was directly behind the driver in the
> quick glance this man Levangie had of the car going
> over when they were going up over the crossing . . .
> I ask you to find as a matter of common sense he was,
> in the light of the other witnesses, in the car, and if on
> the left side that he may well have been immediately
> behind the driver."

But if Levangie could have made so gross an error as putting a back-seat passenger at the driver's wheel, what reliance could be placed in his testimony at all? Moreover, if Vanzetti was in the back seat, nobody could see him, as the curtains of the car were down.

Judge Thayer, who, as we have indicated, had manifested a prejudice against the defendants, collaborated with Katzmann on this point. He instructed the jury:

> "The law does not require that evidence shall be pos-
> itive or certain in order to be competent. Overpositive-
> ness in identification might under some circumstances
> and conditions be evidence of weakness in the testi-
> mony, rather than strength."

Why shouldn't a witness be positive when his testimony may invoke the irrevocable penalty of death? And why would overpositiveness be weakness? Judge Thayer said further: "Any evidence that tends in any degree, however slight, to prove a likeness or similarity between the defendants and the assailants is admissible." This would mean that if a fleeting glimpse of a murderer revealed that he had black hair, then every person with black hair could be accused of the murder!

A judge's charge to the jury must never be an argument for either side. It is intended to be an exposition of the law, and its purpose is to submit in measured language the contentions of both parties. How did Judge Thayer meet this indispensable requirement? The Commonwealth contended for a verdict of guilty on three propositions; namely, identification testimony, inanimate exhibits, and so-called conscious-ness of guilt. Sacco and Vanzetti asked for acquittal on the ground that it was impossible for them to have been in South Braintree at the time of the murder, because on that day they were elsewhere. Their defense was an alibi. The alibi, therefore, was entitled to as much attention in the judge's charge as the Commonwealth's theory of guilt. How did Judge Thayer balance these conflicting contentions? He devoted ten pages to a discussion of identification testimony, inanimate exhibits, and consciousness of guilt. To the defendants' alibi he gave *two paragraphs!*

It was Sacco's hard luck that he should have chosen April 15, 1920, to go to the Italian consul's office in Boston for the purpose of making arrangements for a passport because of his pending visit to Italy. Had he worked at the shoe factory on that day, his shop record would have been a perfect alibi. However, the evidence presented to trace his movements throughout the entire day of April 15, 1920, should have been just as convincing as a shop record. The testimony of eleven witnesses demonstrated that Sacco left his home in Stoughton at seven-thirty in the morning; that he was in East Boston at 11:30 A.M.; ate lunch in a restaurant at noon and conversed with several persons there; called at the Italian consulate at two-fifty; visited a coffeehouse where he remained twenty minutes; stopped at a grocery store to pay a bill, and left Boston at 4:12 P.M., arriving back in Stoughton at 6 P.M.

Vanzetti's movements on April 15, 1920, were equally unimpeachably established. All morning on that day he had peddled fish; an itinerant clothing merchant in Plymouth sold him some clothing material for a suit about noon; in the afternoon he went down to the shore to see Melvin Corl, as heretofore mentioned, and he was with Corl at the exact time of the murders in South Braintree.

This alibi evidence on the part of both defendants, supported by eighteen witnesses in all, built a bulwark of defense against the terrible charge of murder. If true, the men had to be innocent. Vanzetti could not have been at South Braintree and at Plymouth at the same time; Sacco could not have been in Boston and South Braintree at the same time. The Commonwealth did not call one witness to challenge the veracity or the accuracy of recollection of the alibi witnesses. Thus it was highly important that the jury be instructed fully by the trial judge on the importance of the alibi. The jury should have had from the judge at least a résumé of the testimony which, if believed, had to exonerate the defendants completely.

They got two paragraphs.

The defense of Sacco and Vanzetti did not depend alone on an alibi, which, of course, would be all-conclusive in itself. Of those who saw the robbery-murder, more persons testified that Sacco and Vanzetti were *not* among the bandits than those who testified they were. There were a few witnesses who risked their jobs—and lost them—rather than barter human lives. Lewis L. Wade was one of these. On the day of the crime he was standing outside the factory and saw the murderous assault unfold with the clearness of a theatrical production, with him in a front-row seat. He was called as a witness by the Commonwealth to identify Sacco as one of the robbers. He refused to do so. When the trial ended, Wade was discharged by the shoe company to which he had given seventeen years of faithful service.

Two other shoe-company employees who had as good an opportunity to see the man the identifying witnesses said was Sacco declined to so testify. After the trial they both were discharged. One of the vacant positions was given to a juror who had voted to send Sacco to the electric chair.

Another witness of the shooting, John Ningmann, was asked by a defense investigator for a statement as to whether he could identify Sacco or Vanzetti. He replied: "I can't testify; if I do, I am out of a job."

Joe Ticon was an eyewitness called to the police station to look at Sacco and Vanzetti. He studied them and concluded: "They are not the men." When, later on, he was asked by defense counsel to repeat his statement he said he could not do so because he had been warned by a representative of the prosecution that if he testified he would have to look for other work.

Forty-three eyewitnesses to the robbery-murder testified at the Dedham trial. Eleven of them, in one form or another, connected Sacco *or* Vanzetti with the crime. Not one of these eleven identified *both* Sacco and Vanzetti as being present during any one phase of the homicidal drama. Yet, since it was the contention of the Commonwealth that Sacco and Vanzetti were inseparably linked in the holdup, it would be inevitable that if a witness saw one of them he could not fail to see the other. It was like eleven people declaring under oath that they had seen a bicycle, seven of them asserting they saw only a front wheel and four of them averring that they saw only a rear wheel, but not one of them testifying to having seen both wheels at the same time and place, although it is simply incontrovertible that if the bicycle existed at all the wheels had to be together.

But that is not all. As against these eleven witnesses who said they saw only one person of a couple which the Commonwealth claimed were Siamese twins in the perpetration of the crime, the other thirty-two eyewitnesses to the crime testified that they could not identify Sacco or Vanzetti as the bandits they had seen. Thus, with this over-whelming superiority in witnesses that Sacco and Vanzetti were not in the South Braintree robbery, the defendants, in a fairly conducted trial, could hardly have been convicted on identification testimony alone. Certainly one juror at least would apply the doctrine of reasonable doubt and insist to the end on acquittal. The prosecution staff knew this and therefore had to depend on something other than the identification testimony, which was no stronger than a rope of sand.

District Attorney Katzmann and those associated with him in the enterprise accordingly systematically built up in the courthouse an atmosphere of hostility against Sacco and Vanzetti as foreigners and as dangerous radicals and labor agitators. Uniformed guards carrying rifles, shotguns, and pistols patrolled the courthouse, inside and out. The defendants, manacled to officers, were marched from the jail to the court and from the court to jail accompanied by twenty-eight guards conspicuously displaying firearms. Four times a day this miniature army tramped in and out of the house of the law, awing the jury and electrifying the surroundings with suggestions of mysterious foes to be met and combated. Doors were barred and all visitors were searched for concealed weapons. Even defense counsel were subjected to this treatment. Yet at no time before or during the trial did there occur the slightest incident or even the remotest suggestion of threat which justified the parade of armed might. There is no doubt, however, that this spectacular demonstration of protective force achieved the desired effect. Mrs. Lois B. Rantoul, covering the trial as a representative of the Greater Boston Federation of Churches, reported to that organization: "At the opening of the trial I was surprised to find that all the court officers and officials considered the defendants guilty. This meant that the jury was surrounded by that atmosphere even though no words were spoken."

When Sacco and Vanzetti took the stand they were cross-examined on subjects in no way related to the charge in the indictment but which were calculated to stir up prejudice in the minds of the jurors. Firing questions loaded with sarcasm, irony, and ridicule, Katzmann inquired into the defendants' politico-social beliefs, their attitude as pacifists, their reasons for coming to America, how they compared educational opportunities in Italy with those in America, etc., etc. Defense counsel repeatedly objected to this pillorying of the accused on topics wholly irrelevant to the South Braintree crime, but the judge permitted the merciless humiliation, even at times joining in it himself. Then, when Katzmann devastatingly summed up to the jury in his final speech, he called upon the jurors to find the defendants guilty as a matter of local patriotism. "Stand together, you men of Norfolk!" he cried to them.

Following Katzmann's speech, Judge Thayer addressed the jury over a bench banked with flowers. One of the enormous bouquets came from the sheriff, who had custody of the jury and who himself had displayed an unremitting belligerent attitude against the defendants. The combined efforts of the district attorney, the judge, and the foreman of the jury, plus the stage setting of fear, resulted in what, under the circumstances, was inevitable, a verdict of guilty.

In its very early stages the Sacco-Vanzetti case did not arouse any unusual interest except in the towns which were directly involved. However, as the bitterness of the prosecuting authorities seemed to intensify in inverse proportion to the weakness of the evidence available against the accused, workingmen became alarmed. In the plight of the fish peddler from Plymouth and the shoemaker from Stoughton they saw themselves vicariously on trial. Labor organs in all parts of the world wrote about the case. Workers in America and in Europe began to send in modest contributions to the defense fund which had been launched to provide legal counsel for the accused. World figures in labor, literary, and political circles offered discreet protests against what seemed to be a determined effort to punish the two defendants not on evidence of a robbery-murder but on the basis of their political-economic-social views. Instead, however, of urging Katzmann to caution, this world interest only fired in him a greater determination to win in what was now becoming a conflict of gigantic forces: the might of Massachusetts versus the heart of the world.

All of Massachusetts officialdom arrayed itself against the defendants. With but rare exceptions the whole upper stratum of the Bay State industrialists and financiers believed, or affected to believe, that Sacco and Vanzetti were what Katzmann represented them to be, enemies of the established order of things. It was to Katzmann's advantage to triumph in this battle. Once the men were convicted, the convictions upheld, and the sentences fulfilled in the electric chair, Katzmann could expect a laurel wreath in the shape of the attorney-generalship of the state, plus a justified hope for the governorship not far away.

Judge Thayer also looked forward to a cluster of deserving grapes on the vines of his valiant efforts. Had he not legally disposed of two enemies of Massachusetts? Why should he not expect investiture in the silk robes of the office of justice of the Massachusetts Supreme Court? But even if he would never sit on the high court of his state, he nevertheless had molded for himself immortal glory out of the common clay of two immigrant labor agitators. Speaking to a group of people on the Dartmouth athletic field at Hanover, New Hampshire, he exulted: "Did you see what I did with those anarchistic bastards the other day? I guess that will hold them for a while." He also appended to them the title of "sons of——" and boasted: "Let them go to the Supreme Court now and see what they can get out of them."

Chapter XXXV

WHILE THERE'S LIFE THERE'S HOPE

AFTER talking with the defendants, interviewing many witnesses, and reviewing the whole record of the trial, including the proceedings which had followed the conviction, I asked Chief Defense Counsel William G. Thompson if I could be of assistance to him. He recommended that I see Governor Alvan T. Fuller, who had announced he intended to give personal attention to the application for pardon which had been filed in behalf of the two convicted men. Mr. Thompson believed that with my independent study of the case as an attorney from another state I might contribute some observations which could possibly be helpful to the governor. However, when I finally sat down to talk to Governor Fuller in the State House I could see that the fears which Sacco and Vanzetti had expressed had taken form as phantoms behind Fuller's chair. To say that the governor was prejudiced against the two condemned men is to put a slightly tolerable face on the matter. The word "prejudice" could suggest an awareness of truth contaminated by a perverse intention, because of an ulterior purpose, to ignore the truth. But Fuller's hostility, it seemed to me, was compounded of an overpowering conceit, an abysmal ignorance of the facts, and a pathetic inability to grasp the evidentiary issues involved—plus an intellectual sloth to devote himself to the study required to perform the herculean task he had declared he would undertake.

In his lifetime Fuller had been a trick bicycle rider and racer, a bicycle-repair businessman, and an automobile salesman. As New England distributor of the Packard Motor Company, every Packard he touched turned to gold in his pocket. He was jealous of that gold: it represented not only comfort, security, luxury, and the indulgence of every ambition, including political preferment, but his millions were proof of his greatness. They were the fruits of his ability, talents, and genius. Anything that jeopardized those millions attacked the integrity of his genius. In the Sacco-Vanzetti case he appeared to see a challenge not only to what his fortune represented but to what was represented by those with whom he associated on the high plateau of business achievement. In the world-wide sympathy for Sacco and Vanzetti he saw a besieging of the plateau. He conceived it to be his duty to hold the fort.

I told the governor that I did not approve of the political philosophy of Sacco and Vanzetti but that the question before him was not a philosophical one—it was simply the one of determining whether Sacco and Vanzetti were guilty of murder. In my review of the record, I went on to say, I was particularly impressed with the unreliability of the testimony of such witnesses as Splaine, Devlin, Andrews, Levangie, and others. I touched on the equivocating testimony presented by the Commonwealth on the subject of the firearms belonging to the defendants. The governor bridled. "But the Supreme Court passed on all that."

I replied: "Well, if you believe that the Supreme Court cannot err, why then have an investigation at all? The very lodgment of this pardoning power in a governor presupposes the possibility of error on the part of the courts." I explained further that the Supreme Court had not once passed on the sufficiency of the evidence against Sacco and Vanzetti or the credibility of the witnesses because, under procedure peculiar to Massachusetts, it did not have that power of review.

From the governor's reaction to this statement I realized that I was treading on dangerous ground, because anything that his localized mind interpreted as a criticism of Massachusetts only served to stiffen him against any plea in behalf of the condemned men. From that moment I spoke only on objective matters.

When I finally left the governor's office I carried away the impression that not only he but nearly everyone in the State House was feverishly carrying bricks, mortar, and clay to erect a wall around the Sacco-Vanzetti decision to keep out those who might have the temerity to say that Massachusetts judicial procedure had here failed.

Sore at heart, I could not muster the spirit to return to the Dedham prison to tell Sacco and Vanzetti that I had found some ghastly confirmation of their fears. I boarded the train back to Pittsburgh and on the entire trip wondered and worried as to whether there could be found artisans with sufficiently delicate fingers and with the necessary repair parts to mend the broken scales of justice in Boston.

Once back in Pittsburgh, I questioned myself if my care-laden trip had not been a futile venture. But that question was immediately followed by the query as to whether, in fact, I had not made a mistake in returning to Pittsburgh. Sacco and Vanzetti were still alive, and while there was life, there was hope—not to express anything novel or unique. Still, what could I do in Massachusetts? The fate of the condemned pair was in the hands of a man who apparently lacked the capacity to realize that what he was doing violated numerous concepts of American fairness. The governor said he was conducting an impartial investigation, yet he was examining witnesses in the absence of defendants and defendants' counsel. He listened to rumors, he gave ear to conjectures, he hearkened to fantastic assertions. Had he been given to travel throughout the city of Boston or the whole state of Massachusetts picking up stories, observations, and guesses, no great harm could have resulted to the cause of truth because, in that event, the gossip being self-contradictory, it would have neutralized itself or it would have been so confusing that he would have had to start anew each day, and eventually, when the slate of his mind was wiped clean, truth might have a chance. But Fuller lived and moved principally in the realm of wealth and officialdom where no one spoke of Sacco and Vanzetti except as robbers, agitators, and murderers who for seven long years had had the world by the ears and the time had come to end the comedy.

Even so, Sacco and Vanzetti were alive and I could not bring myself to accept that one man, self-opinionated as he was, could put at naught the whole American concept of democratic justice and fair play. I asked friends in Pittsburgh what I should do about the Sacco-Vanzetti case, and many of them said I shouldn't talk about it so much. One of them specified: "While you believe these two men to be innocent, and so does much of the world, the official class of America takes for granted that they are guilty." When I said I might return to Boston he said that doing so would be detrimental from every point of view. "Sacco and Vanzetti are accused of being anarchists, agitators, radicals, and you cannot afford to be defending men with that kind of a reputation." I pointed out to him, as I had stated many times, that I held no brief for Sacco's and Vanzetti's political views, and added: "I know that they are innocent of the crime of which they have been convicted, and I want to see a great injustice corrected. What would you think of a lawyer who looked in on the case of Socrates and left because he thought Socrates had no chance?"

Another friend, Fred Mercer, Sr., a leading lawyer of the Allegheny County Bar, took up a different argument. He emphasized that I had my own professional future to consider and that although I was now

making excellent headway in the practice of the law in Pittsburgh I
could quite easily, by a protracted absence, lose the ground I had
gained. I explained that I could not abandon two men whom I believed to be absolutely guiltless. "Abandon them?" he exclaimed. "No
one has retained you to defend them. You have received no compensation and you have paid your own expenses so far. How can you
speak of abandoning them?"

Nonetheless, it seemed to me that not to return to Boston meant
abandoning not only two innocent men but the concept of justice itself.
Even when I visited our Allegheny County Jail to interview prisoners
I was to defend in court I could not dismiss from my mind the helpless
figures of the two innocent men in Dedham.

At about this time I received in the mail the following letter from
the Dedham prison:

> My dear Mr. Musmanno:
>
>   You can perhaps well comprehend how I and my
> loved ones must feel grateful to those who, in this sad
> and grave moment of my life, hurry in defense of my
> life and of all that in life is worth living, as you hurried
> from a great distance to help us. You well know that
> there are sentiments and things which the tongue and
> words cannot express, and I am sure you will appreci-
> ate my inability and, therefore, my not attempting to
> express to you the innermost feeling of my soul.
>
>   I want to tell you that I desired so much that you
> should go to Plymouth, in order that you could verify
> with absolute certainty and honesty, my complete inno-
> cence of the two crimes* for which I have already

* Prior to the Dedham trial, Vanzetti had been tried for an attempted robbery
in Bridgewater. Katzmann prosecuted and Judge Thayer presided. The evidence
against Vanzetti was farcical. One of the witnesses identified Vanzetti as being
the robber he saw because the robber "ran like a foreigner". Another witness,
prior to the trial, said that the robber he had seen had a "closely cropped"
mustache. Vanzetti's mustache was long and flowing, but he "identified" Vanzetti as the robber principally because of the mustache. Eleven witnesses
testified that during the time Vanzetti lived in Plymouth his mustache was
always long and flowing and never cropped. Eighteen witnesses testified that
Vanzetti was in Plymouth the entire day (December 24, 1919) the crime was
being committed in Bridgewater, twenty-seven miles away. Vanzetti was convicted, and this became the foundation for the scaffold Katzmann prepared to
erect for the Dedham trial. On October 31, 1928, the *Outlook and Independent*,
national periodical, published the authenticated account of the Bridgewater
holdup with sworn affidavits of the men who had actually committed the
crime. They absolved Vanzetti completely.

suffered seven long years in prison and am now on the road to be put to death. Yes, I desired extremely much that you should go to Plymouth, but in consideration of your already tiring labors and the usual exigencies of life, I could not bring myself around to asking you. But now that I have learned you did go, and did learn first-hand of my presence there on the two days that I was supposed to have been elsewhere perpetrating crimes, I will say that only one who has passed through a situation similar to mine can form for himself an idea of the great satisfaction and pleasure I had in hearing of it.

You are optimistic about the final outcome of our case, and it is pleasant to hear optimism founded on reason, because our experiences of the last seven years tend us toward pessimism. But if we are not put to death, if we leave alive the prisons of Massachusetts, we will owe it solely and completely to our companions, to our friends, to wonderful people who, like you, have done so much in our defense.

Grateful for your valuable aid, I wish you health.

Sincerely,

Bartolomeo Vanzetti

I closed my office and the next day appeared in Boston to place myself at the disposition of Chief Defense Counsel Thompson and the Sacco-Vanzetti Defense Committee, with headquarters at 156 Hanover Street, close by the shop in which Paul Revere had hammered out his beautiful silver creations before mounting the steed which carried him to patriotic immortality. The walls of the Sacco-Vanzetti headquarters, which consisted of two rooms, shone with bright posters from all parts of the world proclaiming in the language of each country represented, and in varying styles of lithography, the innocence of Sacco and Vanzetti.

One room was furnished with a table, typewriter, and chairs, the other contained filing cabinets jammed with correspondence and addresses of sympathizers from the four corners of the globe. Piles of pamphlets stacked in both rooms served as seats for volunteer workers and visitors. There was to come a day when the papers in the typewriter room would double as my bed. I came to Boston with all the funds I possessed. In four weeks' time they were exhausted and I had no resources to draw upon for a continued stay at a hotel. I am confident that if Aldino Felicani, chairman of the Sacco-Vanzetti Defense Committee, or Gardner Jackson, brilliant Amherst graduate who had dedicated himself to the case, had known of my depleted exchequer they would have offered to pay my expenses, but as a volunteer in the battle I wished to impose on no one. Moreover, I knew of the tremendous expense to which the committee was put in printing legal briefs, hiring investigators, publishing pamphlets, and making additional similar vital outlays. The defense money came from voluntary contributions sent in by working people from all parts of the world, and I could not think of accepting a dollar of those financial sacrifices committed to the goal of saving the lives of two innocent men in America.

Thus, the first night after insolvency compelled me to give up my accommodations at the hotel, I invented an excuse to remain in the headquarters late, explaining I wished to study the reports of certain investigators. About midnight then, when all had departed, I scattered pamphlets and newspapers on the floor so as to make as even a surface as possible, and on them I rested my tired bones until the following morning. I repeated the performance the subsequent night and then adopted it as regular procedure. Since no one could question my intense devotion to the case, it never occurred to anybody to ask why I remained at the headquarters so late every night. This went on for about six weeks, my back becoming increasingly sore and my legs correspondingly stiff from my unyielding nocturnal couch.

One night Edward H. James, wealthy nephew of the famous philosopher William James, and a staunch adherent to the Sacco-Vanzetti cause, visited headquarters and indicated he would like to accompany me back to my hotel that night as he wished to discuss with me certain features of the case. I urged him to discuss those matters right away as I would not get to my hotel until very late. He said he did not wish to interrupt my work and that he would gladly wait until I started back to the hotel. I begged him not to tarry as I had considerable typing ahead of me and, saying this, I turned to the typewriter. I would be busy until midnight at least, I warned him. James looked at his watch and said it would be no hardship for him to wait until midnight. Adjusting the deed to the word, he proceeded to sit down on a pile of pamphlets which nightly became the mattress for my bed.

Then promply at the stroke of midnight he said: "Well, Mr. Musmanno, let's go. You must be pretty tired by now."

"I am tired, Mr. James, but I repeat that I have an enormous amount of work ahead of me and I wish you would go because I don't want to hold you up."

"Oh, that's all right, Mr. Musmanno, I'll wait."

By now my eyelids were as heavy as stove lids, but I was obliged to convey the appearance of one who had just emerged from a mid-morning shower fresh as a daisy. But by one o'clock it became impossible for me to carry the masquerade further. James noted my sagging back and said: "Come, come, you better get to your bed. You're almost falling over."

"No, thank you," I replied, continuing to type with sleepy velocity: "Now is the time for all good men to come to the aid of their party."

However, since it was now apparent that James was determined to walk me to my nonexistent hotel I finally, at one-thirty raised the white flag. "Mr. James, I must tell you the truth. I can't go to bed because you're sitting in the middle of it."

"Oh, my God!" he gasped. "That's terrible." I couldn't tell from his tone which he was more concerned about: the papers being slept on or my back becoming gradually petrified. However, he then rushed on to say: "I have a spare room in my house and I want you to take it at once. Tonight. I'm certainly glad I waited around or you might have gone on ruining your health."

"Thank you, Mr. James, I will not refuse your kind offer." And so from that night until the end I had an excellent room in Mr. James's exquisite mansion on Beacon Street, which, paradoxically, symbolized the forces striving to send to their death the men we were striving to save.

Canon 5 of the Canons of Professional Ethics of the American Bar Association declares:

> Suppressing facts or secreting evidence which might be
> of assistance to the accused is highly reprehensible.

Was this canon respected by the prosecuting authorities in the Sacco-Vanzetti case? When I first visited South Braintree to reconstruct the crime I found a certain Candido de Bona, who gave me a sworn statement that three weeks after the robbery-murder, which he had witnessed at close range, he called on the district attorney to inform him that the supposed suspects, Sacco and Vanzetti, whose pictures appeared in the newspapers, did not resemble the bandits who had passed before his immediate vision. He said he stood ready to testify to this in court. However, since his testimony would have tended to prove Sacco and Vanzetti innocent instead of guilty, De Bona was never subpoenaed to testify.

This was only a small bruising by the district attorney's office of Canon 5. A more momentous fracturing revolved around the incident of the so-called "bandit cap." From the very beginning of my study of the case I felt there was much more to the story of this cap than had so far appeared. I often asked myself why it was that Jeremiah F. Gallivan, chief of police of Braintree, had not testified at the trial regarding the cap, since it had been in his safekeeping from the day it came into his possession until the day it was produced in court. It is a fundamental rule in trial procedure that, if a physical object connected with a crime or accident is presented as evidence, proof must be submitted that it presently is in the same condition it was when the crime or accident occurred. Why wasn't Gallivan asked about the condition of the cap when it first came into his custody? Was it perhaps because, in the meantime, it had undergone some transformation?

I went to Braintree to talk to Gallivan about the cap. He evinced no reluctance to discuss the subject. Lighting up a large curved meerschaum pipe, he said: "Mr. Musmanno, I'll tell you all about that cap. A great deal was said in court about the hole in the lining having been made by a nail on which Sacco hung the cap at his workshop. That's all nonsense." As I caught my breath, sure of a revelation to follow, he released the thunderbolt: "*I* made that hole!"

The floor danced beneath my feet. Gallivan then narrated how two days following the robbery-murder the superintendent of the shoe-company plant had given him a cap which someone had picked up "last night." It was even possible the cap had been dropped by a sightseer and was thus in no way connected with the bandits. At any rate, when Gallivan got the cap *two days* following the robbery, it was absolutely intact. Thinking that he might find a name or initials under the lining, Gallivan cut a hole in it. And that explained the famous aperture in the cap—not because it had been hung on a nail in Sacco's workshop, as the Commonwealth had contended and as Thayer had accepted, as if the proof had come down from Sinai.

Gallivan's revelation sent shivers of ecstasies through my entire body. This disclosure in itself, combined with the other evidence of Sacco's innocence, would exonerate him, since Katzmann had emphasized that the jury had the right to convict on the cap alone if they thought it was Sacco's. But now, with this unequivocal proof that the only alleged evidence which connected Sacco with the cap was false, the prosecution's case against Sacco had to collapse like a sack from which the contents have been removed.

With wings on my feet I raced to the governor to acquaint him with the momentous exposure of the cap evidence. I thought he might be shaken by what I reported. He was as much shaken as if I had reported to him on the state of the weather. However, he did say that he would talk to Gallivan. But when Gallivan appeared before him Fuller asked: "Did you see a hat mark or a rack mark inside it [the cap]?" Fuller would not give up the prosecution's theory. Gallivan spelled out that there was no hat mark or rack mark or any kind of mark inside the cap and that he made the hole, the only hole which was in the cap when the cap was presented in evidence at the trial. But Fuller refused to be impressed. Here was an officer of the law smashing before his very eyes what was perhaps the most important link of the so-called chain of evidence which was binding Sacco to the electric chair, but Fuller was thinking of other things. Was he casting about in his mind for another link to take the place of the one destroyed in his presence?

I have mentioned that Celestino F. Madeiros confessed to participation in the South Braintree crime, revealing that the crime was committed by the Morelli gang, of which he was a member. Herbert Ehrmann, brilliant Boston attorney and assistant to William G. Thompson, conducted an exhaustive investigation based on the statements made by Madeiros. His investigation produced practically uncontradicted evidence on which any unbiased jury could find the Morelli gang (all five) guilty of the South Braintree crime. Professor Frankfurter, in comparing the possibilities of the Morelli gang as against Sacco and Vanzetti committing the South Braintree crime, said:

> The Morelli theory accounts for all members of the Braintree murder gang; the Sacco-Vanzetti theory for only two, for it is conceded that if Madeiros was there, Sacco and Vanzetti were not. The Morelli theory accounts for all the bullets found in the dead men; the Sacco-Vanzetti theory for only one out of six. The Morelli explanation settles the motive, for the Morelli gang were criminals desperately in need of money for legal expenses pending their trial for felonies, whereas the Sacco-Vanzetti theory is unsupported by any motive. Moreover Madeiros's possession of $2800 ac-

counts for his share of the booty, whereas not a penny
has ever been traced to anybody or accounted for on
the Sacco-Vanzetti theory . . . The character of the
Morelli gang fits the opinion of police investigators and
the inherent facts of the situation, which tended to
prove that the crime was the work of professionals,
whereas the past character and record of Sacco and
Vanzetti have always made it incredible that they
should spontaneously become perpetrators of a bold
murder, executed with the utmost expertness.

Despite the astounding discoveries which came to light in the
Madeiros confession and the Ehrmann investigation, all of which
completely exculpated Sacco and Vanzetti, the district attorney's
office refused to take any action leading to a new trial for the condemned men. Since the whole world knew of the Madeiros confession,
Fuller felt impelled to make at least a showing that he was considering
what Madeiros had said. He decided to visit Madeiros in prison.
Madeiros was under sentence of death for another murder, to which he
had also confessed; namely, the killing of a bank cashier in a robbery
in Wrentham, Massachusetts. It appears that when he was arrested
for the Wrentham crime the police led him to believe that if he confessed they would recommend a second-degree murder penalty and
thus he would escape the electric chair. However, this agreement, if
it was made, was not kept and Madeiros charged that he had been
"double-crossed." Now came the governor to say that if any promise
had been made to him by the police authorities he, the governor,
would see to it that that promise was not ignored. Apparently, however, the governor expected Madeiros to do something for him
first; namely, to renounce his exculpation of Sacco and Vanzetti as
participants in the South Braintree robbery. Thus he began his conversation with the leading question: "Of course you don't know
anything about the South Braintree murder of your own knowledge,
do you?"

Surprised, Madeiros replied, "But I do know about it because I was
there."

"Were you in the car?"

"Yes, I was in the car."

"Oh, I see, so you are a double murderer. In that case, I'll do nothing for you."

If one analyzes this dialogue he will find it not only amazing but grotesquely entertaining. It revealed Fuller directing the millstream of evidence over a logic wheel from which many paddles were missing. By proclaiming Madeiros a double murderer, the governor accepted the truthfulness of Madeiros' confession of the South Braintree crime and he thus, by necessary implication, declared the innocence of Sacco and Vanzetti, since Madeiros had said that Sacco and Vanzetti were not with him at South Braintree. It was generally agreed that if Madeiros actually participated in the South Braintree robbery Sacco and Vanzetti did not. But either Fuller was incapable of perceiving this simple deduction or, seeing it, he refused to act on what his mind told him was indisputable. The mill wheel turned, but it failed to grind the wheat of exoneration into the flour of liberation. During the days of the famous Dreyfus affair of France, the generals of the army denied Dreyfus the right to be innocent because they could not admit an error. In the Sacco-Vanzetti case, Fuller went further: he denied Sacco and Vanzetti even the hypothesis of innocence.

From the day that application for executive clemency had been filed it had been urged on Governor Fuller by defense counsel, civic organizations, and many newspapers that he appoint an advisory commission which would also review the case, hear evidence, and make recommendations to the governor, the commission to consist of learned, honorable men whose names would command immediate and unhesitating respect and confidence. There were many jurists, lawyers, and statesmen of world-wide reputation from whom to choose. Fuller, however, did not lift his eyes beyond the geographical borders of Boston itself. On June 1 he announced the appointment of a commission composed of Abbott Lawrence Lowell, president of Harvard University; Samuel W. Stratton, president of Massachusetts Institute of Technology; and Robert Grant, writer of fiction and former probate judge. It would certainly seem that men holding such distinguished positions, especially the two university presidents, had been ideally chosen for a task calling for undeviating impartiality and scholarly disinterestedness. It was to develop, however, that they were also carrying gilt-edged bricks and fancy stonework for the high wall under construction by Massachusetts' officialdom to shield the fair name of the Bay State from world censure. Judge Grant was particularly well equipped for his part in the bricklaying job. He had already made his opinion known that the judgment in the Sacco-Vanzetti case should not be questioned.

Lowell dominated the commission, and it soon became apparent that he was resolved to go to any length to uphold the infallibility of Massachusetts' justice. At the Dedham trial two witnesses, Felice

Guadagni and Albert Bosco, testified that they had seen and talked with Sacco on April 15, 1920, in Boni's restaurant in Boston. They particularly remembered the date because they had discussed with Sacco a banquet being tendered that day by a group of Italians to James T. Williams, editor of the Boston *Transcript.* Lowell summoned these two men before the commission and annnounced that a fraud had been perpetrated on the Court and jury because there was no banquet to Williams on April 15. He had made an independent inquiry himself on the subject and found, by consulting two newspapers and Williams, that the banquet in question had occurred on May 13 and not April 15, the day of the South Braintree robbery. In view of Mr. Lowell's categorical declaration, Mr. Thompson was for a moment nonplused. I suggested to Mr. Thompson that there might have been two banquets, because Italians are rather expansive on the subject of banquets. However, when Mr. Thompson offered this possible explanation, Mr. Lowell was annoyed and made the gratuitous remark that "I don't know whether you are trying to reach the truth or not."

Nevertheless, the two witnesses insisted that their memory had not deceived them. In fact, Bosco stated that prior to testifying at Dedham he had looked up the date of the banquet in the files of *La Notizia,* an Italian newspaper, and his recollection had been confirmed. And he had so testified. It would appear that the members of the commission, despite their aggressive show of knowledgeableness, had either not read the record of the trial or had forgotten much of what they read.

The day ended with Lowell triumphant. He had singlehandedly demolished Sacco's alibi. He had proved that Sacco was not in Boston on April 15 because there was no banquet on that day, and it was impossible there could have been two banquets. Ergo, Sacco was incontrovertibly guilty. However, on the following day the sun rose on what could never have been imagined possible in Boston: the great Abbott Lawrence Lowell could be wrong! Bosco and Guadagni reappeared before the commission bearing with them the files of *La Notizia.* The issue of April 16 carried an article which described the banquet tendered to Mr. Williams on April *15,* the day before—which was the day of the South Braintree crime. A later issue also described the banquet of May 13, so that there had been two banquets after all.

Mr. Thompson now reminded Mr. Lowell that Sacco's alibi had been rehabilitated by the incontestable proof that Bosco and Guadagni

had told the truth, and he asked that the commission recognize
that fact. Lowell did not exhibit the slightest embarrassment over the
fact that he had been caught knee-deep in fallacy. Not only had he
strayed into the pool of error but he had deliberately left the course
of the tribunal's regular procedure to pick up on his own what turned
out to be misleading and false information. However, secure in his
position and impregnable in his great name (the hearings were held
behind closed doors and he could order, which he did, the stenographer
to make no mention of the contretemps), he did not need to spare any
blushes over what defense counsel was requesting. With a wave of the
hand he "tut-tutted" Mr. Thompson, who now turned to Judge Grant
and asked him whether the restoration of Sacco's alibi by unim-
peachable documentary evidence had not at least raised a reasonable
doubt in the minds of the commission as to Sacco's guilt. Judge Grant
also "tut-tutted" Mr. Thompson, but added: "You are just back where
you were," which meant, of course, helplessly standing by as the bricklaying job proceeded apace.

Jeremiah Gallivan, who had spoken to the governor's deaf ear about
the hole he had made in the alleged bandit's cap, now appeared before
the commission, and the commission was prepared for him. Judge
Grant was determined to save something from the wreckage of
the once damning evidence. He approached Gallivan persuadingly.
"Didn't you say there was a little hole?"—that is, before Gallivan had
torn the lining. Of course Gallivan had said nothing of the kind, but
Grant obviously reasoned that if Gallivan would admit to any kind of
hole in the cap when he first got it, this admission would verify and
authenticate the Commonwealth's theory about the nail. However,
Gallivan rejected the existence of any such prior hole. Lowell now
nudged Grant as if to say: "Here, let me try this." Turning on all his
charm and beaming with engaging amiability, Lowell strove by the
power of suggestion to make a little hole in that cap. With a rising
inflection which dripped honeyed blandishment he ingratiatingly
purred: "There was a little hole?" But Gallivan was not awed or
hypnotized by this obsequious wheedling. He replied with a brutally
frank "No" and explained once again what he had done in seeking an
identifying mark. Then, to remove all speculation about the matter,
he categorically declared: "That lining was perfectly whole when that
hat was given to me."

In Lowell's report to the governor he admitted that Gallivan had
accounted for the hole in the cap but said that it was "so trifling a
matter in the evidence in the case that it seems to the committee by

no means a ground for a new trial." Before the exposure, the hole in the cap was large enough through which to push Sacco to his doom. After the ascertainment of the cruel hoax which had been played on Sacco and the whole world of truth, the hole was of no importance. What, then, was important to the commission?

Lincoln Wadsworth, an employee at the Iver Johnson revolver repair shop, testified at the trial regarding the Berardelli revolver which had been left at his shop for a new hammer. The district attorney had interpreted Wadsworth's testimony to mean that the revolver found on Vanzetti was the same revolver which had belonged to Berardelli and had been repaired at the Johnson shop. I called on Wadsworth. He expressed considerable relief in talking to someone associated with the defense. He said that his conscience had been troubling him because prosecuting authorities were asserting he had testified that the Vanzetti revolver was the same revolver which Berardelli had left in his shop. "That is not so!" he cried, and he denied that he had ever said so in court. He hoped for an opportunity to correct authoritatively the misinterpretation which had been placed on his testimony. That opportunity came before the Lowell Commission. Here he spoke out in strong voice that "there are thousands of times more chances that it [Vanzetti's revolver] was not [Berardelli's revolver] than that it was." But how did Lowell accept this statement of a man who testified not only as an expert in the field but as one possessed of positive, personal knowledge on the particular revolver in dispute? In his report to the governor Lowell said that the defense had given no "satisfactory explanation" that the Vanzetti revolver was not the Berardelli revolver. "It was natural," he said, that "if the bandits saw the pistol they should carry it off for fear of someone shooting at them as they escaped." But how could Berardelli have fired at the escaping bandits? The bandits had killed him and the paymaster Palmenter too.

It almost seemed that the members of the commission were so sure no one would dare question their wisdom to distinguish between reliable and unreliable evidence that they gave credence to stories which, if heard by them in their own respective professional spheres, they would most certainly reject as being idiotic and absurd. For instance, there was Carlotta Packard, who was so irresponsible that even the district attorney would not let her testify at Dedham. She told a story that she had been a fellow employee of Sacco's at the Rice and Hutchins factory in 1908 and had then seen him, twelve years later, on the day of the murder, standing in front of the factory at

11:30 A.M. The truth of the matter—and this was known to the prosecution—is that Sacco did not work at a shoe factory in 1908. He had just arrived from Italy and worked throughout that year at "pick and shovel." When Mr. Lowell asked Carlotta Packard how she had come to know Sacco in 1908, this was her startling reply:

> "Why, I don't know, I couldn't remember. Gentlemen, I talked with Governor Fuller, and I don't remember, my head is too full of music and things like that, to remember."

Police Chief Jeremiah Gallivan, who had known Carlotta from infancy, said of this strange creature:

> "Well, my honest and frank opinion is that that girl is a nut, she is a nut, and I have known her since she was born. She ought to be in the Brookline Psychopathic Hospital. She is a nut. She is crazy, and she has been that way for years. She imagines things. She has pipe dreams."

Her former employer said of her: "I will tell you, I think she is about twelve ounces to the pound."

But in his report to the governor the erudite Mr. Lowell said:

> "The woman is eccentric, not unimpeachable in conduct. But the committee believes that *in this case* her testimony is well worth consideration." (Emphasis supplied.)

It is particularly to be noted from this statement that Lowell was prepared to regard anything that condemned the defendants as "well worth consideration"—even the testimony of one who was "twelve ounces to the pound," whose head was "too full of music and things," who "imagines things" and had "pipe dreams."

Chapter XXXVI

THE LAST STAND

ON THE night of August 3, 1927, Governor Fuller announced what had been obvious from the very beginning—that he would not interfere with the death sentences. The executions were scheduled for midnight of August 10. Mr. Thompson withdrew as chief defense counsel and Attorney Arthur D. Hill took his place. On the morning of August 5, Mr. Hill called a conference made up of Herbert B. Ehrmann, Francis D. Sayre (professor at Harvard and President Wilson's son-in-law), Professor Felix Frankfurter, and myself, later joined in by Elias Field and Richard C. Evarts, lawyers of considerable ability and fine reputation.

We unanimously agreed upon a selected course of action. The first step, obviously, was to obtain the designation of an impartial judge to pass upon all legal motions to be made. Mr. Hill accordingly went to Judge Broadhurst of Superior Court in Boston and requested the assignment of a judge other than Judge Thayer to hear a motion for new trial based on Thayer's demonstrated prejudice and on newly discovered evidence. Broadhurst refused the motion.

Mr. Ehrmann filed a petition with the governor requesting a stay of execution. Fuller did nothing.

I proceeded to the Dedham courthouse and filed a motion for a new trial on the basis that Sacco and Vanzetti had never been accorded the trial to which they were entitled under the Constitution of the United States and the Declaration of Rights of the Inhabitants of the Commonwealth of Massachusetts. I fortified this motion with affidavits and statements establishing that Judge Thayer had been biased against the defendants from the beginning and thus was incapable of presiding as an impartial judge. I pointed out how he had said that he "would get the defendants good and proper," how he had taunted, after his decision, "Let them go to the Supreme Court and see how far they will get," and how he had often referred to the defendants as "anarchistic bastards."

After Judge Broadhurst had refused to assign a judge other than Judge Thayer to hear what we had to present, we asked Chief Justice Hall of the Superior Court, that he, in the name of decency and justice, avert the fantastic spectacle of a judge passing judgment on himself. But Chief Justice Hall saw nothing fantastic about Judge Thayer doing that very thing, and so on August 8, 1927, the world witnessed the grotesque show of a judge deciding for himself whether he had done the right thing in presiding over a trial and sentencing to death two defendants of whom he had said he would "get them good and proper"!

Flanked by motorcycle police and armed guards, Judge Thayer made a state entrance into the courthouse and proceeded at once to the bench where, with beady eye, he looked down at the crowded courtroom. Small of stature, nervous in movement, Judge Thayer scowled at three or four of us sitting at the defense counsel table and asked what we had to present. Mr. Hill immediately rose and said that Judge Thayer should withdraw from the case: "Every consideration of sound sense, good morals, and intelligent administration of law impels you to withdraw."

The judge shifted in his seat, the pallor of his face wrinkling into yellow corrugations, his small eyes blinking unceasingly, but he did not withdraw. He refused also to consider the new evidence presented. Retiring to his chambers, he swore, reviled the defendants and their lawyers, spat on the floor, and ruled against us on every point.

We appealed to the Supreme Court of Massachusetts, but the date set for the execution, August 10—at midnight—had arrived. One would assume that the most obvious thing in the world for the Supreme Court to do, since it had the obligation to decide whether Sacco and Vanzetti should die, would be to keep them alive until they, the judges, had passed on that very question. Small comfort it would be to the defendants if the Supreme Court should decide that they had been illegally convicted if, by the time the decision was rendered, they were legally—or illegally—dead. Nevertheless, Judge Sanderson of that court, to whom we applied for a stay of execution, refused it.

It would also seem like the most obvious thing in the world for the chief executive of the Commonwealth to grant a reprieve, once he knew, as he did know, that the Supreme Court was to pass upon the question of a new trial for the prisoners. However, instead of authorizing a respite at once, Governor Fuller, the ex-trick bicycle racer, with atavistic flavor decided to hippodrome the whole ghastly business. He summoned to the State House all the living ex-attorneys general of Massachusetts, seven of them. He also convened the Governor's Council. They all came, smoked and talked throughout the entire day; talked while the hangman made hideous preparation for the killings only several hours away.

In this grisly state of affairs, which caricatured the whole process of orderly state government, we decided to appeal to the United States courts for enforcement of the due process of law guaranteed by the Fourteenth Amendment of the United States Constitution. The granting of a writ of habeas corpus by a federal judge would take the prisoners out of the death house and sanction an impartial review of the entire case which had so long been desired, so imperatively needed—and, by the state authorities, so constantly refused.

By automobile I raced to the Charlestown prison and there, in the shadow of Bunker Hill, I explained to Sacco and Vanzetti the present state of affairs, proffering for their signatures the petition for the writ of habeas corpus. Sacco refused to sign. "They're going to crucify me, both of us," he said. "They've been driving nails for seven years. Let's get it over with." Despite the depth of his feeling, however, he spoke in a low voice so as to dispel any idea that he was unappreciative of my efforts.

Vanzetti smiled and picked up two books from his cot. In the garish light of the death house the title gleamed: *The Rise of American Civilization*. The books had been given to him by Mrs. Elizabeth Glendower Evans, to whom he had written: "The only trouble is that the Massachusetts hanger may not give me time to finish them." The fish peddler now wrote on the flyleaf of Volume 1: "To my friend and defender, Michael Angelo Musmanno—offered August 10, 1927, Bartolomeo Vanzetti," and proffered the two volumes to me through the bars. I said: "Mr. Vanzetti, you are offering these books as a parting gift, and were I to accept them it would mean I believe this to be a permanent farewell, which certainly it is not."

Sacco smiled. "Mr. Musmanno," he said, "better take the books—I know."

"Yes, I will take the books, but not now and not in this place. I'll accept them when Vanzetti hands them to me outside of prison—when you are both free men. And now that you have the pen in your hand, please sign this petition for habeas corpus." Vanzetti signed. As I prepared to leave, the noises in the adjoining execution room rose to a threatening crescendo. The electric chair was being serviced and tested for action that night. Holding tightly in my grasp the petition for habeas corpus, I said to the men: "This writ or the Council will silence all those mutterings. I'll be back tomorrow to see you."

At eleven twenty-three that night, thirty-seven minutes before Executioner Elliott was to pull the switch which would send thousands of volts of electricity crashing through the bodies of Sacco and Vanzetti, Fuller signed the reprieve which could have been granted long before the mechanicians started to oil up the macabre equipment.

Early the following morning I was at the prison again, but this time my blue serge suit was not taut with anxiety as it had been the night before. It smiled with its wearer, who rhapsodically shook hands with two men who almost challenged the verity of the Bard's lament that no traveler returns from the "bourn" of that "undiscover'd country." Vanzetti picked up the thread of the story stretched almost to the breaking point just a few hours ago. "You must now take the books for sure." He appended another inscription and passed the two volumes through the bars. Again I declined. "No," I insisted, "I will accept them when both of you are free."

That outside world was once more sitting on the edge of seats, following breathlessly the next episode in the melodramatic series which had taken the fleeing fugitives from one hanging cliff of the law to another for seven years. Would they foil the avenging Javert in the end?

We were all helping the fugitives by searching through the lawbooks, digging up precedent and authority which would convince the Supreme Court of Massachusetts—what could not be doubted in the factual world of elementary reasoning and sound judgment—that a judge who prejudges a case so impairs the sanctity of a fair trial that only a new trial can repair the damage. It was easy to find what we were looking for. In fact, it was difficult to select from so many authorities of the law which proclaimed that a judge who wears the dagger of prejudice beneath his robe is no longer a judge.

On August 16 we appeared in the Massachusetts Supreme Court, and Mr. Hill stood before the bench formidably marshaling the authorities which armor-plated our position that, since Judge Thayer had been an adversary rather than an arbiter in the case from the beginning, Sacco and Vanzetti had been denied due process of law, even though the trial in its outer aspects might have seemed to be free of error. Four judges sat and listened. I hoped they were listening. One of them kept stealing glances at his watch.

Three days later they handed down the staggering doctrine that "a motion for a new trial comes too late if made after the sentence has been pronounced." This meant that once a judge hurls the death-charged words at a convicted defendant he is to be regarded as legally dead so far as the courts are concerned, even though it should be established by *newly discovered evidence* that the defendant is absolutely innocent, or even if it should be proved that the sentencing tribunal was prejudiced, biased, or actually corrupt. Of course it was obvious to me that the judges were saying what they could not possibly mean. They had to say something. The Sacco-Vanzetti case had to come to an end sometime. Already it had dragged too long.

But this was not the end. There was still the Supreme Court of the United States to appeal to, and here I doubted not that justice would at last be done. The reprieve had put off the hangman until August 22. That was a good three days away, and by the time he knocked at the door again the Supreme Court of the United States would have served notice on him to avaunt! since his visitation was in violation of the Fourteenth Amendment of the United States Constitution. This we set forth in our petition for writ of certiorari, which would take the entire documentation in the case to a court removed from the political whirlwinds sweeping Massachusetts.

I could feel victory in the air as, traversing ground which had been covered by Paul Revere, I hurried to the Charlestown prison to outline our plans for the next and finally successful offensive. Sacco and Vanzetti noted the flush of happy anticipation on my cheeks as I entered the white-tiled death house with its three cells. Joyous optimism did not desert me even when, through the partly opened door into the adjacent room, I saw the canvas-covered American guillotine. In three days the itching fingers of Massachusetts would come again to tear off the canvas, but in those three days the long arm of the majesty of the United States would halt that poison-ivy hand.

I laughed at the electric chair and all its grim surroundings. They did not seem grim to me; rather they appeared to be the flimsy and make-believe trappings of the stage. I unfolded the petition for the writ of certiorari and spread it out for Sacco and Vanzetti to see as one displays the map which will guide lost travelers out of a pathless jungle. I crackled the paper in joyous gesture. Vanzetti caught the spirit of a realizable hope; even the laconic Sacco vouchsafed a cheerful grin. The piteous wretch of a Madeiros in the third cell smiled. Even the guards relaxed into a gentle good humor. Poor devils, they had no heart in the dirty work of preparing human beings for the butcher's block.

My enthusiasm filled the death house. That was many years ago. I was young. I was always referred to as the "young lawyer" in the case. And my youth scorned all those properties of death; in my hand I held the sword that would at last cut the Gordian knot which for seven years had held two innocent men tied to the tree of ceaseless torment. Blessed be certiorari!

With the momentous papers in my brief case I boarded the Federal Express at eight o'clock on Friday evening, August 19, and arrived in Washington the following morning at seven fifty-two. Numerous newspaper reporters were waiting at the Union Station, but I walked through them unquestioned. Shortly after I arrived at my hotel, however, a dozen men with notebooks and pencils burst into my room, expressing great surprise. "No wonder we missed you at the station," they chorused. "We expected an old man with a beard and mustache." The reporter of the Washington *Times* wrote in the afternoon edition: "Musmanno, despite his Italian name, speaks without the trace of a foreign accent." For an instant I thought of that political meeting in Mount Lebanon where others had thought I should have a "foreign accent." And in his surprise at not finding me "bearded like the pard," the reporter said further: "He is smooth-shaven with skin inclined toward fairness." And to remove all doubt as to whether I was a real American, even though defending Sacco and Vanzetti, he added: "He wears the bronze emblem of the United States Army in his coat lapel." My enthusiasm was apparently still with me, for he said: "He is not tall but is exceedingly brisk in all his movements." Yes, I was brisk—my heart was on fire with hope, confidence, assurance. At last we were coming into our own. I filed my papers with the Supreme Court of the United States, the highest in the land, and felt like exclaiming: "Massachusetts, beware!"

We had now only to obtain a stay of execution from any one of the nine Supreme Court justices because, strangely enough, the filing of an appeal does not of itself act as a reprieve. However, it would be a simple matter to get one of the justices to issue the necessary order in this respect. No justices were in Washington, so I telephoned Mr. Hill, and he immediately set out for Beverly, there to see at his home the venerable Justice Oliver Wendell Holmes, who, with his magnificent background as a defender of human rights, would unquestionably at once gladly offer his signature to the death-arresting document.

With this gratifying reassurance pervading my entire system, I rode back to Boston as happy as an exiled monarch returning to his throne. However, crossing into Massachusetts, a zigzag of chilling disillusionment ripped through my sky of optimism. Mr. Justice Holmes had refused to delay the executions. Still, this did not end the matter. He had no objection to application being made to another justice because, he explained: "I am far from saying that I think counsel was not warranted in presenting the question raised in the application." In effect, Justice Holmes admitted the possibility that the Supreme Court of the United States could well do what we were asking of it.

We now applied to Justice Brandeis, who declined to interfere on the peculiar ground that during the time of the trial Mrs. Brandeis had allowed Mrs. Sacco to tenant a house in Dedham owned by her, and to this extent he said he had displayed a personal interest in the case. Mr. Hill now set out to find Mr. Justice Stone, reported to be vacationing on an island off the coast of Maine. Since it was a question whether he could reach Justice Stone before midnight of August 22, I decided to appeal to the executive branch of the government.

There was precedent for my action. In 1918 President Wilson had requested the governor of California to commute the death sentences of the labor leaders Mooney and Billings on the ground that national welfare was involved. The lives of the men were spared. It appeared to me that with this incident in history to guide him, President Coolidge, as Chief Executive of the nation and former governor of Massachusetts, would need only to send a message to Governor Fuller recommending a postponement of the execution date—and preparatory work on the electric chair would be suspended, at least until the Supreme Court should meet in October to review the entire case. Thus I sent off a long wire to President Calvin Coolidge, who was vacationing in South Dakota, asking that I be allowed to see him to present a petition in the Sacco-Vanzetti case. I made arrangements for an airplane and directed the pilot to stand by. After waiting two hours and receiving no reply to my telegram, I dispatched a second telegram. Still failing to hear from the Summer White House, I now put in a telephone call and finally got one of the President's secretaries on the wire. I asked him whether the President had received my telegram. "What telegram?" he asked.

I read the copy to him. He said he had not seen the telegram. But did the President receive it? He said he did not know. Well, could he find out? He couldn't disturb the President because he was resting.

Well, certainly someone ought to know whether a telegram had been delivered. Would he please inquire? In a moment he explained that, yes, the telegram did arrive, but the matter was outside the President's jurisdiction. May I speak to the President? I now ask. No, the President is resting, he repeats, explaining in detail that the President had a hard day yesterday, fishing, and that as he is leaving for Yellowstone National Park this same evening on his vacation, he cannot be disturbed.

I urge the importance of my mission. I can come at once. An airplane is ready. No, the President is leaving for Yellowstone National Park. But I can fly to any place he goes. No, this is to be a complete vacation and he will see no one on official business. But this is a matter of life and death. All we ask is a stay of execution until the Supreme Court of the United States may pass upon our application for a writ of certiorari.

"The President has no power to stay executions."

"I understand that, but if he telegraphs the governor of Massachusetts that it is his wish the execution be postponed until the Supreme Court hears the case, the Governor will surely honor the request. May I talk to the President?"

"I tell you he is resting."

"Well, wake him up."

"Sir!"—with great severity—"There is nothing more to say."

"I'm sorry, I did not mean to be disrespectful. You must understand how worried I am. Practically the whole world believes these two condemned men innocent, and the United States Government, which assumes and must take world leadership, cannot ignore a situation which at least calls for federal inquiry. It has been our boast that no matter how humble the petitioner he may appeal even to the highest officials in government. This is a just cause. I am sure the President will want to consider it. May I come by plane? I will leave Boston at once."

"If you come, the President will not see you."

There was a click at the other end of the wire, and my further words rebounded from an unseen wall.

Mr. Hill had not yet reached Justice Stone. It was a two-hundred-mile drive to Rockland on the sea, and there he would need to cast about for marine transportation and then, finding it, fogs might hold up the sailing for many hours. We had to locate another justice. The sands of time were running fast. After many inquiries in newspaper offices and of people who might know the whereabouts of the other justices, since it was vacation time, I finally got the address of the Chief Justice himself. Why not contact him? This would be ideal, for who should know better than the Chief Justice the necessity for immediate action which would protect his court from a denial of jurisdiction through the destruction of the very subject matter before it for consideration? Accordingly I dispatched the following telegram:

> HONORABLE WILLIAM HOWARD TAFT,
> CHIEF JUSTICE, SUPREME COURT OF UNITED STATES,
> POINTE-AU-PIC, QUEBEC
>
> YOUR HONOR, WILL YOU KINDLY WIRE WHERE YOU MAY
> BE REACHED FOR THE PURPOSE OF PRESENTING TO
> YOUR HONOR QUESTION OF STAY OF EXECUTION ON
> WRIT OF ERROR IN THE SACCO AND VANZETTI CASE
> BEFORE SUPREME COURT.
>
> > M. A. MUSMANNO,
> > ATTORNEY FOR SACCO-VANZETTI

Fearing I might wait in vain for a reply, as had happened in telegraphing the President, I resorted again to the telephone and, much to my surprise and relief, I heard the Chief Justice's voice at the other end of the wire in Canada asking who wished to speak to him.

"Good evening, Mr. Chief Justice," I exclaimed, overjoyed to reach someone with power to act. "This is Attorney M. A. Musmanno, of counsel for Sacco and Vanzetti. I'm very sorry to break in on you in this manner, but urgent necessity compels speedy communication. However, I would not expect you to dispose by telephone of the matter I will mention to you. I should like to come to present my request in person."

"What is it you would like to present?"

"A request for a stay of execution in the Sacco-Vanzetti case. We have already filed our petiton for a writ of certiorari in the Supreme Court."

"But how can I hear the matter? I am not even in the United States."

"I know, Your Honor, but perhaps you could come to the border. An airplane is in readiness and I can leave at once."

"This is a most unusual thing you are asking."

"I realize that, Your Honor, but the duty that a lawyer owes his client will, I think, fully justify everything that I propose. We must act quickly. Our clients are scheduled to die tomorrow at midnight."

"I do not see why you should come to me. There are other judges in that circuit."

I explained that Justices Holmes and Brandeis had refused the requested relief and that Mr. Hill was on his way to see Justice Stone, but there was the possibility he might not reach him in time. I pointed out that since the case had definitely become part of the business of the United States Supreme Court it would be of particular concern to him as its Chief Justice to know what was transpiring. I asked that he indicate the closest point on the border which could be reached with least inconvenience to himself and I would fly to that place at once. He said that this was not a matter that could be discussed or decided by telephone.

"Your Honor," I pleaded, "that is why I humbly beseech that you allow me to present the request in person."

He asked me to send him a telegram specifying what I wanted. At 9:30 P.M. I sent the telegram and I requested Western Union to telephone me as soon as the reply was received from Canada. I instructed the pilot to stand by at the airport, ready to take off on a minute's notice.

When by midnight I had received no further word from the Chief Justice, my worries began to intensify into agony. Unless officialdom interceded, the ax would fall in twenty-four hours. I tried once more to get the Chief Justice on the telephone, but although I could hear the bell ringing in faraway Quebec I heard no human voice replying. Over and over the intermittent pealing came through the stillness of the night, my soul standing on tiptoe for the sound which would transform the insensate mechanism of instruments and wire into the exchange of miraculous thought between human beings, but the hopeful jingle always ended on the emptiness of hopeless silence.

Every half hour I also called the Western Union office to inquire if a telegram had arrived for me. On another telephone the pilot at the airport kept ringing me up to ask if he should set the propellers whirling. Throughout the night I fought the battle of empty communications. By five o'clock sleep began to claim his rights, but I struggled to deny him recognition, even though for the preceding week I had given him but scant hospitality. . . .

A shrill of the telephone lifted my head from the desk to which it had fallen. Western Union was calling. I looked at the clock. It was seven-twenty. A telegram had arrived for me, the operator said. It contained 430 words and it had been sent collect. If I would pay $19.20, she would have it delivered to me. I paid the $19.20, and

with the telegram in my hand I stumbled into a cab for Charlestown
to show Sacco and Vanzetti how a chief justice could spell out
the answer "No" in 430 words. Had I known that Chief Justice Taft
looked upon Professor Frankfurter's honest and able review of the
court record as a "perverted view of the facts" and that already, three
months before, he had urged the president of Yale University to
silence members of his law faculty who were arguing the issue,* I
would not have agonized through a whole night for an answer which
could scarcely have been a different one.

Crushed as I was by the double defeat administered by the executive and judicial departments of the government, I still managed
to maintain a semblance of hope as I talked to the doomed men in
their cells. I reminded them that the sky was no darker today than it
had been on August 10 when Fuller delayed action until a half hour
before midnight, knowing, as he had to know, that with the case
pending in the Massachusetts Supreme Court he could not have
allowed the death warrant to be executed. I explained that since we
had filed our petition for certiorari in the Supreme Court of the United
States, the state authorities would not dare to destroy the subject of
litigation in the face of that authoritative pendency. Furthermore,
abreast the marching dark clouds moved always the light of reasonable
expectation that Justice Harlan Fiske Stone, on an island in the Atlantic,
physically and emotionally isolated from the continental passions which
the Fullers, Thayers, and Lowells had stirred, would authorize a respite.
Justice Stone's record on the bench justified a boundless confidence
that he would do this.

But even Justice Stone, later to be Chief Justice, did not rise to the
occasion which would have added to his name an additional luster
of demonstrated courage, which had not been previously missing and
which later made him stand out as one of our more distinguished
jurists in American juridical history. Why did Stone turn us down?
Why was it becoming seemingly impossible in New England and all
territory and waters adjacent thereto to get anyone to understand
the sheer absurdity, to say nothing of intolerable injustice, of allowing
two men to be killed before the Supreme Court could determine
whether the application of the men for the Court's jurisdiction had
merit or not? Justice Holmes had said when he turned down the application for a stay of execution that he would be "glad" to see the
application made to another justice. Justice Stone said he turned down
the application "without prejudice to application to any other justice"

* *The Legacy of Sacco and Vanzetti,* by Joughin and Morgan, Harcourt Brace
and Co., 1948, p. 308.

and approved what Justice Holmes had said in that same regard. Chief Justice Taft said that since Justices Brandeis and Stone were within the First Judicial Circuit application would more properly be made to them. We have seen that Justice Brandeis' refusal to act had no bearing on the merits of the case.

No one had conclusively decided that the men were not entitled to a reprieve, but, on the other hand, no one had accepted the responsibility of granting the reprieve. As our hopes seesawed on the plank of expectation that we might yet find a justice who would do more than refer us to another justice, Attorney Ellis Field said to me: "Come, Musmanno, let's try Judge Siske. Since the men were convicted in the Superior Court of Massachusetts, it would seem to me that as a member of that Court he would have the jurisdiction to authorize a stay."

In an unrestrained flow of faith I allowed myself to believe that in this unostentatious Court we had at last found someone who would act. As we entered Judge Siske's chambers, I unclipped my fountain pen, ready to hand it to him for his signature beneath the simple word "Stay!" but in less than 430 words Judge Siske said "No," and the disconsolate fountain pen went back into my pocket.

Although we were within the federal courts because of our petition for a writ of certiorari to the Supreme Court of the United States, that particular procedure was in the nature of an appeal from the highest state court. There was another entrance to United States jurisdiction, which would be on the ground-floor level—the United States District Court. We could seek a writ of habeas corpus in the federal courts on the ground that Sacco and Vanzetti were being illegally detained because of violation of the United States Constitution. I prepared such a petition and, without any awareness as to how I got there, I stood again in the death house, again seeking signatures, again wearing (if somewhat less ebulliently) the same badge of assurance that we would still win the battle. Again Sacco refused to sign and again Vanzetti carefully inscribed his name to the paper I handed him.

While in the death house I encountered the most heart-shattering scene that one could ever witness in a prison. Luigia Vanzetti, sister of Bartolomeo Vanzetti, whom she had not seen for nineteen years, had just arrived from Italy. Grasping the loving hands of this pale, frail creature, the playmate of his faraway childhood, Vanzetti broke down. "Oh, sister of mine, why did you come to give yourself so much pain? How can I say 'Welcome!' and at the same time 'Good-by!' And how does one say 'Good-by' in a place like this?"

Mrs. Sacco was there too, holding tightly the hands of her husband, those hands that had worked in ditches, factories, at the shoemaker's bench, and in the garden, but which had never committed a dishonest act.

"I love you and always will," Sacco was saying.

"Nick, I am dying with you!"

I left the prison, my chest a tormenting void. Clutching desperately the paper Vanzetti had signed, I mounted the steps of the Federal Court in Boston three at a time.

Another legal argument, this one before Judge Lowell, relative of Abbott Lawrence Lowell. He looked through many lawbooks, but he could not find the page which authorized him, a judge of the United States courts, to intercede when a state is charged with ignoring the mandate of the Constitution of the United States, which holds the states together.

When I returned to our law headquarters they were empty. Mr. Fields was absent and Mr. Hill and Mr. Evarts were still in Maine. For a moment I trembled in the awesome realization that responsibility for the remaining legal fight in the world-shaking Sacco-Vanzetti case had now fallen on my shoulders. Praying for strength as I ran, I made for the State House to urge upon the governor his sacred obligation to prevent the loss of life which could never be restored, while the ultimate tribunal in the country had yet to pass upon a vital constitutional issue before it.

The State House was an island in a churning sea of humanity. For several days tens of thousands of people had been gathering on the Boston Common, urging by their presence that the governor exert the mercy for which the whole world was supplicating by telegram, demonstrations, and millions of petitions. Hundreds of pickets were circling the golden-domed capitol. Authors, artists, war veterans, students, workingmen, housewives pleaded with placards and signs that the governor not abandon humanity. One of the pickets stopped me, seized my hand, and wished me success. I rubbed my eyes. Could this be Edna St. Vincent Millay, the greatest American poet of today? Yes, it was she. She carried a placard reading: "If these men are executed, justice is dead in Massachusetts." Later she wrote a letter which should have convinced the governor more than the argument of any lawyer:

> Tonight, with the world in doubt, with this Common-
> wealth drawing into its lungs with every breath the dif-

ficult air of doubt, with the eyes of Europe westward
upon Massachusetts and upon the whole United States
in distress and harrowing doubt—are you still so sure?
Does not the faintest shadow of question gnaw at your
mind? For, indeed, your spirit, however strong, is but
the frail spirit of a man. Have you no need, in this hour,
of a spirit greater than your own? . . .

I cry to you with a million voices; answer our doubt.
Exert the clemency which your high office affords.

There is need in Massachusetts of a great man tonight. It is not yet too late for you to be that man.

With long strides I passed through marble halls and climbed marble
steps, looking for the great man that Edna St. Vincent Millay and
half the world were seeking. I stepped into the governor's office but
found no one there worthy of the Pantheon. The whole world was
worrying, but not Alvan T. Fuller. Cool as the marble floors I had
traversed, he sat at his desk, no mark of care creasing his rounded
face, no preoccupation dimming the brightness of his marble eyes. On
this day of crisis when he was to make the most important decision, not
only of his whole gubernatorial term, but of his whole life, he still
looked what he was: a highly successful automobile salesman. He
received me as if I might have been a likely customer for one of his
luxurious Packard cars. With the maximum urbanity of one inquiring
about the latest score of a current baseball game, he asked for news
on the latest development in the case. I outlined the situation to him
and then added:

"Your Excellency, as attorney for Nicola Sacco and Bartolomeo
Vanzetti, I formally and respectfully ask for a stay of execution."

"I don't understand this procedure, Mr. Musmanno," the governor
replied, still urbane. "First Mr. Thompson bowed himself into my
office and said: 'I am through with the case.' After Mr. Thompson
left, Mr. Hill came in and said: 'This is the last time I will ask for a
respite,' and now that Mr. Hill has gone, in bows Mr. Musmanno and
asks for a respite." He turned to his private counsel, Mr. Wiggin,
sitting in the room with him, and chuckled. Mr. Wiggin understood
that the governor was being quite clever and laughed aloud in appreciation of his boss's superlative wit.

I replied: "Your Excellency, there is no criticism to be made of
your observation, and at the same time I don't think that any attaches

to the actions of my predecessors. After all, it is not a question of personality of counsel but a matter of the lives of two men."

"In other words, if you can't get any help elsewhere, you come here." He chuckled again in the direction of Mr. Wiggin, who, knowing full well on which side his bread was buttered, laughed uproariously. The governor then shot at me what he must have thought was a salvo of destruction: "How about the courts?"

"Your Excellency, we have found four of the nine justices of the Supreme Court. We have not yet ascertained the whereabouts of the other five."

"Haven't your clients received the benefit of all the courts in our state?"

"Yes, Governor, but you are also part of the constitutional machinery of the state for the ascertainment of truth. It is your province to correct any error in this case, no matter where and how committed."

"Mr. Musmanno, if you can convince my attorney general that I should grant a respite, I will do so."

Scarcely feeling the intervening stretch of marble and carpet under my feet, I stood in the offices of Arthur K. Reading, attorney general of Massachusetts, also in the capitol. The attorney general (later, in another connection, to be removed from office and disbarred for accepting a bribe) received me with courtesy and said I could take as much time as I wished in making my presentation. I said that all we were seeking was an opportunity to argue our case before the Supreme Court of the United States. Certainly Massachusetts could be gracious enough to stay the execution until October. It had already waited seven years, it could wait another two months. For two hours I argued to that one man as I might have argued to the world's population, because in him, for the moment, was lodged the right to decide what constituted universal justice. He said he would reflect on what I had said and then notify the governor as to his decision.

I returned to the governor's office and renewed my plea with him. I reviewed the case, pointing out how every bit of accusatory evidence which the prosecution had presented at the original trial had since been repudiated or had disintegrated under inquiry. Why would he want to take the irrevocable step of ordering an execution, with the possibility that he might later be convinced the men were innocent, when he would be powerless to rectify the horrible error? "What can be lost in reprieving the men until the Supreme Court of the

United States passes upon the appeal? Once the highest Court renders a decision, no one can possibly criticize you."

While I was speaking, Mrs. Sacco and Miss Luigia Vanzetti arrived to entreat clemency. I interpreted for Miss Vanzetti. These two sisters in sorrow begged the governor for a word of pity, of mercy. They both wept, I wept, the pictures on the wall probably wept, but there was no weeping in the governor's eyes. He said: "I have gone over all the evidence, and if it can be shown where I am wrong I will willingly change my views, but I feel I am right."

Mrs. Sacco broke in: "Governor Fuller, you say you have gone over all the evidence—but you never visited our home. Why not find out what kind of a life Nick lived? I am not a smart woman, I have no education, but I know that when a man loves a woman like Nick loves me he shares his good luck with her. You say that Nick was in a gang that stole fifteen thousand dollars and that Nick got his share of it. I didn't see any of the money. And if Nick had been in that robbery he would have brought his share home to me. He always gave me his pay to take to the bank. But Nick didn't bring any money home on April 15, 1920, or on any other day except the money he got in his pay envelope as a workingman. Governor! Governor! Won't you see how innocent Nick is?"

Here was an argument! In the acuteness of her grief Mrs. Sacco had risen to the heights of supreme logic. A man may deny everyone, but he will never deny the object of his love. With her he shares everything. But the governor overlooked this unassailable reasoning as he overlooked Sacco's impregnable alibi, as he overlooked Vanzetti's unshatterable exculpation, as he overlooked every piece of proof in the perfect mosaic of innocence of the two doomed men.

Miss Vanzetti prayed with her rosary-filled hands uplifted, while tears flowed to the carpet beneath her knees. The gubernatorial statue spoke: "I am very sorry. There is nothing, absolutely nothing I can do and remain true to the oath of my office."

As I translated the words to Miss Vanzetti, she sought to muffle, with her hands, a shriek which shook her small body like a gale torturing a young tree. Mrs. Sacco, quivering, lent an unsteady arm for support. I supported from the other side, and the three of us stumbled from the room. In the antechamber devoted friends were waiting: Mrs. Jessica Henderson, Aldino Felicani, Gardner Jackson, and his sister, Dr. Edith B. Jackson. In their care I left the two stricken women and returned to the governor's chamber to ask:

"Governor Fuller, when you said you could do nothing, I assume you meant in the absence of a recommendation from the attorney general?"

"Oh yes, if Mr. Reading recommends a respite, that will change the situation. You may wait outside until Mr. Reading reports."

As I waited I thought of all that had happened since I returned from Washington. It seemed that weeks had passed since then. And during that entire frenetic period it appeared that on occasion we could actually slacken the passage of time in order to get into a court, apply to another judge, make another application for reprieve. But now the clock above the governor's door was grimly resolute. The small hand pointed to eleven and the longer hand had started on its journey with a determination to complete, without any further tarrying, the cycle, and thus complete once and for all the seven-year-old Sacco-Vanzetti case. One hour remained until midnight when Executioner Elliott would throw the switch with which he had now been experimenting for many a day. Unless the governor or someone in a black robe scribbled his signature beneath the word "Stay," we had reached Journey's End.

At this moment the governor called me into his office. I did not need to put any question to him because my whole body queried: "Your Excellency, may I hope?"

"Mr. Musmanno, the attorney general has just sent me a letter in which he says that he does not recommend a stay of execution."

"And what do you say, Governor Fuller?"

"That is my decision."

"And on that decision will you stand for all time?"

"For all time."

As I left the governor's office, Joseph Moro, secretary of the Sacco-Vanzetti committee, handed me a letter received at headquarters. Through misty eyes I read, as I faltered over hard floors and down hard steps which yielded no more than had officialdom in seven years' pounding at the doors of justice, the shattering lines penned by the men I now started out to see—I feared, for the last time.

> We have no hope. This morning our brave defender and friend, Michael Angelo Musmanno, was here and told us he would come back this afternoon if he would have time for it. Also Rosa and Luigia were here this morning, and they too promised us to return this afternoon. But now it is 5:30 and no one returned yet. This tells us that there is no good news for us, for, if so, some

of you would have hurried to bring them to us. It almost tells us that all your efforts have failed and that you are spending these remaining few hours in desperate and hopeless efforts to eviate our execution. In a word, we feel lost!! Therefore, we decided to write this letter to you to express our gratitude and admiration for all what you have done in our defense during these seven years, four months and eleven days of struggle.

That we lost and have to die does not diminish our appreciation and gratitude for your great solidarity with us and our families . . .

We embrace you all, and bid you all our extreme good-by with our hearts filled with love and affection. Now and ever, long life to you all, long life to liberty. Yours in life and death.

Bartolomeo Vanzetti
Nicola Sacco

Arriving at the prison at eleven twenty-five I went directly to the office of Warden William A. Hendry, who was then leaving for the death house. I impeded his passage. "Warden, you don't have to do this tonight. The law allows you a week in which to carry out a death sentence. Postpone the execution tonight. I am sure there will be a judicial reprieve tomorrow. Our case is in the Supreme Court of the United States. Don't do what cannot be undone when you are not required to do anything at all."

"Mr. Musmanno, I'm sorry I cannot grant your request. Furthermore, the men are prepared to die."

"Good God!" I exclaimed, " 'Prepared to die'? Do you suppose they'll be disappointed if you tell them now they're not going to die?"

"But they'll only have to die later in the week."

"How do you know that? The case is still in the courts. How can you go about killing two men when the courts may say tomorrow they should not die?"

"All I know is that I have the death warrant and it orders me to put these men to death the week of August 22. That week has begun and I'm going ahead with my duty."

"But your duty, Warden, does not compel you to be a monster. How can you talk of destroying two human beings as if you were killing two chickens or dogs? And even if they were only dogs or chickens and they had an appeal pending in the courts, you couldn't legally kill them until you found out what the Court decided."

"Oh no. They're not going to pass the buck to me." He stepped around me and started down the corridor. I hurried along by his side. Presently he arrived at a door before which he stopped and said I could go no farther. I looked him in the eye and asked: "Warden, what did you mean by saying that they weren't going to pass the buck to you?"

He started, embarrassed, and then slowly spoke: "Suppose something happens tomorrow and the case starts all over again. They'll blame me for not having ended the case."

"Warden Hendry!" My voice went hoarse as I realized the sinister implications of what he was saying. "This is not a race against legality. If something happens tomorrow to reopen the case, you should be happy that you have saved the subject matter of the case. You cannot kill blindly."

"Mr. Musmanno"—his voice became stern—"you know I've been very accommodating to you, letting you see the prisoners three and four times a week and not limiting the time of your visits."

"Yes, that's true, and I thank you for what you have done, and I want to say further that at heart you are a kindly man."

"Well, don't say that I'm killing blindly. I'm not killing at all, I'm only obeying orders."

"But your orders do not command execution tonight."

"Mr. Musmanno, this thing's bigger than you or me. All I know is that I got a job to do—and I'm going to do it."

"But suppose the governor orders you to postpone the execution———"

"Oh, if the governor tells me to hold up the works, naturally I'll do what he says. He's my boss."

It was now eleven thirty-five. I ran to a telephone and put in a call for the governor. The operator fumbled. I pleaded: "Operator, this is a matter of life and death. I know the governor is in his office. Please ring him."

"I am ringing his office, but I get no reply."

"Try his secretary! But please hurry—please."

Several moments of anguished silence and then the operator:

"He wants to know what you wish to speak about."

"Let me speak to him."

"He says he is busy and that you are to give the message to me."

"Tell him that the warden has said that he will postpone the execution if the governor telephones him to do so. The warrant can be executed any time this week so that no official reprieve is necessary. I am certain that within the week we will find one or more of the five justices we have not yet contacted. Please also add that until we exhaust every effort to contact the remaining justices it would be a disparagement of United States authority to execute the men, since their appeal is pending in the Supreme Court, and especially since the death warrant can be executed any day this week." I could tell from noises at the other end of the wire that the secretary and probably the governor also were listening to what I was telling the operator, who now said: "All right, I'll give him the message."

"Shall I wait here?" But she had hung up.

It was eleven forty-five, with the first killing only fifteen minutes away. Frenziedly I rang the State House again. Again I asked for the governor, again I asked for the governor's secretary, again I was told to wait. Again I was requested to give the message to the operator, and again I repeated the message to the operator.

I waited.

Reporters were swarming about. One of them murmured: "They're doing the job now."

I looked at my watch. It was twelve-five.

Yes, they were doing the job, and that's what it was. A job.

I am on the train returning home. We move down the rails through Boston's South Station and head out into the night, a night as dark as my lugubrious soul. I should dismiss the case from my mind, but I hold in my hand the New York *World*, whose editor seems to be speaking for me:

> It is with a sick feeling indeed that one realizes that Sacco and Vanzetti have at last been executed. One's passionate desire is to have faith in the American scheme of things, to be convinced that by the irrevocable step we took . . . we are the authors of a just punishment and not a ghastly fiasco. In a groping toward that faith one finds all arguments one can: one reviews the evidence, and tries to see it as conclusive; one reflects that justice should not be subservient to popular clamor; one tries to believe that after all this investigation we must somehow have got the right men. Yet,

try as one will, one cannot escape a haunting doubt that here we may have witnessed a great miscarriage of justice.

At my side is a package. I break the string and two books tumble out: *The Rise of American Civilization.* They were found in Vanzetti's empty cell, and the warden sent them to me by messenger. On the morning of August 11 I had said that I would accept the then proffered books when the men were free. Were they now free?

I now read again the inscription I had seen in the death house. "To my friend and defender, Michael Angelo Musmanno. —Bartolomeo Vanzetti." And as the train rolls over the rail joints I seem to hear his voice:

"If it had not been for this thing, I might have lived out my life talking at the street corners to scorning men. I might have died unmarked, unknown, a failure. Now we are not a failure. This is our career and our triumph. Never in our full life could we hope to do such work for tolerance, for justice, for man's understanding of man as now we do by accident. Our words—our pains— nothing! The taking of our lives—lives of a good shoe-maker and a poor fish peddler—all! That last moment belongs to us—that agony is our triumph."

I lay aside the books and look out the window of the rhythmically swaying car. The darkness has lessened. The moon, like a freshly crowned queen, is rising in the sky to take her place on a cloud-banked throne to reign as mistress of the night. Eager stars prepare a luminous path of glory before her. Heat lightning supplies a coruscating luster to her royal brow. The trees in the woods through which we are passing have become pillars of silver, the leaves Roman coins.

With a roar the train emerges from the wooded temple and races into open lands bordering the ocean. These waters, which glisten like burnished copper in an ebony frame, form part of the sea for which Vanzetti had cried one day behind the bars which held his spirit in a vise: "Oh, that sea, that sky, those free and full-of-life winds of Cape Cod! Maybe I will never see, never breathe, never be at one with them again!"

I withdraw from my pocket a clipping from the St. Louis *Post-Dispatch.* This I should read in the presence of that sea which, through the ages, has known Socrates, John Huss, Joan of Arc,

Savonarola, Giordano Bruno, and John Brown, conjured forth by the gifted writer whose piece I hold in my hand. The voices of the bronze-crested waves blend with the hymn of the singing train wheels, and as we advance through the night into the dawn of what I hope may be a better day for tolerance, for justice, and for man's understanding of man, I ponder the words:

> Like many of these others, Sacco and Vanzetti were of the lowly of this earth. We do not know if they were guilty or not. They did not die like it. Neither does Massachusetts know. If she had, she would not have waited seven years to kill them.
>
> We do, however, know that they long ago entered that great domain of human psychology in which time at last evaluates all things truly, making the calendar of intolerance and injustice complete from 399 B.C. to 1927 A.D.

Chapter XXXVII

OUT DAMNED SPOT!

I RETURNED to Pittsburgh a failure. The failure was not only a personal vanquishment—the whole human race had suffered a setback and a disastrous defeat had been administered to the forces of humanity which had been marching since the martyrdom of the early Christians. I had discovered with painful disenchantment that time-consecrated proverbs representing eternal truths could still be stained, mangled, and discarded. I found that it was not always true that truth crushed to earth would rise again; I learned that right does not always triumph though the heavens fall; I ascertained that in the law there could be a wrong without a remedy. Nor did it appear that all those entrusted with administering American freedoms were worthy of that trust. In the very cradle of America I had seen individual human liberty and life itself suffocated under the blankets of personal greed, political ambition, and unqualifiable infamy.

And now what was to happen? If our system of jurisprudence developing through centuries of progress could fail where the unreignitible spark of human life was involved, what assurance could we have of its reliability in the field of general legal controversy? The only solace I could derive from this lugubrious thought was the reflection that since all of America now knew of the perfidy that could be perpetrated by the Thayers, the Katzmanns, and the Fullers of society it would be a simple matter to isolate them from the world of respectability and responsibility. A measure of comfort also stole into my being in the realization that the world, grieving over the unspeakable injustice done to two unoffending men, would, to that extent, be prepared to forestall any future attempt to immolate innocence on the block of unconscionable uncontrolled power. However, in all this my eyes were to open on a bleak landscape of disillusionment. Not only within the borders of Massachusetts, but in other states as well, there were many who applauded the Thayers, Katzmanns, and

Fullers and looked with little favor on those who had attempted to prevent the execution of Sacco and Vanzetti, even through constitutional procedure. When not long after my return from Massachusetts I announced my intention to be a candidate again for the Pennsylvania legislature, there were some to say I had defied law and order by appealing to the Supreme Court of the United States in behalf of two murderers.

One evening after the legislative campaign began, finding myself in the vicinity of an opposition meeting in Knoxville, I decided to attend it for the purpose of ascertaining at first hand what program my opponent was advancing for election to the post we both sought. The rally took place in the auditorium of the high school, which had a large outside lobby where I could stand and hear the speeches without being part of the meeting. An able and rather forceful speaker whom I had never seen before was in the process of eulogizing my opponent to the skies, which, of course, was to be expected. Suddenly, however, he departed from eulogy and proceeded to bring me into the gymnasium of his oratorical broad jump. "Do you know," he rhetorically asked the audience, "that this Mr. Musmanno, our opponent, had the audacity to challenge the correctness of the decisions of the highest court of Massachusetts and even attempted to cast discredit upon that sovereign body by appealing to the Supreme Court of the United States? I'm glad the Supreme Court ignored his slurs on the legality of Massachusetts procedure—and yet that man has the temerity to run for office here in Pennsylvania. I say that his actions were censurable. I don't know him and I don't care to know him. I wouldn't know him if he stepped into this hall right now."

I decided to step into the hall right now. I took up a position where the speaker could not help but see me. I folded my arms and looked him squarely in the eyes. He continued to speak, but my concentrated gaze disconcerted him more than he cared to admit—even to himself. In a few minutes he brought his remarks to an abrupt end and rather confusedly sat down. I lifted my voice.

"Mr. Chairman, may I have the floor?"

The chairman did not share the speaker's ignorance of my identity. He knew me only too well. He was my opponent in the legislative fight. "Mr. Musmanno," he said with no attempt to hide his annoyance, "you have no right at this meeting. This is my meeting."

Murmurs of excitement rippled through the hall as I continued: "I don't intend to usurp any privilege, but I heard one of your speakers say that there was something censurable about my defense of two men

I deemed innocent. I believe I have the right to answer that charge. May I ask the name of the man who just spoke? Perhaps he will give it himself."

The man rose. "My name is Robert McClintock, and I don't think you should be here attacking me."

"Attacking you? That is a unique flip of the flapjack. I am replying to your untruthful utterances. You were the one who brought up the Sacco-Vanzetti case, and I would like an opportunity to speak a few words which would introduce some light of reality into the darkness of ignorance in which you speak." I turned to the audience. "Would you like to hear me say a few words on the Sacco-Vanzetti case? I assure you I will not speak about my candidacy."

Of the five hundred people in the hall, at least one half applauded my question. The others remained silent. My adversary in the chair angrily banged the table and above the now-increasing din of applause interspersed with cries of "Yes!" and cries of "No!" he shouted: "Do I hear a motion to adjourn?"

Someone accommodated him with the requested motion and without waiting for a second, he proclaimed: "It has been moved and seconded that we adjourn. The motion is carried, and the meeting is adjourned."

Fifty or more persons came over to me to shake my hand. But while this reassuring gesture was being made, I could hear others yelling: "Throw him out!"

It did not take long for the news to spread through Knoxville that one of the legislative candidates had been maligned at the high school and that when he sought the opportunity to defend himself he was denied the floor. A half dozen war veterans who had been present throughout the meeting and had noted the American Legion button I was wearing made arrangements to obtain the same hall for the following night, and they prepared a large sign which read: "Come listen to Attorney Musmanno discuss the Sacco-Vanzetti case."

When I walked on the stage of the same hall which had absorbed the tumult of the night before, some three hundred people greeted me. I spoke for two hours on the Massachusetts tragedy. I answered many questions put to me from the floor, and at the end of the meeting I was given a standing ovation. But that kind of rapt interest did not last long. Sacco and Vanzetti were dead. The world moved on. It had no time for ghosts—innocent or guilty. I was obliged to wrap up my heartache, store away my grief, and turn to the toils and cares of the day. In addition to campaigning for the legislature, I had to repair and build up a broken-down law practice. My five months' absence had scattered my clientele and depleted my exchequer. Such prosaic items as rent, food, and clothing demanded attention.

The coal miners of Allegheny County had always been very friendly to me and they had apparently followed my defense in the Sacco-Vanzetti case quite sympathetically. Upon my return to Pittsburgh several locals of the United Mine Workers passed resolutions commending my efforts and urged me to take up again the fight I had waged for several years against their mortal nemesis, the Coal and Iron Police. "In many ways," one of the resolutions read, "the brutal deeds of Coal and Iron Police are in the same classification of injustice as that perpetrated on the workmen, Sacco and Vanzetti."

I scarcely needed any urging. It was simply absurd that, in a democracy, sovereign police power should be in the hands of any private organization. For years now the Coal and Iron Police had become increasingly arrogant and brutal, but their depredations always escaped governmental condemnation because they were, by law, part of the government. On June 1, 1927, Patrick T. Fagan, president of United Mine Workers District No. 5, was standing on a sidewalk in Pittsburgh talking to imported miners, asking them not to take the place of his men who were on strike, when he was arrested by Coal and Iron policemen and charged with disorderly conduct. A magistrate found him guilty, but his conviction was reversed by the County Court. Mr. Fagan then sued the Pittsburgh Terminal Coal Company, employers of the arresting Coal and Iron policemen, in an action of trespass for false arrest and recovered a verdict of three thousand dollars. The coal company appealed to the Supreme Court of Pennsylvania, which reversed the verdict on the ground that the police were officers of the state and the company therefore was not legally responsible for their actions.

The laws which permitted this shameful state of affairs had been passed in 1865 and 1866. The benefiting corporations wielded enormous financial-political power in the state, and this power, by 1910, had become so solidified and consolidated that no legislator dared to oppose the Coal and Iron Police system, even though it had by now become a monster of Frankenstein proportions.

I won the 1928 election by a narrow margin, and as soon as I took the oath of office as a member of the House of Representatives I drafted the legislation I had been contemplating for a long time. As if to show their utter scorn for any attempted curb on their iron-fisted domination in the coal fields, two Coal and Iron policemen seized a defenseless coal miner and beat him to death. The story of that horrible killing will never be forgotten by the coal miners of Pennsylvania or lovers of justice anywhere in the world who saw the motion picture *Black Fury*, based on the novel which I wrote on the subject.

On the evening of February 8, 1929, Coal and Iron Policeman Harold P. Watts, in heavy boots, with an ammunition belt strapped around his waist from which dangled an enormous revolver, made his erratic way over the snow-covered roads of the coal territory he patrolled. In order to brighten his night vigil he had partaken of intoxicants, which in that prohibition era were prohibited but not forbidden. With his unsteady gait he tripped over a frozen rut in the road and fell against a plank from which a nail protruded, cutting through his leather jacket and slightly lacerating his shoulder. He regained his feet just as a coal miner, still wearing on his cap the carbide lamp which had lighted his subterranean toil of the day, came plodding by.

Suddenly the miner, later ascertained to be John Barcoski, felt himself seized from the rear while a heavy blow descended on his head. Shouting in alarm, he fled, pursued by the wrathful coal officer. Reaching his home, he tried to lock the door behind him, but Watts, who was on his heels, whipped out his revolver and with the butt end struck the miner, who had retreated to a corner of the bleakly furnished living room and there cowered, with his hands above his head. Several times the heavy weapon descended, and when Barcoski fell to the floor, Watts seized him by the collar as one would take up a dead dog, dragged him to his car, and drove to the Coal and Iron Police barracks several miles away. Arriving there, he threw the miner to the floor and announced to the officer in charge, Lieutenant Walter J. Lyster: "Here's a hunky — — — who stabbed me." And then, to the miner: "Why did you stab me?"

Bewildered and bleeding, the wounded man replied: "I no—no stab nobody. I never see you before. What you talk about?"

Another Coal and Iron policeman, chewing tobacco at a typewriter, thrust a sheet of paper into the machine and, to Watts's dictation, typed out a "confession" which he flung at Barcoski, who had been lifted to a chair. "Sign this if you know what's good for you."

"But I no know what you want. What happen?"

Watts stepped in. "Oh, you want more, do you? Well, I'll give it to you." Whipping a blackjack from his belt, he struck at the captive's head, when Lyster interrupted: "Look here, Watts, I'll take care of this—I'm your superior officer and I feel like having a workout tonight and I don't intend to let you deprive me of the pleasure."

Stripping off his shirt, he grasped the iron poker with which he had just finished agitating the burning logs in the open fireplace. He studied it as a dragoon might regard a saber and then brought it down heavily on the head of the helpless prisoner, who groaned: "Please, please, mister, I no hurt nobody."

"You won't hurt nobody when I get through with you, you hunky —— ——."

Up and down the poker rose and fell on bone, muscle, and cartilage. The poker finally bent and Lyster cursed: "What hard heads these miner b—— have." He straightened out the metal and with the next blow sent his victim crashing to the floor.

As Lyster lunged forward to pounce on the prostrate figure, Watts threw out his arm to hold him back. "Stop! I've got something to say about this. I'm the one he stabbed, you know." Pushing the lieutenant out of his way, Watts moved back to the wall of the room and ran forward, landing with both feet on Barcoski's chest. The sternum snapped like an axletree. He continued leaping as rib after rib broke beneath his feet like kindling wood.

Lyster returned to the picture. "Let's see if he will sign now." The mangled form could only reply with a moan.

"Oh, you won't?" Lyster tore a leather thong loose from a nail on the wall and laid it over the prisoner's back with whistling fury. Watts, however, still regarding Barcoski as his own personal quarry, now re-entered the arena with a pair of brass knuckles. Lifting the groaning quarry to his feet with his left hand, he smashed away with his knuckled right hand. Just as he was landing another brass blow on the nose of the falling sufferer, the doctor who had been called by Watts for his own injury arrived.

Aghast at what appeared before him, the doctor bent over the bleeding figure on the floor, but Watts broke in: "Doctor, you've come here to take care of me, not him," and he bared the scratch on his shoulder. Quickly and mechanically the doctor applied a bit of adhesive to Watts's cut and then turned to the battered hulk gasping before him. "Who is he?" he asked.

"Oh, it's just a damned coal miner," Watts replied.

Taking a pair of scissors from his bag, the doctor cut away the miner's hair in order to bathe and cleanse the deep gashes in his scalp. He treated all the wounds and then bound the whole broken body in bandages. Catching sight of the bloody poker, knuckles, and leather thong, he warned: "Don't you dare strike this man again. Another blow will be fatal—and get him to the hospital at once."

As soon as the doctor closed the door behind him, Watts lifted their bandage-enveloped guest to a stool and thrust the confession before him. "Will you sign this now?" When no reply was forthcoming, he seized one end of the bandage and jerked it forward like a string wrapped around a top. The tormented man spun on the stool and then reeled to the floor with a crash. Bleeding from a hundred gashes and wounds, Barcoski lay senseless at the feet of his tormentors, who, demanding a signature, continued the fusillade of blows with whip, poker, knuckles, and thong.

Corporal Mechling, who sat at the typewriter, mildly bored throughout the gory spectacle, finally suggested that their battered sojourner be taken to a hospital. However, when Barcoski arrived at the hospital and the interns in the emergency room looked at the ruins of flesh and bone before them, they knew that here was a task not for them but for the coroner.

No untoward event stirs people into righteous indignation more quickly than acts of violent inhumanity. The cries of John Barcoski, as they rose above the strident reverberations of the brandished poker, revolver, knuckles, and lash, echoed in the uplifted voices of an outraged citizenry. From one end of the state to the other, but particularly in western Pennsylvania, loud and angry condemnation was heard not only of the Barcoski killing but of the whole system which had made it possible. I introduced a bill to tear out that system by the roots through an outright repeal of the acts of 1865 and 1866 which had engrafted a medieval pattern of baronial armies onto the charter of a democratic commonwealth.

The coal and iron barons of Pennsylvania, however, who continued to enjoy the sovereign police power which made them invincible and untouchable in their industrial domains, did not intend to relinquish their nail-studded scepter of absolute authority. Moreover, they were in a formidable position to resist the demand for demobilization of their private military forces. For years they had been subsidizing the ruling political party in the state; they dominated party councils and effectively operated behind the scenes in electing their chosen candidates to high office. They had been particularly active in behalf of John S. Fisher and had lubricated the wheels of the band wagon on which he had ridden to the Executive Mansion.

Governor Fisher, while acknowledging to himself the debt of gratitude he owed to those who had borne him in a gilded chariot to the governor's mansion, was a lawyer of ability and knew quite well that the bartering of the police power of the state was constitutionally indefensible. When the story of the Barcoski killing burst upon the state like the tale of a hideous Spanish inquisition, he made a statement: "Its viciousness consists of the surrender by the state into private hands of police powers. These powers ought to be jealously guarded by the state and exercised only under its jurisdiction. There ought to be a thorough revision by the legislature of the present methods." In 1929 the Pennsylvania legislature was practically the handmaiden of the governor. Most of the legislators had been elected by the same political organization which had elevated Fisher, and thus they were disposed to regard the governor as the leader of the legislative as well as the executive department of the state.

While determined to work for the repeal of the Coal and Iron Police laws, I realized that industries which were geographically distant from metropolitan police stations were entitled to protection of their physical properties. I accordingly drafted a companion bill which authorized these distant industries to hire "corporation guards" with no state jurisdiction. They would thus in effect be watchmen, unarmed and confined to the property of their employers. I was hoping, in view of what the governor had publicly stated about the evil to be combated, to have his approval of my bills. I was in for a great surprise.

A short time after I introduced my bills I was honored by an invitation from Attorney General Cyrus E. Woods to visit him at his office. He received me graciously at the door, showed me to a large comfortable armchair, and handed me a cigar. "Mr. Musmanno," he said, "the governor and I were talking about your excellent efforts with regard to the Coal and Iron Police business. We congratulate you on your energy and singleness of purpose."

I, of course, was completely aware that a compliment of this size handed by an entrenched administration cabinet member to a first-term member of the legislature was extraordinary and had to cover some latent intent. What was it? I did not have long to guess. "Mr. Musmanno," the attorney general continued, "I am wondering if you are not going too far with your proposed legislation."

"Do I understand that the governor does not like my bills?"

"I can't speak for the governor, but I know from my own experience here in Harrisburg that neither of your bills has any chance of passing the legislature. They are too drastic."

"Why not wait to see what the legislature will do?" I asked as I smelled the cigar.

"That's the point I'm coming to. Why should you subject yourself to a great endeavor, incurring difficulties and even bruises in a legislative battle which is bound to turn out unsuccessfully for you—when it is all so unnecessary?"

"What do you propose, Mr. Attorney General?"

"I propose that you do nothing on your bills, but wait until the Administration prepares a measure which we think will meet the situation to your entire satisfaction."

The next day the attorney general called me again, handed me another cigar, and said that the governor and he had decided to let me present the Administration bill on Coal and Iron Police reform. In view of the fact that most administrative measures had clear sailing through the legislature, sponsorship of an administrative bill was usually a much-sought-after privilege since it meant having one's name attached to a piece of legislation going into the statute books. However, I was not satisfied that I wanted my name associated with a bill whose provisions were still written with invisible ink, and I so indicated to the attorney general.

"Mr. Musmanno," he said, "I know that you are wrought up over the Barcoski killing, but we don't legislate because of one episode. We must always keep in mind the general over-all picture." He then went on to say that he admired my work in the legislature and predicted that if I was not too impetuous I would go far in public life. "There is no reason why you should not, after several terms in the House, be promoted to the Senate, and then," admiringly appraising the rich appointments of his own office, he added: "Someday you may be attorney general." He now paused, as if in doubt whether to throw in the governorship too in the offer he was obviously making to me if only I would not be too impetuous—and would allow my repeal bills to die a natural death.

"And if I don't take up the administrative measure, what will happen?" I asked.

"Oh, nothing will happen. We will simply give the bill to some other representative, and you will only make it more difficult for yourself to be re-elected because the organization is very strong in your district, as, of course, you know."

Which would be stronger in the legislature: public opinion or the organization under the direction and control of the Republican State Committee? The domineering strength of the organization was as obvious as the statue in Capitol Park of "Boss" Boies Penrose which confronted every legislator on his way to his legislative duties. Every committee chairman in both the House and Senate was appointed by the organization; every political officeholder owed his allegiance to the organization; every favor of any consequence granted in the state government was dictated and approved by the organization. On the other hand, the governor could not ignore the awesome force of public opinion. That was the only reason his attorney general was handing me cigars. I was not being deceived on that score. In view of the fact that the Barcoski killing had occurred in my legislative district and I had conducted a personal investigation into the facts of the crime, I had in a measure become a spokesman for the affected area. The governor and the attorney general believed (not without cause) that I was capable of embarrassing them in the event the Administration flouted the demands of western Pennsylvania for Coal and Iron Police correction.

On March 12, 1929, the attorney general handed me a sheaf of papers within an orange-colored cover. "Here, Representative Musmanno, is the Administration bill. I am sure that with your energetic piloting it will pass the legislature and, when signed by the governor, it will be a credit to your name." I took the bill and repaired to my desk in the House chamber to study it. My heart sank into my shoes. I found blighted hope on every page. Apparently Governor Fisher had turned to the wall the mirror of his conscience. After his public condemnation of the Coal and Iron Police evil, how could he countenance a perpetuation of it? All that he had done in this proposed law was to give to the vicious Coal and Iron Police a new name—industrial police. Under the provisions of the governor's bill the state would still invest private police with sovereign police power; it would still immunize corporate employers from liability for depredations committed by their police officers; it would still authorize the governor to issue public commissions to private corporations. As if to atone for its shameful delegation of sovereign authority, the bill limited the arresting jurisdiction of industrial police to one thousand feet beyond the boundaries of the employer's property, but by this very limitation it re-emphasized the sovereign character of the policeman's commission because it placed the imprimatur of the state on his jurisdiction over land admittedly not owned by his employer.

With troubled heart I left the capitol and made my way to the Susquehanna River to think over the exasperating situation now confronting me. Walking up and down its banks, I wrestled with the horny dilemma. In view of what the attorney general had said, it was evident that my own bills had no chance of enactment into law. In fact, they were bottled up in committees whose chairmen even refused to acknowledge their existence. It was also evident that if I angrily returned the Administration bill to the attorney general and refused to have a hand in his legislative plan I would lose considerable voice in the shaping of proper legislation. Then, on the other hand, it was clear that if I accepted and sponsored the governor's bill an avalanche of "liberal" censure would engulf me for advocating so evil-hued a measure after I had so unreservedly castigated the doctrine of the bartering of state powers. As I winced under the prickly thorns of the problem I picked up a pebble, drew back my arm, and sent it skimming over the shimmering surface of the river. As it traveled it seemed to leave on the face of the stream a writing which answered many queries I had addressed to myself. I could introduce the Administration bill, and then in the committee to which it would be referred I could amend it so that it would measure up to the requirements of decency and justice. Of course I could not take anyone into my confidence on such a plan. Rapidly I returned to the capitol, entered the House of Representatives, and dropped the orange-covered sheaf of papers into the legislative hopper.

The storm I had apprehended broke quickly and mercilessly over my head, drenching me in criticism from one end of the state to the other. Two hundred University of Pittsburgh students signed a "round robin" of censure. The American Civil Liberties Union wrathfully demanded an explanation with a resolution which was printed in nearly all the newspapers:

> An explanation is due from Representative Michael A. Musmanno for his change of front. When John Barcoski was murdered, Musmanno expressed abhorrence and introduced a bill calling for the abolition of the coal and iron police. Now he suddenly appears as a champion of an insipid measure, which, according to reports, continues the coal and iron police in full force and power.

I made no reply. I could not afford to defend myself at the expense of disclosing my plan. I sent copies of the Administration bill to the Pennsylvania Federation of Labor, United Mine Workers, civic organizations, educators, and other public-spirited citizens who had shown a profound concern over the subject matter, asking them to write me their views on the proposed legislation, knowing full well that they would be as disappointed with the bill as I was. When I received their replies, which of course in the main coincided with my own estimate of the bill, I publicly stated that I would ask the Judiciary General Committee, to which the bill had been referred, to hold public hearings where opponents and proponents of the measure could be heard. As much as the governor and attorney general hated me for this idea, they could not openly protest against a procedure which would allow all interested parties to be heard. After all, the process of lawmaking is supposed to be one based on the will of the people.

I then called on the attorney general and pointed out that it was absolutely necessary to eliminate the thousand-foot extraterritorial jurisdiction. He said; "As a matter of fact, Musmanno, all the corporations are for its removal too."

When I registered agreeable surprise he explained: "What they mean is that there should be *no limitations whatsoever* on their jurisdiction, since they are state officers."

I threw up my hands in horror. "Oh, that would never do at all."

I hurried to the governor and asked him to notify the House committee that he favored limiting the industrial police to the property of the employers. He replied: "I will sign the bill whether it has the thousand-foot provision or not." Since removing the thousand-foot provision could mean giving the industrial police unlimited jurisdiction or restricting them to the property, it was clear to me that Fisher was here giving an impersonation of the oracle of Delphi. Dignified in demeanor, suave in conversation, and adroit with the use of words, Governor Fisher was pursuing a politician's course in the worst meaning of the term. He could not afford to say anything that would alienate his financial and political supporters, since he had ambitions for advancement to the United States Senate, but, on the other hand, he feared to have the newspapers quote him as being insensate to the public demand for Coal and Iron Police abolition. He had large wide shoulders, and on each he carried a bucket of water.

One evening as I was entering the capitol I encountered him emerging from the building in the company of two men who in themselves perhaps represented more wealth than any other small group of men in the state: W. L. Mellon, the banking king of Pittsburgh and former chairman of the Republican State Committee, and Joseph R. Grundy, head of the Pennsylvania Manufacturers Association and member of the executive committee of the Republican State Committee. I tipped my hat to the governor and bade him a good evening. Quickly he excused himself from his companions, who were well-known champions of the Coal and Iron Police system, approached me, and in a low voice told me to keep up my good work in "ridding the state of the Coal and Iron Police evil." In doing this he did not spill a drop of water from the pails which he fluently, dignifiedly, and suavely bore on either clavicle.

Our public hearing before the House Judiciary General Committee bloomed with success. Speaker after speaker denounced the administrative measure in its present form and called for amendments. The newspapers played up the denunciations. I now got ready to perform one of the most delicate but formidable dental operations ever attempted on Capitol Hill. I prepared amendments which would insert a full set of teeth into the almost toothless Administration bill. My amendments provided that: (1) industrial police be limited to the property of their employer; (2) they be United States citizens (the Administration bill even omitted this obvious requirement); (3) persons arrested by industrial police were to be immediately brought before a magistrate and, if committed, sent to county jail (the Coal and Iron Police took their victims to their own barracks); (4) corporations had to put up a bond of two thousand dollars for each industrial policeman, the corporation itself to be one of the insurers; (5) no industrial policeman was to hold a public position.

With these amendments I appeared at the governor's office, where I was as welcome as a boy with measles entering a girls' school. Mr. Gorman, the governor's secretary, seeing the typewritten sheets under my arm, quickly announced that the governor was very busy and could not see me. I explained that I wished to have the governor's opinion on the amendments. He said the governor would not have time to read them. I said I would leave a set for him to study at his leisure. Gorman, who of course was aware of the governor's penchant for hauling water simultaneously to two different flour mills, said: "You better leave the governor out of this."

At the next meeting of the House committee I presented the amendments and moved their adoption. While the members were impressed with the need for the amendments, they still had no desire to oppose the chief executive, who was, for most of them, the leader of their party. However, since the governor had made several public declarations in favor of a strong anti-Coal and Iron Police bill, they felt they would be justified in approving the amendments. The most effective argument in behalf of the amendments was the fact that the industrial police bill was an Administration measure and I had been chosen to present it. One of the members said to me *sotto voce:* "Musmanno, I know that the Administration looks upon these amendments as poison, but they haven't said anything to me, so I can always say in my defense that I assumed the Administration approved the amendments. Count on me." The amendments were adopted by the committee and on April 2, 1929, the amended bill, now known as the Musmanno Bill, passed the House by a vote of 184 to 0. It was then referred to the Senate, where the Judiciary General Committee of that house took it under advisement.

The advisement was short and bloody. What the coal operators and industrialists had been unable to accomplish on the House side they achieved easily in the Senate with one dagger thrust. Senator Augustus F. Daix, chairman of the committee, announced that the bill had been rejected by the committee, that only one vote had been cast for it, and that he did not intend to have the committee consider it again. Of course, while Daix held the dagger it was obvious that it was the Administration which had supplied the force behind the thrust, even though that force was cloaked.

Cyclonic indignation swept the state from Lake Erie to the Delaware River. Dr. Albert E. Day, pastor of the Christ Methodist Episcopal Church in Pittsburgh, exclaimed:

> "We are left with the conjecture that money counts far more than human welfare in the eyes of the legislators and that the secret influence of powerful corporation is stronger than the voice of an outraged civic conscience."

Philip Murray, international vice-president of the United Mine Workers of America, declared that the action of the Senate committee was "a deliberate affront to the taxpayers." The Pittsburgh *Post-Gazette* in a first-page editorial written by the publisher, Paul Block, demanded to know:

> How long will the public stand for this dictation by certain bosses to the representatives who are supposed to serve the people?

The Pittsburgh *Press* editorialized:

> Pennsylvania will stand ashamed before the other states of the Union if it writes a record of continuing

to tolerate a police system which has brought disgrace upon the commonwealth.

The Pittsburgh *Sun-Telegraph* in a large-type editorial declared:

> THE STATE POLITICAL MACHINE HAS DE-
> CIDED TO KEEP THE VICIOUS COSSACK
> SYSTEM IN FORCE, TO PLEASE A FEW SHORT-
> SIGHTED COAL COMPANIES. THE SHAME OF
> PENNSYLVANIA IS TO BE CONTINUED UN-
> LESS THERE IS AN UPRISING OF THE PEOPLE
> THAT FRIGHTENS THE BOSSES.

Two thousand citizens met in a mass meeting at the Carnegie Hall in Pittsburgh to condemn the high-handed procedure of the Senate committee.

In Harrisburg I asked the senators on the committee why they had killed my bill. Many of them explained they were not present when the rejection occurred and that it was all Senator Daix's doing. Mark Shields, Harrisburg correspondent for the Pittsburgh *Press*, wrote that Senator Daix was "about to be rewarded for his organization stead-fastness by being named as president pro tem of the Senate."

Powerful as were the coal and iron interests which, through the governor, had guided Daix's hand, they still could not stop up their ears to the barrage of censure fired from church groups, civic organizations, labor unions, and other public-spirited bodies. Nor was there any bombproof cellar in which the governor could hide, despite his bleating assertions that he still favored reform in the private police system.

Suddenly, with the same lack of explanation which had attended the smothering of the Musmanno Bill in the Senate committee, it was now released from the committee. This was done quite unconventionally. There was no meeting of the committee, no polling of the senators. Government became a nice, private, sociable arrangement. Governor Fisher called Daix into his office and told him he could release the bill. Daix said it was not necessary to do this, because he would stand by the governor. "I live in Philadelphia," he wryly observed, "and I don't care what the western Pennsylvania newspapers say." Fisher, however, assured him that it was all right, adding: "I know what I'm doing." The governor imposed only one condition; namely, that the bill should not be reported out by Senator Mansfield. (There was a purpose in this.) Daix accordingly handed it to Senator

Leslie of Pittsburgh, and Leslie reported it to the Senate with the approval of the committee—which had never met.

When the news broke that the Musmanno Bill had been revived, the adherents of good government rejoiced, but, as the facts were later to be ascertained, the rejoicing rose from a false armistice. The governor was even praised for having brought about the emancipation of the Musmanno Bill, but it was a praise which was soon to turn to revulsion over a blatant hypocrisy. At the time the attorney general handed me the Administration bill to present to the House, he had given a twin measure to Senator Mansfield in the Senate. But while my bill was being strengthened on the House side, the Mansfield Bill was being emasculated in the Senate in several ways, including the elimination of the thousand-foot restriction, so that the industrial police could exercise sovereign police power *everywhere in the state!* The plan of the governor and his co-conspirators in the closing days of the session was to let both bills pass the legislature, whereupon he could veto the Musmanno Bill and sign the Mansfield Bill. And that is what he did.

Fisher paid dearly for the political support he had received and vainly expected to continue to receive from the spokesmen for the coal and iron barons who had induced him to shatter the mirror of his conscience. They disliked his having released the Musmanno Bill from the Senate committee when the pickling brine had already done its work. Even W. L. Mellon refused to come to his assistance, remarking: "Let him stew in his own juice. He brought on his troubles by his own fault." And thus Fisher's ambition to become United States senator turned to vinegar on his tongue. He was never again to hold public office of any kind when his gubernatorial term expired. Cyrus Hungerford, the gifted cartoonist of the Pittsburgh *Post-Gazette,* portrayed Fisher in the robes of Lady Macbeth, his hands dripping with blood. The cartoon depicted the Musmanno Bill lying prostrate on the ground, a dagger in its heart, while Lady Macbeth-Fisher, seeking to wipe away the dripping blood, kept wailing: "Out, damned spot." That picture stands out in my mind as one of the most powerful political cartoons in American history. It probably did more than any other philippic to relegate Governor Fisher to the private life for which he was more than ripe.

The legislature adjourned and I came back to Pittsburgh stumbling under a sack of disillusionment as heavy as that which had weighted me down at the termination of the Sacco-Vanzetti case. If representative government could fail so completely in its sacred and bounden duty to enact into law the will of the people, what hope could there be for the future? I doubt that ever in legislative chronicles had there been a situation where remedial surgery was more clearly required and where government purposely allowed the patient to die on the table.

Of course it was not representative government which was at fault. A handful of willful men had acted on the assumption that the people could be fooled and, if not fooled, would soon forget what had happened. Thus the willful ones took it for granted that despotism would go on and on because the people would feel too frustrated to resist continuing usurpation. They overlooked Lincoln's keen observation: "It is true that you may fool all the people some of the time; you can even fool some of the people all the time; but you can't fool all of the people all the time."

I nailed that trenchant piece of wisdom as a plank into my platform, and on it I announced that if re-elected I would vigorously renew the battle against the private police system which, in the words of the Pittsburgh *Press,* had "brought disgrace upon the commonwealth." This newspaper, in supporting my candidacy, said:

> Representative Michael A. Musmanno of the Twelfth Legislative District should be re-elected. He was the author of the industrial police bill which was vetoed by Governor Fisher because it was too strong. He was indefatigable in fighting that measure through the Assembly. His potentialities should not be lost. He injects into the Assembly the spirit of discussion and debate revealing issues to the public, an almost lost art in the Assembly which has come to do too much of its legislation in secret committee session.

The Pittsburgh *Sun-Telegraph* said editorially:

> Like a World Baseball Series, the 1929 session brought forth its outstanding character. Michael A. Musmanno, member of the House of Representatives, looms as a big figure in the affairs of the state and county as a result of his energetic service in behalf of the rights of the people. A new member, he rose to the top by trying to be useful from the beginning, instead of accepting the dictum that political little boys, as well as others, should sit back and do the listening.

So he made himself both seen and heard, not obnoxiously, except, perhaps to the bosses, but insistently. With the record he has made, Representative Musmanno should go far in a political career, does he choose to follow it.

My legislative district elected four representatives. I received the highest vote of the four victorious candidates. Of this vote, the Pittsburgh *Post-Gazette* said:

The explanation [of the high vote] is that in the 1929 session Mr. Musmanno represented ably and courageously the most important question, from the standpoint of justice and humanity, before that body. The great vote given Mr. Musmanno, author of the bill that sought to meet the public view, adds in an especial sense to the protest against the executive rejection of it and commissions the Allegheny Countian to take the lead against the abuse that has been demanding correction for years.

Chapter XXXVIII

BATTLING ON THE SUSQUEHANNA

UPON my re-election to the legislature, the newly elected governor, Gifford Pinchot, invited me to his home in Pike County to discuss plans for renewing the war against the Coal and Iron Police. As an ex-Bull Mooser, Pinchot enjoyed a merited excellent reputation for opposing industrial and monopolistic domination of government. He was a liberal in the best tradition, and I felt confident that with him at the head of the state government the shame of the Fisher defection would soon be wiped out. I was to find out, however, that the evil which had been accomplished in the previous administration by a cunning Macbeth was to be repeated in the new administration by a well-meaning but obstinate Othello.

It was Pinchot's idea that the solution of the Coal and Iron Police problem lay in hiring out state police to corporations on a compensation basis. He argued that if the police were under state control and jurisdiction they could not be used by corporations for terroristic or strike-breaking purposes. But with this line of reasoning he overlooked the prosaic realism that a wage earner feels duty-bound toward the person or corporation paying him, especially when the continuing wages depend on service satisfactorily rendered. Aside from this pragmatic observation, however, it was baffling to me why Pinchot, with all his experience in government, could not grasp how indefensible was the concept of the state going into the business of hiring out police—for money! The whole scheme smacked of Hessianism.

I entertained a high respect and personal regard for Pinchot. I could never forget how considerate he had been at his home, where we were now meeting, when I presented the argument in the Valotta case and how his willingness to study and reflect on realities had saved the life of a man who had been unjustly condemned to death. We recalled the Valotta affair on this occasion, and I again thanked him for saving the condemned man's life. He replied: "Mr. Musmanno,

I only did my duty, and you are to be congratulated on your perseverance, without which Valotta might not have been saved."

With this exchange of sincere compliments, I found it extremely painful to tell Mr. Pinchot that I did not like his plan, and I asked him if our friendship would suffer if I had to oppose it. He smiled under his picturesque handle-bar mustaches and said: "Of course not, Musmanno. Every person has the right to express his own views."

On January 6, 1931, when the legislature convened, I presented the first two bills of the session: House Bill No. 1 and House Bill No. 2. No. 1 was entitled the "Property Guard Bill," later to be referred to as the "Musmanno Bill." It specifically declared that the state could not and would not lend, rent, or hire its sovereign police power to anybody. All industries which needed special protection for their properties would be permitted to hire property guards who had to be approved by the Court of Quarter Sessions of the county in which the property was located, after they had qualified as to character, citizenship, and three years' residence in Pennsylvania. The employing corporation was required to put up a bond of two thousand dollars for each property guard, on which bond any person injured by the guards could sue in the name of the Commonwealth. The employing corporation was also expressly to be held liable for any tort committed by its guards, who were to have no power whatsoever off the property of the corporation. For offenses committed within their presence the guards could arrest without warrant, but in all other cases a warrant from a magistrate was required. House Bill No. 2 repealed the Mansfield Act.

Although my Property Guard Bill was a drastic measure, I had no qualms about its severe provisions. Between sessions of the legislature I had communicated with every state attorney general in the country and found that no state in the Union permitted the sale of police power as did Pennsylvania.

Despite the universal condemnation of the private police system, the coal and iron barons were as determined in 1931 as they had successfully been in 1929 to doom all efforts at reform. Their lobbyists moved into Harrisburg to overwhelm representatives and senators with attention and promises. Champagne flowed like water at parties in the Harrisburger and Penn-Harris hotels. The Coal and Iron policemen themselves got into the act, not only by sending me threatening letters but by demonstrating in a physical manner that they were capable of putting their threats into action if I would not be more "reasonable." One evening while I was driving through the coal fields near Imperial, two "koalandirons" (as the miners called them) fired several shots into the tires of my car, compelling me to walk three miles to obtain assistance.

A grotesquely ironical situation arose out of the fact that the forces opposed to my Property Guard Bill found an unexpected ally in Gifford Pinchot, who for years had been one of their most implacable political foes. For a reason which I could never fathom, Pinchot was determined to force upon the Commonwealth a piece of legislation which surpassed in its scope the excesses, brutalities, and horrors of the original Coal and Iron Police system. Through his attorney general he prepared a bill which provided for what he called "trade police." Under this measure the state itself stood at the counter and sold state police power for a consideration. Under its provisions neither the state nor the corporation would be responsible for damages and injuries perpetrated by the police, who were to have statewide jurisdiction. Nor was there any limit to the number of trade police who could be appointed. Thus a governor, if he had a mind to, could recruit a veritable army to be used for strike-breaking purposes or for any other purpose which might appeal to him. On behalf of the governor, this bill was introduced by Representative Thomas Wilson of McKean County and it accordingly became known as the Wilson Bill as well as the Pinchot Bill.

Now again, as in the 1929 session, I faced the power of a hostile administration equipped with patronage, committee chairmen appointments, and a whole armory of favors to bestow in pushing through a legislative program. Now again, as in the past, I had difficulty with the chairman of the committee to which my bills had been referred. He would not authorize a public hearing so that both opponents and proponents of the proposed legislation could be heard. Again I turned to the citizenry of Pennsylvania. I went before civic bodies in different parts of the state; I took to the radio, calling upon the people to write and telegraph their representatives to insist upon a public hearing. The chairman yielded; we got our hearing, at which representatives from labor organizations, church groups, and civic organizations spoke. The bill was released and reported to the House for action.

Legislative procedure in the House requires a bill to be read on three different days, the final vote taking place on the third reading. On the afternoon of Wednesday, March 18, 1931, before my two bills had had even their first reading, Representative Glenn Moore of Washington County, and Pinchot leader in the House, quietly rose and spoke words which sent icy chills chasing down my spine; namely, "Mr. Speaker, I move that House Bills Nos. 1 and 2 be referred to the Law and Order Committee for further consideration." He said this without any suggestion in his voice that he meant more than he said, but in the gentle afternoon light I could see the glint of the guillotine blade. Once the bills got to the Law and Order Committee, execution would follow. This committee was manned by Pinchot adherents, who frowned on all measures which opposed the governor's ideas, which mine certainly did. In that first shocking moment I could see the end of Coal and Iron Police reform, I could see a repetition of the Fisher-Daix treachery. My limbs went cold, but in an instant I could feel warm blood racing to my temples. I bounded into the aisle, knocking books off my desk in transit, and, making no effort to conceal my wrath, I shouted: "Mr. Speaker, last week when my bills were considered before the Judiciary General Committee, no opponents were present, and someone made the observation that there was something ominous in that fact. That ominous something has come into this House, that mysterious something is stalking through these legislative halls, and—as a result—we have this insidious motion to send my bills to the Law and Order Committee. Why to the Law and Order Committee? Are they to be sent there to be smothered? To be killed?"

I asked the House not to be deceived. The purpose of the motion was execution and burial. "Members of the House, if you vote to send these bills to the Law and Order Committee, you vote to kill them . . . I never spoke with more sincerity in all my life than I do on these measures which are based upon the fundamental rights of humanity. I beg of you and I plead with you and I supplicate you to vote 'No' upon this motion!"

Mr. Moore insisted he had in mind only "consideration of the bills," but Representative Turner of Delaware County intervened to say that what was before the House on the Musmanno measures was a question of "fairness." Representative Beyer of Philadelphia joined me with a vigorous speech in which he indignantly observed: "I am tired of this football game which we have been having here for the last few weeks. It has been a case of kicking bills around from one committee to another for apparently no other reason than to stifle the legislation and place them in the hands of 'cats'-paws' for final destruction."

Mr. Moore explained that Governor Pinchot had made certain "campaign pledges" which he wished to abide by. I replied that in advocating Coal and Iron Police abolition I did not speak of "campaign pledges." Lifting my hands high to take in that vast hall now electric with eager attention, I said: "I speak of John Barcoski, who was brutally murdered by Coal and Iron Police only several miles from my own home. I know what Coal and Iron Police are; I know what they have done, and it is high time that something be done to erase the blot of their depredations from the escutcheon of Pennsylvania—and it can be done by the passage of these bills which Mr. Moore seeks to doom."

Moore charged that I was usurping authority in telling the House what the Law and Order Committee would do. However, he said he would be reasonable and agree to let my bills pass their first reading and then he would send them to the Law and Order Committee. In other words, he would grant a respite while the executioner sharpened the ax. I retorted that the "gentleman from Washington knows that he has no authority to refer bills to committee," and that we would see to it that "he shall usurp no authority as to what shall happen to these bills on their first reading, second reading, or before or after second reading." I again asked the House to vote "No."

The vote was put. As the clerk started the call of the roll, I trembled in an agony of suspense. Each name was the sounding of a ship's bell and each response clanged "Aye" or "No." I tried to keep count of the bell's tolling, but the thoughts which whirled through my brain that this might be the tragic tolling as the ship disappeared into the sea, plus the emotional turmoil within me, shook my pencil and I got lost in the count. The House seemed to be rolling in a mist and a fog as the roll clerk droned on with the names. When my own name was about to be reached I prepared to shout a stentorian "No!" but all that emerged from my larynx was a squeaky "No." An icy sweat dotted my forehead. Then through the fog and the mist I heard a voice speaking as if from a great distance: "The ayes are 57 and the nays 84; the question is determined in the negative and the motion is not agreed to."

It was one of the sweetest moments in my whole legislative career. I felt I had fought off the threat of a great wrong and that right had triumphed simply because it was right. Many members came to my desk to congratulate me. Mark Shields of the Pittsburgh *Press*, hurrying out to telegraph his story, seized my hand. "Good work, Mike, good work," he said. Glenn Moore, as the House was now adjourning, came by my desk and asked if I had any hard feelings. I said, "No," but I still shook from the torpedo he had launched at my ship of legislative faith.

On March 24, 1931, House Bill No. 1 came up for final vote. A young personable lady, daughter of Arthur M. Northrup, secretary of labor and industry, and whom I had met several days before, visited the house to witness the debate and vote. Since her father was in Pinchot's cabinet and she was enthusiastic about the governor, she said to me that my bill must surely fail. However, in a spirit of sportsmanship she gaily added she would take an aisle chair next to my desk to comfort me when I should have lost the day. After I finished my speech urging passage of the measure, she remarked: "That was a good speech, but you'll never beat Governor Pinchot in this House." But when the vote tally was completed, she rose, and with icicles dropping from her words commented: "Mr. Musmanno, I'm disappointed in you. This is the first time that Governor Pinchot has been defeated in the legislature, and I regret that it should have been you to administer that defeat." With that remark she stalked from the House chamber while I rubbed my forehead in amazement.

But even Miss Northrup's frowns could not sour the sweet milk of victory which I drank as I contemplated the magnificent vote of 153 to 25 in favor of my property guard measure. It now moved to the Senate for that august body's consideration.

But the battle flags in the House were not yet furled. There was still the actual Pinchot measure (the one introduced by Representative Wilson) to contend with. If it passed the House and Senate and my bill also was approved by the Senate, Pinchot would most assuredly veto my bill and approve his own. I asked Harry Himes of Armstrong County, chairman of the Law and Order Committee and a strong Pinchot disciple, to allow a public hearing on the Pinchot measure now in his custody. "Why should I allow you to bring in people to attack the governor's bill?" he replied acidly.

"I'm not bringing in anyone. If you authorize the hearing, proponents as well as opponents will be heard." He walked away, grumbling.

Meanwhile Representative Wilson was trying to convince me to allow the governor's bill to pass the House uncontested. He explained that by this procedure the Senate would have both bills and the senators could perhaps combine the best merits of each. I smiled as I placed a hand on his shoulder. "Mr. Wilson," I said, "it would be impossible for the Senate or anyone to graft my bill to yours or the other way around. They are of totally different species. You might as well try to create a satisfactory animal by sewing together the forward part of a lion and the rear half of a jackass."

"Musmanno, are you making an insidious comparison?"

"Wilson, it is not vanity which causes me to say that my bill which the House passed despite your opposition can more appropriately be compared to a lion in its defense of the rights of humanity than your bill which, with its stupid bartering of the people's sovereign rights, would make a jackass look like a wise owl."

This zoological discussion got us nowhere, and Wilson summed up: "I understand then that you will oppose my bill?"

"Of course I will oppose it."

"Well, then, we'll beat you on the field of battle and you'll regret, Musmanno, not having accepted this compromise."

Wilson did not exhibit his show of confidence to me alone. He displayed the same cocksureness all over Capitol Hill. To give visual substantiation to his expressions of assured victory he held numerous conferences with groups of members from various parts of the state. He worked on the not unwise theory that the man who desires to impress the market that he will have a bountiful harvest should line up his market wagons in the spring. Thus after each conference Wilson smiled broadly for the benefit of all House members and newspaper reporters. He also called on the governor from time to time as well as the attorney general, and always emerged from the offices of these holier-than-holies with a grin of victory that would have made Lord Nelson's smile of triumph seem wan in comparison.

Of course I tried to smile victory, too, but I was sailing over a more difficult sea than the one which bore Wilson's frigate of war. Furthermore, he was in home waters. The Administration offered shore batteries and a flotilla of Administration favors in support of his efforts. Wilson also commanded respect in his own right. He was a lawyer of ability, a gentleman of excellent character, and had a splendid record as a legislator. He was dignified in demeanor but had a nice, sociable manner about him. Although not the proverbial hail-fellow-well-met, he made friends easily. The newspapermen liked him. He seemed to have convinced most of them that it was all over but the shouting. Mark Shields, expert analyst of parliamentary situations and a most competent writer, wrote that the governor's bill would pass the House without much difficulty. John K. Morrow, another newspaperman and a good friend of mine who favored my bill over the governor's measure, nonetheless wrote:

> What Musmanno will attempt to do Tuesday will be
> to defeat the Wilson Bill on the floor of the House, but
> he probably will not be successful. The Adminis-
> tration forces of the Houses have already proved that

even in their hardest tests they can muster enough majority to withstand the attacks against the Administration.

Many members of the legislature who had stood with me in the
last show of strength began to show uneasiness as the next passage-
at-arms neared. They feared that if they voted against the Pinchot
measure and it passed, they might be marked for reprisal in matters
of patronage and legislative favors. Others argued to me that I was
misreading the barometer in opposing the Pinchot measure because if
I failed to defeat it this would serve notice on the Senate that I had
been repudiated and the Senate would summarily jettison the
Musmanno Bill and accept the Wilson Bill. A story now began to
circulate that I was pondering the possible disastrous results of a
clash-at-arms and that I would most likely not draw my sword when
the Wilson Bill came before the House.

Pinchot sought further to gain labor support for his pet legislation
by adding a provision that labor unions would be accorded the same
right as industry to employ trade police. This, of course, was sheer
demagoguery and I blasted the provision when the bill finally had a
hearing before the Law and Order Committee. "The new Pinchot
Bill," I said, "is worse than the original bill. Under this new draft
he offers armies to both labor and capital so that they may fight
out their differences on sanguinary battlefields. This is the first time
in our industrial history that the state has provided the means for a
civil war. This is not only preposterous but it is an insult to labor.
Labor unions do not want any army. They have no funds with which
to pay for state police, nor should they be required to pay for police
protection. But, above all, police should be impartial."

The Law and Order Committee approved the Pinchot measure and,
by special arrangement, it was placed on the House calendar for final
consideration and vote on May 5.

This became the supreme test. I was now in full opposition to the
governor, the attorney general, the Administration floor leaders, and
all the forces that a party in office may summon to the legislative
arena in a controversy which bears on an Administration's prestige.
My most formidable opponent, however, was the intangible, im-
palpable notion floating through the legislative halls, over the Capitol
Hill greens, and in the lobbies of the hotels that somehow it was wrong
to oppose a governor who was known as a liberal and who had the
interests of the people at heart. No one would ascribe wrong motives

to Governor Pinchot, and yet, purposely or unwittingly, he was embarked on an evil course. That to me was plain.

On Tuesday, May 5, I entered the House of Representatives, my helmet visor up, ready for battle. At 1 P.M. the Speaker announced: "The Chair lays before the House the special order of business fixed for this hour, consideration of House Bill No. 1035, Printer's No. 771, on page 1 of today's calendar."

Every member was in his seat. The gallery was filled to overflowing. Coal miners, ministers, university professors, labor organizers, plant superintendents, coal operators took up every available inch of space in the huge chamber. As proponent of the Pinchot Bill, Mr. Wilson rose to address the assembly. The scene was one to gladden the heart of every lover of popular government, for here truly was democracy in action. In a firm, convincing voice Mr. Wilson began his argument. He said that the Pennsylvania Protective Service, provided for in his bill, would protect "the welfare of the lives, the liberties and the properties of the citizens of this Commonwealth in emergencies where extra police authority is needed." Lifting a professorial finger, he told the House that no one had to fear that this organization could become unwieldy or acquire a power which would get beyond the control of the government. The trade police force, he said, was limited to but 250 men and it could not be used anywhere except by the governor's consent. He emphasized that the bill was fair and that it protected both "labor and capital." He urged the House to pass the bill so that the Senate could consider it with the Musmanno Bill already in the upper chamber. "Unless this legislation is passed," he warned, "we go back to where we were before we passed legislation of this character, and capital and labor will return to the situation where, in the time of emergency, the sheriffs of the different counties will swear in deputies."

Not a representative moved or stirred as Wilson spoke, not a person in the gallery coughed. All the drama of a momentous decision about to be made was absorbed by the House-packed audience. As Mr. Wilson concluded his speech and took his seat, the faces of the House members and all the spectators turned toward me as they do in a tennis match when the opposing player is receiving the serve. It is said that the best of speakers sometimes are nervous before they begin an important speech. If uneasiness is a criterion of speaking ability, then that afternoon I was a Daniel Webster as I stood up on my legs, which seemed to be all hinges. My throat felt parched; my hands became shovels; I expected that at any moment my pounding heart would crash through my chest. If I could have asked myself whether

I had ever felt that way before I would have answered that these were the symptoms I had experienced when I rose to address the jury in my first case as a young lawyer eight years before. Would the fates be with me today as they were on that long-ago day?

I knew I had to master my nervousness and I knew I had to say something that would at once break the spell which Wilson had cast over the House. I could not lead up to my point slowly. I had to place Wilson at a disadvantage immediately. Clearing my throat, I called out: "Mr. Speaker." As I uttered those two words, my self-consciousness dropped from me like an unwanted topcoat, my voice was distinct, my heart went into the even rhythm of a well-lubricated engine. Although the House was not equipped with any public-address system, I knew I could be heard in the farthest corners of that gigantic chamber. After being acknowledged by the Speaker, I addressed myself to Mr. Wilson and asked: "Mr. Speaker, does the gentleman from McKean know how many industries would draw from the Protective Service throughout the state?" Mr. Wilson replied that he did not know.

I followed up with another question: "Does the gentleman from McKean know how many Coal and Iron policemen there are at the present time in the state of Pennsylvania?" To this he also replied that he did not know. I put a third question: "Mr. Speaker, does the gentleman from McKean know if there are Coal and Iron Police in the county which he so ably represents?" To this he replied: "There are no coal mines in McKean County."

Here was a man proposing and advocating legislation without knowing what industries would make use of his "trade police," without knowing how many Coal and Iron Police there were in the state, and probably without having ever seen a Coal and Iron policeman in his life. I promptly proceeded to show that he knew even less than his answers revealed. He had said that the maximum number of trade police would be 250, but if he had studied the very bill he presented he would realize that a force of 250 could be appointed each week, every day, or even every hour! So that in a short time two armies could be created. For what? For industrial warfare? Was that desirable?

I ridiculed his plan to send the Pinchot Bill to the Senate to be considered with the Musmanno Bill. The House had already approved the Musmanno Bill by a vote of 153 to 25. If they now accepted the Pinchot Bill they would inevitably have to rescind their approval of the Musmanno Bill. "You can't have two loves, my friends, on this issue. You are either for property guards or for trade police with un-

restricted police powers; you are either for House Bill No. 1 or
you are for House Bill No. 1035. You certainly cannot be for both,
because they are absolutely incompatible. Two years ago this House
was confronted with a somewhat similar situation. Two police bills
were presented at that session and both were approved, and when the
weaker one was signed by the governor he was subjected to the most
violent denunciation that any governor has ever felt, and the members
of both the House and the Senate were severely criticized for having
approved two bills when they knew only one could be enacted into
law."

I reminded the House that with an adjournment day looming it
would be folly to jam the Pinchot Bill through the House and send it
to the Senate, only to confuse the issue over there. "There will be one
of two results if you pass this bill. It will either go to the Senate, be
approved there, and then be approved by the governor and enacted
into law; and you then will have earned the censure and condemnation
of the people for having put on the statute books such bad legislation.
Or it will go to the Senate, there meet with a deadlock, and both bills
will be jettisoned, and then you will have earned the condemnation
of the state for, in effect, killing a bill that you at one time approved.
The only logical thing to do is to disapprove this measure today."

I pointed out that Mr. Wilson, by his very answers to the questions
I had put to him, had shown that his interest in Coal and Iron Police
was an academic one. But in western Pennsylvania, where we had
felt the fangs of the Coal and Iron Police dragon, the problem was
very real. I spoke for about forty-five minutes and ended by calling
upon the House to vote down the Wilson Bill. "On March 24 you
revealed your courage in honestly accepting a bill which you honestly
believed settled this problem. Today, show by your vote that you have
the courage to stand by your original vote and not pass this bill which
would undo what you did on that day.

"In the name of not only John Barcoski, but in the name of many
people still living who might be subjected to a similar fate if this bill
were to pass, I ask you to vote 'No.' In the name of the sovereign
power of this Commonwealth, which should not be cheapened; in the
name of the dignity of the House, which should not be lowered; in
the name of an honest decision already made by this honorable body,
and which should not be ignored; in the name of consistency; in the
name of that fairness which you hold dear to your hearts, I respectfully ask you on the roll call of this bill to register 'No.' "

Three or four others spoke on the bill and then again came that spirit-stirring moment of the tally. The yeas totaled 43, the nays 142. The clerk simply announced: "Less than the majority required by the Constitution having voted in the affirmative, the question was determined to the negative, and the bill fails." But it was more than the failure of a bill. It was a rebuke to the governor; it was a jolting reminder to the coal and iron barons that the representatives of the people would not tolerate the degrading of sovereign jurisdiction, which is and must always remain in the people themselves. But the lesson imparted by the House vote still made no lasting impression on the barons. They simply moved over to the other side of the capitol and besieged the senators now to take up a knife against the Musmanno Bill already in their tender custody.

The senators in the Senate Judiciary General Committee, to which my bill had been referred, did not fail the barons. They added amendments which cut out the very heart of my bill. The amendments gave to the property guards all the police power of a Philadelphia officer of the law and a constable, which is the greatest cumulative police power in the Commonwealth; they removed the provision restricting the guards to the property of their employer; they eliminated the provision making employers responsible for depredations of the guards.

On May 26, 1931, the Senate passed the crippled Musmanno Bill by a vote of 27 to 15. It was now sent back to the House for concurrence on the amendments. What was I to do? Certainly I could not permit such a monstrosity to become law. In its Senate-amended form the Musmanno Bill had become the very antithesis of everything for which I had been fighting since 1926.

At two o'clock the following morning the bill came before the House for a vote on concurring in the Senate amendments. With a knot in my throat I rose to ask my colleagues to repudiate the very bill which two months before I had pleaded with them to affirm: "Mr. Speaker and members of the House, the Senate has cut out the very heart of this bill; they have mangled it in the same manner that the Coal and Iron Police mangled the body of John Barcoski—and they will answer for this heinous offense to the outraged people of the state of Pennsylvania.

"The conspirators who have committed this treachery have covered themselves with undying infamy and have earned the contempt of mankind. By their amendments which utterly destroy the purpose of the bill, they have placed their stamp of approval on a bloodthirsty system which has disgraced Pennsylvania before the nation, they have

condoned the acts of those gorillas who killed John Barcoski, they
have condoned the conduct of those monsters who shot into a schoolhouse at Bruceton while children were attending classes, they have
condoned the savage deeds of all those thugs, gangsters, and plug-
uglies who have borne the ignominious name of Coal and Iron Police.
On March 24 you passed a bill here, members of the House, which
was a vigorous and healthy measure. The Senate has drained its life-
blood and sent it back to us a corpse."

The House accepted and acted on my plea to turn down the bill as
it had been amended by the Senate, and it did so. This, of course,
meant the end of the battle. We were where we had begun. The
long fight had ended in a complete rout. The forces of democracy had
been defeated. Decency, justice, and truth had been worsted. Two
governors failed to abide by their pledges to the people: one because
he was too weak, the other because he was too strong. One because
he believed in quid pro quo, the other because he believed that he
knew more than the people who had elected him. Of course neither
of these governors could have made a shambles of democratic
processes had it not been for the greed of a few coal operators who
placed profit above humanity and wealth of dollars above riches of
spirit.*

* Going beyond the scope of this book, it may be added here that the Coal
and Iron Police system finally came to an end in 1935 when Governor George
H. Earle signed the repeal measure passed by the legislature that year.

Chapter XXXIX

THE BLUE LAWS OF PENNSYLVANIA

Now that one can attend almost any kind of theatrical entertainment or outdoor sport on Sunday, it is almost incredible that in Pennsylvania, as late as 1929, baseball, movies, and musical concerts were forbidden on the Sabbath by the so-called "blue laws." So hidebound was the Keystone State in this respect that when the Pittsburgh Symphony Orchestra staged a Sunday concert in 1927 its first violinist, Joseph Anderon, was arrested, prosecuted, and convicted of violating the law. At Anderon's trial, the prosecuting attorney questioned one of the witnesses to the concert as if the witness had beheld the commission of a murder. Slowly approaching the witness chair like a prosecutor who is about to draw from its occupant the bloodcurdling declaration that he had seen the defendant plunge a knife into the back of his victim, the district attorney hissed: "And what did the defendant hold in his hand?" The witness, now under the spell of the district attorney's dramatic approach, hesitated, as if ashamed to admit that he had looked upon a scene so brutal and degrading. Then, pulling himself together, he huskily replied: "Mr. Anderon had in his hand—a *violin*."

Ever since 1794, Pennsylvania had been entombed on Sundays as if in punishment for what it had done the first six days of each week. The "blue laws" of 1794 prohibited every type of worldly activity. This included working, playing, entertaining, attending concerts or theaters, traveling, and all buying or selling except "dressed victuals." Although milk could be legally delivered up to 9 A.M. on Sunday, it was illegal to sell it on Sunday. As late as 1891 the Court of Common Pleas of Allegheny County declared that while the Act of 1794 exempted the delivery of milk, "delivery does not in any sense comprehend a sale, and the business of delivering articles is entirely distinct from selling them." This was rather fine-edged reasoning because, with the exception of mothers nursing their infants, it is difficult to imagine the delivery of milk without comprehending a sale thereof. In 1887 a merchant was convicted for selling soda water on Sunday, the Court going to the trouble of explaining that soda water could not come within the concept of "dressed victuals." In 1891 the Supreme Court of Pennsylvania affirmed the conviction of a merchant who sold newspapers on Sunday. By 1929 many of the absurdly restrictive provisions of the law were ignored, but one could still go to jail for playing baseball, performing at a concert, or attending a theatrical performance. Of course those wealthy enough to belong to private clubs could snap their fingers at the blue laws, for the law could not touch their movies, golf, concerts, and other entertainments.

Although unquestionably the overwhelming majority of the people of Pennsylvania favored liberalization of the Sunday laws, the legislature refused to act because, as was true in the Coal and Iron Police situation, the political organization dominating the state opposed liberalization. The political leaders did not resist Sunday entertainment on moral or religious grounds. They hypocritically supported a "blue" Sunday so as not to gain the enmity of the Sabbath Observance Organization, the Anti-Saloon League, and the Lord's Day Alliance, which might expose some of their more flagrant sins.

The very first bill I introduced in the 1929 legislature provided for modification of the 1794 laws to the extent that each community could decide for itself what entertainment it would permit on Sunday after 3 P.M. I did not favor what is known as a "wide-open" Sunday, but I saw no antagonism between spirituality and physical-mental relaxation. I felt that the law should be revised so that Sunday, like one's elementary education, should also have three R's—Religion, Rest, and Recreation.

Governor Fisher, who had pledged himself to the Anti-Saloon League not to touch the blue laws, gave a "thumbs-down" to my bill and accordingly it was boxed and shipped to the Law and Order Committee, the cemetery of all Administration-doomed bills, from which it never emerged.

On the first day of the 1931 session I reintroduced this legislation, giving it the name of the Sunday Observance Local Option Bill. It differed from my previous bill mainly in that the referenda in all communities were to take place simultaneously throughout the state, each municipality being empowered, once the people had approved the measure, to decide what Sunday entertainment they would permit after 2 P.M. The bill was referred to the Law and Order Committee, where ordinarily it would at once be deposited in the vat of pickling brine ever ready for measures of that kind. However, the Speaker, C. J. Goodnough, although opposed to Sunday liberalization, was a just man. I appealed to him personally to use his power and influence to have the committee at least grant a public hearing. The chairman, Representative Harry Himes of Armstrong County, acceded to the wishes of the Speaker, and a hearing was scheduled for March 17, 1931.

In the meantime the "blue" forces got busy. Ministers who opposed any change in the blue laws thundered in their pulpits against this "desecration" of the Sabbath. While of course many ministers, and possibly a greater number, took the opposite position and advocated a change, it seemed that the "blues" were considerably more vocal and vociferous than the "anti-blues." One minister, the Reverend Dr. Robert F. Galbreath of the ——— Church, was so carried away by his own vehemence that he made the absurd charge that all attempts to alter the law of 1794 were "un-American." He went even further. Aiming his bow at me, he released a poisoned arrow by proclaiming: "The assault on this law does not come from native-born Americans. One of our most dangerous foes in this fight is Representative M. A. Musmanno, sponsor of the bill bearing his name."

The Reverend Galbreath assumed, because my name is of Italian origin, that I was not native-born. I replied to him, as I had spoken in Mount Lebanon years before:

"I do not yield to you nor to anyone throughout the universe in my love for and devotion to America. I was born in Stowe Township, Pennsylvania, which has always been my home. There were four boys in our family and we all served in the United States Army: one was killed in France, another was wounded in Cuba, a third received a battlefield commission for gallantry in action. I hold a captain's commission in the United States Army Reserves. My book on the United States Constitution was accepted and published by the United States Congress as a congressional document. Whatever I do, I do for America; whatever I oppose, I oppose because I believe it is injurious to America."

The Reverend Galbreath's personal attack boomeranged against him and the "blue" forces for which he spoke. People who for years had been hoping for a break in the blue-law ice field now cheered the prospect of being heard at a public hearing. In all parts of the state, sports and music lovers prepared for a pilgrimage to the capitol to be seen and heard on a subject dear to their hearts. In Philadelphia,

Pittsburgh, Reading, and Wilkes-Barre, arrangements were made for special trains and buses to arrive in Harrisburg on March 17, and on that day the anti-blue-law enthusiasts, several thousand strong, paraded through the streets of the capital city carrying huge banners: "WE'RE FOR THE MUSMANNO BILL FOR HOME RULE!" Following the parade, as many as could do so crowded into the vast hall of the House of Representatives, where the Law and Order Committee sat on the dais to conduct the hearing. Fifteen speakers spoke in favor of the Musmanno Bill; not one in opposition. Among the speakers were the Reverend Frank Smith of the First Unitarian Church of Pittsburgh and former Governor John K. Tener. A powerful statement was made by Colonel Samuel Harden Church, president of the Carnegie Institute of Technology, who said, *inter alia:*

"The Lord's Day Alliance is composed of rich men who ride in their automobiles, play golf and tennis, and see moving pictures at their clubs—all on Sunday—while at the same time keeping the masses of the people from the enjoyment of these innocent recreations. I hope this bill of Mr. Musmanno's will be passed."

I addressed the committee and called upon it to release the bill: "I ask that you report out this bill, not because under the blue laws Pennsylvania is known as a backward state; not because the blue laws enforce idleness, corner loafing, crap shooting, and other vices; not because in many parts of the state, as in Erie, for instance, the law is openly defied and nullified; not because every member of this House has at some time violated this law—all of which is true. I ask for the release of this bill on a grand and loftier ground—fair play and a square deal, so that this House may vote on the measure and then the people of Pennsylvania may determine the issue for themselves."

Many years have passed since that memorable day in Harrisburg, and now that I have reached the age when one is apt to look back upon his youth somewhat sadly in realization that it is gone forever, it is somewhat comforting to know that in those days of boundless energy one used at least part of this God-given boon to a good purpose. The Philadelphia *Record*, reporting the speeches, said:

> Applause frequently interrupted Musmanno's oration, which was delivered with the fire of enthusiasm burning in every word. It was a magnificent speech, beautifully delivered, and when it was over even the "blues" were moved to admiration for the Pittsburgh

> youngster who had put so much of his soul into
> his words.

But oratory was not to move those picked gravediggers on the Law and Order Committee. The principle of home rule struck no responsive chord in their breast. Most of them were avowed prohibitionists, and they equated Sunday wholesome entertainment with whiskey saloons and all the excesses of the rum trade. One of the most fanatic prohibitionists on the committee, Representative Samuel G. Hartsock of Blair County, said at a committee meeting:

> During the last six years I have traveled throughout
> the United States and I have found that the good
> people—I want to make it clear that I mean the good
> people—all say that prohibition is the best thing that
> ever happened to this country.

That evening I wrote in my diary:

> The presumption of Hartsock in deciding who are
> good and who are bad—and in placing all the good
> people on the side of prohibition—is unfortunately an
> indication of the attitude of the majority of the members
> of the Law and Order Committee.

When we went into executive session, following the public hearing on the Musmanno Bill, Hartsock moved that my bill not be released. His motion was quickly seconded. I argued that the committee deliberate, I pleaded for fairness, I supplicated that the House be given an opportunity to vote on the measure. I pleaded in vain. I could hear the bill dropping into the pickling brine.

A few days later a Hartsock-sponsored bill on raccoon hunting came before the House for debate and vote. I spoke against it. Hartsock declared that my opposition was personal, reminding the whole House of our battle on my Sunday Local Option Bill. He then finished his speech by calling upon the House to give him a "vote of confidence." His hunting eye failed him badly here. He was avalanched by a vote of 140 to 10, and I must confess I laughed heartily to see Sam Hartsock tumble across the puddle into which he had intended to push me.

Although the Law and Order Committee killed my bill, the fight to dissipate the clouds of Sunday-afternoon boredom was not ended. Representative Schwartz of Philadelphia had introduced earlier in the session a bill to amend the blue laws of 1794 by extending the time for milk deliveries on Sunday from 9 to 10 A.M. This bill was referred to the Law and Order Committee, which, in an unusual display of reasonableness, reported it to the House. Once it got to the floor, I saw an opportunity to revive my bill by attaching it to the Schwartz Bill as an amendment. To do this I naturally had to inform some of my friends of the intended plan. The "blues" in the House learned of the maneuver and prepared to outmaneuver us. Representative D. Glenn Moore, always ready to drive a hearse to the Law and Order Committee, moved that the Schwartz Bill be returned to that committee for study. What he meant, of course, was—for burial. We saw through his necromantic stratagem and defeated his motion by a vote of 102 to 91.

Although we won in this skirmish we were fully aware of the formidableness of the "blue" forces when they came out in battle array. Thus, we decided to concentrate on only one feature of Sunday liberalization—baseball. If we were successful on the diamond, then we would later try for movies. Accordingly, Representative Sowers introduced an amendment providing for Sunday baseball and it came before the House for debate on April 28, 1931. Sowers began his excellent speech on the amendment by saying: "It may surprise you to know that I am a "blue", but not, however, an indigo blue. Nobody more than myself desires the suppression of vice and immorality. This amendment I have offered has for its purpose the prevention of vice and immorality. Idleness, you all know, creates vice. Idleness breeds immorality. The Bible has stated that the devil finds plenty of work for idle hands to do. Idleness lures many to places of vice and crime. An honest, helpful, and clean recreation like baseball will employ the idle minds and keep them from places of sin."

Representative Himes, chairman of the Law and Order Committee, lamented that the milk bill which he had released was now becoming the vehicle for something else and asked the House to vote down the amendment. I followed with a eulogy on baseball.

Representative Stevenson of Mercer County, speaking for the "blues," cleverly said: "You would think, from some of the remarks some of the gentlemen have made this afternoon, that the Sabbath day was the only day on which men are permitted to play baseball. There are six days in the week in which boys and men can engage in this pastime and sport if they care to."

This was an astute observation but of course an irrelevant one. Not everyone has the chance to go to baseball games during the week. Representative Thomas C. Evans of Lancaster County, also speaking for the "blues," quoted from the Bible: "Remove not the ancient landmark, which thy fathers have set." Representative Carmany of Venango County likewise called upon the Scriptures to remind the House of the commandment: " 'Remember the Sabbath day, to keep it holy.' There is danger of us as American citizens and legislators forgetting God's day. 'Remember the Sabbath day, to keep it holy.' I am fearful we are allowing the pendulum to swing too far toward a liberalized Sunday."

When he finished I asked him if he was acquainted with Chapter 12 of St. Matthew, in which it was related how the Pharisees wished to destroy Christ because He healed people on the Sabbath. Carmany replied that it was always right to do good on the Sabbath, but he failed to explain how it was wrong to spend an afternoon in the open air watching a good, clean American game.

Representative Stewart of Clearfield County argued that the bill was intended solely "in the interest of those wealthy owners of baseball franchises in the large centers of population. Organized baseball is a highly organized, highly commercialized business . . . and that is why we are here today, and last week devoted so much time in an effort to give a special right and privilege to one of the greatest trusts that we have in this country today."

It so happened that Stewart, who argued so vociferously against the commercialized interests of baseball, was himself in the commercialized publishing business, which operated on Sunday in defiance of law.

Sowers' amendment was adopted by a vote of 103 to 99. However, when the amended bill came on for a final vote on May 4, 1931, one vote changed and the final tally was 102 in the affirmative and 98 in the negative. Since the constitutional majority was 105, we thus lost by three votes.

In the meantime another baseball bill (this one introduced by Representative Denning of Philadelphia) had broken loose from committee probably because the members assumed it was unconstitutional and could never become law. I conferred with Denning and Sowers of Philadelphia and others shepherding the measure and helped to prepare amendments which would assure the bill's constitutionality. At the same time I added the tail of the kite of my bill—the local-option feature. The amendments were adopted and this bill came before the House for final consideration and vote. I was now satisfied that in fighting for this bill we should dwell not so much on baseball as on the right of the people to determine for themselves what they wished.

We should emphasize also that longevity alone of any law did not of itself command reverence and that the age of the blue laws (137 years) did not prove that they were perfect and beyond amendment or even repeal.

The hall of the House of Representatives in Harrisburg is one of the most beautiful legislative chambers in the world. Aside from its massive gold-and-crystal chandeliers, its stained-glass windows and rich architecture, the walls are covered with paintings of superb artistry. The forward wall carries a huge spectacular work of art entitled "The Apotheosis of Pennsylvania" and portrays men and events prominent in the Commonwealth's early history, with emphasis on William Penn, the founder of the Commonwealth. At noon on May 15 I began my address by calling the House's attention to that magnificent mural.

"Each day that we sit here in session we face that stupendous painting, 'The Apotheosis of Pennsylvania,' but if we refuse to pass this bill, which is a measure of and for the people, we make a mockery of the glorious spirit behind that picture. The central figure is William Penn, who said that 'of all injustice that is the greatest which passes under the name of law.' Our opponents say that the law of 1794 is sacred because it is old. Why, Mr. Speaker, as far back as 1700 when our colony was only nineteen years old, William Penn said, speaking of the Constitution: 'There are in it some laws which may be accounted obsolete, others hurtful, others imperfect that will need improvement.'

"And then in the autumn of 1700, when the legislature was convened at New Castle, William Penn said of it: 'Review your laws and propose new ones that may better your circumstances.'

"And now, if you deny to this legislature the right to amend a law which the majority of the people deem obsolete in many particulars; if you deny to the people the right to change a law which, in the words of William Penn, needs improvement; if you deny to the people the right to pass upon any vital measure which is near and dear to their hearts—then at least be consistent: Stand up and tear the noble figure of William Penn from that matchless canvas!

"Rip it out and say to the father and founder of our state: 'Master, although you came to America to found a commonwealth in order to establish religious and civic freedom, although your whole life was dedicated to the cause of the people, we, your official descendants, repudiate the principle of democracy as exemplified in referendum and local option.' "

Representative Flinchbaugh of York County, speaking for the "blues," said that to pass this bill would be to give to Pennsylvania a European Sabbath, which is known as the "Continental Sunday." And he informed us that the Continental Sunday of Europe precipitated World War I! Mr. Flinchbaugh's speech reminded me of a letter I received from a blue-law adherent who said that the North lost the first battle of Bull Run because it was fought on the Sabbath!

The debate was a most interesting one, and several of the speakers rose to splendid heights of oratory on both sides of the question. When the vote was finally taken the ayes tallied 106 and the nays 98. Thus, for the first time in 137 years, the blue laws of Pennsylvania were amended—in the House of Representatives. When the bill, however, got to the Senate side of the capitol, the head mortician of the Senate Law and Order Committee took it in tow and sepulchered it without benefit of clergy—or reason.*

There were moments during my legislative career when I wondered if representatives and senators really represented the people of Pennsylvania. Many of them were so beholden to the political organizations which had sent them to Harrisburg that they exercised no independent judgment whatever on legislative issues. It was enough for them if, like trained bears, they followed the direction of the organization floor leader who pointed to his eye when he wanted an "aye" vote and to his nose when he wanted a "no" vote.

Some of the members voted equally as errantly, not in response to organization leaders, but in obeisance to whim, caprice, or personal conceit. There was one legislator who had an eye for a very attractive girl who often came to the House to listen to the debates. He would visit the gallery to talk to her and on several occasions asked her out to dinner, which invitation she always refused, as he himself told us. At a banquet held at the Penn-Harris Hotel, I found myself sitting at a table next to the one at which sat the lovely lady of the gallery. We exchanged some pleasantries and then, when the floor was cleared for dancing, I danced with her. Mr. Lady-Killer Legislator witnessed all this. The next day, on an important bill, he voted "no" because I supported it, even though he had previously publicly declared that he was in favor of the bill.

There were four lady members in the 1929 session. At the Governor's Ball I danced with three of them, but before I could get to the fourth one the orchestra had put away its instruments and the

---

* Sunday baseball finally came to Pennsylvania in April 1933, and Sunday movies were legalized in July 1935.

ball was over. The lady, who, through no fault of mine, had become a "wallflower" for the evening, blamed me for the sunken garden in which she vainly waited all evening. From then on she opposed nearly every measure I advocated and voted "aye" to most bills I opposed. Her attitude perhaps could be regarded a tribute to my terpsichorean aptitude, but it definitely registered a demerit against parliamentary foresight.

The Baldi brothers of Philadelphia, Charles and Joseph, were two of the most popular members in the House and certainly two of the friendliest to me. When the Philadelphia delegation, by caucus decision, was opposed to some measure I was advocating, the Baldi brothers would split their vote, one voting "Aye" and the other "No" so that if they could not help me, they at least would not hurt me. They exemplified the truism that in any deliberative assembly it is difficult to avoid the human equation, and, indeed, it would not be desirable to do so. A friendship may sometimes achieve what might fail through the processes of ordinary parliamentary procedure. This principle was dramatically illustrated in the 1931 session when the legislature was considering my Barbers' License Bill. Up until that year barbers were not licensed in Pennsylvania, and as a consequence many barbers without proper training and some even afflicted with contagious disease endangered the safety and health of their patrons. On the night of April 13, 1931, when my bill came to a vote, the final tally for passage was 104, with 36 opposed. Since the constitutional majority required for the passage of any measure was 105, the bill thus failed by one vote. Instinctively I hoped that I might get a reconsideration of the legislation and on the next test perhaps pick up one more affirmative vote.

I immediately rose and moved for reconsideration. In doing this I knew I was wrong on two counts: one, new business had to intervene before a motion for reconsideration could be entertained; and, two, since I had voted on the losing side I was not qualified to make a motion for reconsideration. But it was imperative I let the House know I felt keenly the defeat by one vote, and the only manner in which I could acquaint the entire membership with my reaction to what had happened was to stand up at once in that vast assemblage and conspicuously make a motion for reconsideration. Accordingly I rose and announced: "Mr. Speaker, it is quite obvious to me that in the calling of the roll there were many who might have voted 'aye' but were not sufficiently attentive at the time to answer, and I therefore hereby make a motion that the vote by which this bill failed be reconsidered."

Representative Perry of Philadelphia made the proper point of order that new business had to intervene. The Speaker sustained the point of order. New business having intervened, I now took the floor again: "Mr. Speaker, the remarks made by the gentleman from Philadelphia, Mr. Perry, of course were in order, and new business having now intervened, I renew my motion; namely, that the vote on House Bill No. 331, which brought about the defeat of that bill, be reconsidered."

The Speaker ruled that the motion had to come from someone who voted in the negative because that was the winning side—all of which I knew. But my purpose was accomplished. I felt reasonably certain, or at least fervently hoped, that, because of the closeness of the vote, someone who had been recorded as being opposed to my bill would, out of sheer sportsmanship or friendship, now move to reconsider. Representative Emhardt of Philadelphia threw me a life saver. He had voted in the negative, so that he was qualified to move for reconsideration. Then Representative Patterson of Beaver County, who had also voted in the negative, seconded the motion—and the bill was now again before the House for consideration.

This time I made a vigorous plea for approval of the measure: "There is no position in which a man more regularly places himself in danger than when he mounts the barber chair. Not only does he subject himself to the possibility of cuts, wounds, and lacerations at the hands of an inexperienced or untrained barber, but he subjects himself to the greater hazard of incurring some contagious disease which he could unwittingly take home to his wife, children, and other relatives. Twenty-nine states of the Union have passed laws similar to this one now before the House, and in consequence, afflicted barbers in the controlled states come here with their germ-laden bodies to work on our population. Pennsylvania should not be the dumping ground for barbers of undesirable character."

As I finished speaking, several of the representatives put questions to me which I answered. Then Representative Patterson, who had seconded Emhardt's motion for reconsideration, spoke energetically against the legislation. His opposition only emphasized the goodness of his heart in having seconded the motion for reconsideration of a bill which he opposed and which had already been once defeated.

When I rose to reply to Mr. Patterson, Representative Haws of Philadelphia interposed a point of order, saying that I had already spoken twice on the bill and therefore could not proceed. The Speaker sustained his point of order. I appealed from the decision of the Chair, explaining that I had really made only one speech and that on the other occasions when I had the floor I was answering questions. The Speaker consulted the stenographer and announced that the stenographic notes confirmed that I had spoken only once in my own right and that therefore I was entitled to the floor. This was further demonstration of absolute fairness on the part of the Speaker. I made another speech, answered more questions, and then the bill came to a vote the second time. I held my breath as the affirmative votes mounted up to 110, and the bill passed. Both Representatives Emhardt and Patterson voted in the negative, but I shall always remember with gratitude their kindness and sportsmanship which made it possible for me to place on our statute books one of the most important health measures of the generation.

But with the sweet cake of good sportsmanship there went occasionally an acrid lime of unfairness. On December 11, 1930, in Pittsburgh, a World War veteran, Grover Barr, having failed to pay a civil judgment of $250, was sentenced to jail for sixty days. As he was seriously ill at the time, the imprisonment caused his death. It was appalling to contemplate that as late as 1931 we still approved the medieval and barbarous practice of imprisonment for debt. I thought of the *Pickwick Papers* and the inhuman debtors' prison described by Charles Dickens; I reflected on the inhumanity of casting into a stone-and-iron cell anyone whose only crime was that he was less astute than his neighbor in the game of dollars and cents. I assumed that the legislature would eagerly grasp the opportunity to abolish a cruel and archaic procedure which perhaps but few members realized still existed. I introduced a bill to efface from our laws any authorization of imprisonment for civil debt. The bill was referred to the House Judiciary General Committee, the chairman of which thought the bill required so much study and consideration that he referred it to a sub-committee. The chairman of the sub-committee thought the bill required so much study and consideration that he delayed acting on it for weeks. I asked him what there was about this measure that required so much study and consideration. He replied that the legislature had to go slow in changing the ways of business. I said that if his sub-committee did not approve of the bill it should so report to the General Committee, and if the General Committee did not approve the bill it could report the bill to the House with a negative recommendation. But, by all that was honest, fair, and just, the legislature should be given the opportunity to mend a shameful rent in the garment of humanity. The sub-committee, however, insisted on additional time to study and consider. It did take the time, and the bill finally died in its hands from an insolvency of humaneness even as poor Grover Barr died from insolvency of dollars.

During the 1925–27 western Pennsylvania coal strike I uncovered evidence that Communists were agitating for violence in the coal fields as part of their plan for world-wide revolution. Further study proved beyond the shadow of a doubt that the Communist party in the United States was a branch of the Soviet international conspiracy for world domination. I tried to enlist support for legislation to outlaw the Communist party, but my plea fell on deaf ears. Edward B. Goehring, member of the House Judiciary Committee, reflected the general attitude when he said that the law I proposed would be "unconstitutional."

In January 1929 I helped to obtain the job of assistant sergeant at arms in the House of Representatives for the most famous ball-player of our times—Honus Wagner. Ill luck had dogged this hero of American youth and all sports lovers ever since advancing years had retired his resounding bat and ragged fielder's glove. He was induced to enter politics and become a candidate for office, but he could never connect with the curves which were thrown at him in that game. He went into business and was handed a walk each time he came to bat. But he was still famous. No matter where he appeared, he was always greeted with applause, but fame placed no bread on his table. He needed a job. We got him a job. On January 21, 1929, I presented him to the House. The members cheered the bowlegged idol of the baseball world. The cheers, however, soon died away. When Honus later became ill, an ugly rumor circulated through the capitol that he was not ill and was drawing his salary as a political drone. Poor Honus, who had stolen more than seven hundred bases in his big-league career, a wholesale larceny which impoverished no one, found that there were moral plunderers who were ready to steal away the glory of his shining name. Wagner resigned his post as assistant sergeant at arms of the Pennsylvania House of Representatives. Cy Hungerford produced another of his masterful cartoons, this one depicting the immortal Dutchman in his baseball uniform, stained from the mud cast at him by persons not worthy enough even to touch the glove and bat which had brought such wholesome joy to the patrons of America's most favorite game.

As a legislator I felt that Pennsylvania was as much a part of my life as if it were my own family. From time to time I traveled through the state visiting state hospitals, penitentiaries, and other governmental institutions. When a tragic explosion occurred in a coal mine at Kinloch near Parnassus I arrived at the scene of the disaster just as the melancholy operation of raising forty-six dead bodies from the wrecked pit began. I shall never forget the heart-shattering scene of wives and mothers chewing at apron strings as they stood at the mine entrance studying the stilled forms brought to the surface, hoping not to identify features of their own husbands and sons. I can never go by a mine today but that I imagine I can hear the screams and wails of the women who discovered in the flickering torches that night at the Kinloch tipple the figures of loved ones stiffened in death. At the Citizens Hospital in New Kensington an injured assistant mine foreman related how the company had removed pumps* in certain parts of the mine, and as a consequence many of the rescued ones had to wade through flooded underworkings with water lapping at their chins. In some instances survivors traveled three to six miles before reaching safe ground. It was a miracle the fatality list did not reach a higher number.

I called for an investigation by the legislature into the cause of the explosion and introduced a bill requiring coal operators to rock-dust all areas where sparks could ignite explosive coal dust. The legislature as a whole did nothing about my recommendations, but one member from Westmoreland County, within whose borders the disaster occurred, who made no visit to Kinloch and displayed no interest in the catastrophe, criticized me for going into "his" county.

This dog-in-the-manger and provincial attitude often stymied wholesome legislation. When I presented a bill providing for a state study of Pennsylvania floral beauties with the view of recommending an official state flower, two Philadelphia representatives insisted that my recommendation could apply only to Allegheny County and not the whole state.

After an experience or two of this kind one can understand the strange things that happen at the end of a session. One entering the House of Representatives during the closing days of a session (at any rate, it was that way in 1929 and 1931) could believe that he had accidentally stumbled into the recreation room of a home for the feeble-minded. Papers are being torn and thrown about like confetti; missiles sail through the air; grinning members are dodging and hiding under desks for protection from books, calendars, and rulers hurled

* Mine-Company officials denied that pumps had been removed.

with force and violence. Bags filled with water are broken over unsuspecting heads; barbershop quartettes are warbling disharmonious ditties in the many corners of the vast hall. The Speaker raps for order as important bills are to be considered and voted on. He is answered with a chorus of catcalls. I can understand the sense of relief with which members contemplate the ending of a tedious session, but I could never comprehend how that happiness could be translated by intelligent people into such uninhibited buffoonery.

A great deal of legislation is passed in those final febrile, frenzied days. Some of that legislation gets into the appellate courts, and occasionally in analyzing a controversial law the Court is moved to ask the question: "What was in the mind of the legislature when it passed this law?" If the law happened to be enacted during the closing hours of some legislative sessions I have witnessed, the answer could well be: "Nothing."

Chapter XL

A VASE OF FLOWERS

THE Pennsylvania legislature convenes every other year. The session begins the first Tuesday of January and normally lasts from four to six months. Latterly, as is true of Congress, the sessions have been much longer, but in 1929 we adjourned on April 18, and in 1931 the curtain came down on May 28. During the life of the session both Houses meet every Monday and adjourn for the week on Wednesday or Thursday. Thus, the members may still carry on with their regular pursuits at home on a part-time basis. Because of this broken schedule, it is rather difficult for a lawyer to do much trial work, since at least one half of each week's time is devoted to Harrisburg. However, he can, over the three-day weekends, confer with clients, do much of the paper work required of every lawyer, and even try short cases which can be finished in a day or two.

I had by now developed a rather good law practice and had acquired comfortable and even beautiful offices which harmonized with my rise in the legal profession. The person calling on me for counsel and assistance would first meet my secretary, attractive and hospitable, who would show him or her to an armchair in the spacious waiting room laid with deep green carpet and hung with large-framed pictures. Directly before him he would see a superb photograph of the United States Capitol glistening like an ice palace. Then he could visualize himself, if he wished, aboard the U.S.S. *Constitution* riding at anchor on the east wall. A huge parchment would remind him of the liberties of America pledged by the Declaration of Independence, and next to this frame he could read the classic letter written by Edna St. Vincent Millay to the governor of Massachusetts on August 22, 1927, copied by her own hand and given to me.

While engrossed in this historical document or perhaps glancing at a picture of me in a gob's uniform at seventeen when I was a member of the Naval Militia, or at my diploma from the University of Rome,

an inner door would open and he would be invited to enter a cheerful
and capacious room fronting on Fourth Avenue. En route he would
pass under an exquisite arch wrought in mahogany and designed by
myself. He was now in my private office, my sanctum sanctorum, my
haven, my refuge, my workshop, my thinking room. A soft, cushioned
maroon rug, friendly in tone and texture, would all but rise to extend
open arms in greetings. From two large windows suspended damask
beige draperies, pleated at the top and dropping in luxuriant folds.
George Washington and Abraham Lincoln greeted from the wall, and
a vase of fresh garden flowers underlined the welcome the visitor
would now receive from the young lawyer who, rising from his desk,
had taken his hand in salutation.

The client would bring the ship of his life, damaged seriously or
lightly, into the dry dock of the young lawyer's understanding and
leave it with him to repair and prepare for safe journeying again on
the ocean of happy and contented living.

It was a beautiful office and, with the exception of the time I spent
in court and in the legislature when it was in session, I occupied it
every day from early morning until midnight and later.

I enjoyed being there. I could never stop admiring that rug. How
I wished the floor of my first office, on which I had slept so often,
had so soft a mattress as was this carpet. In the evening as I sat alone
working over the problems which had accumulated during the day, I
could always gain a moment of visual and mental relaxation by lower-
ing my eyes to that close-cropped woolen lawn at my feet. How many
other feet, weighted down with worries, had trod heavily across it, and
how many, I was happy to recall, had left this sanctum, their footsteps
lighter, their hearts gayer and freer. How many feet of women whose
sons were facing prison and disgrace, how many feet of workingmen
threatened with loss of wages and property, how many feet of children
brought to re-cement the bonds of mothers and fathers which were
loosening—that good fine carpet had welcomed and comforted.

My desk was large and held not only papers and documents but
mementos of all sorts. Here was a small rubber ball we had used in
court one day to keep a loquacious infant quiet while her parents testified and which the grateful parents had allowed me to keep in re-
membrance; here was a pretty porcelain white pony donated by an
ex-cavalryman I had acquitted in criminal court, where he had stood
trial for knocking down a man who was beating an emaciated, sick,
and superannuated work horse; here was a baton bestowed upon me
by a band leader who had heard the melodious chord of "Not Guilty"

after standing trial for assault and battery—his slide-trombone player in the *andante* part of *Rigoletto* had blown a sharp when he should have blown a flat, and as a consequence my client had flattened the trombone's slide over his head.

A snuffbox used now as a paperweight always released a flood of reminiscence. It came from Tony Monica, a poor little old man who operated a small pretzel stand in one of the more obscure streets of Pittsburgh. He had been attacked one night by a drunken ex-convict who flashed a revolver in his face; and Monica, terror-stricken, had emptied his pockets to him. The robber then demanded whatever money Monica had in his home, which was just a little room facing the sidewalk. In the room at this time was Monica's wife, who, like himself, was some sixty-five years of age. The robber charged into the house, brandishing his weapon. Tony seized him from the rear; they both fell and grappled with one another, rolling over the floor, when the gun went off. The bullet hit the robber in the head, killing him instantly.

Although Monica was obviously free of criminal fault, the processes of law and order required his arrest to answer to a charge of homicide. He was without funds, and when I learned of his plight I volunteered my services free of charge. I applied for his release on bail, which was set at ten thousand dollars. I got a couple of businessmen friends of mine to pledge their properties in this amount, assuring them that they ran no risk, as Monica was not only innocent of criminal purpose but absolutely harmless. I guaranteed to them he would not run away.

Several days before the scheduled trial I wrote Monica to come to my office so we could prepare his defense. To my unutterable consternation my letter came back bearing the disconcerting wording: "Addressee moved. No forwarding address." Nor could I obtain any information as to his present whereabouts when I went to the house which I had visited shortly after the shooting. The house was empty, and no one in the neighborhood could offer any clue as to Monica's current address. I felt a headache coming on when I thought of the ten-thousand-dollar bond. What could I say to the men who stood to lose five thousand dollars each—men who had never seen Monica and had signed the bond only on my guarantee that their money was safe?

Continuing my inquiry in the vicinity of Monica's erstwhile home, I heard of a small boy who was present when the Monicas had left. I located him, and he said he had heard Mrs. Monica say something about moving to "Washington Street." I traversed the length of Washington Street, knocking at every door. Monica was unknown. Could the boy have overheard incorrectly? Possibly Mrs. Monica had said they were moving to Mount Washington, but Mount Washington was a large subdivision of Pittsburgh, a small city in itself, with a population numbering some thirty thousand. It would be impossible for me to visit every house in Mount Washington.

I appealed to the county and city detectives for assistance, but after three or four days they reported they could find no trace of my absconding client.

The day of the trial arrived. I explained my predicament to the Court and, upon request, the Court granted a week's continuance so that I might continue my search. When the week expired and we still had no news of Monica, I asked for another postponement. This was also granted, but the district attorney warned that if I did not produce the defendant at the end of the second week he would move for foreclosure on the bond. Foreclosure meant ten thousand dollars!

I now had in my office two pleasant, amiable, and very able young lawyers, Samuel Albo and Michael Catanzaro. They were splendid youths who have since become highly esteemed and successful practitioners. They were always eager to be of assistance to me, but never was their assistance more welcome and least effective than in the search for Tony Monica. He had apparently disappeared from the face of the earth. Our office underwent a melancholy metamorphosis. Gloom overhung it like impending doom. In the whole building, when tenants spoke of a hopelessly lost article they would say ruefully: "It disappeared like Tony Monica."

The district attorney moved for foreclosure on the bond. The bondsmen served notice that they expected indemnification from me in the sum of ten thousand dollars, plus all expenses to which they were being subjected. Ten thousand dollars! I was ruined. I had just finished paying for the furniture and all the magnificent embellishments in the office. I visualized the crumbling of all I had built up through those struggling years. I could see the exquisite maroon carpet, the draperies, desks, everything being hauled away by the sheriff, while Sam Albo and Michael Catanzaro, at the threshold of their professional careers, looked wonderingly on.

The foreclosure date was now at hand, and if Monica did not appear by nightfall, I would be back to the days of the chair which threw me forward on my face. As I paced the floor, my back cringing against the prospect of returning to the floor-sleeping era, I heard a slight knock at the door. The only assurance I could allow myself that this was not the sheriff calling was the pragmatic knowledge that no sheriff would approach so diffidently. Then the door slowly opened. Framed in the doorway stood my lost client. "Tony Monica!" I cried.

My secretary, thin and delicate, fainted dead away. The pretzel vendor, frightened at our strange reception, wheeled about to take flight. I seized him with one hand as I tried to revive my secretary with the other. "Where have you been?" I exclaimed with emotion, at that moment more disturbed over the trouble he had caused me than elated over the relief I should have felt in realizing that my office furnishings had been liberated from imminent seizure by the ogre sheriff. "Why haven't you given me your new address since you moved from the old one?"

Monica's eyes bulged in astonishment and fear as he stammered but one word: "Why?"

"Why? Don't you know you have to answer to a murder charge? And don't you know that two bondsmen put up ten thousand dollars for your appearance and if you had not shown up I would have had to pay the money—and lose everything, everything I own?"

For a moment I thought the old man would collapse. He buried his face in his hands and burst into unrestrained sobbing as he rocked back and forth. "Oh, oh," he moaned, "Mr. Musmanno, I'ma so sorry I putta you to so much trouble."

"But why did you move?"

"I was afraida the dead man's ganga coma to kill me, so I move away."

"But why didn't you tell me you were moving?"

"I thinka the law knows everything. I'ma so sorry."

His sobbing continuing to progress toward hysteria, I helped him to a chair and urged him to sip at the glass of water I handed him. When he finally quieted down he said: "Mr. Musmanno, I no hava right to live. I wisha you killa me. And if you no killa me, I should killa myself!"

"Now listen, Tony, everything is going to be all right. All I want to be sure of is that you will show up for the trial."

Through the Commonwealth Building the news spread like wildfire that Tony Monica had been found. Tenants on my floor (the fourth) and neighboring floors dashed in to take a look at Monica as if he were an escaped bear just recaptured, all of them asking what I intended to do with him. Some good-naturedly recommended that I lock him in the office until the day of the court appearance. Others suggested I should attach a rope to him and have him follow me, like Mary's lamb, wherever I went. They all agreed, however, that

I should not allow him to depart with no more assurance than his word that he would show up when wanted. I called the district attorney and requested that he set Monica's trial for the very next day, and he agreed to do so. I then said to the crestfallen wanderer: "Tony, I want you here tomorrow at nine o'clock. Can I depend on you?"

"Mr. Musmanno, you can dependa on me lika you can your own father." And with renewed tearful apologies for all the trouble he had caused, he left.

The next morning at seven-thirty as I approached the Commonwealth Building I saw a white-haired man sitting on the curb. He had been there since dawn. We went to court. The trial was over in a couple of hours, and when the jury announced its certain verdict of "Not guilty," Monica sank to his knees and, much to my embarrassment, seized my hand and kissed it. Later he came to my office and presented me with the beautiful ebony snuffbox now resting so tranquilly on my desk. He said it was an heirloom descending from his great-grandfather who had lived in Florence.

The vase which harbored the garden flowers in my office had also been a present resulting from an unusual case. I was walking through the corridors of Criminal Court one morning when a well-dressed woman stopped me and asked:

"Are you a lawyer?"

"That's the impression I'm endeavoring to create around here."

"Well, I could tell from your walk and bearing that you are no ordinary person."

"Madam, there are no ordinary people in Criminal Court, no matter how you look at it. I would say that *you* are far from being an ordinary person."

"You may think me bold to address you like this, but I am going on trial this afternoon and I should like to have you defend me."

We walked to the end of the corridor and she related a rather amazing story. She represented herself as a well-married woman of society who lived in a fashonable section of the city. She said that she had been identified, while shopping in a large store, as a woman who had on a previous day stolen a valuable fur. She pictured the distressing episode as a case of mistaken identity, but, fearing publicity, she had given an invented name when questioned by the store detectives. She said that she allowed the incorrect name to stand because, while positive of an eventual exoneration, it was possible people might still believe she had in some way been implicated in the shameful affair.

She went on to say that she had first intended to go to trial without a lawyer so as to reduce still further the possibility of her friends learning of her humiliating experience, but she was now afraid that without counsel some miscarriage of justice might occur, and it would be unmitigated catastrophe for her if she were to be convicted. She begged of me that I not ask her her real name and pleaded with me to defend her as an act of the purest benevolence. Her demeanor, erect bearing, and clear eye, dimmed only by incipient tears, persuaded me that she was telling the truth. I assured her I would gladly respect her request for anonymity but that I should have to find out something about the case before I could promise to be her attorney. After making some discreet inquiries at the store I concluded that the accusation might well have been one based on mistaken identity. I tried the case and won an easy acquittal. As the jury intoned the words, "Not guilty," my mysterious client grasped my hand, pressed it tightly, sobbed: "Thank you, thank you," and hurried out of the courtroom. I never saw her again.

A year later to the day, there was delivered to my office a magnificent dark yellow marble vase filled with gorgeous red roses. Every year on that day, new roses came. One year—by oversight, I presumed —the name of the donor appeared on the tag. Recalling the promise I had made to the unknown lady that I would never ask for her name, I tore up the tag without reading it. But as I studied the resulting confetti in my hand I wondered: Suppose the sender of the flowers was not the woman I defended in court but someone who liked me for myself.

The mystery was never solved—and the roses ceased their annual visit.

Chapter XLI

A WHITE-THROATED SPARROW

I SAT on the porch of my home in Stowe Township in the shade of the mulberry tree whose branches frescoed the veranda with pictures drawn from the memory of my childhood. In front of me a green meadow rolled to the railroad tracks beyond which the Ohio River flowed serenely on its way to the Mississippi and the sea. At this point Davis Island cut the river in two. From the island to the mainland on our side ran a dike with intermittent piers. Under the main pier passed a conduit which formed part of the river-control system for the accommodation of steamboat traffic. In my boyhood days when courthouses did not exist for me, we swam in the Back Channel, using the large pier for a diving platform. The more daring of the swimmers would dive down to the conduit, there to be sucked into the swift current of the water rushing through to the lower level. The passage from the higher to the lower pool was a thrilling adventure. The aquatic adventurer traveled a vertiginous distance of some thirty feet through an aperture approximately six feet in diameter and finally emerged in a whirlpool of foam on the lower side. The exciting journey was not without danger. It could happen that a log, rock, or debris might impede the flow of water and possibly imprison the swimmer momentarily or even permanently.

One day Elmer Smithers dived but failed to emerge on the lower side in the ten seconds' time usually allotted for the passage. To the two boys on the pier with me, Harry Kengler and Joe Markels, I screamed: "Let's do something! Harry, grab the edge of the pier; Joe, you slide down and grab his legs; I'll dive down and grab Joe's feet and kick into the pipe. If Elmer's stuck close to the entrance we can pull him out or push him through." My pals leaped to the rescue. Harry took hold of the edge of the concrete, while Joe, monkey-fashion, swiftly descended out of sight. I dived and aimed for Joe's feet, but the current was too strong. I missed Joe entirely and was myself forced into the lower violent stream. Borne along in the dark waters, I raced to whatever fate awaited, because if Elmer was stuck I would surely become entangled in the same obstruction. I flailed with my arms and thrashed with my feet, hoping that whatever obstacle I met I might displace or at least break through. Ordinarily one shot through the swirling tunnel with the speed of a rocket, but now the passage seemed a mile long. Suddenly I struck something hard. I felt a suffocation in my chest. Then I heard bells tinkling in the distance.

When I saw light again I was bobbing among other swimmers in the foaming water. Elmer, Harry, and Joe were churning all around me. It seems that Harry had been torn loose from his grasp by Joe's violent exertions, and both of them had been drawn into the conduit. The force of our three bodies against the small log which had clogged the conduit loosened it, freeing Elmer, and the four of us shot out into the lower pool together. . . .

A white-throated sparrow in the mulberry tree chirped and swooped down to the railing on the porch where my rocking chair never failed to stir the pools of nostalgic recollection. I believe my feathered visitor wanted me to admire him. This was easy to do. His throat glistened with the softest white down which fell across his bosom in a fancy dress scarf. On his head he wore a black cap decorated with an arrow. He lifted his voice in song. Motionless on the banister, with his head upraised to the sky, he seemed a pretty toy on a music box producing a sweet-sad concert which was an echo of all the distant sounds of my childhood.

With a cheeping salute he fluttered back to the mulberry tree and I looked out again over the river. Placid and unruffled, it bore on its surface no writing of the drama which had been enacted in its depths twenty years before. The dike and the pier dozed lazily in the summer sun, unconcerned, if they ever remembered, how they had dammed up the stream of the young lawyer's life for a moment; they might have stopped it forever.

In a sentimental mood I appraised not only the majestic and philosophical Ohio but the river of existence itself. Where had it flowed in those twenty years and whither was it destined now? Twenty years! A wave of melancholy rippled up my spine.

I was getting old. Only several weeks before I had had a birthday. There was so much to be done, and I was already thirty-two. This should not have cast too heavy a gloom over the mulberry tree of my life because on my nineteenth birthday I had written in my diary: "Nineteen! and nothing accomplished. At nineteen Alexander was on his way to conquering the world." Was I ambitious? A trifle. Happily, however, I did not emulate Alexander. He was dead at thirty-three. I thus would have had only one year to go.

But at thirty-two I was still not at peace with myself. I felt that it was not enough to be a lawyer, even a successful lawyer. Good and bad fortune had intermingled to provide me with an unusually broad and extensive experience in the law. In only seven or eight years I had handled nearly every type of case that can come to a general practitioner in a lifetime. I had seen in that short period how justice sometimes miscarries not because of any shortcoming in the law but because of some fault present or some virtue missing in the judge. Father Bonaventure of the Immaculate Conception Church of Bloomfield related to me a rather shocking incident. The relative of a parishioner of his had been sentenced to death for murder. The good Father called on the sentencing judge to implore mercy—specifically, to reduce the death sentence to life imprisonment. The judge was indignant. "I certainly will not change my sentence," he raged. "His lawyer thought he was putting something over on me when he had his client plead guilty and thus placed on me the burden of deciding the penalty. Well, I fixed him!" Thus, the controlling factor in the judge's mind at that moment was not whether further consideration might justify alteration of the sentence. His only concern was that the lawyer had embarrassed him, and he would fix the lawyer by hanging his client.

I myself had seen judges impose penal servitude as if they were avenging a personal grievance. There was the case in our courts of a boy seventeen years of age who had been sentenced by the judge to a term of ten to twenty years in the penitentiary after he had been assured by the district attorney that if he pleaded guilty to a charge of burglary he would be committed to a reformatory. It happened to be the lad's hard luck that, on the eve of sentencing, the judge's home was burglarized. The judge stormed into court the following morning with revenge in his eye, and the erring youth, who of course had had nothing to do with the judge's home, received the full impact of the judge's wrath.

There were several judges in Allegheny County who were known at the Bar as "bad-livered judges." If their livers disturbed them at night, woe betide the defendants who came before them the following day. However, if their livers functioned smoothly the defendants could depend on getting off comparatively easy.

As I saw defendants receiving penalties out of all proportion to the offenses committed, I also saw hardened criminals released on parole or given light sentences because the judge was perhaps obligated to some politician interested in the defendant. I do not say that this practice was general, but incidents of this character happened often enough to make me hope that justice might be dispensed in a manner more consonant with social responsibility and criminal rehabilitation.

In the civil branch of the courts I noted judicial attitudes equally inconsistent with the concept of fundamental fairness. I appeared before judges who did not understand the word *courtesy* and who seemingly believed that judicial dignity was synonymous with impatience and arrogance. They forgot that at one time they also were lawyers, and they failed to realize that when they upbraided counsel in court it was not the lawyer who bore the brunt of the resulting harm but the client, whose cause was thus prejudiced before the jury. In such instances the involved litigant could lose his case not because of what he had done or not done but because the judge did not like the lawyer.

What is the Temple of Justice? To one who has never attended in court, the courthouse is the symbol of all that is honest, impartial, and just. And even to those who visit but for an occasion, the awesome administering of the oath to a witness (Do you swear, by Almighty God, that the evidence you are about to give will be the truth, the whole truth, and nothing but the truth, and for which you will answer on the last Great Day?) is enough to assure the novitiate that only righteousness could be the product of so serious, reverent, and solemn a procedure. But we have seen that justice is more than a formal law procedure. Nor is its standard unvarying. It differs according to the personality, the background, and even the whims, caprices, and prejudices of the judicial agencies controlling the decision.

As a lawyer I had sought to gather as much justice as I could from the fields of the law, but no matter how conscientious and energetic were my efforts, the results were bound to be affected by the attitude of the judge. I wondered if I might help to harvest justice in larger and richer sheaves. Perhaps if I lived closer to the field, if I could in some way supervise the sowing of the seed and work with the reapers I might be able to do something, no matter on how small a scale, to assure litigants that there would be less bread of the Ferguson-Stanley brand. Would it be too much for me to hope that I could become——

A judge!

My heart flamed. In my childhood I had built, on the summit of the hills across the Ohio River, a castle of aspirations, but the topmost turret of that castle hardly reached so high as to capture the cloud-capped dream of a judgeship—to sit in judgment, to right wrong, to make people happy, to protect the maligned, to rescue the oppressed . . .

What a dream! It was too wonderful, too grand to contemplate. The Ohio River formed an impassable moat. I could never reach the castle. I had better not tell anyone that I had even yearned to reach it. I might be ridiculed for having entertained such fanciful musings. The white-throated sparrow visited me again. I wondered if he had heard my thoughts. As he tossed his pert and pretty little head I turned an entreating eye to him not to divulge to the world those reveries which he had divined.

For a year or so neither my sparrow friend nor myself told a soul about our dream, and then one day we went into a huddle and talked the matter out at length. Why shouldn't I be a judge? I had now already served two terms in the state legislature, where I had been active on several judiciary committees; I had practiced extensively in all the courts; I had authored several publications on legal subjects. I believed I was thoroughly qualified from the standpoint of education, training, and experience. Judges in Pennsylvania are elected by the people. And if I possessed the qualifications for judicial office and the citizens of Allegheny County believed in me, why might they not elect me judge? I asked the sparrow—and he replied they might.

So we decided to release our secret. He extended his wings and soared away to spread the news. I extended my arms and announced my candidacy. And lo and behold! what a delightful surprise. My candidacy was received with genuine kindness in the community.

I plunged into the campaign with the enthusiasm of a baseball player circling the bases to bring in the winning run. Allegheny County is made up of 126 different municipalities, including the city of Pittsburgh and three third-class cities. Without being the endorsed candidate of any party and without a single financial contribution from any source, I campaigned in every town, township, ward, and precinct. Wherever I traveled I distributed a small pamphlet containing an account of my career up to that time. The shamelessness of a political candidate parading his assumed virtues is one of the fascinating and entertaining phenomena of a true democracy. There was a time when it was assumed the candidate knew nothing of what was being done in his behalf, and in fact custom even recommended that he seem to discountenance the efforts being made to elect him. Of course this was hypocrisy, and we should be grateful that there is less of it today than heretofore. No one asked me to enter the political lists. Being a candidate was my idea alone. When I declared my first candidacy for the legislature in 1926 there were political figures in my town who said that I was too young. I asked them if they would notify me when I was ripe enough to be a candidate. They said they could not take that responsibility. I replied: "Very well, I shall wait on no notification. I am in the race as of now." And since that time no one ever did urge me to be a candidate, except, of course, the sparrow.

When I formally announced my candidacy, volunteer workers sprang up on all sides. Good men and women offered to distribute my campaign circulars, to arrange meetings for me, to supply me with mailing lists. They did this without pay, nor did they expect any patronage in recompense, since a judge has no jobs to dispense. I do not know how I can ever repay with gratitude those kindhearted people who gave of their time and energies to help someone who could not materially reward them in any way. Perhaps their enthusiasm was aroused partly because of my youth. They had been accustomed to seeing graybeards as judges and judicial candidates, but I campaigned for judicial post while springtime was still in my bones. Perhaps, also, considering my background, they felt that in my courtroom justice would never be lost in a labyrinth of bleak technicality and sterile form.

Most of the campaigning took place in the summer and early fall months when outside festivities were the rule of the day. This was greatly to my advantage. Picnics, athletic meets, and baseball games offered excellent opportunity to meet people and to pass around cards. Picnics were a bonanza for me. Contrary to a general impression, outdoor merrymakers enjoy listening to political candidates. At any rate, they did in 1931. The candidate's arrival provided a nice little diversion in the day of pastime and fun, his breezy greetings and short speech harmed no one, and when he had departed the picnickers good-naturedly discussed his personality, his speech, and even repeated a joke or two which he might have dropped.

I outdid myself in speeches during the campaign. I doubt that there is a park, grove, or grassy plot in all of Allegheny County that did not have a Musmanno speech mixed in with the sandwiches, potato salad, foot races, and softball games of the day.

It was not unusual for me to speak at fifteen different picnics on Sundays and holidays. Not a day passed that I did not make at least six or seven speeches. All this required speedy traveling because the county is large (thirty-six miles across at its widest point), and often there was no time to stop to eat or drink. In a continuous speaking campaign of about five months I lost fifteen pounds in weight.

Came election day and victory smiled—I received 250,000 votes out of 296,000 cast.

And thus the young lawyer was about to become the young judge. As I had been the youngest member of the legislature I was now the youngest elected judge in Pennsylvania.

The moat was no longer impassable; a drawbridge lowered and spanned the Ohio River; I prepared to enter the dream castle of my childhood, but it was no longer a dream. It was real, only as dreams can become real in America, the magic land of the world. And yet the magic is not supernatural, nor is it ununderstandable. It is the magic of eager hearts, willing hands, and brotherly souls. It is the alchemy which transforms the blood of patriots shed on countless battlefields into America's most glorious heritage—freedom and opportunity. It is the Aladdin's Lamp which places a key into every boy's pocket with which to unlock the gate of success on the distant hill if he but perseveres in the climb.

Opportunity in America, however, does not mean climbing with escalator ease. America withholds her rewards from the slothful and the easily discouraged, but she is always ready to recognize those who fling themselves with full heart into the never-ending crusade to make our country ever greater; it constantly remembers with affection those who work and fight to right inequalities and correct injustices; it never ceases to bestow the accolade of a nation's gratitude on those who carry oil to the lamp of democracy so that it may never dim its vigil over a free and God-fearing people. . . .

I heard a flutter of wings and a little melody of song at my elbow. My white-throated friend had arrived to congratulate me on the election. I thrilled to his visit but lamented to learn that, according to the laws of birdland, he being a white-throated sparrow, he was required to fly South for the winter. Thus, as he sang his merry felicitations, he added in a minor key that he was sorry he had to say good-by. Yes, winter would soon be here. I had quite forgotten that there could ever be winter again. There was such a riotous joy of summer in my heart; the people had been so wondrously kind to me.

My sweet-voiced friend warbled his keen regrets he could not remain for the inaugural ceremony. Then, lifting his wings and raising his head, he soared above the mulberry tree and, with the directness of the arrow on his cap, he headed for the South. I waved a hand in affectionate farewell.

A month later I sat on a platform in a large courtroom which was a wilderness of flowers. Huge baskets, bouquets, and vases of roses, chrysanthemums, gladioli, dahlias, and snowballs smiled at me along the walls, and from every corner and angle. Hundreds of faces, equally as cheerful as the flowers, smiled in felicitation on this, the biggest day of my life. On the chair next to mine waited my judicial robe, ready for its part in the event of the day. A pretty little girl, all pink and ribbons and as sweet and charming as you would ever see, advanced to the platform bearing a bunch of red roses larger than herself. As she approached the dais, it was difficult to distinguish which was the girl and which the flowers. "Congratulations, Mr. Musmanno," she said. "And now, *Judge* Musmanno!"

Judge Musmanno!

The windows in the castle turret blazed with a golden light.

The president judge prepared to administer the oath. I stood and lifted my hand. As I looked out into the crowded courtroom I saw one face: a kindly, patriarchal, sweet, and handsome face framed in an aureole of white hair—it was my father. My good mother looked on from the ramparts of heaven.

As the president judge intoned the oath and I answered with a firm but heart-pounding "I do," I saw my father take into his hands the folds of the flag which rested in a stand by his side. The silk of rich crimson and pure white glistened, while the stars against the blue lighted up his face in one grand expression of beatitude. Tenderly and reverently he lifted the folds to his lips and kissed them. Then he softly uttered some words which I could not hear.

That night at home as I started for my room I bade my father good night.

He waited until I had about reached the staircase and then replied: "Good night—*Judge*," lingering on the last word. I turned. He was smiling from the depths of his armchair. In his hand he held his old briar pipe.

I walked back, placed my arm around his shoulder, and asked: "Father, what was it you said when you kissed the flag today?"

"My boy," he replied as the curling smoke from his pipe rose to envelop his fine head in a cloud of creamy vapor, "what I said was: 'Thank God for a country where even an immigrant railroad worker-coal miner's son may become a judge.'"